AFTER EXCESSIVE TEACHER AND FACULTY ENTITLEMENT

ADVANCES IN RESEARCH ON TEACHING

Series Editors: Cheryl J. Craig and Stefinee Pinnegar

Recent Volumes

Volume 31: Decentering the Researcher in Intimate Scholarship: Critical Posthuman Methodological Perspectives in Education

Volume 32: Essays on Teaching Education and the Inner Drama of Teaching: Where Biography and History Meet

Volume 33: Landscapes, Edges, and Identity-Making

Volume 34: Exploring Self Toward Expanding Teaching, Teacher Education and Practitioner Research

Volume 35: Preparing Teachers to Teach the STEM Disciplines in America's Urban Schools

Volume 36: Luminous Literacies: Localized Teaching and Teacher Education

Volume 37: Developing Knowledge Communities Through Partnerships for Literacy

Volume 38: Understanding Excessive Teacher and Faculty Entitlement: Digging at the Roots

Volume 39: Global Meaning Making: Disrupting and Interrogating International Language and Literacy Research and Teaching

Volume 40: Making Meaning With Readers and Texts: Beginning Teachers' Meaning-Making From Classroom Events

Volume 41: Teacher Education in the Wake of Covid-19: ISATT 40th Anniversary Yearbook

Volume 42: Teaching and Teacher Education in International Contexts: ISATT 40th Anniversary Yearbook

Volume 43: Approaches to Teaching and Teacher Education: ISATT 40th Anniversary Yearbook

Volume 44: Studying Teaching and Teacher Education: ISATT 40th Anniversary Yearbook

Volume 45: Drawn to the Flame: Teachers' Stories of Burnout

Volume 46: Smudging Composition Lines of Identity and Teacher Knowledge: Cross-Cultural Narrative Inquiries Into Teaching and Learning

ADVANCES IN RESEARCH ON TEACHING   VOLUME 47

AFTER EXCESSIVE TEACHER AND FACULTY ENTITLEMENT: EXPANDING THE SPACE FOR HEALING AND HUMAN FLOURISHING THROUGH IDEOLOGICAL BECOMING

EDITED BY

TARA RATNAM
Independent Teacher Educator and Researcher, India

AND

CHERYL J. CRAIG
Texas A&M University, USA

United Kingdom – North America – Japan
India – Malaysia – China

Emerald Publishing Limited
Emerald Publishing, Floor 5, Northspring, 21-23 Wellington Street, Leeds LS1 4DL

First edition 2024

Editorial Matter and Selection © 2024 Tara Ratnam and Cheryl J. Craig.
Individual chapters © 2024 The authors.
Published under exclusive licence by Emerald Publishing Limited.

Reprints and permissions service
Contact: www.copyright.com

No part of this book may be reproduced, stored in a retrieval system, transmitted in any form or by any means electronic, mechanical, photocopying, recording or otherwise without either the prior written permission of the publisher or a licence permitting restricted copying issued in the UK by The Copyright Licensing Agency and in the USA by The Copyright Clearance Center. Any opinions expressed in the chapters are those of the authors. Whilst Emerald makes every effort to ensure the quality and accuracy of its content, Emerald makes no representation implied or otherwise, as to the chapters' suitability and application and disclaims any warranties, express or implied, to their use.

British Library Cataloguing in Publication Data
A catalogue record for this book is available from the British Library

ISBN: 978-1-83797-878-6 (Print)
ISBN: 978-1-83797-877-9 (Online)
ISBN: 978-1-83797-879-3 (Epub)

ISSN: 1479-3687 (Series)

INVESTOR IN PEOPLE

CONTENTS

List of Figures and Tables	ix
About the Editors	xi
About the Contributors	xiii
Foreword	xvii
Acknowledgments	xxi

Introduction: The Healing Touch to Excessive Entitlement: Bringing Humanity Back Into Education and Society — *Tara Ratnam* ... 1

SECTION I
CULTURAL–HISTORICAL ACTIVITY THEORY (CHAT) AS A WAY FORWARD FROM EXCESSIVE TEACHER/FACULTY ENTITLEMENT

Why Are Teachers Excessively Entitled? Understanding Teachers to Foster Their *Ideological Becoming* — *Tara Ratnam* ... 17

Excessive Entitlement From a Networked Relational Perspective — *Louis Botha* ... 43

The Onto-Epistemological Dimension of Knowledge and Interaction Within Excessive Teacher Entitlement: A Cultural-Historical Activity Theory Perspective — *Cristiano Mattos and André Machado Rodrigues* ... 63

Excessive Teacher Entitlement and Defensive Pedagogy: Challenging Power and Control in Classrooms — *Joanne Hardman* ... 81

Why 'Defensive' Pedagogies Matter: The Necessity of Expanding
Teachers' Agency to Inform Educational Transformation   99
Warren Lilley

Living in Dilemmatic Spaces: Stories of Excessive Entitled
Teachers and Their Transformative Agency   117
Ge Wei

SECTION II
THE YIN-YANG OF *EXCESSIVE TEACHER/ FACULTY ENTITLEMENT* AND THE *BEST-LOVED SELF*

When Not Getting Your Due Is Your Due: Excessive Entitlement
at Work   137
Cheryl J. Craig

Challenging Structures of Excessive Entitlement in Curricula,
Teaching, and Learning Through Dialogic Engagement   149
Richard D. Sawyer and Joe Norris

Generating Living-Educational-Theories With Love in
Transforming Excessive Teacher Entitlement   167
Jack Whitehead

Societal Narratives of Teachers as Nonpersons as an Expression
of Society's Excessively Entitled Attitude   183
Celina Dulude Lay, Eliza Pinnegar and Stefinee Pinnegar

SECTION III
BRINGING TO CONSCIOUSNESS THE *UNTHOUGHT KNOWN*

Troubling Excessive Entitlement: A Teacher's Reflective Journey   197
Jackie Ellett

In the Shadow of Traditional Education: A *Currere* of School
Entitlement and Student Erasure   215
Richard D. Sawyer

A Reflective Look at Excessive Faculty Entitlement in Doctoral
Supervision   231
Marie-Christine Deyrich

Excessive (En)title(ment) Fight? Exploring the Dynamics that Perpetuate Entitlement in Education and Beyond   *249*
John Buchanan

SECTION IV
SYNTHESIZING THE CORE IDEAS

Looking Back to Look Forward   *271*
Cheryl J. Craig

Afterword   *275*
Tom Russell

Index   *281*

LIST OF FIGURES AND TABLES

Figures
Chapter 1
Fig. 1.	Yin–Yang Relationship Between Excessive Entitlement and the Best-Loved Self.	3
Fig. 2.	Vygotsky's Mediational Triangle.	9
Fig. 3.	The Activity System Model.	9

Chapter 2
Fig. 1.	A Conceptual Model of Cycle of Expansive Learning.	28

Chapter 3
Fig. 1.	Entitlement as an Activity Systems Model.	46
Fig. 2.	Drawing of a Networked Relational Model.	51
Fig. 3.	Networked Relational Model for Kate's Academic Activity.	56

Chapter 5
Fig. 1.	An Activity System.	84
Fig. 2.	Reinforcement Pedagogy: Activity System.	91
Fig. 3.	Defensive Pedagogy Episode.	95

Chapter 12
Fig. 1.	Sapelo Island.	210

Chapter 13
Fig. 1.		220
Fig. 2.		224

Chapter 15
Fig. 1.	Jim Crow.	259

Tables
Chapter 5
Table 1.	A CHAT Checklist.	87
Table 2.	CHAT Interview Schedule.	88

Chapter 6
Table 1.	Overview of Change Laboratory Research Intervention.	109

Chapter 7
Table 1.	Summary of the Three Teachers' Narratives.	129

ABOUT THE EDITORS

Tara Ratnam, PhD, is an independent teacher educator and researcher from India. In her work with teachers, the difference she observed between what they advocated and its startling antithesis in their practice led her to study how culture and context interacted and influenced teachers' thinking and practice, creating a gap between their intention and action. A failure to link student learning to their cultural ways of knowing has motivated her to explore forms of pedagogical mediation, relationality, thinking, and development that could support teachers help students, particularly the socioculturally diverse and disadvantaged students, to learn with dignity and possibility.

Cheryl J. Craig, PhD, is a Professor, Houston Endowment Endowed Chair of Urban Education, and Program Lead of Teaching and Teacher Education at Texas A&M University. In addition to being her campus's Founding Director of the Collaborative for Innovation for Education, she is an AERA Fellow, a recipient of AERA's Division B Lifetime Achievement Award and AERA's Division K Legacy and Research Excellence Awards. She is also a recipient of the AERA Michael Huberman Award for Outstanding Contributions to Understanding the Lives of Teachers. Currently, she serves as the Chair of the International Study Association on Teachers and Teaching (ISATT).

ABOUT THE CONTRIBUTORS

Louis Botha, PhD, is a Senior Lecturer at the Wits School of Education at the University of the Witwatersrand in Johannesburg. He teaches sociology of education, inclusive education, and transformative education and research at the undergraduate and postgraduate levels. His research is concerned with the marginalization and transformation of knowledges within contexts of teaching, learning, and research, drawing particularly upon indigenous knowledges in this regard. His research is generally framed within a cultural-historical activity theory (CHAT) approach, using the principles and research interventions developed by CHAT researchers to explore possibilities for innovative change within educational contexts.

John Buchanan, EdD, is an Adjunct Associate Professor at the University of Technology Sydney, where he has worked for more than 20 years. Prior to that, he taught at primary and secondary levels in NSW, Australia, mainly in language education. His main teaching and research interests include self-study and social and environmental education, focusing particularly on intercultural education. He has also researched and published extensively on teacher quality, attrition, and retention. His environmental education interests extend to researching about the conceptualization and uses of place and writing about his hometown, Sydney, Australia, a place for which he holds a deep love.

Marie-Christine Deyrich, PhD, is Professor Emerita of Applied Linguistics, English Studies, and Teacher Education at the University of Bordeaux, France. She is an active member of ISATT and AERA. She has been involved in several collective projects among which include: Language Learning for Active Social Inclusion, Pandemic Pedagogy: Educators' Practices During the Covid-19, and the Invisible College Symposia. Her writings deal with ethical language teaching in intercultural issues, linguistic policy, LSP, and learning and teaching in higher education. Her most recent writings deal with the impact of power imbalances and excessive faculty entitlement on doctoral supervision.

Jackie Ellett, PhD, is an Associate Professor of Art Education at Piedmont University. She taught art in Gwinnett County Schools for 32 years. Her varied experiences as a mentor and state and national leader equipped her with the skills to prepare future classroom educators for success. Her teaching accomplishments and dedication to art education have been recognized with state and national awards, including the Nix/Mickish Award for Lifetime Contribution to Art Education, 2022, and the NAEA National Elementary Art Educator of the Year,

1995. She was a contributing writer for the texts *Exploring Art*, *Art Talk*, and *Art Connections*.

Joanne Hardman, PhD, is a Professor and Deputy Director in the School of Education, University of Cape Town. A Psychologist by training, her research interests include using Cultural Historical Activity Theory to study pedagogy and child development; the use of tools such as ICTs on cognition and the development of Executive Functions in the brain and developing online applications to facilitate conceptual development among primary school children. She is the Secretary of the International Association of Cognitive Education and Psychology and African executive member of International Society for Cultural-Historical Activity Research.

Celina Dulude Lay, PhD, currently teaches as an Adjunct Instructor at Brigham Young University at the David O. McKay School of Education. She majored in Educational Inquiry, Measurement and Evaluation at Brigham Young University. Her research interest is in teacher educator knowledge. She is a regular contributor to the American Educational Research Association, especially in the methodologies of Self-Study of Teaching and Teacher Education Practice (S-STEP) and Narrative Research SIG. She enjoys preparing teacher candidates in assessment, classroom management, adolescent development, TESOL K-12, instructional design, literacy in all content areas and ages, and supporting in-service teachers in professional development.

Warren Lilley, PhD, is a Senior Lecturer in the School of Education within the Psychology of Education stream. Developed through his extensive experience as an educator and teacher-trainer, his research focuses on digital equity and meaningful integration of technology within the classroom. His work empirically and theoretically explores these questions around educational transformation using formative-intervention methodologies, which focus on how educators and students can transform their classroom practices. Additionally, Warren continues to contribute his expertise and experience to the design and facilitation of national teacher development interventions and courses focusing on educational technology integration.

Cristiano Mattos, PhD, studied at the University of São Paulo (USP) investigating artificial cognitive systems. He is an Associate Professor at the Institute of Physics at the USP and currently the leader of the Research Group in Science and Complexity Education (ECCo). He works on the Cultural-Historical Activity Theory from a Freirean perspective, investigating the philosophical, psychological, and pedagogical foundations of teaching–learning of scientific and quotidian concepts, models of dialogic interaction, situated cognition, interdisciplinarity, and activity complexity, developing practical educational activities using science as an instrument to develop citizenship and democratic education for social and economic equity.

ABOUT THE CONTRIBUTORS

Joe Norris, PhD, is a Professor Emeritus at Brock University. He has received the 2015 Tom Barone Award for Distinguished Contributions to Arts Based Educational Research from AERA's Arts Based Educational Research SIG. He also has focused his teaching and research on fostering a playful, creative, participatory, and socially aware stance toward self and other and has taught courses in drama in education, applied theater, research methods (general, qualitative, and arts-based), and curriculum theory, among others at various universities. His book, *Playbuilding as Qualitative Research: A Participatory Arts-based Approach*, received AERA's Qualitative Research SIG's 2011 Outstanding Book Award.

Eliza Pinnegar, PhD, began her research journey while earning her undergraduate degree. She went on to graduate school, working with Dr D. Jean Clandinin. She attended community events at AERA. Her focus has been on school-aged children and their families' experiences inside school settings and outside. She has a passion for and has been an active member of the Narrative Research and S-STEP communities. She teaches for Anchorage School District. She has enjoyed serving in informal and formal capacities, advising budding researchers, reviewing journals, serving as program Chair, and contributing to the overall knowledge of the educational field.

Stefinee Pinnegar, PhD, is a graduate of the University of Arizona and an Emeriti Professor of Teacher Education from Brigham Young University. Her research interests focus on teacher thinking and practical memory, teacher educator knowledge, and teacher development through professional development. She has published articles in *Educational Researcher, Journal of Teacher Education, Studying Teaching*, and others. She has coauthored chapters in the most recent handbooks on teacher education and self-study of teacher education practices. She is a specialty editor of *Frontiers – Teacher Education* and coeditor of Emerald's *Advances in Research on Teaching* series.

André Machado Rodrigues, PhD, spent 10 years teaching Physics at an urban high school in São Paulo before assuming his current role as an Assistant Professor at the Institute of Physics, University of São Paulo. There, he leads the Physics Demonstrations Laboratory and coordinates the Teacher Instruction Program in Physics. As a member of the Research Group in Science and Complexity Education (ECCo), André focuses on science teacher education and scientific concept formation within the cultural-historical activity theory framework. His recent research critically evaluates the science education research field, highlighting the importance of collaborative activities.

Tom Russell, PhD, is a Professor Emeritus, Faculty of Education, Queen's University. He retired in 2019 after 42 years at Queen's. His teaching focused on secondary school science (physics in particular) and the improvement of teaching. His research focused on reflection-in-action, how individuals learn to teach, learning from experience and self-study of teacher education practices. He was a coeditor of the 2004 *International Handbook of Self-Study of Teaching and Teacher Education Practices* and served as a coeditor of the journal *Studying Teacher Education* during its first 15 years of publication. He has published numerous book chapters and coedited more than a dozen books.

Richard D. Sawyer, PhD, is a Professor of Education at Washington State University, where he chairs the MIT Secondary Certification Program. His scholarship intertwines reflexive, dialogic qualitative methodologies with curriculum theory. Working with Dr Joe Norris, he originated duoethnography and has written extensively about it. He has published a number of books and articles on curriculum theory and qualitative methodologies, including duoethnography. With Joe Norris, he was a recipient of the American Educational Research Association's Qualitative Research SIG's 2011 Outstanding Book Award for *Duoethnography: Understanding Qualitative Research*.

Ge Wei, PhD, is an Associate Professor and the Director of the Research Center for Children and Teacher Education, Capital Normal University, China. He is a Visiting Professor of Tampere University, Finland, and also the scientific council member of Center for Activity Theory at University West, Sweden. He draws on cultural-historical activity theory in studies of learning, teaching, and human development in a range of contexts, including schools, families, and societies. Besides, he prefers to inquire narratives to understand experiences of educators. His recent monograph is entitled *Reimaging Pre-service Teaches' Practical Knowledge: Designing Learning for Future* (Routledge, 2023).

Jack Whitehead, PhD, is a former President of the British Educational Research Association, a Distinguished Scholar in Residence Westminster College Utah, and a Visiting Professor at Brock University, Ontario. He is a Visiting Professor at Ningxia Teachers University, China; the University of Cumbria in the United Kingdom and North–West University in South African present. He is a reviewer and member of the editorial board of the *Educational Journal of Living Theories* and a reviewer for *Action Research*; *Educational Action Research*; *Teaching and Teacher Education*; *Practitioner Research in Higher Education*. In 2023, he received an Honorary DLitt from the University of Worcester.

FOREWORD

EXCESSIVE ENTITLEMENT: TRYING TO GRASP THE UNGRASPABLE

At the entrance to Auschwitz, the first thing that stares at you is George Santayana's famous warning to humanity: "Those who cannot remember the past are condemned to repeat it." Wars and pestilence and the pain of hate and oppression that surround us today seem like the price we are paying for not heeding, not listening. What makes us use our human potential for violence and inhumanity rather than for peace and respect? Gunter Grass avers that "Auschwitz can never be grasped." However, what gives me hope and makes me persevere in grasping the ungraspable is the innate human aspiration for the ultimate good, the utopian ideals that every one of us shares regardless of our dystopian actions.

My personal utopia is underlined by the value of inclusivity borne by the Upanishadic mantra of peace, "Om sarve' bhavantu sukinah," which speaks to collective well-being and happiness. However, my appeal to this value did not originate from any Upanishad. It came to me as *living knowledge* witnessing my father's way of life. As a doctor, his healing touch and human concern did not know class or caste differences, the common prejudices of his time. His compassion has left an indelible impression on me.

The human inconsistency between espoused values and actual practice became a matter for sober contemplation in the dissonances I experienced when I attempted to put my values to practice as a teacher, teacher educator, and researcher. Trying to apprehend the seeming resistance by teachers to reform efforts led me to the notion of "excessive teacher entitlement" – a proclivity among teachers to adhere to scripted practice that militates against the need for adaptive flexibility from them. Cheryl Craig enriched this idea by bringing in the perspective of faculty entitlement in higher education settings as a close counterpart. As Dewey (1910, p. 19) points out, naming the phenomenon "helped pin it for investigation, and gave the motive for becoming conscious of our knowledge of experiences to which we had not hitherto applied our own mind."

Studies piloted to uncover the sources of teacher intransigence and the public-deficit image of them revealed the presence of "excessive entitlement" as a critical and pervasive issue in schools and universities (Ratnam & Craig, 2021): it manifests itself as pushing back change, professional jealousy, competitiveness, and aggression among teachers and faculty. These undesirable behaviors perpetuate existing inequities in institutions of education meant to be democratically inclusive. They create a toxic work environment that undermines trust, collaboration, and innovation. However, the studies also laid bare the relational complexity of teachers' and educators' work, exposing the ubiquitous presence of excessive entitlement in the whole system, encompassing all actors working at various levels of educational hierarchy. Everyone is entangled hopelessly in the web of excessive entitlement, consigned to be harmed and to harm others. In these discursive dynamics, teachers and educators fail to get the recognition, respect, and support for their efforts. These unmet expectations make them vulnerable, and they use excessive entitlement as a way to cope, but this also makes them less aware of themselves. When teachers and educators are not self-aware, they judge others harshly. They blame students for their problems and ignore their own shortcomings.

In the Afterword to the book, "Understanding excessive teacher/faculty entitlement: Digging at the roots" (Ratnam & Craig, 2021), Stefinee Pinnegar asked, "After Entitlement What?" This sounded a clarion call to engage further with the notion of excessive teacher/faculty entitlement as a way to address afresh the "conundrums" that have dogged teaching and teacher education such as theory–practice divide and promoting teacher change. In response, the present volume proposes to bring together promising approaches to help teachers/educators negotiate the *living contradictions* (Whitehead, 1989; also, Chapter 10 in this volume) they experience in their sociocultural and institutional milieu and reclaim the agency stolen from them by the excessive entitlement enshrouding their self-awareness. Those living contradictions are the conflicts between what they believe and what they do or what they want and what they have. Such conflicts can harm them by posing a threat to their professional, emotional, and moral survival and by making them recourse to excessive entitlement. The healing touch to excessive entitlement involves importantly the promotion of teachers and educators' "ideological becoming" (Bakhtin, 1981) – a holistic process of learning and development that involves recreating identities and social relationships by changing their "way of viewing the world" (Bakhtin, 1981, p. 333) in dialogue with others' worldviews. The heightened self-awareness and respect for diversity developed through dialogue increases the possibility of cocreating a better learning and working environment for all. Teachers and educators can also achieve the shared utopian goal of fairness and inclusion.

How does the wisdom gained from my lived story connect to the larger human story of hatred, oppression, and violence that I began with? People seem to think that hatred for and destruction of others is inevitable for self-preservation. It has taken me the journey of a lifetime to make sense of the apparently simple but profound Upanishadic aphorism that individual happiness is a collective phenomenon – that is, the path to individual happiness and well-being runs through collective happiness and well-being. Might not this similar realization spur us to expand the space for the utopian vision of human flourishing in communities of educational practice and social life, which are threatened by systemic challenges from poverty, exclusion, climate, war, pandemic diseases, and technological disruptions such as the advent of AI?

Tara Ratnam
Independent Teacher Educator and Researcher, India

REFERENCES

Bakhtin, M. (1981). *The dialogic imagination: Four essays* (M. Holquist & C. Emerson, Trans.). University of Texas Press.

Dewey, J. (1910). *How we think*. D. C. Heath and Company.

Ratnam, T., & Craig, C. J. (Eds.). (2021). *Understanding excessive teacher and faculty entitlement: Digging at the roots*. Emerald Publishing Limited.

Whitehead, J. (1989). Creating a living educational theory from questions of the kind, "How do I improve my practice?". *Cambridge Journal of Education, 19*(1), 41–52. https://www.actionresearch.net/writings/livtheory.html

ACKNOWLEDGMENTS

We, the editors, want to thank Xiao Han for her careful formatting work and her pointing out several important details that escaped our notice. Her tireless efforts are much appreciated.

The world is a better place thanks to people who want to grow professionally and help others grow in their personal development. We have all learned a lot during the peer review process. We appreciate how the exchange of feedback helped the authors create deeper meaning through dialogue with their fellow chapter authors. This has turned the writing of the chapters into a rich and transformative learning and development journey for everyone involved. Our heartfelt thanks go out to all the reviewers who gave their time to engage in the dialogic peer review process: Louis Botha, John Buchanan, Jackie Delong, Marie-Christine Deyrich, Jackie Ellett, Mairin Glenn, Joanne Hardman, Sheila Hirst, Sunil Iyengar, Thuri Jóna Jóhannsdóttir, Celina Lay, Warren Lilley, Cristiano Mattos, Joe Norris, Eliza Pinnegar, Stefinee Pinnegar, André Machado Rodrigues, Richard Sawyer, Ge Wei, and Jack Whitehead.

We especially thank Jackie Ellett for her extra reviews and editorial assistance.

We were delighted when Tom Russell took up our invitation to write the Afterword. We know how busy he is and the extra effort involved in responding to the multidisciplinary orientations of all the chapters.

Finally, we are grateful to all the people who helped us bring this book to life, especially Kirsty Woods, Lydia Cutmore, Pavithra Muthu, Shanmathi Priya, and the entire Emerald publishing team.

INTRODUCTION: THE HEALING TOUCH TO EXCESSIVE ENTITLEMENT: BRINGING HUMANITY BACK INTO EDUCATION AND SOCIETY

Tara Ratnam

Independent Teacher Educator and Researcher, India

ABSTRACT

This introductory chapter begins by outlining the background of this book: how the concept of excessive teacher entitlement took shape and was progressively enriched through my collaborative work with Cheryl J. Craig. Our ongoing informal dialogues gave rise to an invisible college where we co-created new meanings to deepen the understanding of professional inertia. We saw professional inertia as a manifestation of excessive teacher/faculty entitlement constantly adrift in a yin and yang relationship with their best-loved self. This insight came from challenging the narrow mainstream view of the notion of excessive entitlement as a purely volitional act of autonomous individuals which leads to blaming and pathologizing teachers/ faculty. Instead, a Vygotskian cultural-historical perspective is proposed. This perspective facilitates a more complex historicized view of the phenomenon by directing attention to the historically and culturally mediated nature of excessive teacher/faculty entitlement and the means to alleviate it. The healing touch to excessive teacher/faculty entitlement repeatedly surfaces as humanizing pedagogy. This involves helping teachers/faculty develop empowered entitlement *and work towards realizing their dreams, their best-loved self. Finally, this introductory chapter provides a brief overview of the 15 chapters that follow. They explore the notion of excessive teacher/faculty entitlement in diverse sociocultural contexts and examine promising approaches to address* this problem from different theoretical and methodological angles. You are invited to join us in this rich journey of inquiry and transformation.

Keywords: Excessive teacher/faculty entitlement; best-loved self; empowered entitlement; humanizing pedagogy; professional inertia; transformative agency

EXCESSIVE TEACHER ENTITLEMENT: COMING TO THE TERM

Excessive entitlement is a sense of arrogance that stems from a lack of self-awareness. It is about the inconsistency between who people think they are and who they are not. This unawareness makes one's expectations of self and others unreasonable, with one's expectations exceeding the social norms of one's deservingness (Fisk, 2010). For example, teachers feel self-righteous about their established practices and expect students to perform well, although their teaching may not meet the needs and preferences of their students. They may feel victimized by students who, according to them, are lazy and incompetent. A classic illustration of this can be seen in an excerpt from what a teacher I was interviewing on a project with English as Second Language (ESL) teachers said: 'After teaching, explaining both in English and Kannada [Students' vernacular], I ask questions, make them repeat answers. I make them write in class and ask them to write again at home. After all this, I ask them to answer the test, I don't know what happens. They don't remember the answers. I don't know what else I can do. I think I'll have to open their heads and pour it in' (Ratnam et al., 2019, p. 10). I developed the idea of 'excessive teacher entitlement' while trying to grasp this paradox, which has been gnawing at me for decades in my work with teachers – specifically, why are teachers not open to learning and change despite being overly concerned about the success in school and life of the multiculturally diverse students they teach? What prevents them from being flexible, adaptable and responsive to the needs of their students in rapidly changing educational, social, environmental and technological contexts? Why do they blame students, parents or administrators for their own failures or shortcomings (Ratnam & Craig, 2021)?

ENRICHING THE NOTION OF EXCESSIVE TEACHER ENTITLEMENT: THE EMERGENCE OF AN INVISIBLE COLLEGE

The philosophical topic of human inconsistency underlying my preoccupations with the notion of excessive teacher entitlement reverberated with Cheryl J. Craig's and others' experiences in higher education, adding the dimension of 'faculty' to excessive teacher entitlement. The nascent theme of excessive teacher/faculty entitlement knit us informally in our ongoing interactions. Our regular communication and exchange of ideas that took place outside academic walls became what others term an 'invisible college' (Crane, 1972), a productive collaboration where knowledge and practices are advanced outside shared institutional boundaries. Our collaborative work on the concept helped us present to the field of teaching and teacher education a concept hitherto unexplored (Ratnam & Craig, 2021; Ratnam et al., 2019). We were able to co-construct new knowledge in the *third space* created by the diverse locations from which we interacted about our common interest in understanding professional (teacher and faculty) inertia: Cheryl J. Craig joined the inquiry with a research background in studying how pre-service and in-service teachers' 'personal practical knowledge' (Clandinin, 1985) evolved in their knowledge communities (Craig, 1995a, 1995b), and how it influenced their knowledge, actions and identity in context. I worked closely with teachers, using the cultural-historical lens afforded by Vygotsky (1978, 1987) and Bakhtin (1981, 1984, 1986). This showed me that teachers' thinking and action came from a space neither completely personal nor entirely social but a blend of both. That finding made me realize that teachers and educators were not solely responsible for their resistance. It pointed to the need to shift the focus from teachers per se to studying the phenomenon of excessive teacher/faculty entitlement, to understand how it mediated teacher and faculty intransigence. Meanwhile, Cheryl's work on Schwab's concept of the 'best-loved self' – which relates to the ideal teacher identity that they aspire to achieve (Craig, 2020; Schwab, 1954/1978) – helped us use it as the complementary yet contrasting aspect of excessive entitlement, evoking their yin and yang dynamics (Ratnam, 2021), which are always shifting and never fixed.

Fig. 1 helps to position complex concepts of excessive entitlement and the best-loved self with respect to each other. There is no static boundary between them. They are constantly calibrating. Together, the language of 'excessive teacher/faculty entitlement' and the teacher's/faculty's 'best-loved self' reflect the two developmental facets of teachers and educators, shaping their knowing, being

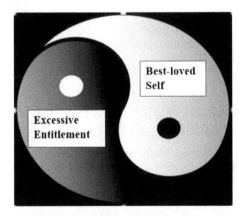

Fig. 1. Yin–Yang Relationship Between Excessive Entitlement and the Best-Loved Self.

and becoming in unique cultural and social contexts (Ratnam, Chapter 2 in this volume). This representation exhibits how expanding the space for one affects the space for the other and helps us assess whether our actions increase excessive entitlement or lead to growth in the best-loved self.

Further explorations and reflections pushed my thinking to see that the exercise of teachers' transformative agency – towards achieving their best-loved self – involved the development of a concept I have named *empowered entitlement*. Empowered entitlement 'comes from being aware of oneself and the consequences of one's actions so that the decision one makes is humane based on an understanding of the other' (Ratnam, Chapter 2 in this volume). Infusing more humanity in teaching through empowered entitlement is an important aspect of remediating excessive teacher/faculty entitlement. It brings teachers and faculty more in tune with their best-loved selves.

THE MAINSTREAM VIEW OF EXCESSIVE ENTITLEMENT AND ITS DRAWBACK

The pervasive feelings of deservingness and the exaggerated expectations that characterize excessive entitlement are seen largely as a personality vulnerability in mainstream psychology (Grubbs & Exline, 2016). This behavioural view is dominant in organized workplace settings such as education and industry (Fisk, 2010). A synchronic view of the phenomenon limited to its individualist psychological dimensions here and now restricts the focus of research to a study of the psychological correlates of excessive entitlement (e.g. Hart et al., 2020), its impact and the strategies to cope with it, without the necessity of analyzing its cultural-historical precursors (Ratnam et al., 2019). Consequently, we are left with a partial view of the problem and with solutions that fail to address the issue at its roots. In teaching and teacher education, this outlook gives rise to a deficit view of teachers and educators (Ratnam, 2021; Chapter 2 in this volume; Lay et al., Chapter 11 in this volume) and serves to reinforce the systemic narrative that legitimizes the neoliberal emphasis on stringent outcome-based accountability of teachers and educators, curtailing their autonomy (Davies & Bansel, 2007; Mikser & Goodson, 2020).

A CULTURAL-HISTORICAL VIEW OF EXCESSIVE ENTITLEMENT AND ITS ADVANTAGE

The cultural turn in psychology made visible the relational and contextual aspects of psychological processes, providing an alternative to unduly 'interiorized' views of how the mind develops (Kirschner & Martin, 2010). The cultural-historical perspective of Vygotsky (1978) emphasizes the constitutive role of others and the world in the formation of our thinking and its transformation as mediated by culturally evolving signs and artefacts (Kozulin, 2024). These culturally evolving signs and artefacts link individual psychological processes to social processes, giving the development of individual mind a cultural-historical dimension. This dialectic between the individual and cultural processes shifts consideration of psychological functions from a synchronic angle to one that is diachronic. It extends our understanding of human thinking 'as inherently situated in social, interactional, cultural, institutional and historical contexts' (Wertsch, 1991, p. 86).

The insights from cultural-historical perspective have implications for not only how we analyze and interpret excessive teacher/faculty entitled behaviour but also how empowered entitlement for realizing one's best-loved self is developed. Teachers' knowledge of teaching does not develop in isolation, but as they contribute to the practical activity of teaching as mediated by culturally available tools and embedded in a 'system of social relationships' (Leontiev, 1981, p. 47). Since cultural tools and social relationships can both facilitate and constrain teacher development and change, a comprehensive study of both manifestations of excessive teacher/faculty entitlement and the development of empowered entitlement needs to be undertaken by considering the resources and constraints of educators' historical, cultural and social contexts (Ratnam, 2021). The major advantage in following a cultural-historical perspective lies in the assistance it provides to unveil the relational and contextual complexity of teachers' and educators' work. By exposing the system and social relationships that mediate to produce the bane of excessive teacher/faculty entitlement, we can stop pathologizing teachers/faculty and consider what might be wrong with the cultural system shaping the context in which their activity is embedded.

THE HEALING TOUCH TO EXCESSIVE TEACHER/ FACULTY ENTITLEMENT

Excessive Entitlement as Teacher Resistance to *Change: Dehumanizing Pedagogy*

The historically and culturally developed thinking and practices, in their current, dominant, neoliberal formation, provide the tools for shaping teacher/faculty thinking and practice. These tools are characterized by competitive educational mores within a context of high-stakes accountability. Competition as the criterion of success makes people antagonize each other and regard every difference as a benefit for one and a loss for another. Teachers are drawn into this vortex of competition as their image of successful teachers is increasingly determined by the measure of success their students achieve (Ratnam, 2021). In the race to prepare all students for a standard test using the prescribed uniform curriculum, the differentiated needs of culturally diverse students are ignored, and their poor performance is seen as a deficiency. Teachers' concern to preserve their self-image in the face of experiences of failure makes them feel excessively entitled to recourse to scripted instruction to fulfil external mandates – overriding the need to become self-aware by questioning those practices critically, as typified by the ESL teacher quoted above. This situation is dehumanizing for both students and teachers as it stifles their human potential for agency and freedom: On one hand, students lose the voice and identity with which to engage in 'educational activity' (Davydov & Markova, 1982) that renders learning personally interesting and relevant – and therefore meaningful to them – while, on the other hand, teachers surrender their agency as 'self-governing agents of their own expectations' (Webb, 2005, p. 204), compromising the professional values of equity and inclusivity they hold as persons.

Humanizing Pedagogy With Resistance for *Change: Developing Empowered Entitlement*

Teachers' work is anchored in the inherent tensions created by the opposition between normative standards and procedures set by the institution of education that concerns itself with objective outcomes on one hand and on the other, the subjective states or personal interests, goals, values, knowledge and beliefs of teachers and students driving pedagogical processes (Olson, 2003). These tensions are swept under the carpet in the vertical relationship established by the hierarchical institutional structure, where compliance is a virtue. Teachers become complicit with the institutional norms and values that cloak larger political and economic interests. These norms and values make believe that equality of opportunity is ensured by subjecting all students to a uniform curriculum. This belief induces a delusive state where teachers lack the motive to disturb the status quo and become critically conscious of the growing inconsistency between what they want and what they do.

In my career-long efforts to demystify this illusion, I have come to understand that teacher resistance *to* change and teacher resistance *for* change are aspects of teachers' excessive entitlement and best-loved self – their *being* and *becoming*. Excessive teacher entitlement, as resistance *to* change towards realizing their best-loved self, binds them to status quo through an unawareness of themselves and their potential for agency and freedom; whereas, resisting externally mandated changes *for* changing themselves – and the situation they are in with students – helps them reclaim their image of best-loved self.

Resistance *for* change leads to humanizing pedagogy as teachers work with a heightened sense of self-realization that includes sensitivity to the unique needs of diverse students within the changing social and educational context. Humanizing pedagogy promotes equity and social justice by respecting and valuing students' culture and experiences and giving voice to students to understand and nurture what they want and find worthwhile based on their interests, potential and aspirations – rather than based on what the system imposes upon them in a banking model of education to serve vested interests (Freire, 1970). This approach positions teachers and students horizontally in a space of *ideological becoming* as they engage in a dialogic meaning-making process with equal rights to pose questions and agree or disagree (Bakhtin, 1981). These dialogues increase the possibility of getting over biases and prejudices by seeing people, situations and things in a new light.

It should be noted that the realization of teachers' best-loved self is also not a static ideal that can be achieved and fixed by a one-time effort. We must remind ourselves here that teachers are not totally autonomous despite their potential for agency and freedom – an insight born from a cultural-historical perspective. Their thinking, like all human thinking, is relational and blooms from interactions with others within a developing cultural historical context. Emerging dissonances created by interacting forces in the discursive context of teachers' practice give rise to fresh gaps between what they want and what they have, thus engaging educators in an ongoing process of becoming as they vacillate between excessive entitlement and the best-loved self. Another point to note is that the move towards the best-loved self, marking a shift in teachers' position from excessive entitlement to empowered entitlement, cannot occur without them owning their excessive self-entitlement and recognizing that it is a barrier to their own and others' growth (Ratnam, Chapter 2 in this volume). Thus, excessive teacher entitlement is an enabling tool for realizing teachers' best-loved self by promoting the development of empowered entitlement through critical self-reflexivity.

THE VOLUME

This volume is a compilation of the work of educational researchers who are passionate about making a difference in the world by helping themselves and their students and colleagues to become more intentional and resist being pushed towards the abyss of excessive entitlement. They uncover the hidden creative potential in the unique situations of excessive entitlement they have experienced. Each chapter has insights to offer for engaging in ways to grow one's sense of empowered entitlement towards achieving an ideal professional identity: the best-loved self.

Peer Review as a Self-Reflexive Tool

The book itself is the result of a process of dialogue engaging the authors in 'soul-searching', as John Buchanan put it. The intense peer review process of evaluating others' work also became a *mirror material* to evaluate the self: '—'s chapter threw me back on my chapter. Here are the questions I did not answer in my chapter' (Cheryl J. Craig). The critical evaluation of the other came from a *position of respect* acknowledging the other's scholarship. This made us willing learners, extending ourselves to new levels of understanding in the presence of the others and the unsettling questions raised by their diverse viewpoints: 'It's a little stressful because of time restrictions, but the challenge and the push to think critically about my work by how others think is transformative. It strengthens my resolve to resist the bureaucratic impositions that curtail our agency' (Cristiano Mattos). Providing feedback was also a deliberate process involving deep reflection: 'I had to reread and allow my thoughts to simmer a little before responding so that I was offering a response of reflection, not haste. Reflecting on this has been exceptionally helpful for me to review my own work from this new angle of vision I have gained – the benefit of the process' (Jacqueline Ellett).

These comments from the authors resonate with what André Sales (2023, p. xxi) points out, '[T]he meanings we create for some words are also constitutive of who we are trying to become'.

The Social Significance of This Book

This book is not a finished product but marks a particular stage in the continuous process of our *becoming*. It raises new questions for us and also for the readers by inviting them to join the conversation with wisdom gained from their own experience. It is through this process of becoming that we recover ourselves from the space of excessive entitlement that we fall into time and again, in the social world that we create and that shapes us.

Excessive teacher/faculty entitlement is a virulent social phenomenon emerging in the discursive context of their work and is not limited to teachers and faculty. It is endemic in the entire education system, in a chain of entitlements (Ratnam, 2021; Chapter 2 in this volume). Excessive entitlement also extends beyond the educational domain. It is a symptom of a wider social issue that can be traced back to the ancient philosophical question of human inconsistency between what people say and do, as raised by Socrates (Cooper & Hutchinson, 1997). This inconsistency lies at the root of discursive dynamics throughout society today, stressing the negative side of social, environmental and technological developments by inflaming bias and human irrationality. The results can be seen in ecological imbalances, poverty, ill health, various forms of oppression we face and the violence and hatred fomented through the use of technology to spread disinformation. Understanding, therefore, what produces excessive teacher/faculty entitlement and how to provide a healing touch to this malady could perhaps also have an ameliorative impact on addressing excessive entitlement as pervasive in the wider society.

LAYING OUT THE CHAPTERS

Section I: Cultural-Historical Activity Theory (CHAT) as a Way Forward From Excessive Teacher/Faculty Entitlement

The authors in this section use CHAT as a framework for analyzing the practices of teachers/faculty to gain a comprehensive understanding of the phenomenon of excessive teacher/faculty entitlement. They offer a multidimensional systemic approach, which includes individuals' motives and mediating tools, as well as the dynamics of power, culture and history (Foot, 2014). CHAT facilitates an analysis of the complex, evolving, contextualized and mediated activity of teachers/faculty, where their tacitly-held excessive entitlement becomes a tool for self-reflection moving them towards transforming both the self and the activity in which they engage.

CHAT is built on Vygotsky's understanding of the mediated nature of individual's thinking and action. As pointed out earlier, cultural tools, artefacts and signs are the means by which individuals and the social world are linked and constituted mutually (Vygotsky, 1978). As Engeström (2001) points out:

> The insertion of cultural artifacts into human actions was revolutionary in that the basic unit of analysis now overcame the split between the Cartesian individual and the untouchable societal structure. The individual could no longer be understood without his or her cultural means; and the society could no longer be understood without the agency of individuals who use and produce artifacts. (p. 134)

Fig. 2 represents Vygotsky's triangular model, which provides a unit of analysis to capture the dialectical relationship between human agency and social structure.

However, Vygotsky's idea of mediated action provides a unit of analysis at the level of the individual. Based on the works of Leontiev (1978) and Engeström (1987), CHAT extends the unit of analysis to the level of a community's collective activity – with the mediating factors of rules and division of labour, as depicted in Fig. 3.

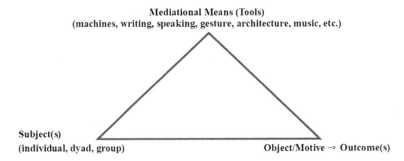

Fig. 2. Vygotsky's Mediational Triangle. *Source:* Edwards, 2005, p. 52.

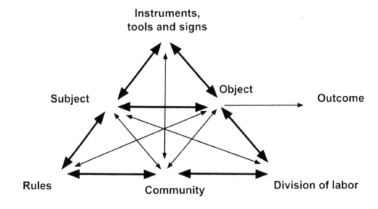

Fig. 3. The Activity System Model. *Source:* Engeström, 1987, p. 78.

CHAT includes all the social and structural elements that define an object-oriented activity system. This model provides a sound basis for understanding and analyzing the phenomenon of excessive teacher/faculty entitlement in all its historical, cultural, social embeddedness and for identifying the internal contradictions that create dissonances, which, in turn, provide the impetus to transformative change towards empowered entitlement. By centring object-oriented action, CHAT makes teachers and faculty consciously aware of the object of the activity they engage in and how this object gets modified by interacting with the discursive dynamics of the context – often moving away from the educators' original intent by responding to changing situational needs (e.g. see Botha, Chapter 3 in this volume; Lilley, Chapter 6 in this volume; Ratnam, Chapter 2 in this volume). When teachers and faculty are not attuned to the evolving nature of the object of the activity and thus experience dissonance, they tend to feel excessively entitled to resist change, holding on to established practices. This is where CHAT's potential for transformation plays an important role – it facilitates self-reflection (Engeström et al., 1999) by directing teachers and educators to the sources of the contradictions they face and increasing their ability to see things differently, including new possibilities for their own practice.

Tara Ratnam's work in Chapter 2 is a real-world application of the principles of CHAT in her practical work with teachers and students in India as an antidote to excessive teacher entitlement. A conceptual model is derived from this concrete example to enable educators to design formative support for using transformative power to challenge excessive entitlement. Her work embodies the vision of a collaborative endeavour in which teachers, teacher educators, educational administrators, students and their local community attain freedom and autonomy towards empowered entitlement through mutual influence, blending one's self-realization with that of the other.

In Chapter 3, Louis Botha proposes an innovative and provocative 'networked relational model of activity' to identify and address the emergence of excessive entitlement. His relational and performative model represents the CHAT activity system as a hand-drawn network of relations between actors and artefacts. This visual representation helps us see excessive entitlement as 'performed into being' in assemblages of relations that develop volatilely around actions and events. This model also provides 'a means for envisioning alternative countercultures into being'. The author illustrates this possibility using data from an empirical study in South Africa.

In Chapter 4, Cristiano Mattos and André Machado Rodrigues from Brazil enrich CHAT with ideas from Paulo Freire and Mikhail Bakhtin to support their theoretical exposition of the phenomenon of excessive entitlement in all its polysemic complexity. They see excessive teacher entitlement as arising in the infusion of the dominant onto-epistemological standpoint of scientific knowledge in teachers' thinking. This standpoint which equates scientific knowledge with absolute truth and influences the organization of educational activity in school gives rise to teachers assuming authoritarian modes of communication in the classroom failing to acknowledge students' diverse ways of knowing. They argue that since excessive teacher entitlement is contingent on educational activity rather than teacher characteristic per se, school reform should focus on redirecting teaching activity and relationships than on remedying some putative deficiency in teachers.

Joanne Hardman's work with mathematics teachers in Chapter 5 which is set in South Africa exemplifies the theoretical argument presented in Chapter 4. Through a fine-grained analysis using a CHAT framework, she reveals how teachers' excessive entitlement leads them to exert complete power over the content taught. It makes them push back reform by adopting a 'defensive posture' with regard to the use of new technology in the classroom.

In Chapter 6, Warren Lilley's work with ESL teachers in South Africa also uses the notion of 'defensive pedagogy' as an expression of their excessive entitlement. He employs a CHAT-informed change laboratory to assist him in supporting teachers to develop an awareness of the sources and consequences of their self-entitlement and exercise their agency and volition to find practices which are optimal for learning in the classroom.

The scene shifts from South Africa to China in Chapter 7. Working with a CHAT-informed understanding of the phenomenon of excessive teacher entitlement, author Ge Wei depicts the accumulated cultural traditions in the Chinese context that binds them to status quo practices. He uses narrative inquiry to unpack teachers' experiences of excessive entitlement and their intentional move to get closer to the values they hold as teachers.

Section II: The Yin–Yang of Excessive Teacher/Faculty Entitlement *and the* Best-Loved Self

The yin–yang metaphor helps describe how the opposing but mutually perpetuating forces of 'excessive entitlement' and 'best-loved self' interconnect. The chapters in this section uncover the yin–yang dynamics involved in teachers' and educators' day-to-day practice as they grapple with excessive entitlement produced mutually in their interactions with diversely oriented others, both at the institutional and societal levels.

In Chapter 8, Cheryl J. Craig, from the United States, narrates her close encounters with faculty entitlement and 'what happens when the excessive entitlement of one educator trumps that of another'. She applies a range of interpretive tools that narrative inquiry offers, such as fictionalization, broadening, burrowing and storying and restorying, to achieve a deeper and richer understanding of the phenomenon and inform her actions beyond excessive entitlement.

Chapter 9, co-authored by Richard D. Sawyer and Joe Norris from Canada, uses duoethnography as a means to examine personal stories, theory and common school practices. With this dialogic analysis, they 'create a collage of thoughts that highlight some of the complex factors that intersect with excessive entitlement'. This understanding helps them move towards realizing their best-loved self which involves creating an ethical habitus, a condition of moral awareness and responsibility towards the Other.

In Chapter 10, Jack Whitehead from the United Kingdom uses Living Educational Theory research as a tool to confront the living contradiction that he experienced from an awareness of his excessive entitlements bestowed by circumstances rather than 'earned' and the accompanying desire to live as fully as possible, values of human flourishing. His story marks a movement from being excessively entitled to *becoming* his best-loved self by exercising his self-accountability in promoting the flourishing of the Other.

The yin–yang dynamics created by the societal narratives of teachers as non-persons as an expression of society's excessively entitled attitude is the focus of Celina Lay, Eliza Pinnegar and Stefinee Pinnegar in Chapter 11. Situated in the United States, their thematic analysis of media narratives imply that teachers are excessively entitled by portraying them in a deficit light, while, as the authors argue, it is a lack of support and recognition of teachers' voice arising from excessive entitlement of others at the societal and institutional level that shrinks the room for teachers' realizations of their best-loved self.

Section III: Bringing to Consciousness the Unthought Known

Naming excessive teacher/faculty entitlement has opened the floodgates of experiences of oppression in schools and universities that were hitherto silenced as non-legitimate. An acknowledgement of the phenomenon as a problem to reckon with has motivated educators to engage in efforts towards resolving it without letting it fester as something to be borne. The authors in this section undertake soul-searching journeys into the self. This helps them become aware of the cultural motifs that influence their actions against reason and intention, so that they do not carry their own complexes into the classroom and victimize their students, even unintentionally.

In Chapter 12, Jackie Ellett from the United States goes on a reflective journey using autoethnography and phenomenology as a means to examine the cognitive and emotional responses to her embodied experience of excessive entitlement and her own implicit role in its production. This awareness opened a world of new possibilities to heal and be healed through a dialogic relationship with the Other.

Richard Sawyer from Canada uses the methodology of *Currere* (Pinar, 1994) to delve into the trauma he was subjected to as a gay high school student by teachers' excessive entitled actions abetted by a belief of their infallibility within the prevalent conservative systemic norms. In Chapter 13, he analyzes the play of excessive entitlement at three levels of curriculum – the formal or explicit, the implicit or hidden and the null or present/absent. He shows how the explicit and hidden curriculum perpetrated oppression while the null curriculum was liberatory offering possibilities to overcome excessive entitlement.

In a self-study of her doctoral supervisory role in Chapter 14, Marie-Christine Deyrich from France investigates the troublesome manifestations of excessive supervisor entitlement arising largely from the power imbalances between supervisors and doctoral students. She employs Bourdieu's theory of social fields to identify the dysfunction in supervisory experiences and the interacting forces that maintain them.

Chapter 15 comes from Australia. Its author, John Buchanan, uses a self-study narrative to understand the limits of his capacity to learn from his surroundings involving events that focus on sexuality, race and gender. This exploration is linked to his career-long struggle to evolve from being excessively entitled – 'a small-minded, small-hearted mini-me' – to exercising his 'responsible autonomy' toward becoming a more enlightened self.

Section IV: Synthesizing the Core Ideas

In this final chapter, Cheryl J. Craig brings us back to the point where we started in the Foreword – the lessons from the Holocaust emphasizing the need to recognize and address excessive entitlement and its inhumane consequences in education and society. She draws logical inferences by connecting the line between the diverse studies in this volume that echo the plea of a holocaust survivor to teachers: teach students to be human. She also reinforces the Upanishadic wisdom arising from these experiences, stating that we can only achieve our best-loved self in harmony with others, not in isolation. It is through this collective endeavour that we can promote human flourishing.

REFERENCES

Bakhtin, M. M. (1981). Discourse in the novel (C. Emerson & M. Holquist, Trans.). In M. Holquist (Ed.), *The dialogic imagination: Four essays by M. M. Bakhtin* (pp. 259–422). University of Texas Press.

Bakhtin, M. M. (1984). *Problems of Dostoevsky's poetics* (C. Emerson, Trans.). University of Minnesota Press.

Bakhtin, M. M. (1986). The problem of speech genres (V. McGee, Trans.). In C. Emerson & M. Holquist (Eds.), *Speech genres and other late essays* (pp. 60–102). University of Texas Press.

Clandinin, D. J. (1985). Personal practical knowledge: A study of teachers' classroom images. *Curriculum Inquiry*, *15*(4), 361–385.

Cooper, J. M., & Hutchinson, D. S. (Eds.). (1997). *Plato: Complete works*. Hackett Publishing.

Craig, C. (1995a). Knowledge communities: A way of making sense of how beginning teachers come to know in their professional knowledge contexts. *Curriculum Inquiry*, *25*(2), 151–175.

Craig, C. (1995b). Safe places in the professional knowledge landscapes. In D. J. Clandinin & F. M. Connelly (Eds.), *Teachers' professional knowledge landscapes* (pp. 137–141). Teachers College Press.

Craig, C. (2020). *Curriculum making, reciprocal learning and the best-loved self*. Palgrave Macmillan.

Crane, D. (1972). *Invisible colleges. Diffusion of knowledge in scientific communities*. The University of Chicago Press.

Davies, B., & Bansel, P. (2007). Neoliberalism and education. *Qualitative Studies in Education*, *20*(3), 247–259.

Davydov, V. V., & Markova, A. K. (1982). A concept of educational activity for schoolchildren. *Soviet Psychology*, *21*, 50–76. http://dx.doi.org/10.2753/RPO1061-0405210250

Edwards, A. (2005). Let's get beyond community and practice: The many meanings of learning by participating. *Curriculum Journal*, *16*, 49–65. https://doi.org/10.1080/09585170420000336809

Engeström, Y. (1987). *Learning by expanding: An activity theoretical approach to developmental research*. Orienta-Konsultit Oy.

Engeström, Y. (2001). Expansive learning at work: Toward an activity theoretical reconceptualization. *Journal of Education and Work*, *14*(1), 133–156. https://doi.org/10.1080/13639080020028747

Engeström, Y., Miettinen, R., & Punamäki, R. L. (Eds.). (1999). *Perspectives on activity theory*. Cambridge University Press. https://doi.org/10.1017/CBO9780511812774

Fisk, G. M. (2010). "I want it all and I want it now!" An examination of the etiology, expression, and escalation of excessive employee entitlement. *Human Resource Management Review, 20*(2), 102–114.

Foot, K. A. (2014). Cultural-historical activity theory: Exploring a theory to inform practice and research. *Journal of Human Behavior in the Social Environment, 24*, 329–347.

Freire, P. (1970). *Pedagogy of the oppressed*. Bloomsbury.

Grubbs, J. B., & Exline, J. J. (2016). Trait entitlement: A cognitive-personality source of vulnerability to psychological distress. *Psychological Bulletin, 142*(11), 1204–1226. https://doi.org/10.1037/bul0000063

Hart, W., Tortoriello, G. K., & Breeden, C. J. (2020). Entitled due to deprivation vs. superiority: Evidence that unidimensional entitlement scales blend distinct entitlement rationales across psychological dimensions. *Journal of Personality Assessment, 102*(6), 781–791. https://doi.org/10.1080/00223891.2019.1674319

Kirschner, S. R., & Martin, J. (Eds.). (2010). *The sociocultural turn in psychology: The contextual emergence of mind and self*. Columbia University Press.

Kozulin, A. (2024). *The cultural mind: The sociocultural theory of learning*. Cambridge University Press.

Leontiev, A. N. (1978). *Activity, consciousness, and personality*. Prentice-Hall.

Leontiev, A. N. (1981). The problem of activity in psychology. In J. V. Wertsch (Ed.), *The concept of activity in Soviet psychology* (pp. 37–71). M. E. Sharpe.

Mikser, R., & Goodson, I. (2020). Narratives of education and curriculum transition in the formerly socialist European countries: The example of Estonia. In G. McCulloch, I. Goodson, & M. Delgado-Gonzalez (Eds.), *Transnational perspectives on curriculum history* (pp. 41–62). Routledge.

Olson, D. R. (2003). *Psychological theory and educational reform: How school remakes mind and society*. Cambridge University Press.

Pinar, W. (1994). The method of Currere. In W. Pinar (Ed.), *Autobiography, politics and sexuality: Essays in curriculum theory 1972–1992* (pp. 19–27). Peter Lang.

Ratnam, T. (2021). The interaction of culture and context in the construction of teachers' putative entitled attitude in the midst of change. In T. Ratnam & C. J. Craig (Eds.), *Understanding excessive teacher and faculty entitlement: Digging at the roots* (pp. 77–101). Emerald Publishing Limited. https://doi.org/10.1108/S1479-368720210000038006

Ratnam, T., & Craig, C. J. (2021). *Understanding excessive teacher and faculty entitlement*. Emerald Publishing Limited. https://doi.org/10.1108/S1479-368720210000038001

Ratnam, T., Craig, C., Marcut, I. G., Marie-Christine, D., Mena, J., Doyran, F., Hacıfazlıoğlu, O., Hernández, I., & Peinado- Muñoz, C. (2019). Entitlement attitude: Digging out blind spots. In D. Mihăescu & D. Andron (Eds.), *Proceedings, the 19th biennial conference of international study association on teachers and teaching (ISATT), "Education beyond the crisis: New skills, children's rights and teaching contexts"* (pp. 210–219). Lucian Blaga University Publishing House.

Sales, A. L. L. de F. (2023). *A political psychology approach to militancy and prefigurative activism: The case of Brazil*. Springer Press.

Schwab, J. J. (1954/1978). Eros and education: A discussion of one aspect of discussion. In I. Westbury & N. Wilkof (Eds.), *Science, curriculum and liberal education: Selected essays*. University of Chicago Press.

Vygotsky, L. S. (1978). Interaction between learning and development (M. Lopez-Morillas, Trans.). In M. Cole, V. John-Steiner, S. Scribner, & E. Souberman (Eds.), *Mind in society: The development of higher psychological processes* (pp. 79–91). Harvard University Press.

Vygotsky, L. S. (1987). Thinking and speech (N. Minick, Trans.). In R. W. Rieber & A. S. Carton (Eds.), *The collected works of L. S. Vygotsky (Vol. 1): Problems of general psychology* (pp. 39–285). Plenum Press.

Webb, P. T. (2005). The anatomy of accountability. *Journal of Education Policy, 20*(2), 189–208.

Wertsch, J. V. (1991). A sociocultural approach to socially shared cognition. In L. B. Resnick, J. M. Levine, & S. D. Teasley (Eds.), *Perspectives on socially shared cognition* (pp. 85–100). American Psychological Association.

SECTION I

CULTURAL–HISTORICAL ACTIVITY THEORY (CHAT) AS A WAY FORWARD FROM EXCESSIVE TEACHER/FACULTY ENTITLEMENT

WHY ARE TEACHERS EXCESSIVELY ENTITLED? UNDERSTANDING TEACHERS TO FOSTER THEIR *IDEOLOGICAL BECOMING*

Tara Ratnam

Independent Teacher Educator and Researcher, India

ABSTRACT

In our societal context, the neoliberal competitive and knowledge-oriented culture still exerts a stranglehold on teachers' sense of professional autonomy giving rise to a deficit image of them as 'excessively entitled'. The purpose of this chapter is to eschew this deficit view of teachers by bringing their agentive side to the fore. First, it explores the concept of 'excessive teacher entitlement' in terms of the prevalent characteristics of the culture of teaching in schools and the nature of authority wielded by teachers in this culture and its negative consequence on student learning using an excerpt from an English as Second Language (ESL) classroom in India where this study is set. This episode helps expose the teacher's unawareness of the gaps between their intention and action, a hallmark of excessive entitlement. Second, it juxtaposes an alternative image of 'teacher as researcher' to foreground teachers' 'transformative activist stance' which revolves around their ideological becoming *in agentively striving to realise their 'best-loved self'. Framed within Vygotskian Cultural-Historical Activity Theory, the principle of 'double stimulation' provides a powerful analytical lens to unpack the complex discursive dynamics of their practice nested within historically developing contradictions. These contradictions work tacitly to drive a wedge between teachers' intentions and action making them feel excessively entitled to passively acquiesce with the existing order of things. This study provides some signposts for teacher education about creating an environment where teachers can reclaim their transformative agency freeing themselves from the 'excessive entitlement' that binds their practice to the status quo and diminishes their relationships with students.*

Keywords: Excessive teacher entitlement; deficit view; transformative activist stance; cultural–historical activity theory; double stimulation; empowered entitlement

Excessive entitlement as an issue associated with teachers poses an anomaly calling for some explanation. Theirs is a 'noble' profession. The 'best-loved self' (Craig, 2020; Schwab, 1954/1978) in every teacher aspires to help all students in their charge to realise their unique potential to do well in school and beyond. Labaree (2000) ascribes the ennobling nature of a teacher's job to its selflessness. He points out that, like most professionals, teachers do not 'rent their expertise', but 'they give it away. A good teacher is in the business of making himself or herself unnecessary, of empowering learners to learn without the teacher's help' (p. 233). In other words, teaching is about helping students become self-evolving learners. However, teachers' practice shows that it is highly straightjacketed to the narrow goals of what students need to know to pass the standard examination relying on a knowledge delivery approach to teaching (Ratnam & Tharu, 2018). There is a lack of affirmation of the conceptual and cultural assets that students bring to school to provide the differentiated support to which they are entitled if they are to connect to the knowledge and concepts presented at school and make them their own (Ladson-Billings, 2014; Ratnam, 2014; Williams et al., 2022).

The gap between the ennobling values teachers hold and their negation in teachers' practice eludes their conscious awareness and manifests itself in the form of 'excessive entitlement' (Ratnam, 2023). Naming this phenomenon of excessive teacher entitlement opens it for investigative analysis presenting it to consciousness (Ratnam et al., 2019). Russell (2021) points to the consciousness raising effect the notion of excessive entitlement had on him: *Until invited to contribute to this collection (*Ratnam & Craig, 2021a*), I had not explored explicitly the idea of teacher entitlement (or student entitlement) in my work as a teacher and teacher educator. Entitlement has been a valuable perspective for reviewing my own teaching experiences between 1963 and 2019 (p. 35).*

I begin this chapter by exploring the concept of 'excessive teacher entitlement' in terms of the prevalent characteristics of the culture of teaching in schools using an excerpt from an English as Second Language (ESL) classroom in India, where this study is set. The defining frame of excessive entitlement used here has to do with the belief that one is inherently entitled to special privileges by virtue of one's position (Craig, 2021; Ratnam et al., 2019). In the classroom context, it refers to teacher authority in their relationship with students and the assumptions made about their role in that relationship and its impact on teaching and learning (McGarr et al., 2017; Petrik, 2019; Ratnam, 2023). Teachers' 'transformative activist agency' (Stetsenko, 2019) lies in developing an awareness of the excessive entitlement encompassing them and the attendant mismatch between their intention and practice. This involves using their capacity to think critically about the values they hold (Delong & Whitehead, 2024), the interests their practice serves (Billett, 2010; Ratnam, 2021b; Ratnam, forthcoming) and how they can realign their practice to pull it closer to their values. The image of 'teacher as researcher' (Stenhouse, 1975) comes to mind here as an alternative for an excessively entitled teacher; one who actively enquires into their practice, its antecedents and consequences (Zeichner, 1983) to transform themselves and their course of action. This possibility is explained through the illustrative case of a small group of teachers whose self-realisation about their excessive self-entitlement, together with a re-evaluation of their past ideas about the 'object' of teaching activity, led to a reconstruction of it 'expansively' (Engeström, 1987/2015; Engeström et al., 2013) making them engage in an effort to realize it in forms of action. The chapter concludes with some thoughts on how teacher education needs to become self reflexively responsive by examining how it is itself a part of the problem of excessive teacher entitlement. It also recognises a need to look beyond teacher education to investigate the emergent contradictions in the diverse interacting activity systems (Engeström, 2001) comprising the entire educational organisation in order to address the chain of excessive entitlement played out on its discursive terrain and to stem its negative consequence on the learning and wellbeing of all stakeholders including importantly, teachers.

INCONSISTENCY BETWEEN TEACHER ESPOUSAL AND PRACTICE, AN EXAMPLE

Teacher resistance to a curriculum reform effort I was involved in the 1980s was the beginning of my long quest to understand what made teachers, who all wanted to do the best for their students, reject something meant to be in students' interest (Ratnam, 2021a). I have had the opportunity to interview and observe the practice of innumerable teachers as part of my field work during my MPhil and PhD studies in the 1990s and beyond to find an answer to this very question. What struck me in my interactions with teachers and observing their classes was the inconsistency between what they claimed about their practice and what they actually did. I accumulated a mountain of data from the many classes I observed that could easily be used as evidence to portray teachers as 'excessively entitled', with unreasonable expectations of high performance from students regardless of their own insensitivity to the subjective needs of learners in promoting their learning. The following excerpt from an ESL class illustrates this.

[T: Teacher; SS: Student]

> *T:* I have given you five questions to answer. Now, I want you to give me the answers. Will you please read the answers along with the questions one by one? Who will start? (A girl makes a movement to show that she wants to answer. Teacher nods) OK.
> *SS1:* Who is the narrator here?
> The barber is the narrator here.
> *T:* The barber is the narrator. Good.
> *SS1:* (Continues unsolicited) Who is the customer?
> Captain is the customer.

T: Captain is the customer. Very good.
(Looks around) Question number three? (Points to a student)
SS2: What did the customer do when he entered the saloon?
The bullet studded.... Studded belt that is the, the holster dangled.
T: Who will give me the correct answer?
(SS1 stands up to read)
SS1: The customer took off the bullet studded belt and hung it upon a wall when he entered the saloon.
T: Repeat, repeat. (To the class) She will repeat the answer.
SS1: (Reads the same answer again)
T: Fine. (To SS2) Please copy down the answer from her.

In his pre-class interview, this teacher claimed, 'All [students] are equal. I don't differentiate among them'. However, the classroom excerpt above betrays a hidden discourse of power at work in the way he used his authority as a teacher that accorded different statuses to students affecting their participation and identity. While SS1 was appreciated for her 'correct' answers that facilitated her participation with an increased sense of importance and confidence, SS2 was positioned as a passive recipient by the teacher asking him to copy down the 'correct' answer from SS1. This denied him his voice to engage in learning conversations.

Teacher Authority and Its Links to Excessive Teacher Entitlement

The authority given to teachers in school settings is based on a recognition of their ability to teach and is consequential for student learning (Pace & Hemmings, 2007). Driven by mounting concerns of equity, diversity and inclusivity, educational reforms in recent decades have been vocal about democratising the teacher–student relationship. This has led to making teacher authority a reluctant topic to be addressed explicitly (Lü & Hu, 2021), giving the term a negative connotation. However, in an educational process, if we dispose with teacher authority altogether, it doesn't remain an educational relationship anymore, but becomes analogous to a relationship among equal partners or friends (Personal communication, Fotis Terzakis, 10 April 2018). Dewey (1902/1990) avers that people require organizational authority within which they find their liberty. He accorded the educational authority of a teacher a high place in their job of leading students and helping them become democratic citizens. While it is important to democratise the teacher-student relationship in nurturing the student voice for their learning and the development of their autonomy, this does not cancel out the educative role of the teacher in promoting this development. The point I want to spotlight here is that whether the position of authority given to teachers is pernicious or beneficial depends upon how it is used in their interactions with students. The distinction Bakhtin (1981) makes between two types of discourses: 'authoritative discourse' and 'internally persuasive discourse', captures these twin orientations to authority dwelling in the teacher's discourse. Authoritative discourse lies within a structure of hierarchical relationship with expectations of passive acquiescence to authority. This authority derives its legitimacy by virtue of teachers' position, while internally persuasive discourse is cognizant of students' voice. Excessively entitled teachers tend to use their authority in ways that constrain learning albeit, unintentionally, while a teacher who listens to students to understand their subjective perceptions, goals and interests is less entitled and more likely to influence students in realizing their own potential to learn. I use the above classroom episode to explain this point.

Uncovering Teacher Authority in Classroom Discourse: The Pernicious Side up

The episode from the ESL class presented earlier illustrates how a teacher's authoritative discourse can hijack the voice students are entitled to and thus inhibit their learning. Teacher authority is closely linked to their view of language learning. In the excerpt, the teacher's appreciation of SS1 for her ability to reproduce the 'correct' answer from the text he had taught reflects his belief that learning is reproducing what is taught. By the same token, the answer given by SS2 was considered a sign of his deficiency in learning. The teacher's transmissional view of language teaching and learning is further evidenced by the means he adopted to remedy SS2's 'deficiency' using SS1 to ventriloquise his corrective feedback. Accordingly, the decisions he made in his position of authority to assist SS2 were mimetic and mechanical: *Please copy down the answer from her*. There was no strategic support to enable SS2 to reflect on the inadequacy of his own answer and reconstruct it through meaning negotiation. By making students simply 'know' the answer by copying it as the teacher did, without providing them the 'growth' experience (Holzman, 2018) of the process of contributing to meaning co-creation, students remain other regulated. Even in the case of SS1, the nature of participatory role assigned to her by the teacher seemed to promote her ability to *adopt* his meaning rather than *produce* her unique meaning, thus limiting her learning to the test rather than expanding it to the generative goal of learning to learn.

Conquering Excessive Entitlement to Develop the Beneficial Aspect of Teacher Authority

Some initial clarifications: My critique of the foregoing classroom episode is not meant to pass a value judgement on this or any other teacher or to show them in a bad or deficit light by labelling them as 'excessively entitled'. Therefore, before I proceed further, it is important to state, in no uncertain terms, that 'excessive teacher entitlement' is a putative concept which, as I have strongly argued elsewhere, 'manifests our understanding of teachers, what we believe them to be, which need not necessarily align with who they are or who they are not' (Ratnam & Craig, 2021b, p. 3). The negative perception of teachers comes from seeing excessive entitlement in psychological terms as a personality trait associated with narcissism (e.g. Jordan et al., 2017). This gives a partial view of the phenomenon of 'excessive teacher entitlement' making it seem as a problem residing in teachers, whereas the real problem lies in our inadequate understanding of the phenomenon. The cultural–historical perspective (Vygotsky, 1978) taken in this study facilitates a more comprehensive view of the phenomenon by exposing the discursive context of teachers' practice that produces the toxicity which triggers excessive entitlement (Ratnam, 2021b).

THE PERSPECTIVE FRAMING THE STUDY

My epistemological orientation in this study is influenced by the cultural–historical perspectives of Lev Vygotsky (1978). Vygotsky's dialectical view draws attention to the mediated nature of our mental functioning. 'The emphasis is on the nexus of people changing the world and being changed in this process of changing the world' (Stetsenko, 2019). This understanding of individual development as dialectically bound up with cultural and historical development is very significant in helping us see the issue of excessive teacher entitlement, not as a problem located within teachers as individuals, but in their interaction with social systems (including the education system) that, in their current formation, pander to the 'naturalisation of neoliberalism' (Harvey, 2007, p. 24). This dialectical view helps dislodge the deficit model of discourse in education that projects 'excessive teacher entitlement' as a personal trait residing in the teacher (Ratnam, 2021b). A dialectical view provides an integrated account of human development that helps us see both excessive entitlement and agency to realise the best-love self as aspects of individual development – the process of our historical and ideological *becoming* (Bakhtin, 1981) – taking place within the resources and constraints of the cultural context and social interactions that they are part of. This opens the possibility of reimagining teachers in a more positive light as competent people working purposefully to meet their commitment to the students they serve.

Cultural-Historical Activity Theory (CHAT), which is grounded in Vygotsky's work and further extended by other scholars' contributions (e.g. Cole & Engeström, 1993; Engeström, 1987/2015; Leont'ev, 1978) provides a methodological framework to this study. It foregrounds the central transformative aspect of human relation to the world. Stetsenko underlines the activist nature of this transformative practice by calling it 'transformative activist stance' (Stetsenko, 2016, 2019, 2020). According to her, 'people never merely react, nor respond, to what exists but agentively act in co-creating both the world and themselves beyond 'the givenness' of the present' (Stetsenko, 2019). It is in and through this process of transforming the world and themselves that people become human, 'gaining self-knowledge and knowledge about the world' (Stetsenko, 2009, p. 137). Becoming human through an 'inward-looking process' is crucial for addressing excessive entitlement and its dehumanising effect not only on teachers and students, but all the people involved in the educational hierarchy (Ratnam, 2021b).

CHAT has been used as an analytical tool to study human activity in diverse contexts with an emphasis on its transformation emerging from the self-reflection of its participants (Engeström & Pyörälä, 2021; Lotz-Sisitka et al., in press; Sannino, 2020). CHAT's object of social transformation centralising the 'formative (or constitutive)' dimension of human development (Stetsenko, 2019) is thus relevant to this study which is about fostering teachers' transformative activist agency through self-realization to overcome excessive entitlement.

Teacher as Researcher: The Transformative Agentive Side up

The idea of teacher as researcher (Stenhouse, 1975) subsumes transformative activist agency because it involves teachers in identifying a problem situation and engaging in transforming it within the resources and constraints of sociocultural interactions and contextual dynamics. This activist endeavour within an 'inquiry as stance' is imbued with values as it reflects teachers' intention to act 'in the best interests of the learning and life chances of students and their communities' (Cochran-Smith & Lytle, 2009, p. 123; also, Delong & Whitehead, 2024).

A lack of acknowledgement in education and teacher education of the capacity of teachers to initiate and sustain transformation to improve the situation they find themselves in is at the root of excessive teacher entitlement (Ratnam, 2021b). An educational landscape dominated by standards movements, and intensified accountability (Hall & Pulsford, 2019) is not conducive to the development of transformative teacher agency.

Teacher as researcher stance upholds the transformative agency of the teacher, which is the better half of excessive entitlement in their yin-yang relationship. The development of transformative activist agency is contingent on access to cultural tools and resources that afford or stifle it (Stetsenko, 2019). A supportive environment with access to resources for the development of teachers' transformative agency will awaken them, in turn, to use their position of authority beneficially to afford agency by creating a similar nurturing environment in which their students can thrive.

BACKGROUND AND QUESTIONS FOR THE STUDY

The Government School in India: An Embodiment of Universal Education

Like most 'new' nations, India, after its independence from British rule in 1947, adopted universal education as a major goal and reflected it as a major concern in its policies (GOI, 1949, 2020; RTE, 2009). Its aspiration to get all children into school has seen a Net Enrolment Ratio of 93.83 girls and 91.63 boys at the primary level (UDISE Plus Report, 2022). Public schools in India, which we call Government schools, account for a little over 143 million children, making up 54 % of the total number (about 265 million) of school going students. The percentage of children enroled in government schools is higher for rural India which is about 74% (Pratham, 2023). The government school providing free instruction, largely in vernacular, is the only option for the socioeconomically weaker sections. These students come to school bearing the deep scar of centuries of the social segregation and educational exclusion their ancestors were subjugated to (Ratnam, 2015). The government schools represent both the perils and promise of achieving equity in education by providing an inclusive learning experience for these historically disadvantaged students.

The government schools are 'layered institutions' that are influenced by bureaucratic administration, the local communities and, not the least, the agency of teachers (Ratnam, 2015; Vasavi, 2015). The quality of education, being essentially a matter of pedagogy, is seen as lying largely in the hands of the teacher (Ratnam, 2015). This makes teacher agency an important aspect of fulfiling the goals of universal education by eradicating illiteracy, and child labour, creating citizenship, fostering democracy, and facilitating upward socioeconomic mobility. The national curriculum framework acknowledges that 'teacher autonomy is essential to ensure a learning environment that addresses the children's diverse needs' (NCERT, 2005, p. 81; also, GOI, 2020). To what extent does the school system as an organizational structure facilitate a hospitable setting for teachers to explore transformative teaching practices for inclusivity and diversity? Vasavi (2015, p. 36) avers that the government schools' effect on society is 'neither reproductive nor transformative, but disjunctive'. Routinisation of teaching and learning practices, training fatigue among teachers whose agency has been eroded, programme overload and disruption of classes by non-teaching work link to learning loss among children (Ratnam, 2021b; Ratnam & Tharu, 2018; Vasavi, 2015). This largely demotivating setting creates a disjuncture between the policy vision and teachers' practice.

Problem Situation: Emergence of a Formative Initiative

The bleak situation described took another beating by the long school closure due to the COVID-19 pandemic. The rural-based children studying in government schools were hit the hardest being on the flipside of the digital divide (Pratham, 2022). Teachers were concerned about the 'learning loss' that would leave their students further behind their more advantaged peers in urban and private schools. Their ethical dilemma was voiced in their worries about connecting to their students online. The control they exerted in the physical space of the classroom seemed to elude them in their efforts to teach remotely online: *Students have become more indifferent and inattentive now than in [physical] class. How can we motivate them to listen to our teaching and answer?* (Asha) This question was posed to my professional colleague, Prema, and me by one of the small group of teachers with whom we were working on a project to enhance their learning and teaching of English. This project, which was initiated in collaboration with the local District Institute of Education and Training (DIET) a little before the onset of the pandemic, came to an abrupt halt with the nationwide lockdown. The teachers came back to us about the end of 2020, wanting us to resume it informally online. They were keen on improving their English besides finding a 'solution' to the difficulties they were facing with engaging their students in learning. Like many other government school teachers, these teachers had to teach English in addition to other subjects even though English Language Teaching was not their qualifying subject in Pre-service Teacher Education. Although we had no readymade answer to the teacher's question, we were willing to explore new possibilities with them by affording 'expanded learning opportunities' (Zeichner, 2010). We wanted them to include a batch of students with the consent of their parents/guardians so that our joint learning would be authentic. We had two groups of students: 14 juniors (Grades 6 and 7) meeting on Saturdays and 10 seniors (grades 9 and 10) meeting on Sundays. We named this informal effort 'We Make' to symbolise its collaborative formative spirit.

As resource persons (RPs), the nature of the learning activity Prema and I facilitated in We Make was different from the standard classroom practice with strict teacher control and transmission forms of pedagogy in a vertical teacher–student relationship. In its 'horizontal social learning' environment, children, teachers, community members and researchers all had a voice (Cole, 2005). The modes of participation gave students the freedom to follow their interests and present their 'authentic selves' (Gutiérrez, 2020). Student contribution was the syllabus for engaging them in a dialogic process of meaning making (Bakhtin, 1981). Language was promoted for students (also teachers) in their efforts to find and express meaning.

We Make put all of us on a robust learning and developmental trajectory, including members from students' local community who were invited to participate in classroom discussions on topics pertaining to their occupations such as farming and cattle rearing. However, in keeping with the scope of this study, the focus here is primarily on illuminating the dynamics that underlie the 'expansive transformation' (Engeström, 2001) in teachers and their activity of teaching by their participation in the cultural space of We Make that afforded an alternative pathway for them to explore. Accordingly, the questions this study seeks to address are:

- What dynamics underlie the transformations in teachers and in their activity from their experience of a new approach to their activity in the cultural space of We Make?
- What implications does the dynamics of teachers' expansive transformation have for how they can be supported to become conscious of their excessive entitlement and agentively transform themselves and their situation?

PARTICIPANTS, SOURCES OF DATA AND ANALYSIS

The Saturday group, which is the focus of this study, consisted of 14 students from grades six and seven and six teachers. Prema and I, in the role of more experienced peers, provided some tools and resources for expanding their thinking about their problem situation. The students came online every Saturday from 6 to 7 p.m. when they could get access to phones after their parents/guardians returned from field work. The rest of us stayed on for another hour to reflect on our experience and observations of the session with students and to discuss other emergent questions, including providing support for developing teachers' English language awareness. The data from the sessions between January 2021 and February 2022 were audio recorded and transcribed. Video recording posed problems due to poor connectivity and network disruptions. Documents, literature, guest appearances of members from the students' community with whom we interacted, my notes on the continuing conversations with teachers beyond the initiative about the sustenance of change in their practice, new challenges they are negotiating, and my reflective diary have also contributed to the study.

'Bathing in the data' (Goodson, 2013, p. 40) through a reflexive iterative process (Srivastava & Hopwood, 2009) has helped identify the salient themes to respond to the questions posed for investigation. I have shared my analysis with Prema and all the teacher participants thus cross-checking its trustworthiness and also enriching it with their comments.

All the names used in the study except that of Prema and me are fictionalised in keeping with the wishes of the participants to remain anonymous.

Double Stimulation as a Method of Intervention

In treating the principle of double stimulation, my focus will be on its interconnectedness with the concepts of transformative agency and 'expansive learning' (Engeström, 1987/2015, 2001). This interconnection is of immediate relevance to the concerns of this study about the development of teachers' transformative agency to fight excessive entitlement.

Double stimulation is a process of agency formation (Sannino, 2015). The dialectical perspective underlying this agency formation foregrounds the role of contradictions inherent in an activity system under investigation as its driving force. It has to do with 'how individuals and collectives perform volitional actions in circumstances of cognitive conflict and ambiguity' (Morselli & Sannino, 2021, p. 2; also, Sannino, 2015). The volitional act of individuals and collectives involved in resolving a conflictual situation renders their transformative activist agency the key mediator of change in initiating new learning. This agentive new learning involves 'examination of disturbances, conflicts and contradictions in the collective activity. Transformative agency develops the participants' joint activity by explicating and envisioning new possibilities' (Haapasaari et al., 2016, p. 233). The process in which participants, through their 'learning actions', seek to overcome the inadequacy of existing relatively stable practices by redefining the object and motive of the activity, and creating new activities is characterised by Engeström as 'expansive learning' (Engeström, 1987/2015, 2001; Engeström & Sannino, 2010; Rantavuori et al., 2016).

Expansive learning is a very useful notion as it addresses the 'prospective' aspect of *learning something that is not yet there* (Engeström, 2001; Sannino, 2015; Sannino et al., 2016) leading to the development of both individuals and the activity. 'Prospective' and 'retrospective' are two aspects of learning (Kozulin, 1998). Retrospective orientation to learning is limited to gaining competence in established cultural practices. Prospective aspect of learning focuses on elaborating/transforming existing cultural tools, meanings and practices. The prospective aspect addresses the activist stance of transformative agency seeking inventive solutions to problems in the discursive context of teachers' practice. It helps overcome 'the residue of passivity' (Stetsenko, 2019) that makes other forms of participatory learning, such as situated learning (e.g.

Lave & Wenger, 1991; Wenger, 1998), largely retrospective with its primary focus on mastering existing cultural tools and practices (Engeström, 2001; Stetsenko, 2016, 2019, 2020).

Methodologically, double stimulation operates on two stimulations. The first stimulation represents the problem situation that creates a 'need state' (Engeström, 2001) prompting individuals and collectives to look for ways to resolve it. The second stimulation is the resources, new models of activity, that help individuals/collectives to break out of the difficult situation and work out a solution (Lund & Vestøl, 2020; Sannino, 2015; Lilley, Chapter 6 in this volume). The new models of activity, with new objects and practices, come with the potential of generating conflicts of motive, colliding with established forms of practice. Identifying these conflicts, tracing their source and agentively taking steps to resolve them are the driving force for change. The inconsistency between the old and new models of activity creates a zone of proximal development for new objects and practices to emerge (Augustsson, 2021; Engeström, 2001; Engeström & Sannino, 2010).

Double Stimulation as a Unit of Analysis

The formative initiative presented in this study was not deliberately designed on the principle of double stimulation. Its use here as a structuring principle for the study of teachers' transformative agency is *post-facto* as it responded to the need for an analytical unit that could help unpack teachers' transformative efforts in resolving a problem situation. It provided an analytical language to capture the movement created in the dialectic between the problem situation teachers faced and their agentive use of resources (Lund & Vestøl, 2020). The focus of my analysis is on identifying the salient features of the dynamics underlying teachers' transformative agency as they navigated through the 'collective ZPD' (Mahn & John-Steiner, 2002) created by the opposition between their old activity, on one hand, and the new model of activity they experienced in the cultural space of We Make, on the other. The findings are presented through quotations that illustrate layers of contradictions identified in the data and analytical comments and concepts behind them (Braun & Clarke, 2013).

Fig. 1 represents teachers' agentive learning actions (A) within an expansive learning cycle set in motion by layers of contradictions they encountered in their efforts to resolve the problem situation. Engestrom's conceptual model of the cycle of expansive learning (Engeström, 2001, p. 152) has been influential in advancing my thinking. I have adapted it to suit the pattern of learning actions that corresponded to the four levels of contradictions explained by Engeström (1987/2015), which propelled these learning actions in this study. Engeström (1987/2015) has identified these contradictions as primary, secondary, tertiary and quaternary.

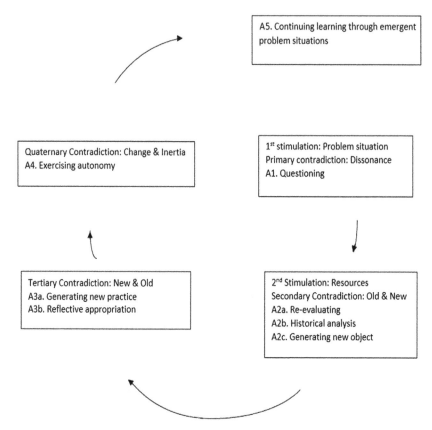

Fig. 1. A Conceptual Model of Cycle of Expansive Learning.
Source: Adapted From Engeström, 2001, p. 152.

FINDINGS

The analysis of the findings will focus on the four levels of contradictions identified in the study and the learning actions ensuing from them. This will help capture the dynamics underlying the transformative agency of teachers in changing themselves and their situation responding to the first question of the study.

Where Teachers Are: Primary Contradiction

Teachers' confirmed practices: The dissonance experienced by teachers during the pandemic created a *need state* raising the question: *Students have become more indifferent and inattentive now [in online class] than in [physical] class. How can we motivate them to listen to our teaching and answer?* This question was driven by concerns of losing their 'grip on students' and the 'learning loss' that would slow their pace in the race to the institutionally set finish line: *Our [rural] students are poor [in learning]. Now they will fall more behind other students in the cities. We have to help them learn and come up* (Tanvi).

The question and concerns voiced by teachers reflected a latent tension between teaching to help students *learn* and *come up*, which points to its 'use value', on one hand, and teaching to fulfil the institutional obligation of promoting students, which points to its 'exchange value', on the other (Engeström, 1987/2015). In achieving the institutionally set object of helping students score on standardized tests, teachers' practice converged with the dominant authoritarian educational practices that marginalised other ways of knowing of the culturally diverse students. Teachers seemed to be unaware of the negative impact of the control they exerted over students through the mimetic practice of making students passively *listen* and *answer*. Their authoritarian discourse failed to acknowledge the plurality of voices, the 'living knowledge' (Vygotsky, 1987) students brought to school as an essential aspect of making learning relevant to them. Remaining 'unaware' of the need to go beyond teaching to the test to teach students how to learn, as Russell (2021, p. 36) points out, is the 'ultimate' form of excessive teacher entitlement. It makes teachers hold a deficit view of students as *poor, indifferent, inattentive*, implying that they are unable (cognitively deficient) and unwilling to learn.

Where Teachers Are Going: Secondary Contradiction

The new colliding with the old: The primary contradiction gave way to secondary contradictions that became apparent in the clash between teachers' established object and practice of teaching, on one hand, and the way learning was mediated in We Make, on the other. The deficit view of students made teachers see students' initial silence in We Make, their appearances and disappearances from the screen, as a confirmation of their appraisal of students: *Same thing happens to us when we try. They just don't bother, they don't listen, simply a waste of our efforts* (Salma). Besides, the time we spent to connect to students, finding and following their interests, warming relationships and earning their trust all seemed to eat into teaching to the test: *We won't have time to finish portions and prepare them for exams* (Salma). We Make was thus a decentring experience for teachers whose main object was directing and controlling students' learning actions, namely, listen and reproduce the given as a means to accomplish the institutional goals. Their scepticism and dismay gave way to interest and self-realization when, gradually students started responding to our overtures: *Miss, I Chaitra. Today my screen name Lingaraju.*[1] In the post class session, teachers observed: *They are picking up words and using it* (Pavana). A major breakthrough came when we invited one of our students from a senior class, Rahul, an avid photographer, to share some of his pictures. The local legends associated with one of the pictures

---

[1]Students' screen names changed depending upon the person they borrowed the phone from, father, grandfather or uncles. In the first few sessions, the class began with identifying the person behind the screen name, which provided all of us an opportunity to familiarise ourselves with who was who.

which he narrated made all of us genuinely involved, and everyone, and students, especially, got drawn into the flow of conversation with our natural curiosity: *won't it get hurt?* [a question from a student, translated from their vernacular]. Prema put the questions posed by students on the whiteboard, and they provided the teaching moments for that session. Other students took the cue from this and from then on, we had no dearth of material for teaching from the many things students were eager to share. In one of the after-class sessions a teacher observed, *Friday morning itself students start calling me about the Saturday class, what they want to share* (Anu). This remark by Anu created an opportune ZPD to provoke teachers to become self-reflexive about their perceptions of students, their practice, and its impact on students. Questions for discussion were raised around who these students were, where they came from, the nature of their competence, and what made school an alienating experience for them. Historical analysis thus became one of the strands of our after-class discussions. These discussions contributed a great deal to teachers developing an empathetic understanding of their students who were disadvantaged by a long history of oppression and exclusion. The realization that they were failing to meet the learning needs of their students by unreflectively following the dominant institutional practices put them in a discomfort zone. It strengthened their resolve to undo this injustice for which they felt partly responsible as cogs in the wheel of the system they were serving.

Discussions around how hidden assumptions of a normal school in the standard curriculum suppressed the rich but different cultural knowledge with little tolerance for students' other interests, talents and styles of learning, helped teachers slowly step out of their 'stuck stories' (Conle, 1999) of students as deficient. An excerpt from teachers' dialogue about Rahul's case is a concrete illustration of this.

> *Asha:* The pictures he [Rahul] takes show how sensitive he is to nature. The way he described them was also interesting.
>
> *Salma:* And he is genuinely concerned. Said he wants to become a forest officer to protect the forest, animals and birds.
>
> *Tanvi:* But in school he fails in both my subjects, English and Maths. We thought he was dull. If he fails in 10th, what happens to his dream? He can't go further. But, here [in We Make] he's picking up so well. That shows he is capable. We teachers, we have to change. I'm helping him and others to learn Maths, means not blindly learning rules to follow, help them to understand mathematical structure and relationships. Another Maths teacher is with me. We plan together, also taking ideas from YouTube.

It is notable how Tanvi's idea of *learning* was gaining a new meaning, that it was not about substituting rules mechanically, but learning to think and reason by revealing the theoretical generalities of mathematical concepts (Davydov, 1990).

Theorising from teachers' firsthand experience of how learning was enhanced in We Make formed a large part of the ongoing post class discussions. This was ineluctably accompanied by teachers evaluating their own practice in relation to the new approach. Questioning their practice in the light of the new, marked a shift from their earlier questioning of the new practices in We Make using their old lens (Engeström et al., 2013): *We used to think inclusion means giving every student the chance to repeat the answers we give them to learn. What I observed here is, everyone is involved, no one is left out because teaching depends on students, what they think, say or do* (Pavana). The phrases 'we thought...', 'now we think/see/understand differently...', appear frequently in teachers' discourse indicating their developing perceptions of teaching and learning.

A new *object* of teaching activity was 'evolving' (Foot, 2002) at the intersection of the old and new conceptions of teaching. Teachers' earlier view of the authority of their position as exerting power over students by controlling what they should learn was making place for authority of reason, the power to influence students through teachers' own learning, experience and knowing, with knowing including a recognition of students' 'funds of knowledge' (González et al., 2005) as a resource for learning. In keeping with this, they started to reconceptualise teaching as a process of knowledge production positioning students as competent 'meaning makers' (Wells, 2009).

Individuating Practice: Tertiary Contradictions

Sannino and Engeström (2018, p. 45) distinguish between 'the generalized object of the historically evolving activity system and the specific object as it appears to a particular subject, at a given moment, in a given action'. According to them, the generalised object is associated with 'societal meaning' while the specific object is associated with personal sense making. This distinction is very relevant here in capturing the dynamics of teacher learning and the development of their transformative agency. At the secondary level, contradictions arose from teachers' object converging with the supposedly benign societal object colliding with the object guiding action in We Make.[2] Tertiary contradictions emerged from a reverse process. Tensions arose when teachers used their evolving object, which deviated from the established institutional object, to generate new practices in school. This also led them to modify their new practice by reflectively appropriating it to balance it with the imperatives of the stagnant institutional demands and expectations. Teachers have become researchers in their own right, studying and acting on the emergent problems in the best interests of the learning and flourishing of their students:

> *Anu:* Every child has to pass up to class X. This RTE [Right to Education] rule has become a big headache for us.
> *Suma:* They [policy makers] think that if they don't detain students, they'll not drop out, they'll learn something sitting in the class. But the reality is opposite. Students don't come regularly. Some are long absentees. They come only for the class test and we have to pass them.

---

[2] A historical analysis reveals how the general societal object of education masks the interests of the dominant sociopolitical and economic groups that tacitly govern institutional practices (Ratnam, 2021b).

Tanvi: Another rule, if students are absent for 1 week continuously, we have to go to their homes and bring them. It's not easy. Children hide or run away. Parents are not at home. How much time can we spend on this? What about our classes? No one understands this. Finally, we have to make them copy some answers, give marks and push them, without learning.

Anu: Earlier, I used to feel bad about it but helpless. Now I'm trying to do something about it. I don't dictate readymade answers. I convert it into a fun activity involving students, like Prema co-constructs summaries with the children. More students participate now and there is more learning, I mean, *meaningful* learning [laughter].

The process of teachers' *ideological becoming* is by no means a linear one. It is a complex, multifaceted process marked by both regression and progression with teachers constantly beleaguered by doubt and dilemmas that make them vacillate between the constraints posed by the authoritative institutional discourse and their own developing internally persuasive discourse. Recurring questions and doubts come to haunt them as they try to generate new teaching actions to accomplish the new teaching object taking shape in them from their participation in the collective ZPD of We Make: *How to follow students' interests and also complete the syllabus? What about exams? Here [in We Make] this problem is not there, but in school we have to think about it (Uma).*

As inquirers, teachers have to strike a balance between making their own choices as 'curriculum makers' and following the rules of the system as 'curriculum implementers' (Clandinin & Connelly, 1992; Craig, 2020). While they negotiate the tensions created by the oppositional pulls exerted by their context and agency, teachers learn to teach in the cracks (Schultz, 2017).

Developing a Professional and Transformative Activist Stance: Quaternary Contradiction

Teachers' personalisation of the object of their teaching created another layer of conflict with the activities of other teachers, administrators, parents, community and policymakers. Teacher change was challenged by the surrounding inertia. Teachers spent much time following student orientation and personalising instruction while all other stakeholders expected them to teach to the test. Uma was admonished by an education officer for having completed only four units out of eight: *Earlier, I would quietly put my head down if any officer found fault. But this time I took him to the class... He was very impressed interacting with the students. He was stunned by the questions children asked him. His tone changed and he told me, 'Very good madam. But also make sure to complete all the lessons for the mid-term test'* (phone conversation with Uma, 19 September 2023).

Teachers are cultivating a professional and activist stance to defend their intentional actions with reasoned justification and exercising their autonomy in dealing with the tensions and disturbances emerging 'in the network relations of involved activity systems' (Sannino & Engeström, 2018, p. 49).

Continuing Learning through Emergent Problem Situation

Contradictions remain as they are rooted in the system that is not easily open to change, where the status quo serves the interests of the dominant group which wants to maintain its power and control (Bourdieu & Passeron, 1990). Teachers experience these contradictions in their day-to-day work in the conflicts created by the top-down mandates limiting their freedom and choices. Teachers' transformative agency lies in their capacity to not only initiate but also sustain change in themselves and their situation (Lund & Vestøl, 2020). In the We Make formative initiative Prema and I were part of the process of provoking and supporting teachers to reflect and act differently. This 'intervention' has shifted to teacher 'intravention' (Sannino et al., 2016), where teachers conduct formative interventions on themselves to address the ever-emergent contradictions in their workplace. They feel morally responsible to do it in the interests of the students they serve. Teachers share their ongoing struggles when we get together or converse on the phone. Teachers' self-regulation is a sign of their transformative activist agency.

REFLECTING ON THE PROCESS

From Excessive Entitlement to Empowered Entitlement

Excessive teacher entitlement manifests itself as a quality of teachers in their unawareness and inability to see themselves from the point of view of others, in particular their students, including the authoritative stance it makes them take towards the students. At a cursory glance, this quality seems to be innate in the teacher, solely intentional and mental, thus trapping them in a flawed frame. This study disputes the static deficit image of teachers as inadequate by showing that excessive entitlement as a phenomenon is generated not exclusively in the mind of the teacher, but in the teacher's dialectical interaction with the historically developing cultural world of schooling and its modes of discourse. This liberating view is backed by Vygotsky's cultural–historical theory, which says that in understanding the 'essence' of a phenomenon, 'historical study of behaviour is not supplementary or auxiliary to theoretical study, but is the basis of the latter' (Vygotsky, 1978, p. 54). Historical analysis is at the core of understanding teachers as well as teachers' understanding of their students. It helps trace the roots of the conflicts that teachers experience here and now to the larger historically developing contradictions and the possibilities and constraints, these contradictions hold for the development of teachers' transformative agency (Sannino & Engeström, 2018). Leveraging the possibilities requires volitional investment of individuals and collectives. This study affirms teachers' capacity for such transformative agency. At the same time, it unravels the dynamics underlying the development of this power motivated by layers of conflicts that create the ZPD for it. Conflicts demand learning actions in creatively fixing them.

The path to the development of teachers' transformative agency lies in an acknowledgement of their excessive self-entitlement. This acknowledgement is voiced in teachers' awareness coming from their self-realization: *Now we think, question and analyse. We thought we were taking so much trouble for the sake of students and still they were not learning. But now we see it is not true. We are not actually helping them but harming them, not allowing them to think and speak, making them simply repeat what we give them. We are not appreciating what they know. We think they are zeros.* (Pavana)

Teachers' honesty in holding their practice to scrutiny is an act of moral 'answerability' (Redder, 2019). This bespeaks their ideological becoming in the commitment they have developed to make a difference to the lives of those who they teach by viewing their practice from the point of meeting their students' needs. This transformative process of teachers' ideological becoming marks a shift from excessive entitlement to what I term 'empowered entitlement'. Empowered entitlement comes from being aware of oneself and the consequences of one's actions so that the decision one makes is humane based on an understanding of the other. People develop empowered entitlement by contributing to empowered entitlement of others, blending one's self-realization with that of others. In my sense of empowered entitlement, agency, determination, and authority are tempered by empathy, compassion, respect and justice such that its assertive and softer attributes hold each other in balance. This balance is important in avoiding the negative import of excessive entitlement that all of these attributes carry with the potential danger of masquerading as empowered entitlement. Agency, determination and authority are important aspects of empowered entitlement to be able to hold one's own moral ground against the self-serving interests of dominant others and their coercion to acquiesce. The positive side of these attributes were reflected in the professional activist stance Uma assumed when she came under censure for not completing the syllabus. She defended her commitment to her students without subordinating herself to the authority of her AEO's superior position. However, the authority exerted by the AEO was the authority of position sourced from domination, coercion, and oppression. His disrespectful and unreasonable behaviour towards teachers like Uma is a symptom of his excessive entitlement, a lack of self-awareness, empathy, compassion and a sense of justice.

Resistance to Excessive Entitlement – An Eye for an Eye or a Lesson in Humility and Humaneness?

An important insight that emerges from the above episode is that the notion of entitlement as good or bad depends on how it is used, just like the notion of 'authority' already mentioned. It suggests that we need to have boundaries to understand what happens when someone's excessive entitlement violates another's legitimate entitlement or the best-loved self (Personal communication, Cheryl Craig, 30 October 2023). Do we need to react with counter excessive entitlement to safeguard our own legitimate boundaries? This is where the distinction between 'excessive entitlement' and 'empowered entitlement' becomes effective. This distinction helps us see how we can respond to others' excessive entitlement in a just way by drawing the line between the positive and negative aspects of the common traits shared by 'empowered' and 'excessive' entitlement. Uma's growing transformative activist stance seems to have offered her another way to cope with the AEO's excessive entitlement. She defended her best-loved self without succumbing to the AEO's authority, and yet, she was respectful and persuaded with reason. Her 'empowered entitlement' not only helped her defend the borders of her 'best-loved self' in the conflict with the AEO, but also influenced his boundary by the good effect she had on him. In summary, excessive entitlement and empowered entitlement are two distinct ways of applying our authority and rights, and they have different consequences for ourselves and others. By preferring empowered entitlement over excessive entitlement, we can resist injustice and promote humility and humaneness in our interactions.

Implications for Teacher Education: A New Evolving Object of Holistic Change

There are two important interrelated elements about the development of transformative agency that have implications for teacher education. One is that teachers need access to cultural resources, and secondly, these need to be 'taken up' by teachers agentively (Stetsenko, 2019). Both these essential conditions for transformative agency provide clues as to how we can create an environment for the development of teachers' empowered entitlement. The resources we provided teachers in the form of a new model of teaching activity in We Make generated disturbances and conflicts confronting their conventionally confirmed ways of teaching. They tended to resist the new model judging it unreflectively using their old lens. What seemed to help them move out of this impasse was the dialectical interplay we helped them establish between their volitional action and the use of resources (Lund & Vestøl, 2020; Ratnam, 2021b). Students' positive response to the new model of teaching made it internally persuasive for teachers, stirring their interest and motivating them to pursue it as a new possibility. Moreover, an acknowledgement of teachers as competent made them feel respected for the knowledge and experience they brought to their learning. This helped us provoke their thinking beyond an obsession with exams and results to think about what learning is and how it takes place, leading to a transformation in the way teachers conceptualised the object of their teaching activity. Parallel to this, the historical analysis we undertook collectively made them reflect on who they were as teachers and what their values were and how their historically developing situation in school helped or inhibited the realisation of the values they held. This awareness was a very important part of teachers' moral growth. It made them determined in their ongoing commitment to place students' interests above the self-serving interests of the neoliberalist school system. The latter, in teachers' newly gained insight, was focused on dehumanising values of productivity, human capital and efficiency (Hall & Pulsford, 2019), neglecting the real learning and life needs of the disadvantaged students.

The path to self-realization is arduous. It runs through a tension-laden path of problems posed by historically developing contradictions. These problems are complex and perplexing. Yet these wicked problems are made to seem straightforward and within easy grasp of solution 'if only the other [the teacher] who needs to act would' (Pinnegar, 2021, p. 285). The perpetual image of teachers as deficient is an inevitable corollary of this sanitized view of the problems that can neither be easily or completely resolved (Pinnegar, 2021; Ratnam, 2020;

Smagorinsky, 2020). A deficit teacher is an asset to the neoliberal project in legitimising its control over education through regimes of audit and accountability, undercutting the apparent autonomy granted to teachers (Davies & Bansel, 2007; Hall & Pulsford, 2019). However, this is not good for teachers; It curtails their motivation to resolve the conflict created by the opposition between the standard solution imposed from above and the unique situated solutions that are required to respond meaningfully to the needs of different students. This demotivation is manifested in their tendency to follow the socially and institutionally scripted practice to avoid conflict (Ratnam, 2021b) instead of embracing it agentively to generate new meanings and solutions.

The Notion of Excessive Entitlement: Insights for Teacher Education

The new angle that the notion of excessive teacher entitlement brings to our understanding of the conundrums of teacher education helps us pose new questions for investigation with possibilities for thinking about the problems in new ways beyond stock responses. One question that follows from the foregoing discussion on the harmful effect of portraying teachers in a negative light as excessively entitled is: To what extent does teacher education help teachers keep their sense of agency alive? This turns the focus of attention on teacher educators and the environment they create for learning that makes this possible. It calls for teacher educators to exert their agency responsibly in influencing the agentive learning of the teachers they teach. However, working within the prevalent theory-into-practice model of teacher education, teacher educators contribute to reducing teachers to unproblematic *adopters* of knowledge produced elsewhere in research (Andreasen, 2023; Darling-Hammond, 2012; Korthagen, 2001) instead of using this available opportunity to promote teachers' capacity to collaboratively and critically produce knowledge (Ratnam, 2020; Zeichner et al., 2015). As with teachers, the space for teacher educators to become self-reflexive through a self-study of their practice (Kitchen, 2023; Russell & Fuentealba, 2023) is constrained by the rules of the system, which, in turn, is governed by the ruling ideology of neoliberalism which is embedded discursively at the global, national, policy and institutional levels (Cahill, 2011). As Hall and Pulsford (2019) point out, collaboration and competition are conflated in policy structures: they promise the potential for social justice and human values through the provision of mechanisms of efficiency and value-for-money (e.g. GOI, 2020). This makes standardisation and accountability seem like a 'common sense frame for conducting and evaluating policy' (Cahill, 2011, p. 487). This frame, which is embedded in the norms of the institutional values, makes it acceptable to all stakeholders in the educational hierarchy, from policy makers to teachers at the chalkface, creating a chain of excessive entitlement (Ratnam, 2021b). Audit and accountability centres education around competition rather than collaboration: it erodes the elevated values educators hold by fomenting undesirable excessively entitled behaviours – greed, arrogance, 'rivalry, pettiness, malevolence and status obsession' (Back, 2016, p. 11). It makes teacher educators (also all other stakeholders) seek to position themselves as most valuable to reap the rewards of a meritocratic system (Craig, 2021).

The chain of excessive entitlement shows that it is complex, interconnected, and requires collective action. It cannot be resolved by a customary focus on *remedying* the putative deficiency in teachers and teacher educators as the object of reform in education. Instead, we need to look wider and deeper at the level of educational activity as a whole. We need to examine how historically developing contradictions thread through and organise relations between diversely positioned stakeholders in the entire educational ecosystem, all purportedly sharing the common object of student flourishing in a factious landscape. Each actor is meant to play their unique but complementary role towards cohesion and cooperation by exercising their transformative agency. However, the hierarchical positioning of these diverse actors creates a top-down flow of authority. This authority of power over those below them leads to subjugation and loss of transformative agency at every level. Therefore, the new object of reform evolving from this understanding points to the need for a more horizontal activity plane. In this plane, the diverse interrelated activity systems can work dialectically and open the possibility for humanising relationships. In a horizontal relationship, every actor can work with dignity and is acknowledged and respected for the agentive contribution they make to the collective educational activity.

WAY FORWARD

Identifying the need for a collective cultural response to address the chain of entitlement, I had put forward the notion of a 'pedagogy of co-authorship' as a possible means to break out of vertical relationships making space for horizontal humanising relationships among diverse stakeholders (Ratnam, 2021b). However, the concrete nature of the activity behind this conceptualisation was still nebulous to me then. Using CHAT as a tool for analysing the formative intervention in this study has awakened me to the rich possibility it holds for actionable intervention. The 'third generation' CHAT was developed by Engeström (2001) to deal with multiple activity systems sharing an object. It has great potential for breaking the educational hierarchy and establishing '*horizontal* and *socio-spatial* relations and interactions' between stakeholders located in different activity systems (Engeström, 2001, p. 144). In Education, these multiple activity systems comprise the diverse stakeholder groups such as students, teachers, parents, administrators, curriculum makers and policy makers all working complementarily towards a common object. The third generation CHAT provides conceptual tools to understand dialogue, multiple perspectives and networks of interacting activity systems (Engeström, 2001). These tools aid individuals to act collectively to resolve the problems they face. The Change Laboratory provides a methodological tool for such formative intervention in activity systems (e.g. see Lilley, Chapter 6 in this volume). Change Laboratory has been found to have great potential to promote a shared sense of purpose and collaboration, strengthening social ties (Augustsson, 2021; Engeström & Pyörälä, 2021; Lotz-Sisitka et al., in press; Morselli & Sannino, 2021).

SIGNPOSTING THE CONTRIBUTIONS OF THE STUDY

Firstly, the study has developed a conceptual model of teacher learning and development by capturing its underlying dynamics in the formative initiative of this study. This move from the concrete to the abstract facilitates a link between theory and practice by revealing the practical activity behind the concept (Davydov, 1990) and opens new possibilities for practice. This model can be used to support teachers and teacher educators on the path of ideological becoming by exercising their transformative agency. Secondly, the study suggests a new way to frame the conundrums of teaching and teacher education using the lens of excessive teacher entitlement and highlights the importance of collective action in breaking out of the chain of excessive entitlement in which teachers and teacher educators are caught with other stakeholders. Finally, 'Empowered entitlement' as a counterforce to 'excessive entitlement' is an idea that emerged in the contemplative process of writing this chapter.

ONE LAST WORD FROM THE SPACE OF BECOMING

The process of human ideological becoming is 'unfinalizable' (Bakhtin, 1981). Trying to puzzle out what made teachers 'excessively entitled' against their valued intention has involved me in a process of becoming through my long career innings as a teacher, teacher educator and researcher (Ratnam, 2021a). Yet, like Pinnegar (2021) and Ellett (Chapter 12 in this volume), 'I find myself once more at the place where I started' (Shammas, 1988, p. 226), 'insistently aware of the problem and promise of teacher entitlement as a venue for research' (Pinnegar, 2021, p. 285). From this position, the systemic effort to quick fix complex educational problems fragmentarily, without acknowledging the human potential for individual and collective transformative agency, seems like an attempt to arrive without travelling.

REFERENCES

Andreasen, J. K. (2023). School-based mentor teachers as boundary-crossers in an initial teacher education partnership. *Teaching and Teacher Education, 122.* https://doi.org/10.1016/j.tate.2022.103960

Augustsson, D. (2021). Expansive learning in a change laboratory intervention for teachers. *Journal of Educational Change, 22,* 475–499. https://doi.org/10.1007/s10833-020-09404-0

Back, L. (2016). *Academic diary: Or why higher education still matters.* Goldsmiths.

Bakhtin, M. (1981). In M. M. Bakhtin & M. Holquist (Eds.), *The dialogic imagination: Four essays* (C. Emerson & M. Holquist, Trans.). University of Texas Press.

Billett, S. (2010). Lifelong learning and self: Work, subjectivity and learning. *Studies in Continuing Education, 32*(1), 1–16.

Bourdieu, P., & Passeron, J. (1990). *Reproduction in education, society and culture* (Trans. R. Nice). Sage.
Braun, V., & Clarke, V. (2013). *Successful qualitative research: A practical guide for beginners.* Sage.
Cahill, D. (2011). Beyond neoliberalism? Crisis and the prospects for progressive alternatives. *New Political Science, 33*(4), 479–492.
Clandinin, D. J., & Connelly, F. M. (1992). Teacher as curriculum maker. In P. W. Jackson (Ed.), *Handbook of curriculum* (pp. 363–461). Macmillan.
Cochran-Smith, M., & Lytle, S. (2009). *Inquiry as a stance: Practitioner research in the next generation.* Teachers College Press.
Cole, M. (2005). Foreword: Why the fifth dimension? In M. Nilsson & H. Nocon (Eds.), *School of tomorrow: Teaching and technology in local and global communities* (pp. ix–xv). Peter Lang.
Cole, M., & Engeström, Y. (1993). A cultural-historical approach to distributed cognition. In G. Salomon (Ed.), *Distributed cognitions: Psychological and educational considerations* (pp. 1–46). Cambridge University Press.
Conle, C. (1999). Why narrative? Which narrative? Struggling with time and place in life and research. *Curriculum Inquiry, 29*(1), 7–32.
Craig, C. J. (2020). *Curriculum making, reciprocal learning and the best-loved self.* Palgrave Macmillan.
Craig, C. J. (2021). Back in the middle (again): Working in the midst of professors and graduate students. In T. Ratnam & C. J. Craig (Eds.), *Understanding excessive teacher and faculty entitlement advances in research on teaching* (Vol. 38, pp. 165–178). Emerald Publishing Limited. https://doi.org/10.1108/S1479-368720210000038011
Darling-Hammond, L. (2012). *Powerful teacher education: Lessons from exemplary programs.* John Wiley & Sons.
Davies, B., & Bansel, P. (2007). Neoliberalism and education. *Qualitative Studies in Education, 20*(3), 247–259.
Davydov, V. V. (1990). *Types of generalization in instruction: Logical and psychological problems in the structuring of school curricula.* National Council of Teachers of Mathematics.
Delong, J., & Whitehead, J. (2024). You and your living educational theory. In *How to conduct a values-based inquiry for human flourishing.* Routledge.
Dewey, J. (1902/1990). *The child and the curriculum.* University of Chicago Press.
Engeström, Y. (1987/2015). *Learning by expanding: An activity theoretical approach to developmental research* (2nd ed.). Cambridge University Press.
Engeström, Y. (2001). Expansive learning at work: Toward an activity theoretical reconceptualization. *Journal of Education and Work, 14*(1), 133–156. https://doi.org/10.1080/13639080020028747
Engeström, Y., & Pyörälä, E. (2021). Using activity theory to transform medical work and learning. *Medical Teacher, 43*(1), 7–13. https://doi.org/10.1080/0142159X.2020.1795105
Engeström, Y., Rantavuori, J., & Kerosuo, H. (2013). Expansive learning in a library: Actions, cycles and deviations from instructional intentions. *Vocations and Learning, 6*, 81–106.
Engeström, Y., & Sannino, A. (2010). Studies of expansive learning; foundations, findings and further challenges. *Educational Research Review, 5*, 1–24.
Foot, K. A. (2002). Pursuing an evolving object: A case study in object formation and identification. *Mind, Culture and Activity, 9*, 132–149.
González, N., Moll, L. C., & Amanti, C. (Eds.). (2005). *Funds of knowledge: Theorizing practices in households, communities and classrooms.* Lawrence Erlbaum Associates.
Goodson, I. (2013). *Developing narrative theory: Life histories and personal representation.* Routledge.
Government of India [GOI]. (1949). *Report of the university education commission.* Ministry of Education.
Government of India [GOI]. (2020). *National policy on education.* Ministry of Human Resource Development.
Gutiérrez, K. D. (2020). When learning as movement meets learning on the move. *Cognition and Instruction, 38*(3), 427–433. https://doi.org/10.1080/07370008.2020.1774770
Haapasaari, A., Engeström, Y., & Kerosuo, H. (2016). The emergence of learners' transformative agency in a change laboratory intervention. *Journal of Education and Work, 29*, 232–262. https://doi.org/10.1080/13639080.2014.900168

Hall, R., & Pulsford, M. (2019). Neoliberalism and primary education: Impacts of neoliberal policy on the lived experiences of primary school communities. *Power and Education, 11*(3), 241–251. https://doi.org/10.1177/1757743819877344

Harvey, D. (2007). Neoliberalism as creative destruction. *The Annals of the American Academy of Political and Social Science, 610*, 22–44. https://doi.org/10.1111/j.0435-3684.2006.00211.x

Holzman, L. (2018). What does it take to be culturally relevant? In *Plenary Address Applied Linguistic Winter Conference (NYSTESOL): Culturally Relevant Pedagogy*, Albany, NY, November 2–3.

Jordan, P. J., Ramsay, S., & Westerlaken, K. M. (2017). A review of entitlement: Implications for workplace research. *Organizational Psychology Review, 7*(2), 122–142.

Kitchen, J. (2023). Improving teacher education through self-study. In R. J. Tierney, F. Rizvi, & K. Erkican (Eds.), *Encyclopaedia of education* (4th ed., pp. 488–496). Elsevier.

Korthagen, F. A. J. (2001). *Linking practice and theory: The pedagogy of realistic teacher education.* Lawrence Erlbaum Associates Publishers.

Kozulin, A. (1998). *Psychological tools: A sociocultural approach to education.* Harvard University Press.

Labaree, D. F. (2000). On the nature of teaching and teacher education: Difficult practices that look easy. *Journal of Teacher Education, 51*(3), 228–233.

Ladson-Billings, G. (2014). Culturally relevant pedagogy 2.0: a.k.a. the remix. *Harvard Educational Review, 84*, 74–84. https://doi.org/10.17763/haer.84.1.p2rj131485484751

Lave, J., & Wenger, E. (1991). *Situated learning: Legitimate peripheral participation.* Cambridge University Press. https://doi.org/10.1017/CBO9780511815355

Leont'ev, A. N. (1978). *Activity, consciousness and personality.* Prentice Hall.

Lotz-Sisitka, H. B., Chikunda, C., Thifulufhelwi, R., & Mponwana, M. (in press). Chapter 10: The emancipatory nature of transformative agency: Mediating agency from below in a post-apartheid land restitution case. In N. Hopwood & A. Sannino (Eds.), *Agency and transformation: Motives, mediation and motion.* Cambridge University Press.

Lü, L., & Hu, J. (2021). Understanding teacher authority. *Journal of Education and Development, 5*(2), 44–52.

Lund, A., & Vestøl, J. M. (2020). An analytical unit of transformative agency: Dynamics and dialectics. *Learning, Culture and Social Interaction, 25*, 1–9. https://doi.org/10.1016/j.lcsi.2020.100390

Mahn, H., & John-Steiner, V. (2002). The gift of confidence: A Vygotskian view of emotions. In G. Wells & G. Claxton (Eds.), *Learning for life in the 21st century: Sociocultural perspectives on the future of education.* Blackwell.

McGarr, O., O'Grady, E., & Guilfoyle, L. (2017). Exploring the theory-practice gap in initial teacher education: Moving beyond questions of relevance to issues of power and authority. *Journal of Education for Teaching, 43*(1), 48–60. https://doi.org/10.1080/02607476.2017.1256040

Morselli, D., & Sannino, A. (2021). Testing the model of double stimulation in a Change Laboratory. *Teaching and Teacher Education, 97*, 1–8. https://doi.org/10.1016/j.tatae.2020.103224

NCERT (National Council of Educational Research and Training). (2005). *National curriculum framework.* Secretary, Publication Department, NCERT.

Pace, J., & Hemmings, A. (2007). Understanding authority in classrooms: A review of theory, ideology, and research. *Review of Educational Research, 77*(1), 4–27. https://doi.org/10.3102/003465430298489

Petrik, S. (2019). Teacher's authority as one of the most important factors in school reform. In *6th International Multidisciplinary Scientific Conference on Social Sciences & Art SGEM.* https://doi.org/10.5593/SWS.ISCSS.2019.4/S13.063

Pinnegar, S. (2021). Afterword. In T. Ratnam & C. J. Craig (Eds.), *Understanding excessive teacher and faculty entitlement (Advances in Research on Teaching)* (Vol. 38, pp. 285–290). Emerald Publishing Limited. https://doi.org/10.1108/S1479-368720210000038001

Pratham. (2022). *Annual Status of Education Report (Rural) 2021.* https://img.asercentre.org/docs/aser2021forweb.pdf

Pratham. (2023). *Annual Status of Education Report 2022.* ASER 2022 – ASER: Annual Status of Education Report (asercentre.org).

Rantavuori, J., Engeström, Y., & Lipponen, L. (2016). Learning actions, objects and types of interaction: A methodological analysis of expansive learning among pre-service teachers. *Frontline Learning Research*, 4(3), 1–27.

Ratnam, T. (2014). Development of oral and written communication in a funds of knowledge approach. *The EFL Journal*, 5(1), 17–40.

Ratnam, T. (2015). Pedagogies of social justice: An Indian case. In L. Orland-Barak & C. Craig (Eds.), *International teacher education: Promising pedagogies (Part B) Advances in Research on Teaching* (Vol. 22, pp. 255–282). Emerald Group Publishing Limited.

Ratnam, T. (2020). Provocation to dialog in a *Third Space*: Helping teachers walk toward equity pedagogy. *Frontier Education*, 5, 569018. https://doi.org/10.3389/feduc.2020.569018

Ratnam, T. (2021a). Foreword. In T. Ratnam & C. J. Craig (Eds.), *Understanding excessive teacher and faculty entitlement, Advances in Research on Teaching* (Vol. 38, pp. xxi–xxii). Emerald Publishing Limited. https://doi.org/10.1108/S1479-368720210000038001

Ratnam, T. (2021b). The interaction of culture and context in the construction of teachers' putative entitled attitude in the midst of change. In T. Ratnam & C. J. Craig (Eds.), *Understanding excessive teacher and faculty entitlement: Digging at the roots, Advances in Research on Teaching* (Vol. 38, pp. 77–101). Emerald Publishing Limited. https://doi.org/10.1108/S1479-368720210000038006

Ratnam, T. (2023). Excessive teacher entitlement? Going inward and backward to go forward. In C. J. Craig, J. Meno, & R. G. Kane (Eds.). *Studying teaching and teacher education: Advances in research on teaching* (Vol. 44, pp. 221–230). Emerald Publishing Limited. https://doi.org/10.1108/S1479-368720230000044022

Ratnam, T., & Craig, C. J. (Eds.). (2021a). *Understanding excessive teacher and faculty entitlement (Advances in Research on Teaching)* (Vol. 38). Emerald Publishing Limited. https://doi.org/10.1108/S1479-368720210000038001

Ratnam, T., & Craig, C. J. (2021b). Introduction: The idea of excessive teacher entitlement: Breaking new ground. In T. Ratnam & C. J. Craig (Eds.), *Understanding excessive teacher and faculty entitlement (Advances in Research on Teaching)* (Vol. 38, pp. 1–13). Emerald Publishing Limited. https://doi.org/10.1108/S1479-368720210000038001

Ratnam, T., Craig, C., Marcut, I. G., Marie-Christine, D., Mena, J., Doyran, F., Hacıfazlıoğlu, O., Hernández, I., & Peinado-Muñoz, C. (2019). Entitlement attitude: Digging out blind spots. In D. Mihăescu & D. Andron (Eds.), *Proceedings, the 19th biennial conference of international study association on teachers and teaching (ISATT), "Education beyond the crisis: New skills, children's rights and teaching contexts"* (pp. 210–219). Lucian Blaga University Publishing House.

Ratnam, T. (forthcoming). STEAM education to unleash students' creativity and knowledge-building capacity: An Indian perspective (Chapter 2). In K. Plakitsi & S. Barma (Eds.), *Sociocultural approaches to STEM education – An ISCAR International collective issue*. Springer Nature.

Ratnam, T., & Tharu, J. (2018). Integrating assessment into classroom instruction to create zones of development for teachers and learners: Some perspectives from India. In H. Jiang & M. F. Hill (Eds.), *Teacher learning with classroom assessment: Perspectives from Asia Pacific* (pp. 119–140). Springer.

Redder, B. (2019). *Teacher pedagogy as an act of moral answerability: A self-study of an infant teacher's answerable acts in infant pedagogy in New Zealand ECEC*. http://researchcommons.waikato.ac.nz/. Accessed on January 1, 2020.

RTE (Right to Education). (2009). http://mhrd.gov.in/rte

Russell, T. (2021). Exploring teacher entitlement: Perspectives from personal experience. In T. Ratnam & C. J. Craig (Eds.), *Understanding excessive teacher and faculty entitlement: Digging at the roots, advances in research on teaching* (Vol. 38, pp. 35–46). Emerald Publishing Limited.

Russell, T., & Fuentealba, R. J. (2023). Self-study of teacher education practices: The complex challenges of learning from experience. In R. J. Tierney, F. Rizvi, & K. Erkican (Eds.), *Encyclopaedia of education* (4th ed., pp. 458–468). Elsevier.

Sannino, A. (2015). The principle of double stimulation: A path to volitional action. *Learning, Culture and Social Interaction*, 6, 1–15.

Sannino, A. (2020). Transformative agency as warping: How collectives accomplish change amidst uncertainty. *Pedagogy, Culture & Society, 30*(1), 9–33. https://doi.org/10.1080/14681366.2020.1805493

Sannino, A., & Engeström, Y. (2018). Cultural-historical activity theory: Founding insights and new challenge. *Cultural-Historical Psychology, 14*(3), 43–56. https://doi.org/10.17759/chp.2018140304

Sannino, A., Engeström, Y., & Lemos, M. (2016). Formative interventions for expansive learning and transformative agency. *The Journal of the Learning Sciences, 25*(4), 599–633. https://doi.org/10.1080/10508406.2016.1204547

Schultz, B. D. (2017). *Teaching in the cracks: Openings and opportunities for student-centered, action-focused curriculum*. Teachers College Press.

Schwab, J. J. (1954/1978). Eros and education: A discussion of one aspect of discussion. In I. Westbury & N. Wilkof (Eds.), *Science, curriculum and liberal education: Selected essays*. University of Chicago Press.

Shammas, A. (1988). *Arabesques*. Harper & Row.

Smagorinsky, P. (2020). *Learning to teach English and language arts: A Vygotskian perspective on beginning teachers' pedagogical concept development*. Bloomsbury.

Srivastava, P., & Hopwood, N. (2009). A practical iterative framework for qualitative data analysis. *International Journal of Qualitative Methods, 8*(1), 76–84.

Stenhouse, L. (1975). *An Introduction to curriculum research and development*. Heinemann.

Stetsenko, A. (2009). Vygotsky and the conceptual revolution in developmental sciences: Towards a unified (non-additive) account of human development. In M. Fleer, M. Hedegaard, & J. Tudge (Eds.), *World year book of education. Constructing childhood: Global-local policies and practices* (pp. 125–142). Routledge.

Stetsenko, A. (2016). *The transformative mind: Expanding Vygotsky's approach to development and education*. Cambridge University Press.

Stetsenko, A. (2019). Radical-transformative agency: Continuities and contrasts with relational agency and implications for education. *Frontiers in Education, 4*, 148. https://doi.org/10.3389/feduc.2019.00148

Stetsenko, A. (2020). Critical challenges in cultural-historical activity theory: The urgency of agency. *Cultural-Historical Psychology, 16*(2), 5–18. https://doi.org/10.17759/chp.2020160202

UDISE Plus Report. (2022). https://udiseplus.gov.in/#/page/publications

Vasavi, A. R. (2015). Culture and life of government elementary schools. *Economic and Political Weekly, 50*(33), 36–50.

Vygotsky, L. S. (1978). *Mind in society: The development of higher psychological processes*. Harvard University Press.

Vygotsky, L. S. (1987). The collected works of L. S. Vygotsky. In R. W. Rieber & A. S. Carton (Eds.), *Thinking and speech* (N. Minick, Trans.) (Vol. 1). Plenum Press.

Wells, G. (2009). *The meaning makers: Learning to talk and talking to learn* (2nd ed.). Multilingual Matters.

Wenger, E. (1998). *Communities of practice: Learning, meaning, and identity*. Cambridge University Press.

Williams, J. A., III, Mallant, C., & Svajda-Hardy, M. (2022). A gap in culturally responsive classroom management coverage? A critical policy analysis of states' school discipline policies. *Educational Policy, 37*(5), 1191–1216. https://doi.org/10.1177/08959048221087213

Zeichner, K. (1983). Alternative paradigms of teacher education. *Journal of Teacher Education, 34*, 3–9.

Zeichner, K. (2010). Rethinking the connections between campus-based courses and field experiences in college and university-based teacher education. *Journal of Teacher Education, 89*, 89–99.

Zeichner, K., Payne, K. A., & Brayko, A. (2015). Democratizing teacher education. *Journal of Teacher Education, 66*(2), 122–135.

EXCESSIVE ENTITLEMENT FROM A NETWORKED RELATIONAL PERSPECTIVE

Louis Botha

University of the Witwatersrand, South Africa

ABSTRACT

As Ratnam makes clear, a cultural–historical perspective on teacher/faculty excessive entitlement is indispensable if we are to use this concept to work with, rather than undermine, education practitioners. In this chapter, a networked relational model of activity is proposed as a tool for understanding excessive entitlement from a cultural–historical activity theory (CHAT) perspective, so that the transformative potential of both entitlement and the modeling of it may be harnessed. The networked relational model, which represents CHAT activity systems as a hand-draw or painted network of relationships between actors and artifacts, allows its creators, in their capacity as researchers or academics, to use it as an imaginative artifact in the Wartofskian sense. That is, by representing activity systems of academic performance as networks of interacting entities, the emergence of excessive entitlement can be traced to, and perhaps mitigated through the relationships that they represent. In this regard, the why, what, *and* how *artifacts proposed by Engeström are taken up as useful means for enhancing the functioning of the networked relational model not just as a tool for analyses of entitlement but also a means for envisioning alternative countercultures into being.*

Keywords: Networked relational model; cultural–historical activity theory; performative; sociomaterial; imaginative artifact; excessive entitlement

As shown in the review by Asadi and Ali (2021), the concept of entitlement has been considered across many contexts, including religious, academic, and organizational contexts. Generally, it refers to, as Kopp et al. (2011, p. 106) phrased it, "not simply the prediction that one *will* obtain a certain outcome, but that one *ought* to obtain a certain outcome." And while most conceptualizations of entitlement tend to emphasize the psychological nature of this phenomenon, such as its rootedness in narcissism manifesting in high self-regard, self-righteousness, harboring grandiose thoughts, hostility, dominance, and being very demanding in relationships (Fisk, 2010; Harvey & Dasborough, 2015; Kopp et al., 2011), in this chapter, I want to highlight broader contextual or social factors.

In this regard, Fisk (2010), for example, refers to an "Age of Entitlement," and relatedly Harvey and Dasborough (2015) locate workplace entitlement with the "Millennial" generation, while Jordan et al. (2017) point out entitlement, following Feather (2003) and Lerner (1987), "is influenced by malleable external factors such as societal laws, rights, and norms" (p. 128). This contextually situated understanding of entitlement is significant, first, for the focus of this chapter, which is on academic entitlement, and second, for the sociocultural framework within which this phenomenon is analyzed, and also elaborated upon in the next section. With regards to the former, though, I turn once again to Kopp et al. (2011) who explain that beliefs about entitlement differ across contexts, and consequently they define *academic entitlement* as context-specific and referring to "the expectation that one should receive certain positive academic outcomes (e.g., high grades) in academic settings, often independent of performance" (p. 106). While they have students in mind, I believe that the link they make between entitlement and the marketization of education is relevant to academics as well. Thus, while students may feel entitled due to the fees that they pay, for academics such entitlement may arise due to the income and recognition that they generate for their institutions through publications and research.

This then brings me to a further refinement, *excessive entitlement*. Here, I will simply rely on an extensive definition from Fisk (2010) from which, I hope, key elements will echo later when I explain the theoretical framing of excessive entitlement in academia:

> ...excessive entitlement is defined as a trait that reflects an aristocratic rather than ambitious personality profile, one that is fuelled by inaccurate perceptions regarding the number or type of outcomes owed to the self (formed in response to distorted views of the validity of one's performance inputs) that exceeds what would be considered normative according to prevailing social allocation rules and that when acted upon, may negatively impact others. (p. 104)

With these definitions in mind, the rest of this chapter will be concerned with showing how an adapted model of Yrjö Engeström's activity systems model, which I refer to as a networked relational model of activity, can be used as a tool for understanding excessive entitlement from a cultural–historical activity theory (CHAT) perspective. The intention with interpreting excessive entitlement in this way is so that this phenomenon can be understood as contextually situated and relationally generated, and also so that the transformative potential of the modeling of it may be harnessed. In pursuing these aims, the chapter is structured as follows:

- First, I will establish the broader societal context within which excessive entitlement is understood, and then, relatedly, show how entitlement (both earned and excessive entitlement), may be represented using a CHAT approach.
- Thereafter, I will translate the relevant CHAT principles and model into a networked relational model that explains how excessive entitlement can be interpreted relationally, as an assemblage (Fenwick & Edwards, 2013) of sources and resources that produce particular affects.
- Finally, I will describe and use data from an empirical pilot study to illustrate the activity system model of excessive entitlement in an academic context as a hand-draw or painted network of relationships between actors and artifacts and show how representing it in this way allows for its use as a healing tool.

EXCESSIVE ENTITLEMENT: CONTEXTUALIZATION WITHIN A CHAT PERSPECTIVE

Drawing on various levels of historical development, Ratnam (2021) situates the development of educators' attitudes of excessive entitlement within the dialectical interaction between social structure and human agency (p. 96). The neoliberal control that she identifies as creating "a chain of entitlement" (Ratnam, 2021, p. 93) also applies to the dynamic pertaining within higher education contexts, where, as Edwards (2022) explains:

> Features include calculative technologies that foster competition such as performance management, target setting and research assessment based on income, publications and impact. Universities have become business-oriented markets and entrepreneurial projects, displacing public good models of governance and collective values with individualized incentives, competitive metrics, monitoring, and targets. (p. 205)

In this educational context which Mayo (2003) describes as "technical-rational" and concerned with "marketability at the expense of, for instance, social justice" (p. 38), much of academics' work has become about learning to perform, participate, and be consumers and producers in a neoliberal knowledge economy. Such a transactional, acquisitive approach to education (Biesta, 2005) profoundly influences what is valued within the educational arena and also how value is assigned. This is evident in the way that, for instance, Hare construes academics' priorities as being largely individualistic. According to Hare (2002, p. 4), in addition to various forms of social pressure from the academic institution, "(o)ther factors influencing the intensity and direction of an academic's work are: their personal satisfaction in knowing they are working well; their own personal ambitions; and the pay and promotion structure." Similarly, Edwards (2022, p. 905) explains that "(w)ithin neo-liberal academia, individual academics embrace or are exhorted to comply with competitive ideas about what constitutes success, with both success and failure framed and understood as personal accomplishment, disconnected from the wider social, economic and political context."

This context of the mutually evolving development of institutions and academics toward measured expectations of performance and reward is the one from which emerges the activity systems which have as their outcomes various forms of entitlement. It is from this perspective that I wish to present entitlement as an outcome of the activity that academics engage in while carrying out their work at a higher education institution. Here, I am concerned with both earned and excessive entitlement (Asadi & Ali, 2021) since, as these authors explain, one can best understand excessive entitlement in relation to earned entitlement.

Consider, then, the classic CHAT diagram in Fig. 1, below, developed by Yrjö Engeström as a model of human activity which presents seven moments (sometimes incorrectly referred to as elements) – subject, object, instruments, outcome, rules, community, and division of labor. Roth et al. (2009, p. 140) explain that "(t)he term 'moment' is chosen deliberately in dialectical materialist approaches, because, as the minimal unit of analysis, activity cannot be properly decomposed into separate 'elements'". For the purposes of the analyses which follow later, I have added to the activity systems model (ASM) examples of each of the moments of activity as they may pertain to a higher education activity system, and the activity of academics specifically. The diagram is intended to depict Leontev's insight of activity as "a relatively durable system in which the division of labor separates different goal-oriented actions and combines them to serve a collective object" (Sannino & Engeström, 2018, p. 45). The two-headed arrows in the illustration represent the dialectical relations, mentioned by Ratnam (2021), that shape and drive the development of the individual and collective moments of activity.

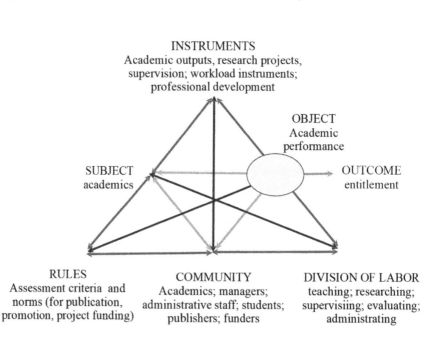

Fig. 1. Entitlement as an Activity Systems Model.

The basic premise is that when academics carry out their roles as lecturers, researchers, and supervisors, we can view this as activity that can be modeled by a CHAT activity system. This implies, firstly, that the academic can be identified as the *subject*, since, conventionally, the activity will be viewed from their perspective. It should be borne in mind, however, that such a subject perspective is de-emphasized later when the activity system is interpreted sociomaterially.

Next, the *object* of the activity needs to be identified. Referring to it as the focal entity and/or desired outcome, Foot (2014) summarizes the significance of the object as follows:

> The object gives an activity system a determined direction, a horizon toward which it orients – but just as a horizon is never reached, an object is never fully accomplished (Engeström, 1999d). The object of an activity – as it grows in intensity as a motivating force – shapes and directs the activity. An activity system constantly generates actions through which the object of the activity is enacted and reconstructed in specific forms and contents. (p. 334)

Broadly speaking, the object of an academic's activity can be said to be commendable or valued academic performance. That is, an academic's performance in terms of developing students' knowledge and learning skills, as well as producing knowledge and insights, is the purpose of the academic's activity, shaping the form and direction that it takes. It is important to further qualify that these knowledge-making activities (which form the object of activity) are those that have value to the academic community within which they are situated and toward which they are directed.

Based upon the earlier contextualization of academic work, we could, therefore, frame the object of academic activity as centered around expectations of recognition and reward. As indicated earlier, the reward that academics seek may take the form of a personal sense of accomplishment, or the awarding of a promotion, funding, or some other means by which the academic institution and others within academia acknowledge the significance of their contributions. Significantly, then, academic performance in the neoliberal context alluded to above is considered to be measurable in terms of outputs according to which money and status are apportioned.

Following from this object, the *outcome* of academic work can then be a sense of entitlement. This outcome is a manifestation of the coming together of the subject, artifacts/instruments, rules, the division of labor, community moments, and the object, implying that the nature of the outcome is dependent upon the ways in which these moments interact. In constructing entitlement in this way, I am proposing that the above moments constitute value-seeking and value-awarding moments. Value-seeking moments would be those that academics enact to try to give value to their academic performance, and would include research outputs, teaching, supervision, and so forth. Value-awarding moments would be those phenomena within an activity system which endorse or assign value to an academic's performance.

I therefore wish to contend that, when there are no significant contradictions between these moments, the outcome of academic activity is likely to be "earned entitlement," a concept which Asadi and Ali (2021) explain as follows:

Earned entitlement points to "deservingness" (Feather, 2003) and is what is due to an individual for the contribution they make to an enterprise and is determined through socio-economic norms (remuneration), socio-emotional norms (respect due to individuals) and rules (accountability). According to Jakiela, Miguel and Te Velde (2015), high academic achievement leads to personal and external acknowledgement of an individual's earned entitlements. (p. 23)

On the other hand, when there is misalignment between the various value-seeking and value-making moments of the activity system, the outcome tends toward excessive entitlement. In this case, "(e)ntitlement is exceeded when one demands outcomes that exceed what is considered socially 'right' relative to entitlements readily given" (Asadi & Ali, 2021, p. 23).

I am therefore suggesting that excessive entitlement from a CHAT perspective emerges as a consequence of the relationships prevailing among the value-seeking and value-awarding moments of the subject and community dimensions of an activity system directed at academic performance. When an academic engages in academic activity with the expectation of this activity being recognized in particular ways by the academic community, and that expected recognition can be considered incommensurate with the academic community's norms, the outcome may take the form of excessive entitlement. To shed light on the nature of these relationships, a sociomaterial performative perspective is proposed.

EXCESSIVE ENTITLEMENT AS A PERFORMATIVE NETWORKED RELATIONAL MODEL

This section builds upon the dialectic relations outlined above by interpreting them sociomaterially in terms of a performative ontology (Fenwick & Edwards, 2013) that is relational. Interpreting activity systems sociomaterially implies considering all of the entities that constitute them, both human and nonhuman, as relevant and capable of exerting agentive force and creating each other as they interact. As Fenwick and Edwards (2013) point out, the more radical versions of the sociomaterial approach to research not only decenter the (human) subject, they also view all matter associated with it, material and immaterial, as "performed into existence in webs of relations" (p. 53). They explain it as follows:

All things – human, and non-human, hybrids and parts, knowledge and systems – emerge as *effects* of connections and activity. There are no received categories. The shift here is what Jensen (2010, p. 7) characterizes as 'from epistemology and representation to practical ontology and performativity'. (p. 53)

Earlier, I alluded to this when I pointed out that, whereas CHAT usually considers activity from the perspective of a human subject, a sociomaterial approach does not preclude a nonhuman subject from its analyses. Importantly, though, such an inclusion should not interfere with the object orientation, historicity, or other key principles of the CHAT approach.

Taking this as my cue, then, I am suggesting that excessive entitlement is an attitude, or a behavior or a label that is variously performed into existence as an effect of the assembling of entities that may be recognized as the ones that make up an activity system. That is, albeit according to a slightly modified dynamic, the subject, object, instruments, rules, and community moments can be viewed as dialectically emerging through intra-actions in assemblages that affect and produce each other in ways that give rise to excessive entitlement.

> *Assemblages* (Deleuze & Guattari, 1988, p. 88) of relations develop in unpredictable ways around actions and events, 'in a kind of chaotic network of habitual and non-habitual connections, always in flux, always reassembling in different ways' (Potts, 2004, p. 19), and importantly, operate as 'machines' (Deleuze & Guattari, 1988, p. 4; Guattari, 1995a, p. 35) that do something, produce something. (Fox & Alldred, 2015, p. 401)

An activity system that is concerned with academic performance can therefore be understood as being made up of assemblages that work to produce knowledge, status, graduates, professors, and all sorts of academic outputs. In producing these outputs, a possible outcome may be that of excessive entitlement. How a particular outcome is produced would be the result of affect – "...an ability to affect or be affected. It is a prepersonal intensity corresponding to the passage from one experiential state of the body to another and implying an augmentation or diminution in that body's capacity to act" (Deleuze & Guattari, 1988, p. xvi).

In other words, within assemblages, value-seeking and value-awarding moments intra-act in ways that nurture or stunt each other's development and the combined effects that they have on the activity system and its outcomes, including those of entitlement and the forms they may take. Thus, we can understand excessive entitlement as manifesting when academics intra-act within assemblages which materialize artifacts, attitudes, ideas, actions, and situations that position these individuals in ways that are perceived by them as incongruent with how related assemblages of rights, rules, and norms have assigned value to them. This implies that excessive entitlement is inherent to the structures of universities and to the performances that make up the institution. By this I mean that entitlement circulates as affective flows within the assemblages that perform the university and its academics into being, territorializing as excessive entitlement through the ways in which particular networks of artifacts, attitudes, ideas, actions, and situations concerned with rights, rules, and norms that assign value (Asadi & Ali, 2021, p. 23), come together, or emerge. These networks may include the moments that make up an activity system of academic performance (outlined earlier), such as *tools* of academia that are used to produce outcomes that are valued by academia, *rules*, and norms that assign value to the outcomes, the various members of the academic *community*, and the roles that they play in evaluating academics and their performances. Examples of these could include *tools* like publications, titles, and funding; *rules* such as those that award titles and evaluate academic contributions; the *community* would be made up of colleagues at the institution, peer reviewers, journal editors, and funders; *the division of labor* would include researching, peer reviewing, committee members awarding titles, promotions or funding, and so forth.

The above performative interpretation of academic activity is framed within a relational ontology. As Barad (2003) argues, adopting such a performative approach necessarily foregrounds the ontological shift that entwines epistemology and ontology, since knowing "the world" cannot be achieved outside of our constitutive relationship with it. To quote Gamble et al. (2019): "This onto-epistemological account, which she calls 'agential realism', leads to a thoroughly 'performative' and relational materialism in which matter just is what it does or how it moves" (p. 123). This relational ontology, which Rosiek et al. (2020) point out, echoes ideas developed by indigenous thinkers and scholars thousands of years ago, insists that we see reality, and our knowing of it, as created in relations performatively enacted through "material practices of intra-action occurring out, within, and as a part of the world's becoming" (Shotter, 2014, p. 320).

Understanding excessive entitlement in this way allows for a focus on how a range of entities from the academic context are implicated in bringing it about. Thus, a relational performative ontological approach avoids viewing excessive entitlement as a quality of, or attitude of academics as individuals, and instead sees it as an outcome or affect/effect that emerges in intra-action. It also opens the possibility for the emergence of alternative forms of entitlement through alternative assemblages. This performative sociomaterial approach will be further illustrated by data collected through an empirical study which I will explain later.

THE NETWORKED RELATIONAL MODEL

Given the above performative, sociomaterial and relational understanding of excessive entitlement, I am proposing, as a reinterpretation of the dynamics of Engeström's (1987) activity systems model, an alternative, complementary form of illustration, namely, a networked relational model of academic activity. This model is intended to, firstly, visually represent, and secondly, support theoretical analyses of the complex ways in which academic activity systems are performed into existence from a relational perspective. In this section, I will attempt to demonstrate how the model maps the network of relationships between the value-seeking and the value-awarding moments identified previously, while also showing how it is possible to plot and analyze the relationships in ways that complement the classic CHAT representations of the activity system.

Reconceptualizing the CHAT activity system from a relational as well as sociomaterial and performative approach demands that we also reconceive it in terms of its representation. While the classic activity systems model, with its symmetrical, bi-directional arrows may very well alert us to the dialectical relations inherent in its Marxist material foundations, I do not believe it sufficiently conveys the messy, rhizomatic nature of the new materialist interpretation that is being proposed here. By contrast, the hand drawn (painted) networked relational model affords researchers or participants who are using CHAT in this relational manner a clearer impression of how the moments in an activity system may appear as nodes in a network, or as assemblages. As will be shown, drawing as a means of representing activity offers a number of possibilities for enhancing insights into these relational dynamics.[1] The upcoming method and application sections will explain how, in advocating for the use of a complementary kind of model of the activity system, drawing is used as a method for representing the networked relational model of activity and understanding how its dynamics apply to the analysis of activity systems such as those of academic activity. Briefly outlined in Botha (2018), this model is thus conceived of here as a hand-drawn representation of an activity system which emphasizes its relational nature while still prioritizing the CHAT principles of object-orientation, historicity, cultural mediation, and possibilities for expansive development through contradictions.

Referring to dialectical relationships of learning and development in an educational context, Botha (2018) explains the model as follows:

> The networked relational model of learning seeks to bring to the fore this fundamental epistemological principle of knowing as relational by identifying the making of connections between its nodes as the primary means by which knowledge is constructed and held, thereby also drawing attention to its networked structure as a representation of knowing. (p. 29)

Applying this beyond learning, the networked relational model of activity (more generally) foregrounds the ontological principle of being and becoming as relational. Thus, the model, illustrated in Fig. 2, below, consists of a hand-drawn

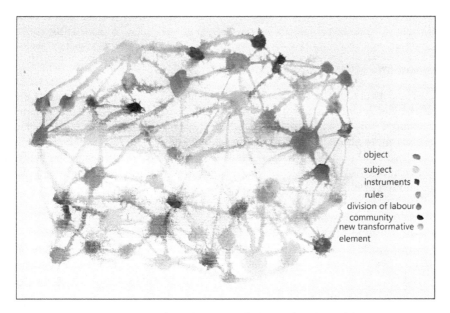

Fig. 2. Drawing of a Networked Relational Model.

---

[1]These insights may be less apparent to readers of this publication due to the use of grayscale rather than color for the images here.

network of interconnected nodes, where the nodes represent the various moments of the activity system, such as the subject, various artifacts, the object, rules, and so forth, and the connectors or inter-nodes depict the relationships between them. Intended to be reminiscent of a brain's neural network, the model not only represents the moments of the triangular CHAT diagram, it also invites one to view the activity system from a relational ontological perspective. This relational perspective implies that the components of the activity system not only produce each other dialectically, but that the relationships between them pre-exist the individual entities and allow them to take shape accordingly (Slife & Wiggins, 2009). In other words, the relations of production, consumption, distribution, and exchange exist prior to the subject, object, artifacts, rules, community, and division of labor, hence the latter emerge from the former.

In addition to facilitating the understanding and analysis of activity systems, the drawing-based network model is also intended to transform our perceptions and praxis. In the first place, as Filippov (2016) suggests, the act of drawing allows individuals "to feel complete in an environment, to navigate and construct it, to keep the records. And, therefore, to design situations, possibilities, next steps" (p. 391). In terms of knowledge environments, Filippov contends that the skills developed through drawing led to geometry, botany, and biology. Thus, I am here pointing to Wartofsky's (1979) observation that representation shapes our understanding of and activity within the world:

> ...our own perceptual and cognitive understanding of the world is in a large part shaped and changed by the representational artifacts that we create...we transform our own perceptual and cognitive modes, our ways of seeing and of understanding, by means of the representations we make. (Wartofsky, 1979, p. xxiii)

The networked relational model therefore does not only serve to illuminate the working of activity systems such as those of the academics but it also functions as a catalyst for the re-imagining of what academic performance, or academic activity more generally, may be. As Asadi and Ali's (2021) review of entitlement concludes: "Mainstream literature tends to see excessive entitlement as largely a personal trait" (p. 29). I will suggest here, however, that it is possible, through the promotion of a networked relational model of academic activity, to encourage a more relational approach to the conceptualization of excessive entitlement. Falling into Wartofsky's category of tertiary artifacts, the networked relational model is viewed as an imaginative artifact which can transcend the limitations of the real world and inspire us to picture alternative realities. "Once the visual picture can be 'lived in', perceptually, it can also come to color and change our perception of the 'actual' world, as envisioning possibilities in it not presently recognized" (Wartofsky, 1979, p. 209).

In the sections which follow, I will demonstrate three ways in which the representation of the CHAT diagram as a hand-drawn networked relational model could assist CHAT researchers with the conceptualizing of excessive entitlement. These include, firstly, how the process of drawing the model may lead to insights about the activity system of academic performance; secondly, how researchers could use the hand-drawn model to express information about the activity system in a readily accessible manner from both a personal and systemic perspective; and thirdly, how the model functions as an imaginative artifact that encourages a relational approach to addressing excessive entitlement.

METHOD: DRAWING THE NETWORKED RELATIONAL MODEL OF ACTIVITY

In this section, I want to elaborate upon the argument initiated above that the ontological and epistemological principles of the networked relational model can be accessed by the researchers or participants through a methodology that employs drawing as a means of eliciting knowledge. Drawings invite participation in the meaning-making of their representation (O'Brien et al., 2012). Thus, Martikainen and Hakoköngäs (2023) point to how the depiction of texture, light, shadow, distance, position, or composition through drawings allows researchers to access their participants' understandings of the world. They go on to say: "In the social representations approach, we understand drawing as a process of meaning construction intertwining subjective experiences with social and cultural meanings" (Martikainen & Hakoköngäs, 2023, p. 8). In this way, drawing resonates with the ways that CHAT is about making sense of activity as a social and cultural process. Notice how Foot's (2014) explanation resonates with that of Martikainen and Hakoköngäs when she says about CHAT: "Cultural points to the premise that humans are enculturated, and everything people do is shaped by and draws upon their cultural values and resources" (Foot, 2014, p. 330). By remaking the classic CHAT diagram as a drawing, the representation would allow for greater freedom in terms of its structure and abstraction, thereby allowing for the one who is drawing to infuse, as well as read into the representation, meanings which may be more personalized, or theoretically or culturally relevant.

In the case of this research, graphic representation is used as a kind of visual elicitation (Fox et al., 2007; Varga-Atkins & O'Brien, 2009). Usually this entails the researcher using visual cues such as photographs, diagrams or drawings to facilitate the construction of data with the research participants. Here, however, I will show how drawing (a networked relational model of academic activity) can elicit insights for the researcher. Furthermore, these insights help to align CHAT with a performative relational approach.

Creating a drawing of the CHAT activity system offers one flexibility in terms of what and how one wishes to represent ideas (Umoquit et al., 2013). The process can also be more interpretative, inviting meaning making (O'Brien et al., 2012) and allowing for the creator to draw on and orient themselves toward preferred cultural and social knowledges (Martikainen & Hakoköngäs, 2023).

Bearing this in mind, I followed a process of reflexively hand drawing the networked relational model in Fig. 2, the way in which I am suggesting researchers or participants of a CHAT-based research project would, noting the ways in which this process allows for them as illustrators to access and construct meanings from the representation of the CHAT diagram according to a sociomaterial and relational approach. Using watercolor painting with a wet-on-wet technique, the illustrators draw the networked relational model of the activity system that they are analyzing.

They would begin by spraying water over the paper so that the entire medium is wet. This is so that the paints will flow and diffuse freely, running beyond the lines that the illustrators make and also running into each other. Because the water serves as a shared, unifying medium that allows the paints to flow through it and mix, it recalls the first principle of CHAT, that the activity system should be understood in its entirety (Engeström, 2001), which also resonates with the principle of the performative sociomaterial approaches that "they take *whole network relations* into account regardless of what small slice of material or activity has been chosen as a primary focus for study" (Fenwick & Edwards, 2013, p. 54). The use of water on the paper medium also recalls the emergent nature of the relational perspective through the way in which it allows the paint to blossom from the connection of the brush and the paint, paper, and water mediums, strengthening the impression of the modes/moments and relationships/internodes emerging in a rhizomatic way from the media, rather than being placed or inscribed upon the paper.

To represent various activity system moments, the illustrators make these blossoming blotches in a variety of carefully considered colors all across the wet paper.[2] For example, by selecting a strong primary color, like red, for the object, one is able to evoke an impression, from the way in which a red color is able to substantially change the color of every other that it comes into contact with, about how the object fundamentally affects all of the other aspects of the activity system, and the shape to the activity system itself. That is, by recording them as blotches of paint, the illustrators can convey the potential "affect" of a particular moment (instrument, rule, etcetera) through the size of the blotch or the quantity or intensity of the color of the paint used. The researchers or participants, as the illustrators of an activity system could then emulate potential assemblages by connecting the blotches (moments) in various ways, either allowing wet blotches of various colors to run into each other, and mix and recolor the connecting relationships and blotches, or allowing the paint to dry so that different effects are produced. In this way, effects are created that are reminiscent of the "affect" economies alluded to earlier where it was suggested that various moments, including the value-seeking and value-awarding moments, of an academic's activity system may interact and allow each other and various other entities and outcomes to emerge. The somewhat unpredictable, irregular shapes that result are intended to spark insights about how the moments of an activity system or assemblage emerge in similar ways, being shaped by "affects" of the activity system in ways that can only be partially foreseen. The deliberate and fortuitous effects of interacting lines and blotches of paint portray the idea of the system's connected, mutually transformative and dynamic nature in ways that bring to

---

[2]Unfortunately, the images for this chapter can only be reproduced in grayscale, and hence, the full effect of using various colors, and their interaction, may not be evident here.

mind Fox and Alldred's (2015) explanation of the affective flows of assemblages, and how, "because one affect can produce more than one capacity, social production is not linear, but 'rhizomic'.., a branching, reversing, coalescing and rupturing flow" (Fox & Alldred, 2015, p. 401). In this way, then, creating the networked relational model is an attempt at "diffractive seeing" (Fenwick & Edwards, 2013), whereby the researchers or participants try to gain access to a relational interpretation of the system dynamics of the CHAT diagram through a performative engagement with representing it.

APPLYING THE NETWORKED RELATIONAL MODEL

In this section, I will offer some brief examples of how the networked relational model may be applied by drawing on an empirical pilot study in which five academics were interviewed about their academic activity. The participants in this small study were selected to be diverse across features that would be considered significant for a South African academic context, and perhaps also in academia generally. However, given the small sample, there is no intention to demonstrate any kind of representativeness. Nevertheless, they included three males and two females, three of whom were black, and two white. They held the following academic positions: three were senior lecturers; one was a newly qualified PhD holding a lecturer's position; and one was a PhD candidate holding lecturer's position. While these different dimensions of their identities significantly impacted the ways in which they perform and experience their academic activity, it is the commonalities around entitlement that I will point to here.

Thus, the interview data from the study is used for purely illustrative purposes, demonstrating how insights about the value-seeking and value-awarding moments of an academic's activity system, along with the relationships between them, may be elicited and applied to represent a relational account of an academic's attempt at establishing their entitlements.

Kate, for example, is a white female senior lecturer from whose interview the following value-seeking moments may be gleaned:[3]

> ...academic qualifications in the form of Bachelor of Science, Honors, Masters and PhD degrees; extensive experience tutoring and teaching at undergraduate and postgraduate level; supervision of Honors, Masters and PhD projects; several publications; involvement in research projects; and participation in professional development courses.

In accordance with the definition of value-seeking phenomena provided earlier, these are aspects of Kate's academic performance through which she seeks to add, in materialist terms, use value and/or exchange value to her activity. In Fig. 3, which depicts a networked relational model of Kate's academic activity, these moments appear as red blotches in digital copies of this book which are signposted by triangles in printed editions and are usually closely tied to the object, represented by yellow blotches labeled as such.

---

[3] All participant names are pseudonyms.

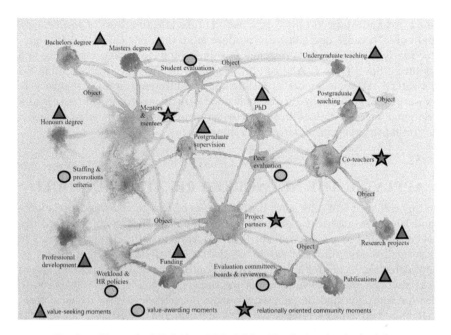

Fig. 3. Networked Relational Model for Kate's Academic Activity.

These value-seeking moments intra-act with value-awarding moments, represented as green blotches in digital copies of this and signposted by circles in print, and include institutionalized time (the ways in which an academic's time is apportioned, valued, and rewarded) in the form of workload policies, supervision agreements, criteria for supervision, and various structures for assessing academic work. Through this intra-action, affects are created that enhance or diminish the capacity of, for example, teaching, professional development, publications, postgraduate supervision, or other value-seeking moments, to generate value. Postgraduate supervision, for instance, may be afforded value by staffing and promotions criteria, and this value could be supported or undermined by student or peer evaluations, thereby affecting how the subject experiences the object of performing valued academic work.

My analysis of Kate's case is that the relationships between these sets of moments, or the ways in which they territorialize, are relatively weak, and this has been represented by the relatively thin connections between them in Fig. 3. By contrast, Kate attributed a greater significance to her relationships with her colleagues and supervisees, as is evident from the following extract of her interview:

> So, for example, I have published on teaching poetry, you know, with one of my Masters students. I also still do some pure humanities publishing. So that usually comes out of the texts and things I prepare for my Honors literature course. Then I'll write a... a sort of a literature paper on one of those, and then a colleague and I, we are sort of...we are working, when we

have moments, on sort of the cultural, culturally responsive pedagogies and decolonizing literacy theory, how to teach literacy theory in our context, you know, in a culturally responsive way.

And then recently I've just been getting so frustrated with how our students, umm, struggle to read academically...you know? So, with the group of colleagues now we've called ourselves a project, and so we want to look at reading...at, umm...reading at higher education? So that's also sort of SoTL...so it's literacy and but also how we as lecturers can scaffold our students reading and transform the way they engage with academic texts, you know, as multilingual global South people reading this... this authoritative knowledge. (Kate)

In the networked relational model, these relationally oriented community moments in the form of co-teachers, project partners, and mentor and mentees appear as significantly larger, as represented by purple nodes in the digital copies of this book (and signposted by stars in print versions), which are intended to convey the impression of being able to profoundly influence the shape of the network. In this way, the model supports my analysis that Kate's focus on collegial relationships as opposed to ones prioritizing more directly value-seeking and value-awarding moments, tends to mitigate against the emergence of excessive entitlement.

The visual representations, therefore, allow for patterns to be readily observable without suggesting that the connections are also qualitatively identical. As can be seen in both Figs. 2 and 3, the shapes of the nodes and connectors vary, as do their color and position, and these variances can be deliberately produced to draw attention to differences in the nature or significance of entities or relationships within the activity system.

From the perspective of identifying excessive entitlement, the intuitive visual cues offer a useful diagnostic tool – like the kind used in image analyses in the biological sciences (Aeffner et al., 2019). By assigning readily recognizable qualities to the various components of the modeled activity system, it becomes possible to identify patterns, strengths, or problematic areas at a glance. By producing various iterations of the model at different historical moments, or agential cuts (Barad, 2003), it would also be possible to easily compare specific aspects of the activity system, so that developments under different conditions can be traced.

The visually accessible networked relational model therefore affords an overview of the activity system within which to situate problems and interventions. This, then, is where the healing potential of the model lies. In a formative intervention situation, the model would be used to represent the activity being addressed, in this case, academic activity that leads to excessive entitlement. For instance, by drawing the model, as I did for Kate, researchers and participants could gain insights into the nature of the activity system under investigation, how to interpret its components, and the relationships governing their development. Kate's model shows, for example, that she has a tendency to align academic performance with relationships that are community-based rather than individualistic. We could therefore infer that, despite engaging in academic activities that are valued within the system, it is unlikely that she will exhibit excessive entitlement as an outcome, and that encouraging similar relationships within an academic setting might similarly mitigate against excessive entitlement. To some extent, this is supported by the interview data from all of the academics whom I interviewed, who tended to look to their colleagues rather than university structures to guide their academic performance.

> I don't think I can speak, you know, to receive the support from the university. I have been fortunate enough that I've received support from particular individuals, but systematically?... I can't think of spaces that I feel like have made my work ...umm, not easier, because easy is not the thing that I'm looking for, but just enabled me to do work and be effective in my work ...and, and of course, when I think of the university, I'm thinking of the structures ..that the university has put in place specifically. So, whether it be a policy, whether it be a particular portfolio that I feel like has been instrumental and in aiding me to do any of these things. (Thembi)

Similarly, Dennis identified his mentors as the most significant contributors to his capacity to carry out his academic activity in an effective manner.

> I think for me the confidence doesn't come through getting formal qualifications, but it comes through mentorship I've received... I was privileged enough to have done a postdoc ...before I came here, I had two very good mentors who allocated me to co- supervise on a series of Masters and Honors students' work. I was also put in touch with the University of Johannesburg, where I was allocated master students there to supervise where I could supervise with support from my mentors and co-supervise to an extent to help develop my skills. (Dennis)

David also credited his development and consequently the way in which he carried out his own academic performance to colleagues and mentors:

> For the teaching roles I drew on... I draw on colleagues, actually, (their) experiences and expertise... And another area, you know, the senior colleagues like where I worked (previously)...because when somebody was appointed to the university as a lecturer, they were attached to a senior colleague and this senior colleague would mentor them. (David)

Like Kate, these academics tended to be aware of, as she put it, "the overvaluing of the research, production kind of side of things." However, they expressed very little dissatisfaction with the extent to which their extensive professional efforts were recognized by the institutions where they worked. By using a networked relational model to trace what the assemblages of these academics' activity systems do, that is, how affects and affect economies are producing capacities through the processes and flows that they facilitate (Fox & Alldred, 2015), we can identify artifacts, actions, community moments, or relationships that account for how excessive entitlement is mitigated in these systems. In this way, academia, academic institutions, or academics as individuals can identify the relationships that are responsible for fostering the development of structures, artifacts, ideas, activities, and other entities that tend to give rise to manifestations of excessive entitlement, and consequently, possibilities for avoiding these. What I am implying is that the hand-drawn networked model offers a way in which to obtain both a system view as well as a personal view of artifacts, which, as suggested by Engeström (1990), allows for a more accurate interpretation of how tools are understood in use.

A *systems* view considers the impact of the artifact on the entire system, whereas a *personal* view considers how the mediating artifact changes the task. Engeström (1990) argues that we can move between these two views by understanding artifacts as "what," "why," and "how" artifacts, since this helps to clarify the multiple ways in which an artifact operates in a system, and how it is conceptualized and materialized by actors so that its collective use in changing an activity system is effective.

Engeström's (1990) categories of "what" artifacts, "why" artifacts, and "how" artifacts were developed from Wartofsky's (1979) primary and secondary artifacts so that researchers may account for the diverse understandings and applications of an artifact within an activity system. The "what" artifacts, like Wartofsky's primary artifacts, are "external physical entities" (Engeström, 1990, p. 188), while the "why" artifacts explain the role of a primary artifact in relation to the object, and the "how" artifact "tells us how a certain object shall be handled with a corresponding primary artifact" (Engeström, 1990, p. 188).

Considering entitlement as an activity system represented by a networked relational model, the "what" artifacts are understood to be the value-seeking moments which manifest as concrete entities in the system. These would be the publications, projects, degrees, supervision, teaching, etcetera, represented as red blotches or triangles in Kate's model.

The "how" artifacts are the value-awarding moments, shown as the green blotches or circles in Kate's model. These include the workload policy, staffing, and promotions criteria and various forms of evaluation, and they basically explain how value-seeking moments operate in relation to the object of performing valuable academic activity. A "how" artifact such as "Evaluation committees, boards and reviewers," for instance, informs us about the way that the "what" artifact of "Publications" may be aligned to the object of Kate's activity.

In an activity system concerned with entitlement, the "why" artifacts would be related to considerations identified earlier where it was suggested by Hare (2002) that an academic's performance is motivated by social pressure as well as expectations of affective and/or material reward. Identifying the "why" artifacts and how they may materialize is key to establishing the character of the activity. For instance, my understanding of Kate's activity system is that her performance is geared toward scholarship that meaningfully develops her own and her students' learning. The way in which this materializes is through the relationally oriented community moments that appear in her model as purple or star-shaped collaborations with colleagues and students. These "why" artifacts are key to understanding why Kate's academic performance does not result in excessive entitlement despite her dissatisfaction with how the university values her work. It is these artifacts that counteract the misalignment between the value-seeking and value-making moments of Kate's activity system that would otherwise have resulted in excessive entitlement. Thus, I would argue that we could influence the activity system and the nature of its outcome of entitlement by anticipating such potentially healing "why" artifacts and introducing them into the system in the form of elements that would intra-act with "what" and "how" artifacts in ways that produce affects that mitigate excessive entitlement.

CONCLUSION

The value of using the networked relational model for understanding excessive entitlement lies with its use of CHAT to emphasize the culturally and systemically situated nature of entitlement. I have tried to do this by representing the CHAT model and all its inherent principles from a sociomaterial perspective that interprets its dialectical relations as performative, where the primacy of relational dynamics is made explicit. I have also attempted to demonstrate how this model may be constructed more generally as well as by drawing on empirical data. This is a very early attempt at applying these approaches, and like Hultin (2019) my intentions are developmental – "I hope to be able to increase awareness of what assuming a relational or becoming ontology can imply for our epistemological practices, and the production of knowledge, and to inspire greater diversity in the epistemological practices of researchers" (p. 94). While I hope that this has been helpful for illustrating the value of the model as a tool for analyzing work activity and instigating change, I believe that it is only through a deeper performative engagement that researchers will be able to fully explore the potential of the networked relational model and its capacity for eliciting insights in the rhizomatic manner anticipated by Deleuze and Guattari (1988).

Nevertheless, it should be clear from the sociomaterial, performative, and relational ontological orientations offered by the networked relational model of activity that excessive entitlement can most productively be viewed as the outcome of a collective performance. As we develop the methodological and epistemological tools to investigate the make-up and workings of this multiplicity, so too will we be able to embrace the complicity of all entities in manifestations of excessive entitlement. Already, however, I can gratefully acknowledge that it is through the generous and constructive engagement of the editors and reviewers that the potentials of this chapter have been nurtured and our collective efforts at healing excessive entitlement brought into conversation.

REFERENCES

Aeffner, F., Zarella, M. D., Buchbinder, N., Bui, M. M., Goodman, M. R., Hartman, D. J., Lujan, G. M., Molani, M. A., Parwani, A. V., Lillard, K., Turner, O. C., Vemuri, V., Yuil-Valdes, A., & Bowman, D. (2019). Introduction to digital image analysis in whole-slide imaging: A white paper from the digital pathology association. *Journal of Pathology Informatics*, *10*(1), 9.

Asadi, L., & Ali, S. (2021). A literature review of the concept of entitlement and the theoretical informants of excessive teacher entitlement. In T. Ratnam & C. J. Craig (Eds.), *Understanding excessive teacher and faculty entitlement: Digging at the roots* (pp. 17–34). Emerald Publishing Limited.

Barad, K. (2003). Posthumanist performativity: Toward an understanding of how matter comes to matter. *Signs: Journal of Women in Culture and Society*, *28*(3), 801–831.

Biesta, G. (2005). Against learning. Reclaiming a language for education in an age of learning. *Nordisk Pedagogik*, *25*, 54–66.

Botha, L. R. (2018). Developing epistemologically diverse learning frameworks. *Journal of Education (University of KwaZulu-Natal)*, (73), 20–37. https://doi.org/10.17159/2520-9868/i73a02

Deleuze, G., & Guattari, F. (1988). *A thousand plateaus: Capitalism and schizophrenia*. Bloomsbury Publishing.

Edwards, R. (2022). Why do academics do unfunded research? Resistance, compliance and identity in the UK neo-liberal university. *Studies in Higher Education*, *47*(4), 904–914.

Engeström, Y. (1987). *Learning by expanding. An activity theoretical approach to developmental research*. Orienta-konsultit. http://lchc.ucsd.edu/mca/Paper/Engeström/expanding/toc.htm

Engeström, Y. (1990). *Learning, working and imagining: Twelve studies in activity theory*. Orienta-konsultit.

Engeström, Y. (2001). Expansive learning at work: Towards an activity theoretical reconceptualization. *Journal of Education and Work*, *14*(1), 133–156.

Feather, N. T. (2003). Distinguishing between deservingness and entitlement: Earned outcomes versus lawful outcomes. *European Journal of Social Psychology*, *33*, 367–385.

Fenwick, T., & Edwards, R. (2013). Performative ontologies. Sociomaterial approaches to researching adult education and lifelong learning. *European Journal for Research on the Education and Learning of Adults*, *4*(1), 49–63.

Filippov, O. (2016, December). The fundamental role of drawing as a method of cognition and creative development of reality. In *2016 3rd international conference on education, language, art and inter-cultural communication (ICELAIC 2016)* (pp. 391–394). Atlantis Press.

Fisk, G. M. (2010). "I want it all and I want it now!" An examination of the etiology, expression, and escalation of excessive employee entitlement. *Human Resource Management Review*, *20*(2), 102–114.

Foot, K. A. (2014). Cultural-historical activity theory: Exploring a theory to inform practice and research. *Journal of Human Behavior in the Social Environment*, *24*(3), 329–347.

Fox, N. J., & Alldred, P. (2015). New materialist social inquiry: Designs, methods and the research-assemblage. *International Journal of Social Research Methodology*, *18*(4), 399–414.

Fox, A., McCormick, R., Procter, R., & Carmichael, P. (2007). The design and use of a mapping tool as a baseline means of identifying an organization's active networks. *International Journal of Research and Method in Education*, *30*(2), 127–147.

Gamble, C. N., Hanan, J. S., & Nail, T. (2019). What is new materialism? *Angelaki*, *24*(6), 111–134.

Hare, P. (2002). *Why do academics work? Institutions and incentives*. Mimeo, Herriot-Watt University.

Harvey, P., & Dasborough, M. T. (2015). Entitled to solutions: The need for research on workplace entitlement. *Journal of Organizational Behavior*, *36*(3), 460–465.

Hultin, L. (2019). On becoming a sociomaterial researcher: Exploring epistemological practices grounded in a relational, performative ontology. *Information and Organization*, *29*(2), 91–104.

Jordan, P. J., Ramsay, S., & Westerlaken, K. M. (2017). A review of entitlement: Implications for workplace research. *Organizational Psychology Review*, *7*(2), 122–142.

Kopp, J. P., Zinn, T. E., Finney, S. J., & Jurich, D. P. (2011). The development and evaluation of the academic entitlement questionnaire. *Measurement and Evaluation in Counseling and Development*, *44*(2), 105–129.

Lerner, M. J. (1987). Integrating societal and psychological rules of entitlement: The basic task of each social actor and fundamental problem for the social sciences. *Social Justice Research*, *1*, 107–125.

Martikainen, J., & Hakoköngäs, E. (2023). Drawing as a method of researching social representations. *Qualitative Research*, *23*(4), 981–999.

Mayo, P. (2003). A rationale for a transformative approach to education. *Journal of Transformative Education*, *1*(1), 38–57.

O'Brien, M., Varga-Atkins, T., Umoquit, M., & Tso, P. (2012). Cultural–historical activity theory and 'the visual' in research: Exploring the ontological consequences of the use of visual methods. *International Journal of Research and Method in Education*, *35*(3), 251–268. https://doi.org/10.1080/1743727X.2012.717433

Ratnam, T. (2021). The interaction of culture and context in the construction of teachers' putative entitled attitude in the midst of change. In T. Ratnam & C. J. Craig (Eds.), *Understanding excessive teacher and faculty entitlement* (Vol. 38, pp. 77–101). Emerald Publishing Limited.

Rosiek, J. L., Snyder, J., & Pratt, S. L. (2020). The new materialisms and Indigenous theories of non-human agency: Making the case for respectful anti-colonial engagement. *Qualitative Inquiry*, *26*(3–4), 331–346.

Roth, W. M., Lee, Y. J., & Hsu, P. L. (2009). A tool for changing the world: Possibilities of cultural-historical activity theory to reinvigorate science education. *Studies in Science Education, 45*(2), 131–167.

Sannino, A., & Engeström, Y. (2018). Cultural-historical activity theory: Founding insights and new challenges. *Cultural-Historical Psychology, 14*(3), 43–56.

Shotter, J. (2014). Agential realism, social constructionism, and our living relations to our surroundings: Sensing similarities rather than seeing patterns. *Theory & Psychology, 24*(3), 305–325.

Slife, B. D., & Wiggins, B. J. (2009). Taking relationship seriously in psychotherapy: Radical relationality. *Journal of Contemporary Psychotherapy, 39*(1), 17–24. https://doi.org/10.1007/s10879-008-9100-6

Umoquit, M., Tso, P., Varga-Atkins, T., O'Brien, M., & Wheeldon, J. (2013). Diagrammatic elicitation: Defining the use of diagrams in data collection. *Qualitative Report, 18*(30), 1–12. https://www.proquest.com/scholarly-journals/diagrammatic-elicitation-defining-use-diagrams/docview/1505321137/se-2

Varga-Atkins, T., & O'Brien, M. (2009). From drawings to diagrams: Maintaining researcher control during graphic elicitation in qualitative interviews. *International Journal of Research and Method in Education, 32*(1), 53–67.

Wartofsky, M. W. (1979). *Models: Representation and the scientific understanding.* Springer Dordrecht.

THE ONTO-EPISTEMOLOGICAL DIMENSION OF KNOWLEDGE AND INTERACTION WITHIN EXCESSIVE TEACHER ENTITLEMENT: A CULTURAL-HISTORICAL ACTIVITY THEORY PERSPECTIVE

Cristiano Mattos and André Machado Rodrigues

University of São Paulo, Brazil

ABSTRACT

In this chapter, we examine the negative impact of excessive teacher entitlement on school life. We argue that teacher entitlement goes beyond individual traits, intricately linked to sociocultural processes and power dynamics within and outside educational institutions. The focus is on theoretical foundations to understand pedagogical practices in science education, highlighting two key components contributing to excessive teacher entitlement. First, we discuss the relationship between teachers and scientific knowledge, emphasising that a narrow view of science may create a strong hierarchical dynamic in classrooms, with teachers positioned as knowledgeable authorities and neglecting students' needs. Second, the organisation of interaction between teachers and students is explored, emphasising how teachers perceive and wield authority. We recognise the limitations of common critiques of authority in science education, as they may lead to excessive indulgence or indifference. We propose a teaching framework based on cultural-historical activity theory to address or prevent excessive teacher entitlement in science classrooms. While acknowledging the phenomenon's complexity, the framework is presented as a pedagogical reorientation addressing identified underpinnings. The study concludes by suggesting that the proposed framework, grounded in science education experiences, could serve as a foundation for understanding and addressing excessive teacher entitlement across various academic fields. We suggest that the authoritative teacher style aims to balance extremes, providing an alternative to authoritarianism while avoiding carelessness. Additionally, the scientific-cultural inquiry promotes a pluralist approach to knowledge, challenging the notion of absolute truth in science education.

Keywords: Excessive teacher entitlement; science education; dialogue; authority; teacher's style; scientific-cultural inquiry

Excessive teacher entitlement can have harmful consequences for school life. This is especially the case in times of school change in which a diverse range of students' learning needs must be addressed. An inclusive school experience creates different ways of knowing and being. However, excessive teacher entitlement could be understood as a protective blockage that pushes the students' learning needs aside.

Ratnam et al. (2019) and Ratnam (2021; Chapters 1 & 2 in this volume) showed that excessive entitlement goes beyond individual traits. Moreover, the conceptualisation should encompass how teachers' excessive entitlement is embedded in the sociocultural processes and shaped by the power dynamics in and outside the institutions. The critical point lies in the term excessive, in which teachers act with a privileged aura and cross the boundaries of a well-deserved entitlement. In this case, teachers look down on students, parents and the whole school community. Eventually, it leads to unhinged behaviour marked by arrogance and complete disregard for students' learning needs.

While excessive teacher entitlement may appear symptomatically in teachers' unreasonable behaviour, its underlying causes can be traced across various analytical levels. Broadly speaking, this phenomenon may stem from responses to strongly controlled educational systems that reinforce stringent accountability mechanisms (Ratnam, 2021). Additionally, institutional factors contribute, particularly when educators are placed within fiercely competitive school environments where excessive entitlement is deemed essential and, to some extent, even rewarded. Furthermore, the origins of excessive teacher entitlement may be rooted in everyday educational practices. In such scenarios, teachers may be perceived as the paramount authority in the learning environment, displaying an unwillingness to entertain questions or criticism. This posture, in turn, tends to attribute educational shortcomings solely to students, leaving minimal space for self-reflection and substantive changes. Teachers' excessive entitlement springs from an unawareness, resulting from a lack of self-awareness (Ratnam, 2021; Chapter 2 in this volume). In the realm of science education, the issue of excessive teacher entitlement becomes entwined with educators' perspectives on scientific knowledge, the role ascribed to students and the overarching pedagogical practices. As we delve into this discourse, it becomes evident that a critical examination of these interconnected aspects is imperative to understanding and addressing the complexity of excessive teacher entitlement in science education.

In his characterisation of Banking Education, Freire (2005, p. 73) underlines that the 'teacher knows everything and the students know nothing' and 'the teacher confuses the authority of knowledge with his or her own professional authority, which she and he sets in opposition to the freedom of the students'. In a reinforcing cycle, excessive teacher entitlement impacts and is impacted by such necrophilic educational practice, in which teachers' and students' agencies are not aligned, instead in permanent contradiction.

Here, we will discuss some theoretical foundations that enable teachers and school leadership to better grasp the pedagogical practice in science education. We focus on two components that combined shape excessive teacher entitlement within science teaching. On the one hand, it is important to consider the relations that teachers establish with scientific knowledge. A narrow-minded view of science that takes it as a collection of well-defined concepts, correct answers and absolute truths might sneak into the classrooms, even in the case of the most progressive teachers. It creates a podium where the knowledgeable teacher looks down at students and colleagues. We briefly discuss such worldview's ontological and epistemological roots and its impact on excessive teacher entitlement.

On the other hand, we put forward the issues around the organisation of the interaction between teachers and students throughout the teaching–learning process. It is critical to frame how teachers perceive and retain authority in the classroom. We discuss the interactive models and discursive mechanisms that teachers use to enable their excessive entitlement. We examine how the discursive interaction in science teaching can reinforce excessive teacher entitlement. However, the criticism of authority commonly found in science education is limited and may lead to excessive indulgence or indifference.

Finally, we present a teaching framework grounded in cultural-historical activity theory (CHAT) that can work as a starting point for teachers and school leadership to tackle or prevent excessive teacher entitlement to flourishing within science classrooms. We acknowledge that excessive teacher entitlement is a multi-determined phenomenon and may have factors deeply embedded in the societal and institutional organisation that go far beyond the science classrooms. Nevertheless, our proposal should not be perceived as a universal solution to excessive teacher entitlement but rather as a reorientation of pedagogical practices that address the foundational aspects, namely the role of knowledge and interaction.

Such theoretical endeavour is firmly grounded in teaching experiences in science education and may work as a frame to structure the bases of excessive teacher entitlement. Thus, this study opens the opportunity to inquire about excessive entitlement and its roots and nuances across different academic fields and disciplines. The relationship between participants, students and teachers, as well as the relations established with knowledge, might vary depending on the academic field, exerting distinct influences on the development of excessive entitlement.

TEACHERS' COMMITMENT TO THE ABSOLUTE TRUTH IN SCIENCE EDUCATION

Despite the research efforts in science education, particularly in the field of the nature of science, it is reasonable to state that science educators have systematically dismissed the problem of ontology. Generally, they take reality for granted, holding a naive realist perspective. Moreover, science teachers' naive realism often unfolds in more complex perspectives such as positivism or instrumentalism. In this case, the ontology becomes unproblematic, and the view of science development slides to dogmatism, ultimately undermining any possibility for pluralism in science and science teaching.

The lack of systematic reflection on the problem of ontology eventually leads science teachers to uncritically embrace an epistemological potpourri, which, in turn, makes the teaching models inconsistent, unreliable and unable to deal with complex socio-scientific issues. Nonetheless, we see science education as a privileged field to ground the ontological debate since science classrooms and curriculum are arenas where the quotidian knowledge (wild) and the school science knowledge (school) counterpose, blend and often merge into new ones.

To conceptualise excessive teacher entitlement, we must address the dichotomic form in which the problem of ontology is commonly posed in science education. On one hand, it is possible to find the notion of a static and absolute reality to which many realists subscribe. On the other hand, postmodernists approach both science and science education with the notion of fragmented and unbonded reality. It might bring pernicious consequences to teaching, particularly fostering a view of scientific knowledge anchored in *absolute truths* (see Mattos et al., 2022).

The historical development of science education has often been marked by naive realism and a commitment to absolute truths. The emergence of the science, technology and society (STS) approach serves as a response to the predominant focus on canonical scientific knowledge, challenging narrow views of science's role in society and emphasising the complex nature of societal problems (Aikenhead, 2006). This approach has been a counterforce to positivist science perspectives, illustrated in contemporary contexts such as teaching climate change, where a broader consideration of diverse knowledge is essential (Levinson, 2012).

Scientific instrumentalism and other derivations from positivism have been a resilient underlying view within science education. Its implications can be found across different science teaching practices. A prevalent issue in science education is the tendency to depict scientific concepts as an assemblage of disconnected formulas or schemas. Teachers often introduce the laws of motion, stoichiometric calculations, Linnaean taxonomy and similar topics in isolation, divorcing them from any societal problem. Consequently, the learning experience for students seems reduced to the mechanical memorisation of symbols and rules, devoid of meaningful context.

In turn, the purported attributes of objectivity, neutrality and rationality form the foundation for an instrumentalist perspective that lends certainty to decision-making processes and encourages technocratic decision-making models. As a result, many proponents of this scientific fundamentalism resort to authoritarian rhetoric to articulate their viewpoints, partially because they regard their epistemological stance as qualitatively superior to alternative perspectives. Some science educators may perpetuate the conception of science that is couched within this *mythological ethos*. Camillo and Mattos (2014) delineate the repercussions for science education as manifesting in several dichotomies: between the products and processes of science, between the individual and collective subjects of scientific activities and between the alienation and emancipation of the subject within the context of such activities.

The first dichotomy refers to the presentation of science as a compilation of pre-established facts intended to unveil the essence of natural phenomena. According to the authors, teaching science as solely an ontological entity, separate from its epistemological dimensions, exemplifies a rupture between the product and process of science. In this approach, science is conveyed as a static set of factual truths rather than an evolving process of understanding reality. Despite minor variations among scientific disciplines, a notable instance of this dichotomy in science education manifests in laboratory work. Even when teachers are keen to overcome the lack of laboratory work, the prevailing approach often involves using experiments to merely validate theories or universal principles delivered beforehand. Paradoxically, the potential for genuine inquiry becomes overshadowed by a series of mechanical procedures, with questioning replaced by data manipulation to align with predetermined answers. Motivated students may initially approach laboratory work with enthusiasm, but the repetitiveness of such meaningless cycles over several months tends to erode their interest, reducing their perception of science to a monotonous pursuit. In this context, students are not encouraged to engage in meaningful inquiry, where the process of questioning plays a central role. Instead, their interaction is limited to the static end product of scientific knowledge. When students encounter Newton's law of motion for the first time, it is typically presented as a finalised concept rather than something to be actively questioned or explored. This approach diminishes the opportunity for students to appreciate scientific knowledge's dynamic and evolving nature, hindering their ability to participate in the inquiry process.

The second dichotomy refers to the notion that scientific activities are exclusively the purview of individual agents, who can make new discoveries under their unique cognitive attributes such as memory and intelligence. This perspective consequently positions science education as reliant on the historically entrenched contributions of *past geniuses*. This approach perpetuates an uncritical and allegorical account of the history of science, eschewing a more nuanced understanding of its cultural and historical development. While examining science textbooks at both high school and university levels, one is likely to be struck by the conspicuous absence of the history of science. In those rare instances where historical narratives are included, they often revolve around portraying the lonely genius. Noteworthy figures such as Newton, Einstein, Darwin and Marie Curie, while inspiring, are frequently presented to reinforce students' perception of the scientist as an isolated individual.

Moreover, it influences the collective imagination regarding the nature of science itself. The emphasis on solitary brilliance can inadvertently contribute to a competitive atmosphere among students, fostering a reluctance to engage in collaborative endeavours in favour of pursuing the goal of becoming the next lonely genius. Such a perspective may inadvertently undermine the collaborative and collective nature of scientific inquiry, hindering the cultivation of a more holistic understanding of the scientific process. This mindset, notably prevalent among highly engaged students, has the potential to shape their perception of science teachers as living models of the lonely genius archetype.

The final dichotomy addresses the overarching goal of science as seeking a fixed, immutable understanding of natural reality. This viewpoint effectively stifles individual agency in engaging with science and precludes the capacity to conceive alternative interpretations of established scientific truths. According to the authors, this dichotomy, in alignment with the first, alienates the agents involved in scientific activities from the products of their endeavours. Unfortunately, students aspiring to pursue a scientific career often encounter a climate with no tolerance for questioning, mistakes and exploratory thinking. From the outset of their academic journey, attempts at even minor interventions are met with discouragement, as they are told, 'Stop making silly questions; here it is like a cinema, you buy your ticket, you sit in silence, and enjoy the movie' or faced with overt gender bias such as, 'The girls' mind is not shaped for science, doesn't matter how hard you try'. These explicit expressions of prejudice add up to more subtle and implicit messages, undermining any sense of agency and belonging among students. Such messaging stifles students' intellectual curiosity and fosters an atmosphere that hinders their sense of ownership and participation in scientific activity. This dominant stance establishes a barrier between students and educators in the classroom. Science is portrayed as a domain exclusively enacted by others – whether scientists or teachers – something to be observed but never actively engaged with.

The underlying structure of these dichotomies hinges on the interplay between epistemology, ontology and axiology to include a third dimension. A complete severance between these aspects gives rise to various forms of positivism, wherein epistemology and ontology are treated as isolated domains. Conversely, a direct and simplistic conflation of these elements paves the way for naive realism.

In the realm of science education, we contend that the historical progression of science and the associated challenges play a pivotal role in shaping educational practices. As mentioned earlier, conventional teaching methods frequently reinforce a perspective on science that alienates students from the production of scientific knowledge, casting the act of discovery as the domain of an exclusive group of *geniuses*. This perspective forms the foundation upon which excessive teacher entitlement can thrive within educational institutions. Reinforcing such relation with knowledge becomes a vicious cycle within schools and universities. From our perspective, the urgent challenges confronting pluralism in science education today include critically examining these entrenched views and proposing alternative perspectives.

AUTHORITATIVE DISCOURSE AND DIALOGICAL SCIENCE EDUCATION

Our exploration into excessive teacher entitlement begins with our delving into the concept of teachers' authority. Understanding the dynamics of authority is crucial for unravelling the concrete conditions of its development within classrooms. Throughout history, the notion of authority has been present in science education, teacher education and parenting studies. This thorough examination will serve as the foundation for constructing a model that transcends the traditional dichotomy between authoritarianism and indulgence, offering a nuanced perspective on the complexities inherent in teacher–student dynamics.

Studies from diverse perspectives have emphasised the significance of looking at classroom dialogical interaction (see Howe & Abedin, 2013). This research trend denotes a shift away from studies highlighting students' individual comprehensions of particular phenomena into those studies related to how understandings are formed in the classroom collective environment.

Considering a dialogic interaction, attention is paid to more than one point of view, more than one voice is heard, and there is an interanimation of ideas (Bakhtin, 2010). Therefore, classroom interaction is considered 'more dialogical the more it represents students' points of view, and the discussion includes both their ideas and the teacher's' (Mercer et al., 2009, p. 354). Aguiar et al. (2010) developed a multi-level framework for analysing teacher–student discursive interactions in science education. This framework explores how teachers support students in creating meaning through various discourse patterns. While introducing dimensions related to dialogic and authoritative speech, it falls short in adequately addressing the complexity of excessive teacher entitlement.

We understand that lumping dialogism and authority within the same dimension hides the multiple ways to understand those complex concepts. Hence, we propose enhancing its complexity by scrutinising the dimensions of authority and dialogue, aiming to establish a robust foundation for conceptualising excessive teacher entitlement within the teaching–learning process.

Authority vs Authoritarian

The polysemy of the concept of authority is notorious for going from positive to negative meanings, but it is central to be discussed considering the excessive teacher entitlement. Its positive meaning derives from the idea that:

> A person has authority if he or she can command someone to do something without having to do anything other than issue a command; which is to say that the person who obeys recognises the authority of the person who commands as legitimate or correct (Meng, 2017, p. 1008)

However, like every concept, authority's nature is historical and complex, and its meanings are developed within collective human practices – activities. The concept of authority expresses its mediational nature since no authority is recognised by another person who trusts in the authority (Pace & Hemmings, 2007). This mediational characteristic is fundamental to understanding the processes of students recognising the teacher as an authority in a given field of knowledge. Thus, for instance, a teacher with authority in science is respected as such by his students, who become confident to follow the teacher's lead in their scientific education.

In situations when trust is substituted by fear, for instance, when the authority uses physical force or persuasion, it means 'that the authority of the one in command is no longer recognised as legitimate or correct by the one being commanded' (Meng, 2017, p. 1009). Despite being physical and symbolic, the force of violence makes authoritarianism 'the advocacy of authority as a source or origin that compels voluntary obedience without question' (Meng, 2017, p. 1008).

The instruments of force and power are varied and act at different scales of social relations and lead, through a dialectical process, ultimately to the interactional condition of oppressor–oppressed. Then, the 'authoritarian act is distinguished from all other acts by the fact that it does not encounter opposition from the person or persons towards whom it is directed' (Kojève, 2014, p. 35). Additionally, a contemporary layer that is widely recognised involves the rise of authoritarian political ideologies, posing a threat to established democratic systems. These ideologies advocate for a voluntary and conscious submission to a purportedly enlightened despot. Subsequently, interactional processes operate unilaterally, excluding dialogue from the communicative process.

Dialogue vs Monologue

The examination of dialogue is crucial as it lies at the heart of investigative human interaction. Considering dialogic approaches in teaching and learning, Matusov (2009) distinguishes between dialogue as a tool for knowledge production and as a goal unto itself. The former is labelled as *instrumental* dialogue since it is considered a 'pedagogical method aimed at enhancing the effectiveness of learning' (Matusov, 2009, p. 6), while the latter is *ontological* dialogue since it focuses on the nature of relationships participants develop among themselves and has an open orientation without a predefined endpoint.

Another conceptualisation of *dialogue* elaborates it as a human activity that emerges as a collaborative-oriented interactive dynamic process where the common objective takes shape during dialogical activities unfolding, involving transformations of the interacting individuals and the mediating tools (Wells, 2002). In this case, dialogue does not exclude its instrumental aspect; the development of dialogic activity responds to motives that may evolve through the changing mediations between subjects and objectives, encompassing the instrumental requirements of communication (Santiago & Mattos, 2023).

More notably, emancipatory dialogic activity entails individuals recognising the dialectical interplay between identity and alterity – 'the recognition of ourselves within the others' (Santiago & Mattos, 2023, p. 4). This perspective underscores the political dimension inherent in dialogic activity, emphasising the necessity of taking a stance and opposing collective ways of being in the world. Freire's work inspires this perspective (see 2005), where the educational process is based on active agents of social and political transformation. According to Freire, dialogue is underpinned by elements such as love, humility, faith, trust, hope and critical thinking, while their absence contributes to monologue (Santiago & Mattos, 2023). Consequently, dialogue built upon this framework nurtures trust between persons engaged in interaction. According to him (Freire, 2005), dialogue is praxis embodying an onto-creative act where humans continually recreate the world and themselves. We could not dissociate the dialogicity and authority dimensions of human interaction from this conception of dialogue.

As elaborated by Freire (2005, p. 72), 'In the banking concept of education, knowledge is a gift bestowed by those who consider themselves knowledgeable upon those whom they consider to know nothing'. Banking education provided a radical criticism of the basis on which education was carried out. Although it is possible to indicate some advancements and changes since then, its sharp criticism remains powerful to examine some underlying tenets that remain alive and resilient in education today, particularly in scientific education. It is worth noticing that Freire never used the term excessive teacher entitlement. Nonetheless, we argue, he was aware of the consequences of such practices and conceptions regarding excessive teacher entitlement to educational changes.

Dialogue, Authority and Teachers' Styles

If one isolates the instrumental dimension of dialogue, it might lead to the perception of independence between the dimensions of authority and dialogue in interactive processes. In this way, it is difficult to conceive dialogical-authoritarian relationships since dialogue is apparently just an instrument to communicate. However, when one takes dialogue from an ontological perspective, power relations appear more clearly in interactive processes.

In order to pinpoint interactional situations between teachers and students that exemplify excessive teacher entitlement, we introduce categories of teacher styles, adapted from the parenting styles proposed by Baumrind (2005). The author categorises parents into three styles: authoritarian, permissive and authoritative. Each of them represents a different form of interaction between parents and children. The *authoritarian* style is characterised by demanding and controlling actions. Parents set strict rules and have high expectations for their children, expecting obedience. Arguably, in this case, interaction lacks open and affectionate communication. In the *permissive* style, parents are characterised by being affectionate and indulgent, establishing few clear rules or limits. They seek to avoid conflicts and allow their children to make their own decisions, even if they are not age-appropriate. Finally, in the *authoritative* style, parents are both demanding and responsive. They establish clear rules and provide emotional support and open communication, allowing children to develop self-control, self-esteem and independence.

Numerous educational researchers have proposed an essential similarity between parenting and teaching styles (Bassett et al., 2013), and, typically, four categories of teacher styles are proposed as follows.

The *authoritarian teacher's style* involves a teacher exerting complete control over the classroom, emphasising strict rules and expecting unwavering compliance. Any deviation from expected behaviour results in strict punishment, regardless of circumstances. These teachers tend to have limited involvement with students, which creates a sense of intimidation and distance. Authoritarian teachers prioritise a quiet, structured environment and favour direct instruction over cooperative learning. They do not promote collaboration or active discussions, leading to a tense classroom atmosphere and a lack of student engagement.

The *authoritative teachers' style* balances maintaining control in their classrooms and fostering student involvement. They establish and consistently enforce rules while valuing students' input, encouraging collaboration and clear communication. These teachers nurture autonomy and responsibility and are committed to their student's success, considering various factors, tailoring expectations and providing positive reinforcement.

In contrast, *permissive teachers* exhibit low control and involvement, lack lesson planning and structure, allow excessive freedom and result in a disorderly classroom. They neglect students' needs, hinder academic and social growth and struggle to unlock their students' full potential due to their disengagement.

A final style is *indulgent teachers*, like permissive ones, exhibit limited classroom control, allowing students excessive freedom, often leading to a lack of boundaries. However, unlike permissive teachers, indulgent educators are highly involved with their students and genuinely care about their lives, fostering a friendly atmosphere where students feel comfortable. This likability, though, sometimes comes at the cost of their authority, as students view them primarily as friends.

Teacher and Student Power Relations

Here, we will consider only two authoritative and authoritarian teachers' styles to deal with excessive teacher entitlement since the tension that emerged with authoritarianism is spread through various hierarchical levels of society and particularly concretised in power relationships among school participants.

When considering the activity system in which the school is immersed, we identify hierarchies of power relations. The discussion of power relations in schools must be instantiated in the broader dispute to build a democratic society that addresses the systemic conditions for a democratic school to exist. The diverse influences of political and economic fields play a crucial role in shaping school structures and curricula, influencing either the empowerment of individuals through educational activities or their adaptations with more immediate practices to the job market.

Within the social activity, the schools' activity regulates teacher and student interactions, providing or taking away their freedom of choice by enforcing routines and rules, dictating the official curriculum and determining how their school days are organised (Winchester, 2003). Thus, significant distinctions exist between traditional schools, which tend to be bureaucratic institutions and uphold a clear power hierarchy with the teacher positioned above the student, and democratic schools, where this hierarchy is downplayed and opportunities for collaborative decision-making throughout the school's activities are encouraged (Apple & Beane, 2007).

Looking specifically at discursive interactions inside the classroom, we necessarily go to the power relations between teachers and students. These power relations have been historically developed and attributed to teachers, especially in traditional education, where the relationships between teachers and students are dominantly formed within unequal power dynamics. These are of utmost importance because teachers can either positively uplift or negatively impact students, shaping students' attitudes, classroom performance and academic achievements (Camp, 2011).

Teachers' Style and the Epistemological Dimension of Science Teachers' Power

Research has primarily focused on exploring the relationship between teacher styles and the quality of teaching and learning, particularly emphasising dialogic interactions in the classroom, especially concerning scientific content (Amodia-Bidakowska et al., 2023). Here, we emphasise that a relevant dimension supporting excessive teacher entitlement is their specific knowledge of science.

The centrality of science content in science education is underscored when contemplating the teacher's specialised knowledge and the extent of alignment with a particular perspective on the nature of science that could serve as a basis for excessive teacher entitlement. For example, a teacher who takes science as truth finds in his students a group of subjects to be convinced or indoctrinated in this truth, leaving little room for diverse onto-epistemological positions. Here, the teacher's authority manifests itself in authoritarianism.

Elsewhere, we have examined how the conversations and disputes about scientific knowledge can assume the form of an epideictic discourse. In particular, in the current affairs of social media and scientific dissemination, the scientific truth is seen as something absolute that must be protected or, to some extent, imposed at all costs. In battling *fake news* and any attack against science, the most enthusiastic defenders assume a position akin to a religious one (Mattos et al., 2022). Polar opposite positions are taken, making any middle or common ground impossible.

Considering science, Gramsci (1977) introduced the concept of *scientific Esperantism* to express that a specific group of persons, whether scientists or not, believe that science functions as a universal and neutral language. According to this perspective, humanity could potentially transcend cultural barriers through science. The conviction that the sciences, viewed as impartial and objective forms of knowledge, can resolve all global issues, thereby enhancing society's overall well-being, is conveyed through a fundamentalist and dogmatic fanaticism.

Furthermore, in a monological-authoritarian teacher–student interaction, discourse happens with no opposition, leading the scientific content to be announced as an unquestionable universal truth. This kind of discourse could be identified as the Epideictic discourse, which often invokes science as a universal order, almost divine, reinforcing unchallenged truths that align with the values upheld within a specific community. This type of discourse highlights this particular science conception, employing a rhetoric of praise to facilitate the reinforcement and amplification of these scientific values within the discourse, allowing them to circulate effectively. Perelman and Olbrechts-Tyteca (1973) emphasise that epideictic oratory plays a pivotal role in persuasion, and any misunderstanding of its significance stems from a mistaken perception of the impact of argumentation, i.e. when students fail to learn, they are always held accountable for their inability to comprehend teachers' arguments.

The Epideictic-Esperantist discourse can be related to educational discourse, where the science teacher's statements in the classroom are seldom contested or seen as controversial. The science teacher fades counterpoints, transforming their words into universally accepted truths, like historical indubitable facts (Mattos et al., 2022).

Roughly, the strong commitment to scientific truth and authoritarianism in the student–teacher relationship can be formulated as one of the foundational practices for conceptualising excessive teacher entitlement. Regarding the teaching–learning process, they compound a fertile environment to flourish excessive teacher entitlement. However, CHAT can provide a way to tackle it by reframing and reorienting the teaching–learning process. Instead of focusing too much on the teacher's behaviour, we advocate for teaching practices that can work as a platform for teacher and student development while preventing problematic levels of excessive teacher entitlement in the first place.

SCIENTIFIC-CULTURAL INQUIRY

Given our position within a dialogical–authoritative educational framework, it is imperative to instrumentalise classroom interactive processes for cultivating both dialogical and authoritative educational practices and fostering the emergence of diverse epistemological and ontological perspectives. This situation does not mean that teachers passively accept an onto-epistemological potpourri, but they manage the different positions aiming to allow contradictions to emerge to transform the activity and, consequently, subjects' consciousness awareness.

To this end, we propose the scientific-cultural inquiry (Lago et al., 2019) as an instrument to overcome 'school encapsulation' (Engeström, 1991). The "school encapsulation" expresses the educational situation in which the content of the school – historically produced and consensually stabilised human knowledge – is disciplinarily recontextualized and loses the historical development of the construction of its meaning. In other words, in traditional, non-dialogic-authoritarian education based on *Esperantist-Epideictic* discourse, scientific knowledge retains little of its multiple cultural-historical meanings, becoming hermetic and oriented to answer questions exclusively related to the disciplinary school activity.

From here, we shall present the foundations of the educational practice grounded on CHAT that could redirect science teaching and tackle the problems discussed. Although the overall perspective is nurtured by teaching experiences in different scientific contents within various school settings, we will focus on the core theoretical concepts. Ultimately, it will provide a platform for teachers and the school leadership to act upon their concrete educational practices.

The Concept Activity

It is common for Vygotsky's propositions, such as cultural mediation, to be put forward as a psychological tool. Moreover, some scholars push this position further, introducing the analogy of psychological tools as material tools. It leads to an inconvenient split between what could be considered internal and external tools to the subject. This type of conceptualisation reframes and aggravates the discussed issue of dual ontology. In this case, one ends up with the object and the material tool as external, whereas the object's representations are internal to the subject. Interpretations of Vygotsky's works emphasising language and concepts as tools for thought often reinforced such an imbroglio. This position is commonly known in literature as semiotic mediation (Wells, 2007).

From our perspective, Vygotsky uses the unit of analysis, which cannot be understood from its decomposition in parts, as a key to examining the process of human development. He also advocates that the mediation, i.e. the subject–object unity, can only be understood as historical. In this regard, reality is not subjective or objective – the reality is subjective and objective, unlike the postmodernist trends that, despite claiming itself as historical, water down the issue to a particular and abstract subjectivism, the Vygotsky position stems from the radically historical and finite subject–object unity.

Although Vygotsky had occasionally mentioned *systems of activity*, Leontiev pushed forward the notion of activity (Engeström & Sannino, 2020). Hence, the binomial unity of subject–object becomes explicitly embedded in a collective dimension, i.e. community. This activity unity is now a trinomial that mediates each other, subject–community–object, and cannot be taken in isolation. In this sense, science teaching is much more complex than the student interacting with the surroundings, as some constructivist trends would like (Leach & Scott, 2003). When examining or intervening through teaching, it is essential to broaden the teaching-learning process to encompass the entire community: the school, out-of-school, scientific communities, and so forth. This approach ensures that learning is intimately connected to the learners' experiences within the activity. Then, through the activity, the subject–object mediation is produced and reproduced within the collective practice – the subject–community–object mediation.

Such a trinomial is also expressed in the action coordination to reach common goals. As discussed, learning in the school activity requires a transformation in action coordination and a complexification in the subject–community–object mediation. Consciousness development shapes novel ways of being with and within the world through the activity movement and entails an ontological complexification of the activity. Thus, without killing the pluralism, the different ontologies coalesce into a complex ontology, from which the complex meanings are forged within the historical limits of the system of activity development. Educational practice can be a path from fragmented ontologies to a complex, delimited and historically determined ontology.

It is possible to find some recent efforts in science education to put this theoretical framework into motion. For instance, Lago and Mattos (2021) named activity complexification as the evolution of concept activity. Ortega and Mattos

(2018) conceptualised the activity's features as hierarchical levels, feedback loops and different modes – as modes of human being-with-and-within-the-world – stabilised through history as genre activity.

Mediation and Conceptual Complexification

For quite some time, the genesis and development of higher mental functions were central to Vygotsky's research endeavour. He focuses on typically human processes such as 'voluntary attention, to logical memory, to the formation of concepts, and the development of will' (Vygotsky, 1997, p. 106). For him, such processes were not innate, yet they had been developed in his interaction with others. In the production and reproduction of activity, new mediations and meanings emerge as complexification, not only for the particular concept but for the systems of concepts. According to Vygotsky, 'every concept arises already connected with all others and, having arisen, seemingly determines its place in a system of previously recognised concepts' (Vygotsky, 1998, p. 4). From the activity, a conceptual system is generated that is marked by a dynamic among a system of conceptual systems, in other words, a complex of conceptual complexes that makes the fabric of ontology.

As Lago and Mattos (2021) indicate, one of Vygotsky's advances lies in his concept of generalisation as a movement between the concrete and the abstract. The concept formation ceases to be a simple reflection of an ideal essence to become part of reality development within human activity. According to them, concept activity entails that the word and meaning should not be taken as ready-made products but as a specific moment of continuous generalisation. Mattos (2014) underlines that concept formation dynamics is not a mere quantitative increment in mediations but a qualitative change. The concept's complexification can be understood as a movement of resignification in the conceptual ecology system's space. Therefore, comparing concepts as more or less complex could be meaningless if they emerge in different activities and have different complexities, i.e. different meditations. The foundations of concept formation, genesis and development are taken as the movement of concept activity (Lago & Mattos, 2021).

According to Lago and Mattos (2021), if science teaching aims at conceptual complexification, it should accommodate the transitions between operation, action and activity levels. Tasks should range from problems that must encompass, in a coming and going movement, from immediate quotidian problems to more complex social problems. This activity movement drives students through levels of volition and conscious awareness, connecting from more immediate situations to more meaningful objects to the subject of the community.

Towards Overcoming the School Encapsulation: The Scientific-Cultural Inquiry

The conceptual investigation approach refers to the method of ascending from the abstract to the concrete, which, as seen before, is a genetic method of a specific concept based on the study of its particular relations and successive generalisations and reductions (see Lago et al., 2019). This teaching–learning context emphasises the development of more complex mediations so that the object of study is understood in increasingly broad totalities.

On the one hand, focusing on scientific practice is informed by the concept of a *community of practice*, where learning occurs through a subject's continuous and increasingly central participation in social practices (Lave & Wenger, 1991). This paradigm is grounded in analysing individual learning within specific, often non-formal, activities – such as the roles of healers, butchers, midwives, tailors or members of Alcoholics Anonymous. In these settings, individuals acquire knowledge through active participation in community practices, beginning peripherally and gradually becoming more central contributors. In this context, science education is conceptualised as a process of enculturation where students are inducted into the practices of knowledge creation, utilising the tools and procedures inherent to scientific activity.

On the other hand, the cultural inquiry approach is rooted in Engeström's (1987) concept of 'learning by expanding', originally conceived to describe and analyse collective learning within organisations. This approach emphasises communal learning and the emergence of new concepts or practices. In this framework, the object of study is expanded to encompass the immediate subject matter and the learning context itself, subject to critical scrutiny from a historical perspective. Engeström (1991) posits that such critical evaluation should occur within the educational environment, thereby integrating a historical understanding into the schooling process. However, Lago et al. (2019) broadened the notion of expansive learning to criticise the scientific object within scientific school practices – learning contexts, including scientific investigation of other spheres of cultural production.

Lago et al. (2019) consider that the basis of scientific-cultural inquiry: (i) the *conceptual inquiry* emphasises modelling, analysis and knowledge production; (ii) the *scientific inquiry* focuses on the epistemic practices developed by science; (iii) the *cultural inquiry* brings to light contradictions of production, circulation and knowledge in society.

Considering the pedagogical proposition of scientific-cultural inquiry implies taking it as an activity, whose necessary conditions for its completion were presented throughout this chapter. This means that it is a condition to understand that in a dialogic–authoritative process, there is a need to consider that there are other commitments to the production of knowledge beyond its epistemological dimension. The ontological and axiological commitments are also dimensions to be considered when identifying the contradictions experienced by the subjects of this activity. These contradictions must become problems, not just any problem, but an initial problem recognised as everyone's own, starting the ascension and descension movement between abstract and concrete. This dialogical and authoritative form establishes the conditions for teaching–learning around mutual productive engagement based on recognising that individual needs are also social.

CONCLUDING REMARKS

This chapter presents an argument that complexifies the concept of excessive teacher entitlement. In pursuit of this objective, we begin with the premise that the entire concept is polysemic and contingent on the supporting activity (Lago & Mattos, 2021). Hence, diverse interpretations of excessive teacher entitlement are identified in the literature, ranging from its economic origins in shaping forms of teaching and learning in educational activity systems to its roots in interpersonal relationships within the classroom.

This text focuses on teaching–learning activities in the classroom, particularly in science teaching. This disciplinary specificity arises from systemic contradictions in science teaching associated with the dual ontology that stems from the idea that social and natural sciences deal with different realities. The object of the first is typically considered dialectical, while that of the second has been treated within a metaphysical realism.

This contradiction has enabled natural scientists to regard their epistemology as more 'true' than others, leading to an extreme stance that equates scientific knowledge with absolute truth. This epistemological standpoint gives rise to communication and science education modes that closely resemble religious propaganda (Mattos et al., 2022). The contents of science teaching become truths to be memorised through an authoritarian relationship that demands submission from students to such truths presented as irrefutable. This epistemological understanding bestows upon the teacher the perception of an indisputable oracle, resulting in a pedagogy that renders students' needs and curiosities inconsequential in the face of the significant questions posed by science, regarded as an institution in this context. Teachers' imperviousness to students' needs manifests their excessive entitlement.

To understand the complexity of the concept of excessive teacher entitlement, we brought CHAT, associated with the perspectives of Freire and Bakhtin. With this theoretical unit, we aimed to concretely elucidate the concept of teacher excessive entitlement within the realm of interpersonal relationships between educators and students. With CHAT as a background, we introduced the concepts of authority associated with the concept of dialogue, determining dialogic styles of teachers – authoritarian, permissive, authoritative and indifferent. With these styles, it was possible to deal with the power dimension of the teaching–learning relationship of scientific concepts. We proposed scientific-cultural activity aimed to overcome contradictions arising from an epistemology and ontology axiologically based on dogmatic scientific knowledge conditions. The activity introduced the notion of 'problem' as a dialectical expression of the simultaneity of the concept meaning for particular individuals and their collectives. Scientific-cultural activity seeks to overcome the dichotomy between the production and consumption of scientific knowledge, considering students, individually and collectively, as producers and agents of knowledge production. Hence, scientific-cultural inquiry serves as a means to rebuild the connections formed by students with scientific knowledge and to move beyond the perception that science teachers communicate from a pedestal of absolute truth. This approach introduces a pluralistic perspective on knowledge, steering towards a complex ontology. The authority of the teacher, scientific knowledge and the students themselves becomes relative to a domain of validity.

Finally, our approach to teacher excessive entitlement focuses on how school activity is organised and carried out today. Thus, we do not focus on teacher excessive entitlement as a specific characteristic of the teacher but rather an emergence of educational activity at its different hierarchical levels. This allows us to avoid the problem of blaming teachers, as those are solely responsible for the phenomenon and opens up a range of possibilities for analysis and actions to redirect teaching activity and relationships between teachers and students.

REFERENCES

Aguiar, O. G., Mortimer, E. F., & Scott, P. (2010). Learning from and responding to students' questions: The authoritative and dialogic tension. *Journal of Research in Science Teaching*, 47(2), 174–193. https://doi.org/10.1002/tea.20315

Aikenhead, G. S. (2006). *Science education for everyday life: Evidence-based practice*. Teachers College Press.

Amodia-Bidakowska, A., Hennessy, S., & Warwick, P. (2023). Disciplinary dialogues: Exploring the association between classroom dialogue and learning outcomes within and between subjects in English primary schools. *Learning, Culture and Social Interaction*, 43, 100742. https://doi.org/10.1016/j.lcsi.2023.100742

Apple, M. W., & Beane, J. (2007). The case for democratic schools. In M. W. Apple & J. Beane (Eds.), *Democratic schools: Lessons in powerful education* (2nd ed., pp. 1–29). Heinemann.

Bakhtin, M. M. (2010). *Speech genres and other late essays*. University of Texas Press.

Bassett, J. F., Snyder, T. L., Rogers, D. T., & Collins, C. L. (2013). Permissive, authoritarian, and authoritative instructors: Applying the concept of parenting styles to the college classroom. *Individual Differences Research*, 11(1), 1–11.

Baumrind, D. (2005). Patterns of parental authority and adolescent autonomy. *New Directions for Child and Adolescent Development*, 2005(108), 61–69. https://doi.org/10.1002/cd.128

Camillo, J., & Mattos, C. R. (2014). Making explicit some tensions in educational practice: Science education in focus. *Cultural Historical Psychology*, 10(2), 110–115.

Camp, M. D. (2011). *The power of teacher-student relationships in determining student success*. Thesis, University of Missouri–Kansas City. https://mospace.umsystem.edu/xmlui/handle/10355/11358

Engeström, Y. (1987). *Learning by expanding: An activity-theoretical approach to developmental research*. Orienta-Konsultit.

Engeström, Y. (1991). Non scolae sed vitae discimus: Toward overcoming the encapsulation of school learning. *Learning and Instruction*, 1(3), 243–259. https://doi.org/10.1016/0959-4752(91)90006-T

Engeström, Y., & Sannino, A. (2020). From mediated actions to heterogenous coalitions: Four generations of activity-theoretical studies of work and learning. *Mind, Culture and Activity*, 1–20. https://doi.org/10.1080/10749039.2020.1806328

Freire, P. (2005). *Pedagogy of the oppressed* (M. B. Ramos, Trans.). Continuum.

Gramsci, A. (1977). *Gramsci, A. Quaderni del Carcere* (2nd ed., Vol. 2). Giulio Einaudi.

Howe, C., & Abedin, M. (2013). Classroom dialogue: A systematic review across four decades of research. *Cambridge Journal of Education*, 43(3), 325–356. https://doi.org/10.1080/0305764X.2013.786024

Kojève, A. (2014). In F. Terre (Ed.), *The notion of authority: A brief presentation* (H. Weslati, Trans.) (1st ed.). Verso.

Lago, L., & Mattos, C. R. (2021). Bridging concept and activity: A proposal of a first-step dialectical synthesis. *Cultural-Historical Psychology*, 17(2), 29–36. https://doi.org/10.17759/chp.2021170203

Lago, L., Ortega, J. L. N. A., & Mattos, C. R. (2019). A investigação científica-cultural como forma de superar o encapsulamento escolar: uma Intervenção com base na teoria na atividade para o caso do Ensino das fases da Lua [Scientific-cultural inquiry as a way to overcome school encapsulation: An intervention based on activity theory for the case of the moon's phases]. *Investigações em Ensino de Ciências*, *24*(1), 239–260. https://doi.org/10.22600/1518-8795.ienci2019v24n1p239

Lave, J., & Wenger, E. (1991). *Situated learning: Legitimate peripheral participation.* Cambridge University Press.

Leach, J., & Scott, P. (2003). Individual and sociocultural views of learning in science education. *Science & Education*, *12*(1), 91–113. https://doi.org/10.1023/A:1022665519862

Levinson, R. (2012). A perspective on knowing about global warming and a critical comment about schools and curriculum in relation to socio-scientific issues. *Cultural Studies of Science Education*, *7*(3), 693–701. https://doi.org/10.1007/s11422-012-9418-y

Mattos, C. R. (2014). Conceptual profile as a model of a complex world. In *Conceptual profile: A theory of teaching and learning scientific concepts* (Vol. 42, pp. 263–291). Springer. https://doi.org/10.1007/978-90-481-9246-5_10

Mattos, C. R., Lopez, F. S., Ortega, J. L., & Rodrigues, A. (2022). The public discussion on flat earth movement. *Science & Education*, *31*(5), 1339–1361. https://doi.org/10.1007/s11191-022-00321-7

Matusov, E. (2009). *Journey into dialogic pedagogy.* Nova Science Publishers.

Meng, M. (2017). On authoritarianism. A review essay. *Comparative Studies in Society and History*, *59*(4), 1008–1020. https://doi.org/10.1017/S0010417517000354

Mercer, N., Dawes, L., & Staarman, J. K. (2009). Dialogic teaching in the primary science classroom. *Language and Education*, *23*(4), 353–369. https://doi.org/10.1080/09500780902954273

Ortega, J. L., & Mattos, C. R. (2018). A hipertrofia de um gênero no ensino de física: Aspectos da sintaxe e da semântica na produção de conceitos científicos [The hypertrophy of genre in physics teaching: aspects of syntax and semantics in the production of scientific concepts]. In M. I. B. Campos & G. T. Souza (Eds.), *Mídia, discurso e ensino* (pp. 75–94). FFLCH/USP.

Pace, J. L., & Hemmings, A. (2007). Understanding authority in classrooms: A review of theory, ideology, and research. *Review of Educational Research*, *77*(1), 4–27. https://doi.org/10.3102/003465430298489

Perelman, C., & Olbrechts-Tyteca, L. (1973). *The new rhetoric: A treatise on argumentation* (J. Wilkinson & P. Weaver, Trans.). University of Notre Dame Press. https://doi.org/10.2307/j.ctvpj74xx

Ratnam, T. (2021). The interaction of culture and context in the construction of teachers' putative entitled attitude in the midst of change. In T. Ratnam & C. J. Craig (Eds.), *Advances in research on teaching* (pp. 77–101). Emerald Publishing Limited. https://doi.org/10.1108/S1479-368720210000038006

Ratnam, T., Craig, C., Marcut, I. G., Marie-Christine, D., Mena, J., Doyran, F., Hacıfazlıoğlu, O., Hernández, I. & Peinado- Muñoz, C. (2019). Entitlement attitude: Digging out blind spots. In D. Mihăescu & D. Andron (Eds.), *Proceedings, The 19th Biennial Conference of International Study Association on Teachers and Teaching (ISATT), "Education beyond the crisis: New skills, children's rights and teaching contexts"* (pp. 210–219). Lucian Blaga University Publishing House.

Santiago, A., & Mattos, C. (2023). From classroom education to remote emergency education: Transformations in a dialogical pedagogy proposal. *Dialogic Pedagogy: An International Online Journal*, *11*(1), DT1–DT21. https://doi.org/10.5195/dpj.2023.462

Vygotsky, L. S. (1997). Mastering attention. In *The collected works of L. S. Vygotsky: The history of the development of higher mental functions* (M. J. Hall, Trans.) (Vol. 4, pp. 53–77). Plenum Press.

Vygotsky, L. S. (1998). *Child psychology* (M. J. Hall, Trans) (Vol. 5). Plenum Press.

Wells, G. (2002). The role of dialogue in activity theory. *Mind, Culture and Activity*, *9*(1), 43–66. https://doi.org/10.1207/S15327884MCA0901_04

Wells, G. (2007). The mediating role of discoursing in activity. *Mind, Culture and Activity*, *14*(3), 160–177. https://doi.org/10.1080/10749030701316300

Winchester, I. (2003). Editorial: Democracy and education. *The Journal of Educational Thought (JET)/Revue de La Pensée Éducative*, *37*(1), 1–4. https://www.jstor.org/stable/23767170

EXCESSIVE TEACHER ENTITLEMENT AND DEFENSIVE PEDAGOGY: CHALLENGING POWER AND CONTROL IN CLASSROOMS

Joanne Hardman

University of Cape Town, South Africa

ABSTRACT

South Africa lags significantly in mathematics achievement on international benchmarking tests, which has led to several interventions aimed at improving mathematics attainment in the country. Drawing on the theoretical work of Vygotsky, Leontiev and Engeström, this chapter reports on one such initiative that implemented computer technology into disadvantaged schools in the apple growing district of the Western Cape. Contrary to expectations, the object of the lesson became control over students' actions, rather than a mathematical object aimed at developing students' understanding of the subject. The teacher adopted what I call a defensive position in relation to the novel technology, tightening pace and sequencing in these lessons. I draw on Ratnam's work into 'excessive entitlement' to illustrate that this teacher's defensive posture regarding technology emanates from a need to exert complete power over the content taught in a lesson and leads her to reject the novel technology in favour of traditional methods. While interviews with the teacher in this study indicated that she felt she promoted student dialogue and more symmetrical power relations in her classes through group work, this is not seen in the data. This is explained in relation to teachers' excessive entitlement to 'owning' the knowledge in their classrooms through maintaining control over the rules of the system. I pull on Cultural-Historical Activity Theory (CHAT) to illuminate how the activity of teaching in a classroom affords and constrains what the teacher is able to achieve, often making them feel excessively entitled to push back reform.

Keywords: Primary school; mathematics; pedagogical change; excessive teacher entitlement; defensive position; cultural-historical activity theory

South Africa consistently lags behind the rest of the world in mathematics performance as measured on international benchmarking tests, such as the Trends in International Mathematics and Science Study (TIMSS) tests. In fact, in the last TIMSS results, South Africa was third from last in the sample, followed only by Pakistan and the Philippines (Mullis et al., 2020). This is an alarming result given that South Africa is a middle-income country that consistently spends over 20% of its annual GDP on education. Understandably worried about these results, the government has rolled out many interventions in schools to assist teachers and students with mathematics in South Africa. Many initiatives rely on the use of information and communication technologies (ICTs) where students can use devices to work through mathematical problems online. Software such as Master Maths and Cami Maths have been introduced in the Western Cape from as early as 2002 under the Khanya initiative (Hardman, 2007a). The premise underpinning the use of technology to aid in mathematics teaching and learning assumes that the use of ICTs can positively impact on students' attainment in mathematics when used as cognitive tools by teachers (Hardman, 2023). The empirical evidence for this, however, indicates clearly that it is not the hardware or software itself that leads to attainment but rather how teachers use technology as pedagogical tools (Hardman, 2019). Specifically, where ICT use is underpinned by a 'constructivist' type pedagogical approach, where children are seen as active cognising agents engaged in co-constructing knowledge with the teacher, there is evidence to suggest that mathematical gains can be made (Hardman, 2019). The question that animates the debate in this chapter is whether ICTs:

- Change pedagogy (and consequently learning) in mathematics and if so
- How pedagogy shifts with the use of novel technology.

In a bid to understand pedagogy as contextually embedded, I draw on the cultural-historical work of Vygotsky (1978) as well as new-Vygotskian work.

THEORETICAL FRAMEWORK

For Vygotsky (1978, 1986), cognition develops through social interaction between a culturally more competent other and a novice. In interaction, a uniquely social space, which he calls the zone of proximal development (ZPD), is opened, and it is here, through guided instruction, called mediation, that meaning is developed and co-constructed. It is in this developmental zone that the student/novice comes to understand and become embedded in the meaning of what is being learnt. For Vygotsky (1986), language was the primary mediating tool that guides cognitive development. In the sense that a more culturally experienced other can guide a novice in learning, the teacher, then, as the more expert other, is not simply a guide on the side or a 'nice to have'; teachers are absolutely essential in the teaching/learning dyad.

While clearly recognising the importance of the social context, Vygotsky's focus on language leaves a gap in conceptualising how activity shapes cognitive development. It was his colleague, Leontiev (1981), who theorised the impact of activity on development, illustrating his approach by reference to a primeval hunt.[1] Leontiev (1981) asks the audience to imagine a primeval hunt, where the actions of individuals can only be understood in relation to the entire activity. For example, watching a beater light a fire to chase the game out of hiding tells you nothing about what the activity is, the action of beating the ground to make the fires larger seems puzzling in the absence of an understanding that this forms part of a larger activity, the activity of obtaining food through hunting. Focusing on the collective activity, according to Leontiev, is the only way to make sense of individual actions. For him, an activity is conceived of as a triad.

For Leontiev, the activity is sparked by a motive, while individual actions and fossilised operations are the mechanisms for addressing the motive and obtaining an outcome. While this model of collective activity helps to situate individual actions within a cultural context, it does not go far enough in providing an analytically useful mechanism for studying the social context in which actions are shaped and reshaped during any activity. For this elaboration, I turn to the work of Engeström (1987) and his articulation of human activity as based in activity systems.[2] Fig. 1 is a graphic representation of Engeström's notion of human activity represented as an activity system.

What we see in Fig. 1 is that a subject (in our case, a teacher) is motivated by an object (in this chapter, the stated need/motive to develop students' understanding of mathematics) to achieve an outcome (mathematically adept students, in our case). The subject uses material artefacts (tools such as a computer or language) to act on the object which is shared by the community, in our case, the students and the teacher. As this model of human action is based in dialectical logic, where apparent opposites are seen as two sides of one whole, the notion of contradictions is used in Cultural-Historical Activity Theory (CHAT) to illustrate how dynamic change happens in and across activity systems. Contradictions refer to double binds, where a level of dissonance is introduced that requires action.

---

[1] While Leontiev's work focuses on collective activity, the move away from Vygotsky's focus on language needs to be understood against a background of oppression and, specially, the banning of his own work, in the Soviet Union. Had the imperative to move towards collective activity not been paramount, one wonders what more could have been done with Vygotsky's focus on signs and symbols in his time.

[2] I note that Vygotsky's work is often referred to as the first generation of activity theory; Leontiev's work is referred to as the second generation of activity theory and Engeström's cultural-historical activity theory (CHAT) is often referred to as third-generation activity theory. I do not draw these firm distinctions in this chapter, but rather trace the historical trajectory of CHAT.

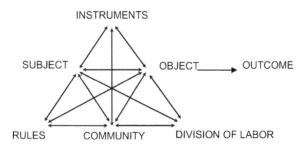

Fig. 1. An Activity System. *Source:* Engeström, 1987, p. 63.

That is, a contradiction is a dynamic site of change. It is important to note, however, that the resolution of contradictions should not be viewed as primarily progressive; a contradiction can, indeed, lead to a regression and a narrowing of the activity system. An example animates this: if there is a secondary contradiction between the subject and the tool, for example, using the computer, the teacher may resolve this conflict by simply choosing not to use the technology. Indeed, in the case study reported in this chapter, this is exactly what we see. No change, then, happens with the introduction of the novel tool as it is not taken up as a tool. Moreover, it is important to note that individual actions do not take place in a vacuum; there are rules that mediate between the community and the subject, and division of labour mediates between the community and the object. The fact that individual actions are curtailed by rules, tools and division of labour will become important when we turn to the notion of excessive teacher entitlement in the following section of this chapter.

Engeström notes that no activity system happens in isolation; indeed, any activity system is integrated and informed by other activity systems. For example, the teacher who forms the focus of this chapter is not only part of the activity system of the mathematics lesson; they are also possibly a parent and are, thus, part of another, family, activity system. They are also part of other institutional activity systems in the school. The multiplicity of activity system indicates that a minimum of two activity systems is in play at any given time. In this chapter, I draw primarily on Engeström's (1987, 1999) notion of activity systems to illustrate how teachers' pedagogical practices shift with the introduction of novel technology into a classroom. Before discussing the case study presented in this chapter, the notion of excessive teacher entitlement is outlined to attempt to understand the patterns that emerge in the data presented here.

Excessive Teacher Entitlement

> It is called praise. It is supposed to be a small act of kindness [but] you could feel the fear from the one she had praised. Not a big fear [...]but a subtle, little fear that would only be obvious to someone who had never received much in the way of praise[...]when one praises, one also judges. (Høeg, 1993, p. 47)

This quote from Høeg's novel *Borderliners* is interesting because it highlights the normative nature of something as apparently innocuous as praise in a classroom, illustrating how someone exercises control over the one being praised. I use this quote to signal that even praise is a normative endeavour, and when we speak about teachers and their praxis, we need to be cognisant of implied judgements. This is especially so when we use the term 'excessive teacher entitlement' which forms the crux of this book. In this chapter, excessive teacher entitlement can be said to relate to the teacher's pedagogical approach to learning in the presence of novel technology, such that the teacher's pedagogy alters, shifting the object of the lesson. Ratnam's work (2023) poses the question of why, faced with new innovative practice, teachers appear to sabotage the innovation, rather than picking it up and running with it to better praxis. In the case of this chapter, we will see how the introduction of novel technology meant to improve mathematics attainment in grade 6, fails to take hold as the teacher does not relinquish her control and power in the computer-based lesson.

However, a brief caveat is in order before I continue; the very term 'excessive teacher entitlement' appears to place the teacher as a central determiner of their own actions in relation to those they teach. It is the teacher who acts volitionally, wielding the curriculum as a tool to transmit knowledge to students. And it is the teacher who is almost always pathologised when students fail to perform. Teachers lack content knowledge; they lack the ability to teach; they are not well versed in science or mathematics (Spaull, 2013). These are just a few of the things we can trace in the abundant literature that indicates how teachers fail in their pedagogical task. For Feather (2003), entitlement is influenced by societal norms, rules and the roles one enacts in society. It is here, in this space of casting an analytical gaze on the teacher, that CHAT becomes a valuable theoretical tool for understanding how teachers act in contexts where they do not have the power and control that one assumes they do. The rules of the school, of the curriculum and even of the classroom impact on how teachers can act. The idea that teachers are autonomous in either their choice of what or how to teach fails to recognise that they are constrained by the contexts they work in (Mooney Simmie & Moles, 2020). Where teachers are equipped with novel technology to aid in teaching, as in the case reported here, the expectation is that they will take this up seamlessly, with little attention paid to the overall context of where and who they are teaching. This anticipated outcome fails to appreciate that in a context where one is not in control over whether a tool is introduced or not (computers, in the case reported in this study) can have unexpected outcomes. A teacher who feels threatened by novelty will revert to a stance that elicits excessive entitlement over knowledge, as this is where they feel they do have power and control. As we will see in the case study in this chapter, one cannot simply intervene in a school, placing novel technology or a novel intervention into the classroom, without having a sense of how teachers already teach and investigating their *own* needs, which may or may not require novel tools to facilitate praxis. Moreover, what strikes a researcher as excessive entitlement needs to be read against the actual activity system the teacher inhabits. Schools are rule-bound institutions where asymmetrical power ensures a firm divide between teacher and taught; the idea that a teacher acts autonomously in this hierarchical system needs to be critically engaged with. By providing an understanding of how human actions unfold in activities, mediated by rules, tools and division of labour, CHAT gives us both a theoretical and an analytical mechanism for understanding entitlement as an effect of an activity and not an individual. In the remainder of this chapter, I draw on a case study to illustrate how the notion of excessive teacher entitlement needs to be seen against the activity systems that a teacher inhabits, which afford and constrain actions.

METHODOLOGY

The study reported here takes the form of a case study. While I report on only one case in this chapter, this chapter forms part of a larger study that investigated the impact of computer technology on pedagogy in grade 6 mathematics lessons in underprivileged schools in the Western Cape Province of South Africa. The case presented in this chapter is largely representative of what was found in the larger study. As the overarching question informing this chapter is a qualitative 'how' question, the study lends itself to a qualitative approach to data collection and analysis (Denzin & Lincoln, 2011; Yin, 2012).

Research Participants

This study took place in grade 6 mathematics lessons. The reason for choosing grade 6 students lies in the fact that they are on a developmental cusp between concrete thinking and more abstract thinking. While this leans heavily on the Piaget (1978) notion of development, Vygotsky himself recognised that schooling was a developmental process wherein abstraction develops over time. The focus on mathematics is because schools were given mathematics software and computer hardware specifically for mathematics and not for other subjects. Students discussed in this chapter were on average 11.8 years of age and there were 23 girls and 17 boys in the class observed. The class teacher, Ms Todd, is 34 years old and has been teaching for 7 years. She has a bachelor's degree in education and a higher certificate in teacher training. She does not have a computer at home, and her use of the computer as a teaching tool was novel at the time of this study. Ms Todd is an Afrikaans first language speaker but teaches in both English and Afrikaans, as two of the grade 6 classes are taught in English and 2 in Afrikaans. The class observed for this study was taught in English although all children were Afrikaans first language speakers. Both teacher and students identify as 'coloured'.[3]

---

[3] The use of racial categories is recognised as problematic. However, as these categories continue to have salience in South Africa and continue to materially influence schooling provision, these categories are used in this chapter.

Context

Siyazama Primary School is in an urban area 37 kilometres outside of Cape Town.[4] This is a large, clean urban primary school, situated in an area that has a history of gang activity. Reflecting the dangers of the area, the school is surrounded by a two-metre barbed wire fence and access is strictly controlled. School fees are R240 (GBP 10.37) per year, and the principal reports that two-thirds of the parents pay the fees. The community in which the school is located is not affluent, and many parents are unemployed. The school has many after-school programmes in place and is particularly proud of its ballet and jazz club. There is a feeding scheme in the school that ensures students get peanut butter and jam sandwiches at interval. While a school uniform is prescribed, during the observation period, students were observed wearing jumpers that were not prescribed by the school. Students not wearing the correct jumpers had them confiscated. The school is a dual-medium school offering classes in both English and Afrikaans. In the classroom, students sit in teacher selected pairs, with their desks facing the blackboard as is the case in the computer laboratory.

Analytical Framework

I drew on the nodes of the activity system outlined in the theory section of this chapter to develop a checklist to analyse the data in terms of subject, object, rules, tool, division of labour, outcome and community. This checklist is outlined in Table 1 below. Video data of both face to face and computer-based lessons were collected, and the checklist in Table 1 indicates how I went about analysing the data for CHAT categories in the lessons observed.

Table 1. A CHAT Checklist.

AT concepts	Questions to ask when analysing evaluative episodes
Outcomes	What is produced in the episode?
Mediating artefacts	What tool(s) is/are used?
Object	What is the object/focus of this episode? What is the purpose of the activity for the subject? What is the teacher working on? Why is s/he working on it?
Division of labour	Who does what in this episode? Who determines what is meaningful?
Community	What community is involved in this episode? What group of people work together on the object
Rules	What kinds of rules: Instructional rules = evaluative rules and pacing rules Social order rules = disciplinary rules and communicative interaction rules

Source: Hardman (2007b, p. 7).

---

[4]All names used in this chapter are pseudonyms.

Table 2. CHAT Interview Schedule.

CHAT Code	Question
Subject	1. How do you think children learn mathematics (probe for theory of teaching)? 2. How do you think children learn mathematics with computers?
Object	1. What were you teaching in the lesson? 2. Is this a typical lesson?
Outcome	1. What do you hope to achieve teaching these mathematical concepts?
Division of labour	1. What is your role in the classroom? 2. What roles do the students occupy?
Rules	1. Are there specific rules in the lesson? Can you explain these?
Community	1. Who shares your motivation to teach mathematical concepts?
Tools	1. What do you use when you teach? Why?

What one can see in Table 2 are the various CHAT overarching categories and more specific analytical questions, in the second column. The 'subject' node remains unpopulated in Table 2 because the subject in this study is the teacher, which was established before the observation as pedagogical praxis is the focus of the chapter. I note here that in relation to 'rules', I distinguish between instructional rules that are related to teaching and social order rules, that relate to classroom management. Instructional rules relate to rules of evaluation, that is, who determines what counts as a valid answer, as well as to rules of pacing and sequencing of work. Social order rules carry with them disciplinary norms as well as rules regarding interaction. While rules facilitate control in an activity, division of labour, enacted in roles, carries with it the power in a system. It is in the sense of who determines what counts as knowledge in the classroom that the division of labour indicates who establishes the meaning of what is taught. The object, shared by community members, motivates the activity and is transformed into the outcome of the activity.

Four lessons were videotaped across a 6-week period. Two lessons were face-to-face lessons and two were computer-based lessons to enable a comparison between pedagogy with and without novel technology. The teacher was interviewed twice, using a semi-structured interview schedule which is reproduced below. Interview 1, which happened after the face-to-face lessons were taught lasted 37 minutes and interview 2, which was recorded after the computer-based lessons, lasted 43 minutes. Interviews were audio recorded and transcribed. Ethics clearance for the study was obtained from my institution, and all students gave assent to the study while their parents filled in consent forms for them to participate. The teacher filled in a consent form to participate.

The above table indicates the kinds of questions used to probe the teacher's understanding of teaching and learning with computers. The schedule is designed specifically to address CHAT concepts. The question around the subject position enables the researcher to elucidate a teacher's theory of teaching/learning. This gives an idea of the teacher's intended pedagogy. What happens in an actual classroom gives a picture of enacted pedagogy.

FINDINGS AND DISCUSSION

Face-to-Face Lessons

Ms Todd indicated in her interview that she believed children learn through activities. In her first interview, she indicated that 'children learn by doing it, by the actions. It must be active' (Interview 1). Her theory of pedagogy, then, assumes that children are active cognising agents who acquire knowledge through interacting with their surroundings and other people. Her subject position, then, in face-to-face classes can be described as based within a constructivist view of learning. Extract 1, below, illustrates a section of a lesson on fractions where Ms Todd is engaged in teaching equivalent fractions. The lesson is a 1-hour mathematics lesson on fractions and is midway through when she begins to elaborate what an equivalent fraction is.

Extract 1. Equivalent Fractions

(1) Ms Todd: Come, now I'm going to tell you what an equivalent fraction is.
(2) An equivalent fraction is a fraction.
(3) Come let me write it down *goes to the board and writes the definition down.*
(4) Is a fraction that is equivalent.
(5) Or we can say is a fraction with the same value.
(6) So, it's the same size or the same value *writes this on the board.*
(7) Come let me tell you again.
(8) Equivalent fractions are fractions that are the same size.
(9) Or fractions with the same value.
(10) Now it's a big word.
(11) But it's really quite easy.
(12) Come I'll show you.
(13) If I have my whole.
(14) And I cut it into two halves (*draws a square on the board and divides it into 2 ne*).
(15) And I take this blockie.
(16) And I cut him into two.
(17) Now I have a quarter. *While she is talking, she is demonstrating on the blackboard. She goes on to show them that ½ is the same as 2/4.*

Extract 1 is illustrative for two reasons: first, the extract illustrates how Ms Todd uses language as a tool to develop students' understanding of equivalent fractions using definitions (lines 4–6) and examples (13–17). The teacher reinforces the definition of an equivalent fraction by repeating it in lines 8–9. Taken together, the definition, repetition and concrete examples provide an *elaborated* explanation of mathematical content, in this instance, equivalent fractions. Rules of the instructional order, then, are elaborated in this lesson, and the criteria for arriving at a correct answer are made visible. The explanation is elaborated because the teacher defines what an equivalent fraction is, repeats this definition and uses abstract as well as concrete examples to illustrate her point. Second, the extract is of interest because it highlights the teacher using the blackboard as a tool to *represent* the explanation that she is verbally giving the students, thereby drawing on a material tool to aid in elaborating content under discussion. The primary tool used in this lesson is language, which is used to elaborate and reinforce content knowledge of mathematics. This is a typical example of the kind of teaching Ms Todd enacts in face-to-face lessons. The object of this lesson is the development and reinforcement of students' content knowledge in mathematics (fractions), and the outcome is mathematically literate students. The community in this lesson is the teacher and students who share the common object. In Extract 2, below, we get a sense of instructional rules, as the teacher slows pace to address a question from a student.

Extract 2. Instructional Rules

(1) Ms Todd: Does everyone understand? *Sizwe puts up his hand; teacher smiles at him inviting him to talk.*
(2) Sizwe: the simplification Miss.
(3) Ms Todd: Right, let me go over simplification again.
(4) Come let's get another example, a big one 21/28 × 7/14. *Teacher writes this on the blackboard and begins to explain both how to complete the problem by first simplifying it.*

In Extract 2, the teacher has been explaining the multiplication of fractions by focusing on simplification as a mechanism for solving these problems more efficiently. She is about to move onto new work (a mathematics task), and as she hands out pieces of cardboard, she asks students if they understand. Sizwe's statement indicates he has insufficient understanding about simplification of fractions, and the teacher takes the opportunity to begin to restate these criteria at some length. What is also evident in Extract 2 is an elaboration of evaluative rules, that is, an elaboration of what counts as a correct answer in this context. Pacing, then, slows to take account of the student's needs for elaboration. Division of labour is asymmetrical, with the teacher in power and occupying an instructor's role. Students enact a respondent role, only venturing to speak to respond to the teacher's questions. I have called this kind of pedagogy 'reinforcement pedagogy' as the object lies in reinforcing content knowledge, rather than developing deep conceptual understanding of mathematics. Below is a graphic representation of this kind of pedagogy as an activity system.

In Fig. 2, the teacher (subject) in the role of instructor (division of labour) elaborates mathematical content knowledge using language and various material tools to reinforce students' mathematical content knowledge (object) to develop mathematically literate students (outcome). This is done in an environment that is animated by instructional rules that incorporate weak teacher control over social order rules and the pace of transmission and explicit elaboration of the rules regarding how to produce a legitimate mathematical text (evaluative criteria).

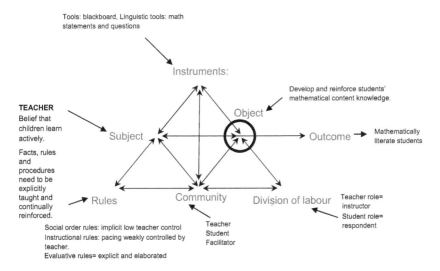

Fig. 2. Reinforcement Pedagogy: Activity System.

In sum, then, reinforcement pedagogy aims at reinforcing students' mathematical content knowledge and is characterised by the teacher in the role of instructor, using tools to reinforce students' mathematical content knowledge in a context where evaluative rules are elaborated, and social order and pacing rules are not rigidly controlled by the teacher. The object of these lessons is to develop and reinforce students' content knowledge using direct teaching methods. Direct teaching has, unfortunately, become associated with the simple transmission as opposed to meaningful acquisition of knowledge. However, didactic approaches do not necessarily imply a dull transmission of facts, but, at their best, these approaches involve children in actively learning concepts (Siraj-Blatchford, 1999). Reinforcement pedagogy is characterised by structured pedagogic communication in which the teacher guides and overtly structures students' engagement with the task through setting up a dialogical space in which structured, cueing questions guide students' engagement. We can, however, see a clear disjuncture between the teacher's intended pedagogy (which is in a constructivist mode, with a focus on children as active cognising agents) and the pedagogy that she enacts in the class, which is didactic and relies more on enlightenment notions of 'true knowledge', held by the teacher; this gives us insight into the teacher's actual pedagogical beliefs about student learning, which appear to lean more towards a behaviourist pedagogical style than a constructivist one. Holding these enlightenment ideas of knowledge and truth leads to a sense of entitlement in relation to the teacher as knower of knowledge and the student as passive recipient of knowledge.

Computer-Based Mathematics Lessons

When asked about teaching/learning in a computer-based mathematics lesson, Ms Todd indicated:

> I think they can try go at their own pace, but I don't think there is more control in the hands of the learners here. ... Discipline will just not work if you let them do their own thing, uhm, work on their own.

For Ms Todd, control over pacing is related to discipline, and a perceived weakening of teacher control over pacing in the computer-based lessons is seen as allowing students to 'do their own thing'. There is a secondary contradiction, then, between the need to use a computer as a tool, with the teacher's subjective positioning of classrooms as controlled and disciplined spaces. This contradiction is resolved by the teacher choosing not to use the computer as a tool for learning mathematics. While a first glance at the teacher's refusal to use novel technology may lead one to view the teacher as excessively entitled due to her refusal to utilise the novel technology and insistence on reverting to a traditional script, this is only understood if one appreciates the contradiction in this system. It is not the teacher herself who autonomously rejects the intervention but rather the activity of teaching mathematics in a classroom with its rules and norms that determine her behaviour. The teacher perceives a potential weakening of control in her computer-based lessons and responds by tightening control over pacing and evaluation rules. Given the perceived shift in rules in the computer-based lesson, the interview probed for teachers' perceptions regarding other changes to their pedagogical practices facilitated by the computer. In relation to what the object of a computer-based mathematics lesson is, Ms Todd said the following:

> ... In the classroom that's where I do the teaching, you know, the expositions of concepts. In the computer lab that's where they get to practice and learn new skills. So, I think that's also a thing a, a factor, that I have to teach them basic things like how to use the computer. ... I can't say that the computer is developing their mathematics. ... [using the computer] is the expected thing to do in this atmosphere of this IT technology thing. (Interview 2)

For Ms Todd, the object of the computer-based lesson is apparently twofold: first the object is to reinforce students' knowledge through practicing what they learn in the face-to-face lesson and second, the object is to develop students' technical skills. Note, however, that the object is not the development of students' mathematical understanding. Ms Todd's motive for using the computer is a desire to follow current trends that see ICTs being used in schools as she herself indicates when she says:

> This is the new thing. Everyone must use it now. (Interview 2)

However, while acknowledging that everyone needs to use technology, Ms Todd goes on to explain that:

> ... it's a tool for the children, not for me to use. It would be too confusing for them if I was also using the computer. ... I have to walk around and check that they are doing their work;

otherwise, they will get too noisy. So, I haven't got time for that also [using the computer]. (Interview, 2)

What this statement points to is that the computer hardware and software in Ms Todd's lessons is not used as a tool by her; rather, she feels that if she were to use the computer, this would confuse children. While one would expect the novel technology to be used as a tool to develop mathematics understanding, then, this is not how Ms Todd views it, and this mitigates against the use of the novel technology to aid in developing mathematics. If a teacher does not view the tool as potentially useful, they will not use it. Here, we can think again of excessive teacher entitlement; what looks, at first sight, to be a teacher merely ignoring a potentially useful intervention is informed by the teacher's subject position and beliefs about the use of the technology. Moreover, in the extract above, the teacher indicates that she needs to control behaviour quite rigidly as the students will 'get too noisy'. One of the clearest rules about schooling, traditionally, is that classrooms must be quiet. Ms Todd is aware of this rule which constrains her ability to enable the children to use the novel technology to explore because they may become too noisy when doing so. Therefore, what we see as excessive teacher entitlement in this instance needs to be re-envisioned as a teacher not having autonomy over either what tools she is given, how to use them or what to do in an instance where rules prohibit certain actions, like making a noise.

The tightening of rules over pacing, sequence and selection of work coupled with a need to be seen as an expert in order not to lose face in the presence of novel technology impact on what the object of the activity system is in the computer-based lessons. The object of the computer-based lesson is not mathematics, as one would expect but rather the regulation of students' behaviour. Here, we begin to see excessive teacher entitlement to the knowledge being taught, through control over behaviour. Extract 3 below illustrates the object of a computer-based lesson for Ms Todd.

Extract 3. The Object in a Computer-Based Lesson

(1) Ms Todd: People, you know what I am asking you. *Not a question as no response is anticipated or offered.*
(2) You not doing what I asked you. *Raises her voice.*
(3) You know what you supposed to be doing. *Again, not a question as no response offered or elicited.*
(4) You must do what I say.
(5) You are copying from each other now.
(6) You are copying! *Raises her voice and stresses this. She walks around the class stopping at Nongazi's workstation.*
(7) Don't take his mouse.
(8) You can show him.
(9) But you mustn't do it for him.
(10) Yis people.

(11) You must listen man!
(12) And then you wonder why you wrong.
(13) Who are finish people. *Although this utterance is potentially a question, the teacher does not actually look up to see who has put their hands up. Five hands are up.*
(14) That is correct, *stands behind Joe's computer.*
(15) That is correct *Points at two screens. Six hands go up. Looks at her watch.*
(16) Right people.
(17) We gonna move onto the next exercise.
(18) Quickly!
(19) Now scroll up.
(20) Quickly!
(21) All together.
(22) Stop what you doing.
(23) All together.
(24) Next one.

This extract contains many behavioural rules: students may not copy from each other; they may not look at each other's work; they may not use each other's mouse; they must listen; they must work quickly and at the same pace. Although there is a large body of research indicating that novel technology such as computer software can lead to learning in mathematics, this is not what we see above (Hardman, 2019; Webb & Cox, 2004). In extract 3, we observe how the teacher exercises a greater degree of control over pacing and social order rules to direct students' behaviour. Students are explicitly warned not to look at other students' work or talk to each other. Those who do so are 'copying'. In line 4, the teacher makes it explicitly clear that students must listen only to her and do exactly as she tells them. There is no freedom of action for students' here and no space to ask questions. The object here is not related to students' content knowledge or indeed to technical task skills. The object here is the regulation of students' behaviour to produce appropriate conduct. What we have here, then, is a primary contradiction in the object of the lesson: mathematical understanding versus behavioural regulation. The contradiction is resolved by the teacher reverting to using tight control and hierarchies, focusing on the object of behaviour regulation. To this end, the teacher uses language as a tool to control students' actions. The teacher uses regulative language as a tool to regulate students' behaviour to arrive at her desired outcome: appropriate conduct in a computer laboratory. Rules of the rules of the social order are directly controlled, in a tight manner, by the teacher who tells children in lines 16, 17, 18, 19 and 21 to move at the same pace and to hurry up. Instructional rules are not elaborated as can be seen in lines 12, 14 and 15 where the teacher notes that the work is correct but does not elaborate on why it is correct. Moreover, in line 12, the teacher indicates that the work is incorrect but gives no elaborated feedback on why this is so. Division of labour in this instance sees the teacher's role as manager of student behaviour, and the students adopt a passive role of performing the actions required by the teacher.

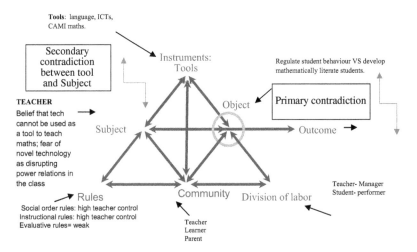

Fig. 3. Defensive Pedagogy Episode.

In Fig. 3, the teacher, in the role of manager, regulates students' behaviour to cover the curriculum. This takes place in a rule-bound context in which evaluative criteria are not elaborated, and the teacher exercises strong control over pacing and rules of the social order. I have called this pattern of pedagogy 'Defensive pedagogy' as it entails the teacher defending asymmetrical power relations and is characterised by the teacher in the role of manager, using regulative language to control students' behaviour in a context in which social order and pacing rules are strongly controlled by the teacher but where evaluative rules are unelaborated. In these kinds of lessons, the teacher is guarding against the fact that students may know more about how to use the computer than she does, which threatens her asymmetrical epistemic position as it potentially highlights her lack of technological knowledge, and she is defending against this. Defensive pedagogy is characterised by a general dearth of student interaction with the teacher and tightened control over the classroom context. This kind of pedagogy can be understood by drawing on the notion of excessive teacher entitlement (Ratnam, 2023). The teacher, in this instance, faced with novel technology with which she is not familiar (she does not own her own computer at home) does not want children to be able to challenge her dominant position in the classroom. However, if we draw on CHAT to understand excessive teacher entitlement in this case study, we can begin to see that the teacher is not the autonomous individual we imagine she is; she is bound by rules that demand that she uses novel technology, even when she is not comfortable or familiar with it. A secondary contradiction arises between her subject position and the tool (computer) leading her to refuse to use the computer as a novel tool. It is worth noting that this teacher received only 1 hour of training in using the computer as a teaching aid. When one is unfamiliar with something, a level of fear can be expected in using the novel tool. The students, on the other hand, although from disadvantaged backgrounds, were much more readily able to engage with the novelty of the computer because they did not feel threatened by it and had, in fact, no reason to fear a challenge to their position as students in the classroom. The teacher, however, had every reason to fear that her position of power, entailed in her knowledge of the mathematics content being taught, could be shifted by the computer because she was unfamiliar with its capabilities and was being forced to use it.

CONCLUSION

This chapter began by posing two questions: Does novel technology such as a computer alter pedagogy? And if so, in which ways does it do this? Findings reported above indicate that pedagogy in this context shifts with the introduction of novel technology but not in ways that one would anticipate. The rationale for using computers as mathematical tools lies in research that indicates its potential beneficial impact in terms of student attainment. However, technology alone can achieve nothing; rather, how it is used determines its ultimate success as a developmental tool. Where technology is underpinned by a constructivist type pedagogy (Hardman, 2019), we can anticipate student gains. This is not the case in the data reported here. What we see in this case study is that pedagogy shifts from a reinforcement type pedagogy to a defensive pedagogy when the teacher moves the class from a face-to-face to a computer-based lesson. Rather than the computer becoming a tool for developing students' mathematical understanding, the computer-based lessons become spaces where the teacher's object is behaviour regulation. In the computer-based lesson, the teacher enacts a defensive pedagogy that sees her tighten control over the classroom rules and become a manager of student behaviour. Looking at the teacher's praxis without reference to CHAT leads us to ascribe excessive teacher entitlement to the teacher; she resists change and adheres to a traditional classroom management pattern. However, the use of CHAT as a theoretical and analytical lens enables us to appreciate that the teacher is not acting autonomously; her behaviour is governed by rules in the activity system and contradictions that arise in the activity system led to a regression in her pedagogy, rather than to a novel, developmental pedagogy.

The picture is not, however, as gloomy as one imagines. Teachers can, and do, take up novel initiatives in their work in classrooms. The case of defensive pedagogy needs to be read against a lack of training, in the first instance, a lack of immersion in new technology and the consequent fear that students may know more about how to use the technology and, therefore, threaten the teacher's position as 'knower', and that they may become unruly, leading to a lack of discipline in the class. These issues are easily addressed through in-depth teacher training when novel initiatives are being launched in schools so that teachers feel empowered to use the novelty provided as developmental tools, rather than viewing them as threatening the teaching position.

REFERENCES

Denzin, N. K., & Lincoln, Y. S. (Eds.). (2011). *The Sage handbook of qualitative research*. Sage.
Engeström, Y. (1987). *Learning by expanding: An activity – Theoretic approach to developmental research*. Orienta-Konsultit Oy.
Engeström, Y. (1999). Activity Theory and individual and social transformation. In Y. Engeström, R. Miettinen, & R.-L. Punamaki (Eds.), *Perspectives on activity theory* (pp. 19–38). Cambridge University Press.
Feather, N. T. (2003). Distinguishing between deservingness and entitlement: Earned outcomes versus lawful outcomes. *European Journal of Social Psychology, 33*, 367–385.
Hardman, J. (2007a). Towards a methodology for using activity theory to explicate the pedagogical object in a primary school mathematics classroom. *Critical Social Studies*, (1), 53–69. ISSN 1904-0210.
Hardman, J. (2007b). Making sense of the meaning maker: Tracking the object of activity in a mathematics classroom using activity theory. *International Journal of Education and Development using ICT*. http://ijedict.dec.uwi.edu/viewissue.php. ISSN 1814-0556.
Hardman, J. (2019). Towards a pedagogical model of teaching with ICTs for mathematics attainment in primary school: A review of studies 2008–2018. *Heliyon*, 1–6.
Hardman, J. (2023). *A cultural-historical approach towards pedagogical transitions: Transitions in post-apartheid South Africa*. Bloomsbury. ISBN 978-1-3501-6470-3.
Høeg, P. (1993). *Miss Smilla's sense of snow*. Picador. ISBN 1250002559.
Leontiev, A. N. (1981). The problem of activity in psychology. In J. V. Wertsch (Ed.), *The concept of activity in Soviet psychology*. M.E. Sharpe.
Mooney Simmie, G., & Moles, J. (2020). Teachers' changing subjectivities: Putting the soul to work for the principle of the market or for facilitating risk. *Studies in Philosophy and Education, 39*, 383–398.
Mullis, I. V. S., Martin, M. O., Foy, P., Kelly, D. L., & Fishbein, B. (2020). *TIMSS 2019 international results in mathematics and science*. Boston College, TIMSS & PIRLS International Study Center. https://timssandpirls.bc.edu/timss2019/international-results/
Piaget, J. (1978). *Piaget's theory of intelligence*. Prentice Hall.
Ratnam, T. (2023). Excessive teacher entitlement? Going inward and backward to go forward. In *Studying teaching and teacher education: ISATT 40th anniversary yearbook* (pp. 221–230). Emerald Publishing Limited.
Siraj-Blatchford, I. (1999). Early childhood pedagogy: Practice, principles and research. In *Understanding pedagogy and its impact on learning* (pp. 20–45). Sage Publications Ltd.
Spaull, N. (2013). South Africa's education crisis: The quality of education in South Africa 1994–2011. *Johannesburg: Centre for Development and Enterprise, 21*(1), 1–65.
Vygotsky, L. S. (1978). *Mind in society. The development of higher psychological processes* (M. Cole, V. John-Steiner, S. Scribner, & E. Souberman, Trans.). (Eds.). Harvard University Press.
Vygotsky, L. S. (1986). *Thought and language* (E. Hanfmann & G. Vakar, Trans.). (Eds.). MIT Press.
Webb, M., & Cox, M. (2004). A review of pedagogy related to information and communications technology. *Technology, Pedagogy and Education, 13*(3), 235–286.
Yin, R. K. (2012). *Case study research*. Sage.

WHY 'DEFENSIVE' PEDAGOGIES MATTER: THE NECESSITY OF EXPANDING TEACHERS' AGENCY TO INFORM EDUCATIONAL TRANSFORMATION

Warren Lilley

University of Cape Town, South Africa

ABSTRACT

In an age of educational reform which incentivises increased digitisation and standardisation, teachers are expected to embrace the rise of 'new' tools and pedagogies with limited agency to inform, question or direct what 'newness' must be brought into their classrooms. Drawing on my research with English as a Foreign Language (EFL) educators in South Africa and using an 'excessive entitlement' lens, I showcase how teachers' lack of agency can result in 'defensive' and 'coercive' practices in the classroom which are a far cry from the education transformation imagined according to either global and local imaginaries for teaching and learning. If we are interested in an educational revolution, I argue that a fundamental reorientation in education recognising teachers' agency in informing change is necessary. To do so requires theoretically driven intervention methodologies which view the competing demands placed on teachers as entry points to developing their agency and volition to find practices which work for them and their students in the classroom. To that end, I illustrate how Cultural-Historical Activity Theory (CHAT) informed interventions like Change Laboratories could aid in this fundamental repositioning for teachers regarding transformational efforts and their far-reaching potential for educational revolution becoming conscious of and overcoming their feelings of excessive entitlement.

Keywords: Defensive pedagogies; teachers' agency; cultural-historical activity theory (CHAT); excessive entitlement; educational transformation; English as a Foreign Language (EFL)

Education is in crisis. Faced with the (looming) demands of a Fourth Industrial Revolution (4IR) and the difficulties in developing the skills and capacities to meet them, educational systems, especially those in the Global South, are under immense pressure to transform (World Economic Forum, 2015, 2020). In South Africa, these fears and concerns become cyclically most pronounced around the release of the Progress in International Reading Literacy Study (PIRLS) and Trends in International Mathematics and Science Study (TIMSS), which consistently find that South African learners significantly underperform in literacy and numeracy in comparison to their global peers. These identified 'deficits' in students' fundamental literacies have led to a renewed focus on the familiar scapegoats of educational underperformance – teachers.

To illustrate, following the release of the 2016 PIRLS results, teachers' competencies, pedagogies and professionalism were signalled as crucial areas of transformation (Department of Basic Education, 2017). Similarly, upon publication of the 2023 PIRLS results, while recognising the impact of the COVID-19 pandemic on student performance, language teachers' pedagogy was still highlighted as needing significant attention, with reforms focused on reskilling, increased testing and more extensive monitoring of teachers (Department of Basic Education, 2023). A pertinent example is the Western Cape Education Department's (WCED) *#BackonTrack* programme, which aims to reverse learning losses experienced over the COVID-19 pandemic and respond to poor TIMMS and PIRLS results (WCED, 2023).[1] The intervention is marked by several critical features: its enormous scope, including all educational stakeholders and phases, feedback mechanisms, emphasis on digital technologies, close performance monitoring and developing 'new ways of teaching and learning' for educators (WCED, 2023). As well-intentioned as this programme may be, underlying these reform endeavours, there is still a noticeable emphasis on monitoring teachers' performances and reshaping their practices through technologies and systemic testing to improve educational quality, accountability and performance in the classroom rather than on promoting teacher agency.

The increasing use of digital technologies to monitor and improve teacher performance and accountability symbolises more significant international education trends in schooling. Critics, such as Murphy (2018), highlight how, globally, education systems are becoming increasingly characterised by neoliberal values of *accountability* and *performance*, where educators' autonomy in directing their classroom practice is being systemically undermined in favour of *standardised* pedagogies, curricula and assessments. He traces this rise in widespread neoliberal education reform to the 1970s and 1980s, where increased

---

[1] The consistently highest performing province in terms of PIRLS and TIMMS student results in South Africa.

deregulation, privatisation, technologisation and focus on marketable (now '21st century') skills were seen as integral for developing a *quality* education system which could meet the needs for the global economy. Under this view, increased standardisation and systemic testing are interrelated drivers that can identify performance gaps and propel competition to improve the system. For 'developing' or 'Southern' countries, like South Africa, this line of thought is especially pervasive as this neoliberal refashioning of the educational system has been directly tied to bringing 'developing' educational systems' performance in line with their 'developed' counterparts (Lingard et al., 2013).

However, rather than driving these reform aims towards improvement, researchers increasingly find that teachers feel compelled to *teach to the test* instead of developing students' deep and meaningful understanding of curricula (Baidoo-Anu & Baidoo, 2022; Burns, 2016). In other words, these reforms link the *quality* of teachers and their practice to students' results on systemic tests; the *value* of teachers' work is *seen* in what they produce and cover (output) in the classroom rather than the understanding and skills (input) they develop with students (Holloway & Brass, 2018; Scott & Dinham, 2002). Moreover, by quantifying teaching, teachers' professionalism and practice are opened to much wider scrutiny and criticism, with teachers feeling incentivised to make their pedagogy *visible* to demonstrate their worth (Simmie & Moles, 2020).

The contradictions inherent in teachers' *teaching to the test* and rendering their work *visible* are most persuasively illustrated in McNeil's (1988a, 1988b, 1988c) and Ratnam and Craig's (2021) research. Faced with the competing responsibilities of needing to teach the required content while at the same time ensuring that students perform well on standardised assessments, McNeil (1982, 2000) showcased teachers adopting 'defensive' teaching styles. According to Ratnam (2021), the pressure to produce results makes teachers 'excessively entitled' to hold on to scripted 'defensive' teaching. These pedagogies are characterised by teachers heightening their control over school knowledge, resources, student participation and assessment to ensure their 'efficiency' in meeting bureaucratic rules and assessments. Equally, teachers' adoption of these pedagogies is located in the de-professionalism of their practice, wherein the increased deployment of 'standardised' teaching and learning materials further contribute to feeling excessively entitled to hold on to 'defensive' positions in needing to make their worth and value in the classroom be 'seen'.

Sadly, as Hardman (in this volume) and others illustrate (see Garrison & Bromley, 2004; Honan, 2010; Lilley & Hardman, 2017), the rise of digital technologies in schooling can push them further towards excessive entitlement and intensify teachers' 'defensiveness'. Rather than support teachers in their practice, these technologies are often purposed to hold teachers even more accountable for their classroom performance (Craig, 2020), placing even greater surveillance and demands on teachers to showcase their value (Gore et al., 2023). Faced with such increased systemic pressures on their practice, it is, then, no secret why so many teachers around the world are finding the contemporary demands on them untenable (Heffernan et al., 2022; Marshall et al., 2022; Siddiqui et al., 2023). Ratnam and Craig's (2021) research on 'excessive entitlement' highlights this breaking point in contemporary education. Their work evidences teachers' agentive ability to reclaim their voice, power and authority against the subjugation of top-down, bureaucratic change mechanisms that always project a deficient image of them.

To be clear, it is perfectly reasonable for the public to hold teachers accountable for the quality of teaching and learning in their classrooms. Ensuring teachers cultivate within their students the knowledge and skills to thrive in society is central to our profession. What is problematic, and what I find profoundly ironic, is that teachers are held wholly accountable for the flaws of an entire system in an educational era characterised by reforms which have systematically worked to undermine teacher agency and autonomy over the quality of 'how' and 'what' they teach their students in the classroom. Under such Orwellian conditions, one can understand why teachers may adopt 'defensive' pedagogies (McNeil, 1982, 2000) and believe themselves to be 'excessively entitled' to more empathetic understandings of the contradictory and complex systemic pressures surrounding their work (Ratnam & Craig, 2021).

While local/national educational interventions (like those in the Western Cape) can be applauded for their focus on broader stakeholder participation and incorporating teacher-feedback mechanisms, one has to question their relevance when these reforms are still fundamentally premised on top-down, technological controls aimed at heightening teacher surveillance and performance to account for teachers' 'deficiencies' in their practice. As illustrated above, the transformative value of such endeavours is questionable if the only pathway to reform is to further de-professionalise teachers and curtail meaningful education to additional standardised instruction and quantifiable results. Surely, there must be alternative ways of re-conceptualising reform that see teachers as fundamental to informing educational transformation rather than viewing them as a problem of the educational crisis that must be fixed.

PURPOSES

In this chapter, I offer possible insights into how positive educational transformation efforts can be realised in forms of action. Drawing on my participatory formative-intervention research with South African English as a Foreign Language (EFL) teachers, I demonstrate how, by expanding teachers' agency to inform transformation at their institution, teachers could realise a more meaningful pedagogy with digital technologies. Central to developing such a pedagogical approach, I will argue, was teachers' engagement and reflection on their 'excessive entitlement' underlying the 'defensive pedagogies' they were deploying in the classroom. This awareness formed the basis of teachers' re-conceptualising how technologies could support and enhance their instruction (and their students' learning) rather than be further measures which impinged on their autonomy and expertise in the classroom.

To fully illustrate these transformative potentials, this chapter makes three central moves. I first engage with how Cultural-Historical Activity Theory's

(CHAT) dialectical understanding of activity and development offers fertile theoretical and methodological terrain to inform educational interventions. Under this view, I then engage with how the contradictory aspects of teachers' activity, seen in their 'defensive pedagogies' emanating from 'excessive entitlement', can be utilised as a means for teachers to unpack broader systemic pressures influencing their agency in classroom settings. Specifically, by re-examining excerpts from a more extensive study, I illustrate that while 'defensive pedagogies' are conceptually helpful to distinguish 'how' teachers' *practices* are contradictory, an 'excessive entitlement' lens allows insight into how teachers *personally* experience these systemic contradictions compelling them to adopt defensive pedagogies. Thus, defensive pedagogies can be seen as a manifestation of teachers' excessive entitlement. Through this reappraisal, I demonstrate how, by unpacking their 'excessive entitlement' within a participatory-formative research intervention, teachers could meaningfully identify pathways to integrate digital technologies to support their activity rather than undermine it. In short, this chapter aims to showcase how interventions premised on expanding teachers' voice, power and agency can provide robust pathways to re-conceptualise educational transformation. Crucially, as I next argue, this rests on viewing teachers as *agents* of change rather than the *objects* of it. In other words, view teachers as 'curriculum makers' rather than 'curriculum implementers' (Connelly & Clandinin, 1988).

THEORETICAL FRAMEWORK

I have pointed out how intensifying digitisation and systemic testing can restrict teachers' activity and agency in the classroom, resulting in teachers adopting 'defensive' teaching styles and expressing discourses of 'excessive entitlement' concerning their work. I have argued that these insights call for a conceptual shift in educational interventions that move beyond holding that such practices merely symbolise what teachers *do* and *who* teachers are. As Ratnam and Craig (2021) warn, such understandings:

> ...[slap] a deficit view on teachers by invoking a constellation of negative behavioural attributes such as being irresponsible, rigid, egoistic, uncaring, and incompetent... [and miss] the interacting factors beyond teachers' individualist characteristics that impinge upon their thinking and action. (p. 3)

What we need, then, are theoretical and methodological perspectives which can situate findings of teachers' 'excessive entitlement' and 'defensive pedagogies' within broader societal, cultural and historical framings. I would also add that these perspectives need to view these contextual factors not only as 'impinging' teachers' thinking and actions but critically view them also as drivers of transformation. To this end, I pose CHAT, in its dialectical materialist understanding of human activity and development, as having much to offer.

As a dialectical perspective, CHAT holds that any phenomenon and its development should be studied as a 'whole unit' of analysis. Using water as an illustrative example, Vygotsky (1986) points out that if we strictly study water in terms of its elemental properties (hydrogen and oxygen), water's unique properties would be incomprehensible. While hydrogen is a highly inflammable substance, oxygen supports burning. These properties are completely different from that of water, which extinguishes fire. It is only when we analyse water as the unification of these opposing elements, as a molecular 'whole' (H_2O), we get to understand its extinguishing capabilities.

For Vygotsky (1986), water's unique properties demonstrate two critical interrelated directions for research and analysis. His example illustrates how the unification of two opposing elements (hydrogen and oxygen) can transform into distinct phenomena with unique properties. This basic unit lies within water's formulation as a molecule (H_2O), which facilitates analysis of all its phases and characteristics, whether water presents as (or changes to) ice, a droplet or an ocean. In this sense, only water's molecular form facilitates the ability to analyse its properties and trace its development. In other words, to abstract water back into its constituent, opposing elements would remove the possibilities of understanding its development and how it might further diversify and change over time (Hegel, 1974; Virkkunen & Newnham, 2013). In short, to research and analyse a system means engaging with the essence of its living qualities as a whole. For social phenomena, this means understanding them as a collection of human actions imbued with cultural values that are, and continue to, historically develop as a cultural-historical *activity* system.

Guided by these principles, CHAT-informed educational research then highlights that inquiries must: '[firstly] identify basic relations in a phenomenon and [secondly] explain the development of phenomena as a consequence of the movement in these relations' (Chaiklin, 2019, p. 265). In other words, just as we cannot separate water into hydrogen and oxygen to understand its nature when researching pedagogy, we cannot reduce education to its constituent elements like the teacher, the learner and the curriculum. We need to see them as an inherent part of the cultural-historical context which informs them. Otherwise, we would miss how, in their opposition, these elements not only construct pedagogy as it appears at a particular point in time but also critically miss insight into how these internal conflicts will further inform development (Wertsch & Sohmer, 1995). CHAT then offers a valuable paradigm that moves research and theorisation into teachers' 'defensive pedagogies' and 'excessive entitlement' away from deficit views and grounds them within the systems in which they are embedded.

In facilitating CHAT's tasks of identifying the unit of analysis and offering explanatory capacities for its development, Engeström's (2014) subsequent elaborations of Vygotsky's theory are particularly well-suited. Often denoted as 'third generation', Engeström's work marks a formalisation of Vygotsky's theoretical and methodological concerns while significantly expanding their scope.

Crucially, his engagement emphasises that while socially situated understandings of human actions can provide insight into describing 'how' and 'what' people do, they offer little insight into 'why' individuals feel compelled to take these actions in their work nor how their collective actions and practices facilitate systemic change (Engeström, 1999). To this end, Engeström's (2014) elaborations prioritise the need to establish participants' *object motive*, which denotes their shared motivation, i.e. the 'problem-space' which compels participants to engage in their activity (Engeström, 2014; Virkkunen & Newnham, 2013). From here, all other constituent elements of collective activity are discernible: the subjects (*who are acting in the activity*), mediational artefacts (*tools and signs* participants purpose to achieve their object), rules (*institutional and cultural controls* which allow or limit participants actions), community (those *other than the subject* who participate in the activity), and division of labour (*how* participants' different actions and roles facilitate their approach towards the object motive).

This ability to 'map' an activity system is essential in identifying the fundamental relations within an educational phenomenon. For instance, in our pedagogical study on South African EFL teachers' and learners' use of mobile dictionaries, our mapping of classroom activity illustrated that introduction of these tools (as mediational artefacts) into classroom activity potentially restricted the object (what lessons were approaching) and division of labour (teachers' and students' role) in the classroom (see Lilley & Hardman, 2017). To explain, teachers' and students' shared object motive was established as developing learners' abilities to communicate in English. However, when students used their mobile dictionaries to clarify unfamiliar words, teachers interpreted these actions as undermining the communicative focus of the language lessons. For teachers, the communicative aim of the lesson could only be realised if students followed the established classroom rules and division of labour where if they came across an unfamiliar word, students should ask the teacher or other students. The *potential* conflict mobile dictionaries posed to the lessons' object of communication led teachers to directly prohibit students' mobile device use, further emphasising their 'control' of learning actions within the classroom.

These findings are noticeably reminiscent of McNeil's (1982, 2000) identification of teachers 'defensive' teaching styles in response to the introduction of systemic testing and standardisation. McNeil noted how, in response to these measures being introduced, teachers used strategies to heighten their control and efficiency in delivering content. For instance, to cover the curriculum efficiently, she found teachers employing fragmentation (through lectures and lists) to uphold their authority of the content and reduce student questioning. In response to her findings, she noted the need for perspectives which could 'examine historical, organisational, and personal dynamics that underlie' (McNeil, 1988b, p. 438) teachers' adoption of these strategies. CHAT provides such a theoretical framework through its ability to 'map' the internal dynamics and its underlying systemic contradictions that make teachers feel excessively entitled to adopt 'defensive pedagogies'. I will illustrate this next.

The introduction of a new tool like mobile dictionaries or standardised materials into an established activity system brings out the latent internal dynamics between its constituent elements. Notably, in our study, mobile dictionaries were seen by teachers to impact the communicative aspects of the EFL classroom, leading them to restrict the division of labour, rules and object in these lessons (Lilley & Hardman, 2017). These insights emphasise how CHAT, as a dialectical *materialist* perspective, views a system's historical development as intricately tied to its mediational artefacts:

> ...the introduction of new tools into human activity does more than improve a specific form of functioning, it transforms it... and [tools] are in turn shaped and transformed through their use in human activity. It is through tool use that individual/ psychological and cultural /historical processes become interwoven and co-create each other. (Daniels, 2010, p. 378)

In other words, mediational artefacts unite the subject and object motive in co-development. As our object motives change, so too will our search for tools to meet them; and as new tools are introduced, so too will our object motive(s) progressively shift (Engeström, 2014). Vygotsky (1978) demonstrated these co-development capacities within his double stimulation experiments wherein individuals were presented with problem situations beyond their present ability to solve. Critically, these situations identified as 'first stimuli' specifically facilitated participants questioning the 'usefulness' and 'value-in-exchange' of existing mediational artefacts to resolve this problem situation (i.e. object). For instance, participants would be left in a room and told that a researcher would be with them shortly. Initially, they waited without any complaints, but they started to wonder about the duration of the wait as time went by (use-value) and what value would there be if they continued to wait for the experimenter versus leaving (value-in-exchange). This 'conflict in motives' (should I stay, or should I go) eventually led participants to reach out for an external stimulus (a second stimuli), an alternative mediational means, to help them make their decision such as a strike of a clock hand on the wall or the temperature of their coffee in aiding their decision to eventually get up and leave (Sannino & Laitinen, 2015). In effect, by the participants becoming aware of the (internal) conflicts of their present activity and the difficulty of their current mediational means to approach them, they were able to develop new mediational means to overcome them (Virkkunen & Newnham, 2013).

For Engeström (2014), Vygotsky's double-stimulation experiments provide a potent means of surfacing the internal contradictions of a collective activity system and critically developing meaningful understandings to trace their historical development. His theoretical elaborations in *Expansive Learning* (Engeström, 2014) elaborate on how an activity system historically develops as a consequence of these latent dialectical (use-value versus value-in-exchange) contradictions surfacing with increasing intensity over time (Virkkunen & Newnham, 2013). As Vygotsky's double-stimulation experiments illustrate, participants need to reflectively engage with the current problem situations, to identify the underlying contradictions which give rise to these problems and in doing so can make movements towards developing new means to overcome them. Participatory formative interventions, such as *Change Laboratories*, provide a formalised methodology which comprises a series of double-stimulation workshops focused on aiding participants in identifying and remediating their contradictory experiences and facilitate collective organisational change (Engeström et al., 2014; Virkkunen & Newnham, 2013).

To support researcher-interventionists in facilitating participatory formative interventions, Engeström and Sannino's (2011) work has distinguished four levels in which participants discursively manifest contradictions as they try to articulate, describe and resolve the difficulties they experience within their work activity:[2]

- *Dilemmas* are identifiable in expressions citing the everyday difficulties or irreconcilable valuing within current working situations.
- *Conflict* is discerned through explicit expressions of disagreement ('no') or criticism.
- *Critical conflicts* are seen in highly emotive and metaphorical language emphasising guilt, violation or the need to find an alternative.
- *Double-binds* wherein participants express the impossibility of taking actions alongside a collective need to transform.

Of central importance to this chapter's focus on teachers' expressions of 'excessive entitlement' is how these discursive manifestations resonate with *critical conflicts*. As Ratnam and Craig (2021) highlight, teachers' expressions of 'entitlement' are 'excessive', specifically in how deeply they are felt or experienced. Frequently documented in their collected research are vivid, emotive metaphors teachers used to describe their problematic educational activity. For instance, a beginning teacher declared she was learning 'to teach in the "eye of a storm"' (Craig, 2013) and another teacher who said she felt like a *Butterfly under a Pin* (Craig, 2020) while recounting how school reforms were crushing their creativity and expertise as curriculum developers. In each of these examples, we see highly metaphorical accounts emphasising educators' paralysis in the face of broader systemic pressures on their practice, which under a CHAT lens are key features of how 'critical conflicts' manifest systemic contradictions (Engeström & Sannino, 2011). At the same time, other examples of 'excessive entitlement' illustrate more narratively charged expressions of historically accumulated feelings of 'helplessness', 'inability to understand', 'inner doubts' or 'frustration':

> I can understand a change in textbooks. You need to update knowledge. But change in method, are you saying that all that we've been doing in the past 25 years and what our teachers did before that is all wrong, a waste? (Ratnam, 2021, p. 78)

Engeström and Sannino (2011) highlight that critical conflicts are difficult to identify due to their personal and emotional nature, especially as they do not present with specific linguistic cues other than a narrative structure and/or vivid metaphor. In this sense, a CHAT analysis of 'excessive entitlement' in teachers' discourse as 'critical conflicts' could be useful in helping guide the identification

---

[2] The use of the word 'manifest' is critical. As contradictions are systemic and emerge through an activity's historical development, they can never be 'seen' or 'touched'. However, they can be 'traced' through how their practitioners articulate them (Engeström & Sannino, 2011).

of how contradictions may manifest in educators' discourse and pedagogic practice.

In sum, a CHAT understanding of 'defensive pedagogies' and 'excessive entitlement' helps us avoid 'deficit' views of teachers by allowing us to 'map' the internal relationships producing these phenomena and 'trace' the historical contradictions which have led to their development. A CHAT-informed analysis and methodology can offer unique opportunities for unpacking and remediating teachers' contradictory experiences through participatory-formative research interventions, providing pathways for teachers to reclaim greater agency in response to, and in the reform of, growing digitalisation and standardisation of schooling practices.

METHOD, DATA SOURCES AND ANALYSIS

The data cited in this chapter draw from a larger Change Laboratory intervention conducted at a South African higher educational institution's English Language Centre in Cape Town (Lilley, 2020). The centre generates profit for the broader university, focusing on developing students' proficiency in English for higher education studies. At the time of the intervention, there was increasing pressure to remain 'competitive' with similar organisations focusing on digital technologies. This participatory formative intervention was guided by the organisation's dilemma in figuring out how, or if, digital technologies could support language instruction.

In line with Change Laboratory protocols, a preliminary ethnographic study was conducted at the site to identify specific disturbances and collect 'mirror data' to act as 'first stimuli' to inform formative research intervention (Virkkunen & Newnham, 2013), which included lesson observations (management, teacher and student), interviews and document collection. An overview is provided below in Table 1. This initial study identified that the centre's teaching/learning was centralised around the 'standardised' use of international language coursebooks, which functioned as the centre's syllabus and classroom material. Teachers were expected to 'cover' this material within a particular time, after which the students would be tested using several 'standardised' language skill tests. Digital technologies were considered imperative, especially considering the centre's need to remain 'competitive' in fulfilling its profit motive to the university.

The reappraisal of data below is drawn from my original analysis of participants' expansive learning actions during the Change Laboratory session, which used Engeström and Sannino's (2011) discursive framework to identify contradiction sites and track participants' progress through the expansive learning process. Data selected for reappraisal are drawn explicitly from two episodes demonstrating 'critical conflicts' in participants' discourse. The first excerpt is drawn from a *Charting the Situation* session wherein participants' analysis of a colleague's use of digital technologies in a lesson facilitated insight into the 'defensive' nature of their pedagogies. Unpacking the elements of this practice led

Table 1. Overview of Change Laboratory Research Intervention.

Research Methodology	Data Collection	Analysis	Aim
Exploratory, ethnographic case study	• Non-participant observations • Organisational artefact collection (handbooks, lesson plans, etc.) • Lesson observations • Interviews of teachers, students and managers	Identification of critical episodes/disruptions	Identification of potential contradiction sites Collection of mirror data
Change Laboratory Research-Intervention	• Participant observation • Video recordings of 13 intervention sessions • Observation notes of sessions • Participant digital artefact collection • Participant's disruption diary • Researcher-intervention diary • Final session recording • Post-intervention tracking of developments at site • Artefact collection	Engeström and Sannino's (2011) framework of discursive manifestations of contradictions	Track development of participants' expansive learning actions throughout the intervention Identify changes in work practices

Source: Adapted from Lilley (2020).

to participants' discussion exhibiting the emergence of 'excessive entitlement' discourse.

Through this, I argue, the beginning of participants' ability to unpack the systemic contradictions informing their 'excessive entitlement' becomes noticeable. These early moves later influenced participants' ability to identify critical features to support teachers to develop a pedagogy that could use digital technologies to help their practice.

FINDINGS AND DISCUSSION

As highlighted in the theoretical framework, the expansive learning process is predicated on participants engaging in a series of double-stimulation tasks specifically aimed at facilitating their reflection on the problem areas they encounter in their work practices. The beginnings of this process occur within 'Charting the Situation', where sessions are aimed at evoking participants' *questioning* of the present practice of their activity (Virkkunen & Ahonen, 2011). By allowing participants to engage with and reflect on concrete instantiations of the critical issues they face, this questioning phase aims to uncover the commonplace assumptions, practices or understandings which make teachers see these problems as 'one-time' issues or 'individual' discrepancies (Virkkunen & Newnham, 2013).

In this session, mirror data of a video excerpt of a teacher, Majorie (all names used here are pseudonyms), experimenting with Google Classroom, were used as the 'first stimulus'. This Change Laboratory was premised on engaging the extent to which possibilities for using digital technologies could support teachers in their practice. Critically, the episode was selected because in the post-observation interviews, Marjorie had highlighted the lesson had not worked as she had intended. Furthermore, to help Marjorie and her colleagues 'distance' themselves from close emotional responses (Virkkunen & Ahonen, 2011), participants' reflections were guided by the following questions: (i) what was the teacher trying to achieve/develop? (ii) What was the teacher's role? and (iii) what was the students' role?

After watching the excerpt together and giving all the participants time to review the lesson material and collect their thoughts, the session was opened for discussion. Immediately, Marjorie engaged with the difficulties she had encountered in the lesson, particularly how she had thought that posting questions from the class textbook on Google Classroom would make the students speak more, but that had resulted in them speaking less. In unpacking why she had decided to do this activity, Marjorie highlighted that she wanted the Google Classroom question to function as a prompt, which would then be displayed to the class, leading students to discuss what they had written. She followed this by looking at her colleagues and asking: 'my, sort of, comments or questions here is when to use a bit of Google Classroom and for what?'

In her description of her lesson using Google Classroom, Marjorie thought she had planned everything meticulously. She had set up the class correctly, planned it with students in mind and had used technology. Her 'helplessness' here, following this reflection, suggests a 'paralysis' in not knowing what to do or how to include technology to support the communication she desired in the classroom. The 'helplessness' in her discourse suggests the emergence towards a potential contradiction in her practice: she is caught wanting to use technology, but in doing so, she feels she is compromising her communicative aims with students.

Engeström and Sannino (2011) highlight in their discussion that at the beginning of Change Laboratories and when first encountering ruptures in their activity, participants usually rationalise or subvert these initial eruptions by relying on commonplace understanding already present within their activity. In Majorie's case, her colleagues immediately suggested that the inclusion of Google Classroom had made the classroom too 'open'. Instead, they suggested students should still submit their answers but that, critically, the screen should stay off until all the students had responded. Only then should Marjorie project the answer and get students to discuss it. In this way, her colleague Ned stated that by separating these two modalities (course book and Google Classroom), students would realise online communication's 'public' nature. John further supported this notion, highlighting how it would further aid students' accuracy. Noticeably, however, in both of their suggestions, we see a concern over the 'openness' digital technologies invite in the classroom, leading to suggest that Marjorie's lesson would be noticeably improved if she had more 'control' over what information be seen and that her communicative aims would be better supported if this move between modalities was simplified. Teacher-participants' suggestions here concur with notions of 'defensive' teaching (McNeil, 1982, 1988b) — simplifying these modalities' introductions and carefully controlling their release would help support Marjorie's communication aims.

Following this, Marjorie began questioning the value of the video she had played in the lesson, which the coursebook provided. The video depicted an interview with a fashion company, which Marjorie thought would significantly engage students' interest. However, in reflecting upon her lesson with us, she expressed her doubts about the extent to which engaging 'authentic' materials had interested her learners or even supported the lesson's learning aim, leading to her to exclaim: 'So, I don't know if we're [teachers] ahead. I thought what we think is relevant. I mean completely different, [than] ah, students...' to which her colleagues agreed. Again, within Marjorie, a 'helplessness' is present as another solution she had posed towards developing students' interest in using authentic examples in this lesson had once again negatively impacted the communication aims of her classroom.

Marjorie's expression of the futility of all her attempts to create an engaging, communicative language-learning lesson through technology and authentic materials highlights the quandary she faces in her work. Despite all her attempts to get students to engage in the coursebook material they are required to cover (through using its questions as prompts on Google Classroom and using its multimedia), students were still not 'speaking' enough. 'Excessive entitlement' is highlighted in how individuals can become blinded by their own assumptions and unreasonable expectations (Ratnam & Craig, 2021). In Marjorie's case, this can be seen to be expressed in 'helplessness' and 'paralysis' that her inclusion of digital tools and authentic materials were not solving the issue of lack of student engagement/speaking in the classroom. In other words, the 'excessiveness' of her 'entitlement' lies in her perceived assumptions that using technology as a substitute for the standardised coursebook and its use of its prescribed video would implicitly lead to heightened student engagement. However, by reflecting on the lesson and its internal relations, critical insight into the importance of student engagement is starting to become discernible. They also see how teacher selection of authentic, engaging material can become problematic without proper mediation. In effect, teacher-participants are beginning to question their commonplace assumptions surrounding their practice in the use of standardised coursebooks, teachers' and students' roles and student engagement.

While *Charting the Situation* sessions focus on participants' *questioning* of the current formulation of their system, in the sessions on *Analysing the Situation*, their ability to engage in *analysis* is emphasised. Specifically, by allowing participants to 'map' their activity (actual-empirical analysis) and 'trace' its historical antecedents (historical-genetic analysis), critical movements towards engaging participants' volition towards identifying new ways of working are emphasised (Virkkunen & Newnham, 2013). In essence, these sessions are aimed at participants articulating the contradiction(s) they experience in their activity and heightening their search for a secondary stimulus to overcome it.

These central conflicts came to the forefront within the *Analysing the Situation* sessions, i.e. in the course of 'mapping' their activity system and discussing the lessons used as mirror data over the *Charting the Situation* sessions. Marjorie lamented: 'it's a war, it's a challenge they [students] do not communicate'. This described teachers' frustrations in developing students' communication skills. The metaphor of a 'war' is especially interesting as it clearly illustrates teachers' extreme conflict in engaging learners at the centre and the 'excessiveness' of how the system they worked within placed them at odds. In mapping their activity, participants noted how, in their system's current formulation, they were expected to be, as Ned proclaimed, 'the all-singing and dancing conversationalist' in response to students' lack of engagement and willingness to participate in the classroom. Notably, he expressed his guilt in how 'he can't keep talking and talking' in lessons. Following CHAT principles, I asked them where they think this emanates from, looking at the 'map' of their system. Marjorie attributed this to students' entitlement and expectation arising from having paid for their services. Ned clarified: 'You [the teacher] need to handle...the product [the course offering]'. John added to this by narrating how difficult it was for him to have lessons that built on each other with students' not attending classes regularly. Pretending to be a student, he stated: 'You [the teacher] should have foreseen this happening, that I wasn't gonna do the work, so where's your Plan B?' with Marjorie adding that even when students were present, they were often on their devices and distracted from the lesson.

In the aforementioned analysis, we see the value of teachers' 'mapping' internal relations, which give rise to their pedagogies, notably 'pedagogies', which emphasise high teacher control and performance within the classroom. As teacher-participants realise, these strategies are 'defensive' in that they directly respond to a systemic pressure which emphasises education as a product and locates the accountability of teaching/learning solely on them as a teacher. This, in turn, makes teachers feel that they are entitled to a better system. This is seen in the teachers' extensive metaphorical and emotive language, highlighting their dissatisfaction with the commodification of their practice, which relies on them to fulfil the centre's learning object of 'communication'.

However, at the same time, teachers are 'tracing' where these negative experiences are originating in their practice. For instance, students 'passivity' and 'expectation' (division of labour) are seen to disrupt their shared object in developing English language skills or how mobile devices (as mediational tools) further reinforce students' disengagement. By doing so, teachers articulate secondary contradiction sites in how two interrelated elements of their activity conflict. Upon further analysis, teachers predicated their negative experiences on their centre's emphasis on communicative language pedagogy (rule) and standardised coursebook (mediational artefact) they were expected to use. Ned described these as 'survival tools', which helped teachers to cope with long teaching days, adding how the standardised coursebooks they were made to use were 'not for anyone'.

In this 'tracing' of the origins of their excessive entitled beliefs, we see teachers' engagement with the more profound contradictions of their activity. In earlier sessions, Marjorie's 'excessive entitlement' was located in her feeling of 'helplessness' with digitally engaging students in her classroom while still covering the coursebook. The initial way participants engaged with this was to suggest 'defensive teaching' strategies that would place Marjorie in more control. What we see now, in teachers tracing the origin of this dilemma, is that the issue of student engagement could be with the coursebooks they are required to teach and the strict emphasis on the pedagogies they were expected to enact. In other words, teachers are looking beyond themselves and their disruptions to the historical antecedents, giving rise to their feelings of 'excessive entitlement' and need to enact 'defensive pedagogies'.

These teachers' further engagement with their pedagogic practice eventually led to the development of a new teaching/learning model for language learning with technologies which emphasised 'co-creation' rather than 'communication' as the object of their activity, with an emphasis on technologies being used to bring students' experiences into the classroom. Notably, rather than 'control' students' use of these technologies or completely disregard the coursebooks they were required to teach, the model emphasised how teachers and students leveraged both in supporting a reciprocal language instruction in meeting their goals for improving English language skills. To illustrate, John's 'co-creation' lesson on the coursebook topic of 'Sustainable Cities' utilised technology to centre students' experiences and language skill development. In his reflection, John noted how by the lesson being 'completely up to them [students]' heightened engagement. According to Ned, collaborating with students offered 'another opportunity to kind of, like, reformulate and correct language as well... [as] they're picking ideas up...'. Similar insights were also seen in the other teacher-participants' lessons with this model. As a result, teachers' 'co-creation' pedagogical approach was then used to inform the Centre's approach to technology integration in their practices, professional development and the development of new courses (see Lilley, 2020, 2022).

CONCLUSION

This chapter set out to discuss why defensive pedagogies matter. In an age of growing neoliberal education reform, I have argued that teachers and their professionalism have come under fire through an emphasis on standardised (increasingly digitised) instruction and measurable educational results. Teachers' deployment of defensive pedagogies highlights how deeply antithetical these reforms are to pedagogies purposed towards developing deep and meaningful learning. They prioritise strategies geared towards efficient curricula coverage and the superficial transmission of it. In doing so, teachers are placed in a contradictory position that holds them accountable for educational outcomes with limited agency to inform and direct them.

Within this space, I have argued for a radical reorientation to educational reform and research. As I have illustrated, teachers' feelings of 'excessive entitlement' and their 'defensive pedagogies' do not exist independently of their broader cultural-historical context. They come from systems which ignore or curtail their voice and agency. What we need, then, are theoretical and methodological perspectives, like CHAT, which can draw on teachers' contradictory experiences to identify their systemic development and utilise these insights to drive novel educational reforms. As can be seen in the reappraisal, while 'defensive pedagogies' offered an entry point for these teachers to re-examine problems surrounding their use of digital technologies, they became conscious of their excessive entitlement when they started analysing the wider systemic contradictions informing their work. These insights, in turn, spurred teachers to develop a novel language pedagogy with digital technologies at their site, which moved beyond teacher control and coursebook coverage to the use of digital technologies premised on co-creation, centred on students' experiences.

As I have shown in this chapter, when education reform and research are reoriented to give voice to teachers' concerns, difficulties and struggles with spaces for teachers to deeply engage with them and become aware of their excessive entitled beliefs, emancipatory pathways for teachers to develop practices which support them and their students can be identified. These practices move beyond teacher 'accountability' or 'performativity' and are centred on cultivating teachers' agency to find and develop meaningful ways to support educational transformation. Crucially, this means reorientating educational reform and research on expanding teachers' agency to direct it.

REFERENCES

Baidoo-Anu, D., & Baidoo, I. E. (2022). Performance-based accountability: Exploring Ghanaian teachers perception of the influence of large-scale testing on teaching and learning. *Education Inquiry*. https://doi.org/10.1080/20004508.2022.2110673

Burns, G. (2016). Relationships of surveillance, assurance and recognition: Early career primary teachers' engagement with discourses of accountability and performance. *Irish Educational Studies*, *35*(3), 269–288. https://doi.org/10.1080/03323315.2016.1175768

Chaiklin, S. (2019). Units and wholes in the cultural-historical theory of child development. In *Cultural-historical approaches to studying learning and development. Perspectives in cultural-historical research* (pp. 263–277). Springer. https://doi.org/10.1007/978-981-13-6826-4_17

Connelly, F. M., & Clandinin, D. J. (1988). *Teachers as curriculum planners: Narratives of experience*. Teachers College Press. Columbia University. OISE Press, Ontario Institute for Studies in Education.

Craig, C. J. (2013). Coming to know in the 'eye of a storm': A beginning teacher's introduction to different versions of teacher community. *Teaching and Teacher Education*, *29*, 25–38.

Craig, C. J. (2020). "Data is [G]od": The influence of cumulative policy reforms on teachers' knowledge in an urban middle school in the United States. *Teaching and Teacher Education*, *93*. https://doi.org/10.1016/j.tate.2020.103027

Daniels, H. (2010). The mutual shaping of human action and institutional settings: A study of the transformation of children's services and professional work. *British Journal of Sociology of Education*, *31*(4), 377–393. https://doi.org/10.1080/01425692.2010.484916

Department of Basic Education. (2017). Minister Angie Motshekga: Release of 2016 progress in international reading literacy study results. https://www.gov.za/speeches/minister-angie-motshekga-release-2016-progress-international-reading-literacy-study-results

Department of Basic Education. (2023). Minister Angie Motshekga: National seminar on reading literacy. https://www.gov.za/speeches/national-seminar-reading%C2%A0-16-may-2023-0000

Engeström, Y. (1999). Expansive visibilization of work: An activity-theoretical perspective. *Computer Supported Cooperative Work, 8*.

Engeström, Y. (2014). *Learning by expanding*. Cambridge University Press. https://doi.org/10.1017/CBO9781139814744

Engeström, Y., & Sannino, A. (2011). Discursive manifestations of contradictions in organizational change efforts: A methodological framework. *Journal of Organizational Change Management, 24*(3), 368–387. https://doi.org/10.1108/09534811111132758

Engeström, Y., Sannino, A., & Virkkunen, J. (2014). On the methodological demands of formative interventions. *Mind, Culture and Activity, 21*(2), 118–128. https://doi.org/10.1080/10749039.2014.891868

Garrison, M. J., & Bromley, H. (2004). Social contexts, defensive pedagogies, and the (Mis)uses of educational technology. *Educational Policy, 18*(4), 589–613. https://doi.org/10.1177/0895904804266643

Gore, J., Rickards, B., & Fray, L. (2023). From performative to professional accountability: Re-imagining 'the field of judgment' through teacher professional development. *Journal of Education Policy, 38*(3), 452–473. https://doi.org/10.1080/02680939.2022.2080274

Heffernan, A., Bright, D., Kim, M., Longmuir, F., & Magyar, B. (2022). 'I cannot sustain the workload and the emotional toll': Reasons behind Australian teachers' intentions to leave the profession. *Australian Journal of Education, 66*(2), 196–209. https://doi.org/10.1177/00049441221086654

Hegel, G. W. F. (1974). In F. G. Weiss (Ed.), *Hegel, the essential writings*. Harper & Row.

Holloway, J., & Brass, J. (2018). Making accountable teachers: The terrors and pleasures of performativity. *Journal of Education Policy, 33*(3), 361–382. https://doi.org/10.1080/02680939.2017.1372636

Honan, E. (2010). Mapping discourses in teachers' talk about using digital texts in classrooms. *Discourse, 31*(2), 179–193. https://doi.org/10.1080/01596301003679701

Lilley, W. (2020). *English language instruction as 'co-creation': A new CHAT model for integrating mobile technologies in advanced TEFL* [PhD]. University of Cape Town. http://hdl.handle.net/11427/32386

Lilley, W. (2022). Cultivating locally transformative digital pedagogies: The need for formative-intervention research. In J. Olivier, A. Oojorah, & W. Udhin (Eds.), *Multimodal learning environments in Southern Africa. Digital education and learning* (pp. 9–30). Palgrave Macmillan. https://doi.org/10.1007/978-3-030-97656-9_2

Lilley, W., & Hardman, J. (2017). "You focus, I'm talking": A CHAT analysis of mobile dictionary use in an advanced EFL class. *Africa Education Review, 14*(1), 120–138. https://doi.org/10.1080/18146627.2016.1224592

Lingard, B., Martino, W., & Rezai-Rashti, G. (2013). Testing regimes, accountabilities and education policy: Commensurate global and national developments. *Journal of Education Policy, 28*(5), 539–556. https://doi.org/10.1080/02680939.2013.820042

Marshall, D. T., Pressley, T., Neugebauer, N. M., & Shannon, D. M. (2022). Why teachers are leaving and what we can do about it. *Phi Delta Kappan, 104*(1), 6–11.

McNeil, L. M. (1982). *Defensive teaching and classroom control*. Routledge.

McNeil, L. M. (1988a). Contradictions of control, Part 1: Administrators and teachers. *Phi Delta Kappan, 69*(5), 333–339. https://about.jstor.org/terms

McNeil, L. M. (1988b). Contradictions of control, Part 2: Teachers, students, and curriculum. *Phi Delta Kappan, 69*(6), 432–438. https://about.jstor.org/terms

McNeil, L. M. (1988c). Contradictions of control, Part 3: Contradictions of reform. *Phi Delta Kappan, 69*(7), 478–485. https://www.jstor.org/stable/20403683

McNeil, L. M. (2000). Contradictions of school reform: Educational costs of standardized testing. In *The Phi Delta Kappan*. Routledge.

Murphy, J. (2018). Neoliberalism and the privatization of social rights in education. In *Economic and social rights in a neoliberal world* (pp. 81–102). Cambridge University Press. https://doi.org/10.1017/9781108284691.005

Ratnam, T. (2021). The interaction of culture and context in the construction of teachers' putative entitled attitude in the midst of change. In T. Ratnam & C. J. Craig (Eds.), *Understanding excessive teacher and faculty entitlement: Digging at the roots, advances in research on teaching* (Vol. 38, pp. 77–101). Emerald Publishing Limited. https://doi.org/10.1108/S1479-368720210000038006

Ratnam, T., & Craig, C. J. (Eds.). (2021). *Understanding excessive teacher and faculty entitlement: Digging at the roots*. Emerald Publishing Limited.

Sannino, A., & Laitinen, A. (2015). Double stimulation in the waiting experiment: Testing a Vygotskian model of the emergence of volitional action. *Learning, Culture and Social Interaction, 4*, 4–18. https://doi.org/10.1016/j.lcsi.2014.07.002

Scott, C., & Dinham, S. (2002). The beatings will continue until quality improves: Using carrots and sticks in the quest for educational improvement. *Teacher Development, 6*(1), 15–32. https://doi.org/10.1080/13664530200200154

Siddiqui, S., Arif, I., & Hinduja, P. (2023). Technostress: A catalyst to leave the teaching profession – A survey designed to measure technostress among teachers in Pakistan during COVID-19 pandemic. *E-Learning and Digital Media, 20*(1), 53–79. https://doi.org/10.1177/20427530221107506

Simmie, G. M., & Moles, J. (2020). Teachers' changing subjectivities: Putting the soul to work for the principle of the market or for facilitating risk? *Studies in Philosophy and Education, 39*(4), 383–398. https://doi.org/10.1007/s11217-019-09686-9

Virkkunen, J., & Ahonen, H. (2011). Supporting expansive learning through theoretical-genetic reflection in the change laboratory. *Journal of Organizational Change Management, 24*(2), 229–243. https://doi.org/10.1108/09534811111119780

Virkkunen, J., & Newnham, D. S. (2013). *The change laboratory*. Sense Publishers. https://doi.org/10.1007/978-94-6209-326-3

Vygostky, L. S. (1978). In M. Cole, V. John-Steiner, S. Scribner, & E. M. Souberman (Eds.), *Mind in society. The development of higher psychological processes*. Harvard University Press.

Vygotsky, L. (1986). In A. Kozulin (Ed.), *Thought and language* (Revised). MIT Press.

Wertsch, J. V., & Sohmer, R. (1995). Vygotsky on learning and development. *Source: Human Development, 38*(6).

Western Cape Education Department. (2023). Massive R1.2bn #BackOnTrack campaign launched to reverse learning losses. https://www.westerncape.gov.za/gc-news/408/59820

World Economic Forum. (2015). *New vision for education unlocking the potential of technology*. www.weforum.org

World Economic Forum. (2020). *The global competitiveness report special edition 2020: How countries are performing on the road to recovery*. World Economic Forum. https://www3.weforum.org/docs/WEF_TheGlobalCompetitivenessReport2020.pdf

LIVING IN DILEMMATIC SPACES: STORIES OF EXCESSIVE ENTITLED TEACHERS AND THEIR TRANSFORMATIVE AGENCY

Ge Wei

Capital Normal University, China

ABSTRACT

This chapter presents three Chinese teachers' narrative accounts about how they live in dilemmatic spaces due to excessive entitlement. Still, the teachers move forward with transformative agency. The thick description of the three teacher participants has been reported elsewhere as the narratives of Lee – a math teacher, Ping – a Chinese language teacher and Wang – a school principal. In this chapter, however, 'excessive teacher entitlement' is used as a new lens to assist me in revisiting their stories of living in dilemmatic spaces. Narrative inquiry as a method unpacks the three teachers' life experiences. Although Lee, Ping and Wang encounter different entitlements and various dilemmas, their transformative agency in transitioning from a survival mode to thriving human beings brings out the similarities in their experiences. Using Vygotskian philosophy and cultural-historical activity theory (CHAT), this chapter focuses on the teachers' transformative agency as breaking away from given boundaries in their professional lives and taking up initiatives that confront the tacit excessive entitlement in and around them. Furthermore, transformative agency is promising in that it helps develop new practices in teacher education. Finally, the new understanding emanating by viewing the three subjects' experiences from the angle of excessive entitlement has the potential to inspire teachers in other contexts to become conscious of manifestations of excessive entitlement not only in themselves or others they interact with but also in the macro context we live in. This consciousness also increases the likelihood of the urge to find ways to ameliorate excessive entitlement and to move closer to one's cherished professional values.

Keywords: Excessive teacher entitlement; dilemmatic spaces; transformative agency; cultural-historical activity theory (CHAT); professional living; narrative inquiry

> Uniformed assessment is measuring students with one ruler. –Lee
>
> The teacher image was self-sacrificing, like a silkworm. –Ping
>
> The religious doctrine conflicts with the government policy. –Wang

The above comments uttered by the three featured Chinese teachers – Lee, Ping and Wang – name dilemmas they encountered in their educational settings. Lee is a mathematics teacher at a primary school in Beijing, who experiences a dilemma between standardized assessment and her students' differentiated development. Ping is a Chinese language teacher at a primary school in Beijing as well, who has been constrained by stereotypic teacher images in Chinese traditional culture. As for Wang, a female principal at a K-12 school in Macau, a special administrative region of China, she struggles to balance the local authority's accountability system with her campus's Catholic single-sex school tradition.

As for me, as the researcher, I have known all three teachers for more than 15 years. Their narratives have been part of my academic research; I have previously 'travel[led] to [their] worlds' (Lugones, 1987, p. 8). When I look back to my interactions and continuous experience with Lee, Ping and Wang over time, several queries have emerged during my continuous narrative journey: How do the teachers enter dilemmatic spaces in their educational settings? And, how do the teachers move beyond dilemmatic spaces in their professional lives?

Although the thick descriptions of the three research participants have been reported elsewhere (Chen et al., 2017; Wei, 2021, 2023a), in this current chapter, I adopt two new concepts, excessive teacher entitlement (e.g. Ratnam, 2021; Ratnam & Craig, 2021; Ratnam et al., 2019) and transformative agency (e.g. Haapasaari et al., 2016; Lipponen & Kumpulainen, 2011; Sannino et al., 2016), to rethink the stories of the three Chinese teachers, in response to the questions listed earlier.

This chapter deals with excessive teacher entitlement in educational contexts. It offers teachers new ways to view and address the problems in their professional living. Similar to Ratnam (2021; also, Chapter 2 in this volume), I access excessive entitlement of teachers from a cultural-historical activity theoretical (CHAT) perspective (Engeström, 1987/2015). Unlike the individualist psychological view (c.f. Farmer, 1999; Levin, 1970), this chapter claims that excessive entitlement is not merely expressed as an individual attitude, personality or emotional character. Rather, it stems from individual's interaction with the external socialcultural context (Ratnam & Craig, 2021); in other words, the excessive entitlement, in fact, is tightly bound by the accumulated cultural-historical traditions, contradictory policies within rapid reforms and unreasonable accountability under neoliberalism in education and beyond (Ratnam, 2021), which fabricate teachers' 'pseudo-selves' (Horney, 1950), a false version of themselves that is created as a defence mechanism to cope with emotional distress caused by the unreasonable demands placed on them in the workplace. It results in a sense of disconnection or alienation from one's true desires and values.

From the perspective I have adopted, I scrutinize how excessive teacher entitlement produces a deficit image of teachers, how the historically accumulated contradictions and contemporarily reform-related policies in education become a trap and, more importantly, how excessively entitled teachers can overcome the trap through transformative agency, which enables them to move from survival to thriving. This chapter examines the 'narrative resonance' (Conle, 1996) among the three teachers' stories; that is, how Lee, Ping and Wang transcended the external demands from contradictory policies, variable reforms, heavy societal requirements and unreasonable expectations of teachers. Their transformative agency authentically reveals their 'best-loved self' (Schwab, 1954/1978; see also Craig, 2013, 2020) and their personal desires to make a difference in their milieus.

THEORETICAL UNDERPINNINGS

This chapter illustrates how the three Chinese teachers' stories exemplify the theoretical underpinnings of this study: excessive teacher entitlement, dilemmatic spaces and transformative agency. These concepts form a niche in the literature that addresses the challenges and opportunities of teacher development in China.

Excessive Teacher Entitlement

In individualist psychology, 'entitlement' refers to individuals' beliefs about what they deserve and how they should be treated by others (Levin, 1970). These beliefs lead to a set of attitudes that influence people's perceptions of themselves, others and the world (Kriegman, 1983). Excessive entitlement is identified by an exaggerated sense of self-importance: individualized characteristics (Farmer, 1999) cause people to demand special treatment and privileges. Similarly, as Fisk (2010) noted, '[it] describes [those] who perceive themselves as deserving of organizational rewards that exceed what would be considered normative in light of their contributions' (p. 109). Excessive entitlement is about the position one gives oneself that blots out one's assumptions and makes one's expectations of oneself and others unreasonable (Ratnam & Craig, 2021; Ratnam et al., 2019).

The above individualist stance blames people for what happens. As a result, excessive entitlement is associated with a lack of personal politeness, empathy or respect for the other. Following this line of thinking, excessive entitlement gives teachers a deficit image without any affordances (Ratnam, 2021). However, it is not enough to only describe the manifestations of teachers' excessive entitlements and then denounce teachers' irresponsibility. On the contrary, we need to also take into account: Where do excessive teacher entitlements emerge? This reflective inquiry helps us review the discourses of educational reform, for instance, neoliberalism and its connection to teachers' individualist attitudes or behaviours

(Ratnam, 2021). By doing so, this chapter moves beyond the individualistic conceptualizations of teacher excessive entitlement, which means that it can take diverse manifestations depending upon the 'social interaction' and relationships in the discursive context of teachers' practice (Ratnam et al., 2019, pp. 211–212).

As Ratnam and Craig (2021) aver, the notion of excessive teacher entitlement does not necessarily point to teachers' deficiency; rather, 'it points to an inadequacy in our interpretation of teachers, by missing the interacting factors beyond teachers' individualist characteristics that impinge upon their thinking and action' (p. 3). When Western neoliberal education reform spread around the globe, education became tightly linked to economies. The free market and individual rights, freedom and autonomy are taken to extremes. Collective welfare and the common good become lost as an individual's excessive entitlement manifests itself in education.

This chapter defines excessive entitlement as a form of 'pseudo-self' (Horney, 1950) based on external demands emanating from policies, reforms and accountability systems. The pseudo-self becomes a cover story (Clandinin & Connelly, 1995; Crites, 1979) teachers tell. Teachers' cover stories are helpful narrative lenses that illuminate how some of the tensions and entailments that ensue are initiated and perpetuated by teachers rather than interrogated and discussed (Wei, 2021). Stemming from institutional prescriptions situated at the juncture between teacher stories and school stories and arising from the conflicting philosophies of educational change (Olson & Craig, 2005), these cover stories are composed by teachers to cope with tensions between themselves and society. Excessive teacher entitlement within cover stories often emerges in dilemmatic spaces they encounter. Contradictory demands, conflicted policies and tension-filled relationships always push teachers into dilemmatic spaces, stoking teachers' pseudo-selves.

In this work, I analyze the concept of 'excessive teacher entitlement' from a cultural-historical perspective to examine and understand what makes teachers excessively entitled and how they can overcome it.

Dilemmatic Spaces

A dilemma is 'a situation in which the [teacher] participants are required to manage competing alternatives' (Flett & Wallace, 2005, p. 190). According to Lampert (1985), educators must balance various interests, often resulting in practical dilemmas. Within a dilemma, 'no right choice is available, and one has to make a compromise' (Honig, 1996, p. 258). Thus, educators need to acquire paradoxical frames embracing a 'both/and' rather than an 'either/or' logic (Engeström & Sannino, 2011). The existence of competing priorities requires the balancing of inconsistencies in specific contexts; this is the recommended way to deal with dilemmas.

Stemming from Lefebvre's (1991) spatial sociology, dilemmatic spaces instantiate where the actions and interactions of agents take place. Dilemmatic spaces are a natural part of the school environment, where micro-politics reveal both educators' internal operations and their interactions with the external environment (Kelchtermans & Vanassche, 2017). The interwoven tensions experienced in dilemmatic spaces shape teacher participants' thinking and actions, which, in turn, shift the boundaries of these dilemmatic spaces. Through this dynamic process, the meaning of a dilemma may become redefined by the teacher participants involved (Chen et al., 2017). Usually, individuals deploy all available resources when seeking alternative strategies; this process helps to redefine their work and professional identities (Foster & Newman, 2005). The dynamic processes generated by these concerted efforts indicate that dilemmatic spaces are not only embedded in daily work but also socially constructed in broader contexts (Fransson & Grannäs, 2013). These processes can be linked with a socially relational conception of power, which may be attained by educators and deployed to affect how key issues are understood and governed. However, they can also encompass how educators' agency enables them to live with dilemmas and, finally, how they may transcend the spaces.

In this chapter, excessive entitlements as an interpretive concept provide a new angle to understand the three teachers' professional living, why and how they lived in dilemmatic spaces.

Transformative Agency

Agency has been regarded as critical capacity for teachers encountering educational reform and change (e.g. Lipponen & Kumpulainen, 2011; Tao & Gao, 2017). Transformative agency within the strand of CHAT (e.g. Sannino et al., 2016) emphasizes the subject's transformation of the current situation by responding to pressing societal needs. CHAT has its roots in Marxist developmental psychology, specifically in the works of Vygotsky, which place primacy on participation in cultural practices as the basis of learning and development (Engeström, 1987/2015).

Transformative agency, in CHAT, is explained in Vygotsky's waiting experiment (Vygotsky, 1931/1987; see Lilley, Chapter 6 in this volume). When the research participant goes beyond the constraints of certain circumstances by use of the affordance of the second stimuli, transformative agency emerges (see also Sannino, 2015). Compared to other forms of agency, transformative agency emphasizes the process of and the capacity for transformative change, both individually and institutionally. In the contemporary fourth generation of CHAT (Engeström & Sannino, 2021), transformative agency is regarded as a quality of 'expansive learning' (Engeström & Sannino, 2010; See Ratnam, Chapter 2 in this volume) because learning expansively requires breaking away from the given frame of action and taking the initiative to transform it. The new ideas and practices generated in an expansive learning process carry future-oriented visions loaded with initiative and commitment by the actors (Sannino et al., 2016). In CHAT literature, transformative agency is not seen as a primary characteristic of an individual but rather a dynamic, complex, relational and cultural process, mediated by conceptual and practical signs and tools (Vygotsky, 1978). In other words, CHAT emphasizes that transformative agency never occurs in a vacuum or merely on individual characteristics; rather, possibilities for transformative agency are created and bound by other people, cultural artefacts and the shared objects of activity in a community. In this line, CHAT offers a cultural-historical perspective on excessive entitlement, which helps us to reflect on teacher excessive entitlement within a broader horizon alongside critical activism.

NARRATIVE INQUIRY AS RESEARCH METHOD

Narrative inquiry, which is anchored in Dewey's (1938) experiential philosophy, focuses on the relationship between narratives of life experience and educators' professional development; Dewey understood the origin of experience to be 'a resolution of unsettled problems or crises' (p. 229). This view of experience relates to the idea of dilemmatic spaces. In dilemmatic spaces, an individual seeks coherence between conflicting stories. This need for coherence resonates with Dewey's (1938) suggestion that an experience is 'educative, or promotes growth, only when it continues to move us forward on the experiential continuum' (p. 28) through a process of reflection on these experiences.

Narrative, as 'the closest we can come to experience', serves as a window through which a person enters the world and interprets and gives meaning to their experiences there (Clandinin & Connelly, 2000, p. 188). Narrative inquiry focuses on how human lives and experiences are constructed and restructured by narratives. Connelly and Clandinin (1990) outlined four key terms in narrative inquiry – live, tell, retell and relive – that emerge from the view of experience as comprising storied phenomena. It is understood that people *live* their stories and *tell* stories of their living. When narrative inquirers accompany participants and inquire into their lived and told stories, this is called *retelling* stories. Finally, because we see how we are changed as we retell our lived and told stories, we then begin to *re-living* our stories. Thus, by thinking narratively, an inquirer can describe the actors' 'experience in the world, an experience that is storied both in the living and telling and that can be studied by listening, observing, living alongside another, and writing and interpreting texts' (Clandinin, 2013, p. 18).

I illustrate the teachers' stories in a metaphorical three-dimensional narrative inquiry space that was temporal (time), personal–social (interaction) and spatial (place) (Clandinin & Connelly, 2000). The recognition of these three dimensions emerges from the fact that each story can be situated within social, cultural, economic and institutional narratives (Clandinin & Caine, 2008). I define the scope of the narrative inquiry to include where the teachers' excessive entitlements are expressed, shaped and how the teachers' transformative agencies are enacted by recognizing the social, temporal and spatial elements of each story.

When I introduce the three teachers in the next section, I include the plotlines of their narratives by contextualizing them into rich story constellations (Craig, 2007). The teachers' stories are selected to demonstrate their experiences with excessive entitlement and how they transformed the situation through enacting their agency in dilemmatic spaces.

- Lee, a primary school teacher teaching mathematics, was told by more experienced teachers that her duty is only to teaching the subject matter well. However, when experiencing the dilemma between subject-knowledge-centred teaching and educating humanity at the same time, Lee's transformative agency introduces her to a teachable moment.
- Ping, a Chinese language teacher, grew up in a rural town in the northern mainland. The traditional image of teacher as being silkworm-like, always sacrificing, changed in the 21st century. Ping's transformative agency helped her to overcome the stuck traditional image of a teacher that blocked her development.
- Wang, a principal of a K-12 school in Macau's Catholic girls' school, faced a dilemma between the religious and the secular and instantiated her transformative agency at the intersection of school, family and government.

To analyze the stories from an emic stance, which places teachers' stories at the centre of the research (Caine et al., 2021), I used three interpretive strategies from narrative inquiry: broadening, burrowing and storying/restorying (Clandinin & Connelly, 2000; Connelly & Clandinin, 1990). Broadening locates the study in an authentic milieu that includes macro–meso–micro contexts, which primarily goes beyond the individualistic stories. Burrowing entails a closer look at a series of the teachers' lived experiences, by unfolding the social dimension of narratives. Storying and restorying reorganize narratives to investigate an agent's thinking and actions, by going backward and forward. My retelling of the three Chinese teachers' narratives make them relive them as experiences again. This narrative inquiry seeks the resonance among the stories (Conle, 1996), which reveals a collective landscape of Chinese teachers' living in dilemmatic spaces and their transformative agency within.

It should be noted that narrative inquirers are not objective researchers but are relational in that they are attentive to the intersubjective, connected and embedded spaces in which lives are lived (Clandinin, 2013). The trustworthiness of narrative inquiry is based on the demonstration of rigour and transparency in offering a vivid and insightful interpretation of narratives; such an inquiry must be grounded in the dependability of the methodological procedure (Clandinin & Rosiek, 2007). My inquiry regarding the three teachers involved a series of narratives, which are 'concrete examples elaborated so that members of a relevant research community can judge for themselves their trustworthiness and the validity of observations, interpretations, etc.' (Lyons & LaBoskey, 2002, p. 20). Through this narrative inquiry, which is a collaborative endeavour employing a co-composition process, I share my understandings of the threes' narrative accounts with my teacher participants, thereby achieving narrative truth from a methodological standpoint. The trust and rapport that built up with the informants during the process of (re-)storying enhanced the trustworthiness of this inquiry as well. Finally, readers are also invited to co-compose their narratives to inform their own lives and education and generate actionable truths in their future endeavours (Lyons & LaBoskey, 2002). I vetted the three teachers' experiences in a responsive community (Caine et al., 2021) which hopefully provide enriched insights to this book's readership.

Ethical issues are very critical in narrative inquiry because the research method is a way of understanding experience through 'collaboration between researcher and participants, over time, in a place or a series of places, and in social interaction with milieus' (Clandinin & Connelly, 2000, p. 20). As narrative inquirers, we become part of participants' lives, and they become part of ours. Therefore, our lives – who we are now and who we are becoming in our own and our participants' landscapes – are also being studied. Accordingly, being a narrative inquirer and thinking narratively is a risky endeavour; the researcher must be attentive to their own 'unfolding and enfolding storied life and the lives of those with whom [I] they engage' (Clandinin, 2013, p. 23). I used fictionalization (Clandinin et al., 2006), a fourth research tool, to mask the three teachers' identities and their schools' identities in keeping with their desire for anonymity, a major ethical consideration.

(RE-)TELLING AND (RE-)LIVING IN THE STORIES OF TEACHERS

Among the three teachers' stories, their excessive entitlements were manifested in the following themes: (1) knowledge-centred teaching and uniformed assessment leads to teacher blindness where student differentiation is concerned; (2) traditional images of Chinese teachers advocating for teachers as self-sacrificing results in teacher burnout; and (3) a single-sex school's religious tradition empowers teachers to resist education reform in Macau. However, their transformative agency enables them to transcend their dilemmatic spaces and assume new professional avenues of life in their educational milieus.

Lee's Narrative Account

Lee is a mathematics teacher at a primary school in Beijing. The experienced teachers at the school, including Lee's mentor, once told her that the most important task for Lee is to teach math well. This knowledge-centred tradition in Chinese basic education system, and the micro circumstance in Lee's school, made her feel excessively entitled to believe that her duty was teaching only what the subject matter and the textbook say. However, after a decade of teaching, Lee gradually became aware that teaching knowledge is not enough. This was especially true when she encountered a situation which implied that 'uniformed assessment is like measuring students with one ruler'. As a result, students' differentiation was not taken into account. This produced a huge gap between what Lee enacted and what she experienced every day.

One day, as usual, Lee distributed the math exam papers to her fourth grade students before announcing the names of those who got the highest scores. As she read the names of the first few students, all expressed admiration, and this was reflected in her students' facial expressions. However, as she read 'Zhao Bo, 98', there came a loud exclamation in the classroom, followed by a clap of hands. She instantly sensed that something had gone wrong. Lee retells that moment as following:

> I supposed that there was some kindness in this clap of hands, but Zhao Bo's facial expression changed from happiness to unease when he heard 98 and then the clapping.

Lee did not continue to read the names of the next high scores but asked the students directly, 'Why did you applaud?' 'Zhao Bo got 98! Zhao Bo got 98!' The classroom was filled with such statements. After the noise finally subsided, Lee said to her students:

> I know you clapped your hands out of good will, but why could Zhao Bo not get 98? My view is just on the contrary. I think your clapping revealed some bias, contempt, and lack of understanding of Zhao Bo. You don't know how hard he has been working with his brain! Many times, when everybody finds a math problem difficult, he will dig into it persistently. I think he is not inferior at all. Instead, he is excellent. He has great potential to become somebody in the future.

Upon hearing this statement, the students' surprise changed into a mixture of puzzlement and admiration, and the expression in Zhao Bo's eyes also changed. He was more self-assured now. Afterwards, Lee told me:

> The expression in Zhao Bo's eyes really changed. I know this so well. He needs to be treated in the same way as the other kids. You shouldn't treat him as inferior or disadvantaged. He needs this fair treatment. In fact, his Chinese language is rather weak, ranking in the last few in his class, and his math was similarly weak. However, after a long period of hard work, his math has caught up now.

Although 'education for student quality' advocated by China's national curriculum reform has become a vogue in the past years (China Ministry of Education, 2001), the school where Lee worked was still implementing 'education for exams' as most of the schools in China. Thus, Zhao Bo, having obtained a high score, should be celebrated, and his peers should show respect for him. The purpose of Lee announcing Zhao Bo's score was obviously to praise him and, at the same time, to encourage the other students to learn from his example. However, it seemed that things did not turn out as she had wished. The students clapped their hands, which made Zhao Bo feel uneasy and made Lee worry.

In Lee's fine-grained accounts, the high-stakes exams in China are at the root of her excessive entitled attitude. She initially thought that she was only a math teacher who did not have to care for students' emotions and morality. However, the situation in the above narrative account put Lee into a dilemmatic space. On the one hand, she could not possibly ignore this incident as if it had not happened at all because she sensed the complexity of the reactions of the clapping students. On the other hand, she realized that whichever side she took would hurt the other side. If she only acknowledged the good intentions of the clapping students without paying attention to Zhao Bo's feelings, she would have hurt Zhao Bo's self-esteem. If she only took Zhao Bo's self-esteem into consideration and negated the other students' clapping, she would also have hurt those other students. She was now facing a dilemma caused by a high score of a low-achieving student.

As a tool of external accountability demanded by administration, the exam system is a harsh reality with which all Chinese teachers have to comply. Even if this practice is far from ideal in reaching the goals of the reform, Lee, like the majority of Chinese teachers, could not help it. Here, the uniform exam system and the students' differentiated capacities produced a more complicated dilemma for Lee. When she was pondering how to respond to the different reactions of her students, Lee had already created a dilemmatic space for her own sense of agency to emerge. Lee's transformative agency revealed itself as her caring for Zhao Bo's differentiated learning. Lee, in fact, created a safe space for low-performing students, like Zhao Bo, to learn math and be themselves as persons.

Ping's Narrative Account

Ping was born in 1974 in a remote county in Hebei Province, located in the middle-north part of China. Ping's parents were both farmers who made their living from corn and wheat. When Ping was a child, she had a dream to be a teacher. In traditional Chinese sociocultural discourse, in particular those influenced by Confucianism, intellectuals are considered prestigious and have high social status. Born in the 1970s, Ping was familiar with the traditional metaphors pertaining to the teaching profession in the Chinese context. For example, the image of 'soul engineers' suggests that teachers' major responsibility is to cultivate students' morality, while the metaphor of 'silkworms' portrays teachers working like the worm that self-sacrificingly produces silk until its death. Teachers are also depicted as 'candles', generously burning themselves out to afford light for their students (He, 2002). These metaphorical images, which foreground self-sacrifice and altruism, present the Chinese public's traditional perceptions of teachers and the teaching profession.

At the beginning of her career, Ping felt obliged to live up to the traditional image of Chinese teachers devoting themselves selflessly to teaching. She soon realized that she was being unjust to herself, and that she was entitled to her own agency when she compared her situation with that of her husband. Ping once intended to abandon her profession, which became her story to live by (Clandinin et al., 2006). Influenced by her husband, she began noticing various social professions other than teaching. Compared to her spouse, Ping told me that she 'earned a low salary but did much more work':

> In the first two years of teaching, I felt good. Later, I faced a major "bottleneck"... I began to doubt myself... For a while, I felt that teachers were very tired and busy every day... Compared with them [people in my husband's profession], our working conditions were not good.

Ping thought she had worked hard in her job but earned very little in return. This imbalance between input and output made her doubt her professional identity. However, the new national curriculum reform in 2001 triggered her motive to make a change. As a result, in 2009, Ping and her colleagues developed a school-based curriculum, 'Sinology and Chinese Culture'. Ping used academic reading to explore approaches to developing a school-based curriculum and thus collected materials from Chinese philosophy, history and literature to construct a teachable knowledge landscape of Sinology for her students. This kind of bottom-up exploration of designing curriculum crossed the limitations of being a Chinese language teacher and enabled the rebirth of Ping's professional career. Ping's new image of the teaching profession unfolded in an interview:

> *Ping:* I really thank Ms Lee, my director back then. She trusted me and gave me opportunities.
> *Ge:* Right...
> *Ping:* Although I am always busy with my teaching, my students, and their parents, which resulted in an ambiguous boundary between life and work, I think that I could grow with the children and keep their enthusiasm for learning. I think that is the most valuable thing in my work.
> *Ge:* You once complained...
> *Ping:* Oh, I have. But now... I talked with my friends who are officials some days ago. They even complained to me that they are too idle to get something meaningful out of life. I reflected on their words and agreed afterwards. If you stay idle in a position for long, you will lose your creativity and imagination.
> *Ge:* You did great work in this curriculum reform.
> *Ping:* In terms of this, I should thank my students as well. My students teach me that a teacher is not a candle burning itself. Teaching and learning are co-developing processes. [A second's pause]
> *Ping:* I would like to say that a school is a forest. The teacher is tree, and the student is grass. Teachers and students grow together in the sunshine. I, as a teacher, just grew earlier [than my students]...We should not look down on the children, who bring their own experience to school as very important curriculum resources.

The metaphor of the 'school as a forest', where teachers and students develop together, further revealed Ping's newly developing professional identity. A questioning of the traditional image of a teacher she had assumed that had made her slog mindlessly led her to find a new purpose and life as a teacher. Now, she was on a path of lifelong development in which learning from her students formed a large part of her learning.

Wang's Narrative Account

Before the 2000s, Macau's religious private schools administered their own institutions and teaching subjects. However, the Basic Law of the Non-Higher Education System (Macau SAR Government, 2006) and the Institutional Framework of Teaching Staff in Non-Higher Education Private Schools (Macau SAR government, 2012) instituted interventions in private schools. While the new policies limited the autonomy of private schools, they also allocated more public funding: the Macau government's financial grants to private schools increased from 23 billion MOP in 2008 to 69 billion MOP in 2017 (Department of Statistics and Census Service, Macau, 2021). Nevertheless, Wang said the Catholic sisters were initially rather worried about the reform movement. The excessive entitlement, stemming from the religious tradition, legitimized Wang's resistance to the educational reform. Wang once said:

> S.T. School is a Catholic school where sisters have more discursive power [than me]. At the beginning of 2012, the sisters did not want to receive government funding. They were afraid that Macau's government would intervene in Catholic schools. However, financial support is critical to improve schooling conditions and to reduce students' tuition fees. Thus, I persuaded our sisters to enrol in the regulation. Two years later, the government started to account for our students' academic performance, which was contradictory to the idea of Catholic education.

As a school leader, Wang must abide by the Macau government policy. However, as a Catholic school principal, Wang must consider the sisters' opinions and Catholic education traditions. Additionally, it was difficult to coordinate Catholic school development with modern education governance. In both secular and religious contexts, accountability can have a negative meaning. In the tradition of Catholic education, discovering children's spirituality is the foci of school education. However, in the context education reform in Macau, cultivating students' core competence increasingly became the dominant discourse.

Wang interpreted the dilemma as follows:

> The dual allegiance is one of the biggest dilemmas; if you are not performing well, the education sector is on your back, and if you are not doing things according to the expectations of the responsible Catholic authority, you are in trouble. So, you are caught in between.

In the dilemmatic spaces between religion and the secular, Wang worried that 'Catholic education might seem too old fashioned to the public'. Moreover, it may seem out of alignment and even contrary to the professionalism that leadership practices require (Madero, 2021). Addressing S.T. School's accountability to the local authority, Wang's principalship shows her 'finding a middle ground between governmental policy-based reform and religious schooling ideas'. Accordingly, Wang believes that she is 'not a copy machine that simply mimics educational authorities' discourses'. Rather, in her view, she maintains her human-centred beliefs when implementing policies:

> Policy should serve people. We are not slaves of rigid documents. The government issues a policy due to macro-considerations, such as economic development, high ranking performance, or some political value. I am a principal facing actual children. I must judge whether a policy is beneficial to their development. It is the only standard for me when considering the value of education reform.

During the past 7 years, Wang has actively engaged with the education sector administration to prevent direct political interference in schooling. Wang believes that in Macau, you should 'know how to manoeuvre [...and] should be able to transform passive implementation into active reflection and appropriate negotiation'. Her principalship is an effort to balance the conflicting priorities in schooling:

> It is good to push us to improve teaching and learning. However, the purpose of education is not to receive higher scores but to enlighten people. I was trying to find a middle ground between government policy-based reform and religious schooling ideas. Now, I can state with confidence that both teachers and authorities seek our kids' well-being. We are accountable not only for education reform but also for student development.

Mandated testing for accountability purposes has long been considered a vehicle and a measure of school success. Wang's reaction to this policy not only presents her meaning-making but also how she puts policy into action. Wang's wisdom represents her response to Macau authorities' discourses while maintaining her educational beliefs in which she sees herself first as an educator and then as an administrator. Once in an interview, Wang described her understanding of the relationship between school and government as 'belonging, but not too much'. She refuses to make schooling chaotic due to short-term policies. The long-standing mission of schooling is to help children grow. In short, Wang's courageous principalship is centred on resisting short-term reforms, maintaining initial ideals and smartly negotiating with authorities through her principalship.

DISCUSSION

In summary, we need to rethink where excessive entitlements in China come from, and how it impacts teachers. By reflecting on the stories of Lee, Ping and Wang, it is clear that the teachers' excessive entitlement does not exist in a vacuum (see Table 1). From a narrative analysis, the external policies as unreasonable expectations are a critical source of teachers' excessive entitlement. What is worse, docile and well-behaved teachers acknowledge and legitimize the excessive entitlement through their individual acceptance of it. When unreasonable demands conflict with teachers' original education ideals or student needs, teachers enter dilemmatic spaces. In a nutshell, teachers are prepped to be excessively entitled. The clashes described in this chapter unfurl in dilemmatic spaces, and the teachers transcended the dilemmas through their transformative agency.

From the three teachers' narratives, it is not hard to find that the excessive entitlement is largely produced by external policies, pressures from reforms, social expectations, accountability, ranking students and the effects of neoliberalism on teaching and teacher profession. The external pressures produce the

Table 1. Summary of the Three Teachers' Narratives.

	Excessive Entitlement	Dilemmatic Spaces	Transformative Agency
Lee	Only teaching the subject matter without educative enactment	Uniform assessment versus student differentiation	Using an ethics of caring and empathy to enlighten youth
Ping	Taking the traditional image of teacher self-sacrificing for granted	External stereotypical demands on teachers versus teachers' personal development	Bravely engaging in educational reform and becoming a lifelong learner
Wang	Emphasizing spirituality in Catholic education but resisting education reform	Accountability imposed by the government versus teacher accountability to the students they serve	Finding a third way through adopting a children-centred approach

image of teachers' pseudo-selves, which, as a result, pushes them into dilemmatic spaces. However, the dilemma, as CHAT makes us see, also includes the potential of change. Teachers' transformative agency emerged and overcame the dilemmas, making them more humane and approachable.

Excessive teacher entitlement emerges in dilemmas. However, transformative agency helps teachers to go beyond the dilemmatic spaces. It is a relational achievement (Wei, 2023b) that creates opportunities for them not only to copy or repeat activities but also to transform activities and even create new ones and to contribute to their own development with unexpected outcomes (e.g. Chen et al., 2017; Wei, 2021).

CONCLUSION

This chapter features how the three teachers' stories of experience within their school contexts increase the possibilities of co-creating a better learning and working environment for all. These possibilities are based on their understanding of themselves and the dilemmas they experience in their respective milieus that often make them take refuge behind the veil of excessive entitlement through the pseudo selves they develop. Moreover, methodologically speaking, teachers' transformative agency seems to emerge in the reliving and retelling of their dilemmatic space stories. Convincing accounts like these teachers' restorying illustrate the potential for research centred on excessive entitlement to move beyond descriptions of how excessive entitlement manifests itself towards how these experiences can be mediated. By doing so, we can see the potential of the narrative inquiry research method to contribute to future research on excessive entitlement and to systematically challenge – and ultimately undo – the excessive entitlement experienced in schools by teachers.

This chapter shows that excessive entitlement is not solely an individual attitude, personality or character. Rather, it stems from the external context, the reforms, policies and accountability, which result in teachers developing pseudo-selves. The dominant control of neoliberalism in education and its implications for teacher professionalism, educational practice and social relations need to be critically examined in order to break the 'chain of entitlement' that Ratnam (2021) describes. Also, what needs acknowledgement, as Ratnam (2021, pp. 94–95) points out, is that excessive teacher and faculty entitlement is not their individual problem but a relational one, encompassing all stakeholders in the educational policy and practice landscape. As for the teacher education system both in China and internationally, more affordances are needed so that teachers' stories can be voiced. These teacher voices bring out the tension between teachers' pseudo-self which they develop as they try to fulfil institutional demands and which makes them excessively entitled, although unintentionally, on the one hand, and their authentic selves wanting to exercise their transformative agency for student well-being, on the other hand (Ratnam & Craig, 2021). This study illustrates how teacher narratives provide a way for them to become conscious of the excessive entitlement that they are veering towards in the dilemmatic spaces that emerge in their work context. It also helps them to negotiate these spaces agentively and to move their practice closer to their authentic self.

ACKNOWLEDGEMENT

This work is funded by the Beijing Social Science Foundation (Grant No. 22JYC016). I would like to express my special thanks to Tara Ratnam and Cheryl Craig, who have assisted me with writing my chapter by their feedback that pushed my thinking to new levels of understanding. I really learned a lot from the cyclically revising process and the email exchanges I've had with them. My thanks also go to the reviewers for their comments on the initial version of this chapter.

REFERENCES

Caine, V., Clandinin, J., & Lessard, S. (2021). Considering response communities: Spaces of appearance in narrative inquiry. *Qualitative Inquiry*, *27*(6), 661–666. http://doi.org/10.1177/1077800420948105

Chen, X., Wei, G., & Jiang, S. (2017). The ethical dimension of teacher practical knowledge: A narrative inquiry into Chinese teachers' thinking and action in dilemmatic spaces. *Journal of Curriculum Studies*, *49*(4), 518–541. https://doi.org/10.1080/00220272.2016.1263895

China Ministry of Education. (2001). *Outline of curriculum reform for basic education (experimental)*. http://www.moe.edu.cn/publicfiles/business/htmlfiles/moe/moe_309/200412/4672.html

Clandinin, D. J. (2013). *Engaging in narrative inquiry*. Left Coast Press.

Clandinin, D., & Caine, V. (2008). Narrative inquiry. In L. M. Given (Ed.), *The Sage encyclopedia of qualitative research methods* (pp. 542–545). Sage Publications.

Clandinin, D. J., & Connelly, F. M. (1995). *Teachers' professional knowledge landscapes*. Teachers College Press.

Clandinin, D. J., & Connelly, F. M. (2000). *Narrative inquiry: Experience and story in qualitative research*. Jossey-Bass.

Clandinin, D. J., Huber, J., Huber, M., Murphy, S., & Steeves, P. (2006). *Composing diverse identities: Narrative inquiries into the interwoven lives of children and teachers*. Routledge.

Clandinin, D. J., & Rosiek, J. (2007). Mapping a landscape of narrative inquiry: Borderland spaces and tensions. In D. J. Clandinin (Ed.), *Handbook of narrative inquiry: Mapping a methodology* (pp. 35–76). Sage Publications.

Conle, C. (1996). Resonance in preservice teacher inquiry. *American Educational Research Journal*, *33*(2), 297–325. https://doi.org/10.3102/00028312033002297

Connelly, F. M., & Clandinin, D. J. (1990). Stories of experience and narrative inquiry. *Educational Researcher*, *19*(5), 2–14. https://doi.org/10.3102/0013189X019005002

Craig, C. J. (2007). Story constellations: A narrative approach to contextualizing teacher's knowledge of school reform. *Teaching and Teacher Education*, *23*, 173–188.

Craig, C. (2013). Teacher education and the best-loved self. *Asia Pacific Journal of Education*, *33*(3), 261–272. https://doi.org/10.1080/02188791.2013.788476

Craig, C. (2020). "Data is [G]od": The influence of cumulative policy reforms on teachers' knowledge in an urban middle school in the United States. *Teaching and Teacher Education*, *93*. https://doi.org/10.1016/j.tate.2020.103027

Crites, S. (1979). The aesthetics of self-deception. *Soundings*, *42*(2), 197–229.

Department of Statistics and Census Service, Macau. (2021). *2020 population by-census: Detailed results*. https://www.dsec.gov.mo/Statistic.aspx?NodeGuid=ee77eb29-fd1b-4f13-8a2d-3181e93adb05#P84acedfb-21f9-4a30-8ba4-5e3f66857f89

Dewey, J. (1938). *Education and experience*. Collier Books.

Engeström, Y. (1987/2015). *Learning by expanding: An activity-theoretical approach to developmental research*. Cambridge University Press.

Engeström, Y., & Sannino, A. (2010). Studies of expansive learning: Foundations, findings and future challenges. *Educational Research Review*, *5*(1), 1–24. https://doi.org/10.1016/j.edurev.2009.12.002

Engeström, Y., & Sannino, A. (2011). Discursive manifestations of contradictions in organizational change efforts: A methodological framework. *Journal of Organizational Change Management*, *24*(3), 368–387. https://doi.org/10.1108/09534811111132758

Engeström, Y., & Sannino, A. (2021). From mediated actions to heterogeneous coalitions: Four generations of activity-theoretical studies of work and learning. *Mind, Culture and Activity*, *28*(1), 4–23. https://doi.org/10.1080/10749039.2020.1806328

Farmer, S. A. (1999). Entitlement in codependency: Developmental and therapeutic considerations. *Journal of Addictive Diseases*, *18*(3), 55–68. https://doi.org/10.1300/J069v18n03_06

Fisk, G. M. (2010). "I want it all and I want it now!" An examination of the etiology, expression and escalation of excessive employee entitlement. *Human Resource Management Review*, *20*, 102–114. http://doi.org/10.1016/j.hrmr.2009.11.001

Flett, J. D., & Wallace, J. (2005). Change dilemmas for curriculum leaders: Dealing with mandated change in schools. *Journal of Curriculum and Supervision*, *20*(3), 188–213.

Foster, T., & Newman, E. (2005). Just a knock back? Identity bruising on the route to becoming a male primary school teacher. *Teachers and Teaching*, *11*(4), 341–358. http://doi.org/10.1080/13450600500137091

Fransson, G., & Grannäs, J. (2013). Dilemmatic spaces in educational contexts–towards a conceptual framework for dilemmas in teacher's work. *Teachers and Teaching*, *19*(1), 4–17. http://doi.org/10.1080/13540602.2013.744195

Haapasaari, A., Engeström, Y., & Kerosuo, H. (2016). The emergence of learners' transformative agency in a change laboratory intervention. *Journal of Education and Work*, *29*, 232–262. http://doi.org/10.1080/13639080.2014.900168

He, M. F. (2002). A narrative inquiry of cross-cultural lives: Lives in China. *Journal of Curriculum Studies*, *34*(3), 301–321. http://doi.org/10.1080/00220270110108196

Honig, B. (1996). Difference, dilemmas, and the politics of home. In S. Benhabib (Ed.), *Democracy and difference: Contesting the boundaries of the political* (pp. 235–256). Princeton University Press.

Horney, K. (1950). *Neurosis and human growth: The struggle toward self-realization*. W. W. Norton & Company.

Kelchtermans, G., & Vanassche, E. (2017). Micropolitics in the education of teachers: Power, negotiation, and professional development. In D. J. Clandinin & J. Husu (Eds.), *The SAGE handbook of research on teacher education* (pp. 441–456). Sage Publications.

Kriegman, G. (1983). Entitlement attitudes: Psychosocial and therapeutic implications. *The Journal of the American Academy of Psychoanalysis*, *11*(2), 265–281.

Lampert, M. (1985). How do teachers manage to teach? Perspectives on problems in practice. *Harvard Educational Review*, *55*(2), 178–194.

Lefebvre, H. (1991). *The production of space* (D. Nicholson-Smith, Trans.). Wiley-Blackwell.

Levin, S. (1970). On the psychoanalysis of attitudes of entitlement. *Bulletin of the Philadelphia Association for Psychoanalysis*, *20*(1970), 1–10.

Lipponen, L., & Kumpulainen, K. (2011). Acting as accountable authors: Creating interactional spaces for agency work in teacher education. *Teaching and Teacher Education*, *27*, 812–819. https://doi.org/10.1016/j.tate.2011.01.001

Lugones, M. (1987). Playfulness, world-travelling, and loving perception. *Hypatia*, *2*(2), 3–19. https://doi.org/10.1111/j.1527-2001.1987.tb01062.x

Lyons, N., & LaBoskey, V. K. (Eds.). (2002). *Narrative inquiry in practice: Advancing the knowledge of teaching*. Teachers College Press.

Macau SAR Government. (2006). Basic law of the non-higher education system. https://bo.io.gov.mo/bo/i/2006/52/lei09.asp

Macau SAR government. (2012). Institutional framework of teaching staff in non-higher education private schools. http://bo.io.gov.mo/bo/i/2012/12/lei03_cn.asp

Madero, C. (2021). Because I am called: How a calling to teach emerges and develops in teachers working in catholic high schools. *Teaching and Teacher Education*, *101*, 103319. https://doi.org/10.1016/j.tate.2021.103319

Olson, M., & Craig, C. (2005). Uncovering cover stories: Claiming not to know what we know and why we do it. *Curriculum Inquiry*, *35*(2), 161–182. https://doi.org/10.1111/j.1467-873X.2005.00323.x

Ratnam, T. (2021). The interaction of culture and context in the construction of teachers' putative entitled attitude in the midst of change. In T. Ratnam & C. J. Craig (Eds.), *Understanding excessive teacher and faculty entitlement (Advances in Research on Teaching)* (Vol. 38, pp. 77–101). Emerald Publishing Limited.

Ratnam, T., & Craig, C. J. (2021). Introduction: The idea of excessive teacher entitlement: Breaking new ground. In T. Ratnam & C. J. Craig (Eds.), *Understanding excessive teacher and faculty entitlement (Advances in Research on Teaching)* (Vol. 38, pp. 1–13). Emerald Publishing Limited.

Ratnam, T., Craig, C., Marcut, I. G., Marie-Christine, D., Mena, J., Doyran, F., Hacıfazlıoğlu, O., Hernández, I. & Peinado-Muñoz, C. (2019). Entitlement attitude: Digging out blind spots. In D. Mihăescu & D. Andron (Eds.), *Proceedings, the 19th biennial conference of international study association on teachers and teaching (ISATT), "Education beyond the crisis: New skills, children's rights and teaching contexts"* (pp. 210–219). Lucian Blaga University Publishing House.

Sannino, A. (2015). The principle of double stimulation: A path to volitional action. *Learning, Culture and Social Interaction*, *6*, 1–15. https://doi.org/10.1016/j.lcsi.2015.01.001

Sannino, A., Engeström, Y., & Lemos, M. (2016). Formative interventions for expansive learning and transformative agency. *The Journal of the Learning Sciences*, *25*, 599–633. https://doi.org/10.1080/10508406.2016.1204547

Schwab, J. J. (1954/1978). Eros and education: A discussion of one aspect of discussion. In I. Westbury & N. Wilkof (Eds.), *Science, curriculum and liberal education: Selected essays* (pp. 105–132). University of Chicago Press.

Tao, J., & Gao, X. (2017). Teacher agency and identity commitment in curricular reform. *Teaching and Teacher Education*, *63*, 346–355. https://doi.org/10.1016/j.tate.2017.01.010

Vygotsky, L. S. (1931/1987). In R. W. Rieber & A. S. Carton (Eds.), *The collected works of L. S. Vygotsky* (Vol. 1). *Thinking and speech* (N. Minick, Trans.). Plenum Press.

Vygotsky, L. S. (1978). *Mind in society: The development of higher psychological processes*. Harvard University Press.

Wei, G. (2021). Imagined professional identity: A narrative inquiry into a Chinese teacher's perezhivaniya in life. *Teaching and Teacher Education*, *102*, 103337. https://doi.org/10.1016/j.tate.2021.103337

Wei, G. (2023a). Principalship in dilemmatic spaces: A narrative inquiry at a Catholic girls' school in Macau. *Asia Pacific Journal of Education*. https://doi.org/10.1080/02188791.2023.2183490

Wei, G. (2023b). Children agency in the Covid-19 pandemic in China. In N. Hopwood & A. Sannino (Eds.), *Agency and transformation: Motives, mediation, and motion* (pp. 336–354). Cambridge University Press.

SECTION II

THE YIN-YANG OF *EXCESSIVE TEACHER/FACULTY ENTITLEMENT* AND THE *BEST-LOVED SELF*

WHEN NOT GETTING YOUR DUE IS YOUR DUE: EXCESSIVE ENTITLEMENT AT WORK

Cheryl J. Craig

Texas A & M University, USA

ABSTRACT

Located at the place where excessive entitlement and the "best-loved self" intersect, this research illustrates what happens when the excessive entitlement of one educator trumps that of another. Then, in a perverse sort of way, those who are excessively entitled may even imply that the other is acting excessively entitled. This is how the "not getting your due is your due" theme emerged in the two exemplary cases that are spotlighted. Excessive entitlement is the belief that one's voice, opinion, and assessment hold more weight than others, whereas the best-loved self is the image to which educators ideally aspire. Given the contested nature of universities, it is not surprising that tensions occur around due – with due being the scholarly attention one legitimately expects to receive. The two featured narratives of experience present "amalgams of experience" lived in multiple academic contexts – with both narrative accounts not turning out as expected. The first story chronicles the choosing of an outstanding doctoral student for a prestigious award; the second one tells how a professor who received two national honors was celebrated at her institution. Through using narrative inquiry as both a research method and a form of representation, the researcher also was able to suggest how people might move beyond excessive entitlement. Narrative inquiry's well-known interpretive tools of fictionalization, broadening, burrowing, and storying and restorying, employed repeatedly throughout this chapter, produced deeper meanings and richer understandings that could result to more generous and informed actions for everyone involved.

Keywords: Excessive entitlement; best-loved self; due; academia; contested academic context; narrative inquiry

Situated at the intersection where excessive entitlement (Ratnam & Craig, 2021) and the "best-loved self" (Craig, 2013, 2017, 2020a; Schwab, 1954/1978) meet, this chapter captures what transpires when the excessive entitlement of one educator trumps the legitimate entitlement of another, detracting from the latter person's sense of best-loved self. Tara Ratnam coined the phrase, excessive entitlement, while observing a teacher demand more of a minoritized student than the student should have to give. Ratnam theorized that similar transactions happen in higher education in professor–student and professor–professor relationships. International case studies involving professors and graduate students have since been created (Ratnam & Craig, 2021), and a scoping literature review (Asadi & Ali, 2021) has been compiled.

This chapter delves further into excessive entitlement and how it inevitably brushes against educators' best-loved selves. The work investigates the place where greediness (excessive entitlement) and longing (best-loved self) intersect in academia. It focuses on what constitutes one's due – that is, what one is entitled to – versus the denial of due that happens when others act – often indirectly behind-the-scenes – in excessively entitled ways that do not leave space for others to thrive. It also addresses the possible directions the field can move to curb excessively entitled behaviors.

BACKGROUND LITERATURE

Key concepts underpinning this chapter's two storied accounts are excessive entitlement, best-loved self, experience, the higher education milieu, and due. Each major idea will now be unpacked.

Excessive Entitlement

Excessive entitlement is the belief that one's voice, opinion, and assessment hold more weight than others with the same or similar expertise. Most fields and professions involve privilege. This means "presidents, priests, princes, presiding judges, police and…pedagogue[s] [have opportunities to] pervert privilege" (Buchanan & Holland, 2021, p. 117). The perversion of privilege afforded by roles, gender, and power dynamics form the seedbed for excessive entitlement. In such instances, outputs are expected that "exceed…inputs" (Craig, 2021, p. 168). As earlier suggested, very little room remains for others to professionally exist. For instance, where progress toward gender equity is concerned, the *Harvard Business Review* reports that it will take 124 years for females to reach parity with males in the workforce (Gallop & Chamorro-Premuzic, 2022), given females are compensated less than males at every faculty rank and receive lesser awards and a lesser share of total awards than their male counterparts (Colby & Fowler, 2020; Hopkins et al., 2019; Meho, 2021). The lightning rod progress of males cumulatively exceeds the snail's change rate for females, as this small example demonstrates.

Best-Loved Self

The best-loved self is the image of self to which educators aspire. This preferred self (Craig, 2023) is part of one's "story to live by" (Clandinin & Connelly, 1998; Connelly & Clandinin, 1999), which is one's identity expressed in narrative terms. The best-loved self is shaped by Eros – the energy of wanting. To Schwab, the teacher's best-loved self seeks "to liberate, not captivate students" (Schwab, 1954/ 1978, p. 125). As for professors, they aim to work alongside students as:

> ...possessor[s] and imparter[s] of disciplines...mentor[s], guide[s], and model[s]; all[ies] of the student[s] against ignorance, participant[s] with student[s] in high adventures into the worlds of intellect and sensibility. (Schwab, 1969, p. 20)

Experience

The greed of excessive entitlement and the longing of the "best-loved self" meet face-to-face and breath-to-breath in the throes of human experience. Experience reaches into the past and is grounded in the present as it presses toward the future. Experience can be educative (productive) or noneducative (nonproductive) (Dewey, 1938). Reflecting on noneducative experience can, however, make it educative, albeit after-the-fact (Lyons, 2010). Thus, experience is both a happening and an undergoing (Dewey, 1938) – all-in-the-same. To demonstrate, humans can simultaneously listen and hear just as they can feel and act (Dewey, 1934).

Higher Education Contexts

Universities are elite institutions that thrive on competition. Those teaching and researching inside of them are considered meritorious if they outperform those who are less meritorious. These faculty advance in position and receive merit pay based on the rank-ordering of their publications and citations and according to their positions and levels of authority. They become increasingly entitled and are provided with additional opportunities for excessive entitlement. This makes university environments highly convoluted and contested, especially when there are two ways one can be considered an outstanding faculty member. The first route is through scholarly achievements that bring honor to the university and increase its standing with respect to other research-intensive places of learning. This is the academy's historical pathway. However, a second route emerged later in the history of academia. This path is the grant route, an approach that does not exist universally across the disciplines – even for those most able (i.e., history, philosophy, physical education, music, multicultural education, etc.). Faculty members who excel in attracting grant (i.e., Science-Technology-Engineering-Mathematics [STEM]) can bring multi-million-dollar awards to their institutions. In the United States, these grants generate indirect costs (IDC) that become divvied up between the university, college, department, and self. Because governments have greatly reduced the amount of state and/or federal support given to higher education, those who bring IDC to their places of work have gained increased prominence and power through their principal investigator (PI) status.

This becomes problematic when PIs earmark a portion of their IDC for their chairs and deans that some then use to curry favor (Campbell-Meiklejohn et al., 2010). Also, some grant-generating faculty produces less top-tier scholarship, which erodes the traditional scholar plotline. Furthermore, the power that IDC wields can have more impact on leaders' decision-making than the research contributions of those advancing their campuses' reputations through scholarship, especially in the case of high achieving scholars who do not ask for or expect special treatment. Given this ramped up neoliberal environment (Peters, 1999), some holding grants act and make demands in extremely excessive ways. This causes excessive entitlement to run wild in academia, particularly when checks and balances have not been put in place.

Due

Entitlement has to do with value distributed along an imagined continuum within a university faculty. On one end of the continuum are those who are benevolent: these faculty members contribute and do not expect much in return. On the other end of the spectrum, however, are professors who are excessively entitled. In contrast to those who are the benevolent, the expectations of the excessively entitled far surpass what would be reasonable for them to ask. They want all the attention – not just a share of it – placed on them. Then, in-between these opposites are faculty who are equity sensitive (Roehling et al., 2010). This group of professors gives respect to their peers and receives respect from their peers in return. Distilled to the essence, they give others their due and anticipate that due will be accorded them when their accomplishments meet the national and international benchmarks of their profession. Faculty on the excessively entitled end of the imagined continuum may become upset by both oblivious and equity sensitive individuals as well as by others excessively entitled like themselves who additionally provoke them. The oblivious and equity sensitive faculty may simply be attempting to live their best-loved selves, but their pleasure in their work coupled with their top-notch performances may be interpreted as them taking up space not meant for them. This, in turn, produces a backlash from their excessively entitled peers who feel jealous of and/or threatened by their excellence.

NARRATIVE INQUIRY RESEARCH METHOD

In lay terms, narrative inquiry conveys "an experience of an experience" (Clandinin & Connelly, 2000). It is "both a view of experience and a way of inquiring into experience;" it is "a methodology that lets experience lead the way" (Pinnegar & Craig, 2023, p. 8). Narrative accounts typically unfold in a three-dimensional inquiry space, patterning Dewey's (1938) philosophy of experience, which simultaneously intertwines temporality, sociality, and place. This narrative inquiry extensively uses fictionalization (i.e., Murphy, 2004), along with the interpretative tools of broadening, burrowing, and storying–restorying

(Connelly & Clandinin, 1990). Together, these devices dig at the roots of due – that is, they query what one is legitimately entitled to.

To further explain, fictionalization masks the identity of key characters in one's research narratives. Sometimes, fictionalization is used to protect the identity of one participant from another. Other times, lifelike accounts from multiple individuals are folded together to form "amalgams of experience" (Craig, 2023), like those shared later. Ultimately, the campuses where my experiences unfolded are never publicly disclosed. Pseudonyms are always used for them. As for individuals, their identities are anonymized.

Broadening is the interpretive device that establishes the broad backdrop of a narrative inquiry. It includes historical facts and points to other cases or even mentions other people who have experienced similar situations. Burrowing, by way of contrast, is the tool that tills the soil of experience to ascertain, through rigorous reflection, details not visible in broad-brushstroke descriptions.

Broadening and burrowing – aided by fictionalization – give way to storying and restorying in narrative inquiry research. When narrative inquirers story and re-story, they add further layers of interpretation to the initial experience. Each time an experience is revisited, it is reinterpreted in a subtly different way. Repeated layers of interpretation reveal back stories that contribute to the understanding of how change happens in context and across time. Change becomes captured through working and reworking the same plotline to identify subtle and not-so-subtle shifts that have taken place.

POSITIONALITY

As the author of this chapter, I am a tenured senior faculty member who has worked in six research-intensive universities in two North American countries, sometimes as a citizen, other times as an immigrant, and still other times as a dual citizen. I have been president of the American Association of Teaching and Curriculum (AATC) and am the current chair of the International Study Association on Teachers and Teaching (ISATT). For years, I have had close contact with many national and international colleagues. From these relationships, for example, I have learned that professorships are only available when a full professor retires or dies in countries like Turkey and Portugal, for example, this means that unlike the United States, the highest ranked position is not always available to those able to earn the promotion, which especially is the case with women.

Another experience I bring to this work is the fact that I have served as the chair of the teaching and teacher education program area and have been a longstanding member and chair of promotion and tenure committees. With my support and supervision, 97 doctoral students have graduated, along with 30 master's students with theses. This means I have been involved in as many high-profile graduate student decisions as I have been part of influential faculty decisions.

It is important for readers to also know that I annually am awarded a moderate amount of grant funding, which generates IDC that is assigned to my department, school, university, and personal research program. I additionally have been awarded noteworthy honors and have served as an editor of some of the field's most prestigious journals. Overall, my career continuum has followed the conventional scholar route.

Because of the background and experiences that I have had, I necessarily present narrative accounts whose stories have been mingled to create amalgams of experience, as foreshadowed. With the intent of uncovering narrative truths (Nelson, 1990; Spence, 1982), the two narrative amalgams I have fictionally created (from numerous possible instances) interlace experiences in multiple milieus lived by other females and me. Also, thinking about my career retrospectively, I have witnessed some administrators, some males, a handful of females, and some of both genders in the STEM and literacy disciplines who, in my view, have expressed excessive entitlement on more than one occasion. Also, at one university, several in the educational psychology department expected due beyond that to which they were entitled because of their elevated view of their discipline. Furthermore, on another campus, the kinesiology faculty placed a higher value on its IDC contributions to the college than they placed on the honorific and financial contributions of other departments. In the latter examples, the fact that educational psychology and kinesiology faculties conducted their investigations using quantitative research methods may also have contributed to their aggrandized views of their disciplines.

The first amalgam of experience I present has to do with the awarding of a graduate student honor; the second experiential amalgam revolves around a planned celebration for a female faculty member who received two national awards in the same year.

AMALGAMS OF EXPERIENCE

Amalgam 1: Graduate Student Example

Background: At the end of each semester, each department in the colleges of the university recognize one graduating PhD student with a scholarly excellence award. The award acknowledges the student's research and community achievements. It includes grades, participation, publications, presentations, group leadership, planning of student events, and the like. The committee is composed of faculty members elected to represent their peers. The awards are announced for the first time at prominent pre-graduation events, which means family members celebrate the happy occasion with those selected to be honored.

Story: Most times the decision as to which graduate student should receive the department award is a tight competitive race. This is particularly the case when the STEM and literacy groups have candidates in the running, due to their underlying belief that their students are more qualified than the others because they represent the core disciplines and attract large grants. But this time around, it was an entirely different matter. One female candidate from another program area appeared head-and-shoulders above the rest. Faculty around the department largely agreed among themselves that the high-achieving/high-contributing female was the clear winner. In fact, some professors openly shared that they were among those who nominated her for the award. Imagine everyone's surprise when another PhD recipient – one whose name had not been mentioned – received the award, which detracted from the best-loved self of the other PhD candidate – the one who was expected to win, given all the hype generated around the honor.

Restorying the story: When the award was announced at the ceremony, it was a moment of awakening for most students and faculty. How could sense be made of a female graduate not receiving an anticipated honor while another unexpected individual received the due?

Many convoluted circumstances may have come into play in this highly competitive decision-making situation. Let us cast a wider net and consider what may have happened. Could it have been that the first student was meant to receive the honor, but the committee discovered in its deliberations that the student's advisor had had another graduated PhD student who was the honoree at the immediate past graduation? This repetition would surely have triggered a hostile response from the excessively entitled faculty members in the department. From this perspective, it simply was not that professor's turn to have a second-in-a-row PhD award-winner – despite it being the female student's fundamental right to receive the honor. The next best thing the selection committee may have wanted to do was to seriously consider the candidates ranking second and third in line for the award. But candidates two and three were very close in their achievements and choosing one over the other would put members of the two most excessively entitled disciplinary areas (i.e., STEM, literacy) at loggerheads with one another. This was not a good solution either. So, then, what might be a satisfactory conclusion to this troublesome circumstance? Could it have been that the decision eventually became one of conferring the award on the right program area (the one from which the multiple nomination letters emanated), but awarding a different graduate student within it? We will never know the logic behind the unanticipated choice as it is always possible that the college or university interfered in the department decision making process. But what we do know is that a female graduate student who was expected to receive her due did not receive it, while another student who possibly never anticipated recognition received the honor many had already associated with someone else.

This is how the phenomenon of not getting your due unfurled in this amalgam of stories from multiple institutions of higher education. This is how the attention given to the excessive entitlement of some ultimately conflicted with the best-loved self of another.

Amalgam 2: Faculty Member Example

Background: In research-intensive universities, faculty are expected to compete for and win awards at state, national, and international levels. These prizes add to their university's ranking and expand its reputation. Such acknowledgments are typically announced at department and college meetings and are shared widely via the university and local media. On this occasion, the awards in question were bestowed on a female professor by a national organization held in highest esteem by the profession.

Story: This story unfolded at the end of the COVID-19 pandemic when large, face-to-face conferences had not yet resumed. Thus, the faculty member received the two awards at a virtual Zoom meeting of an organization attended by national and international colleagues but not by local leaders, although they were welcome to attend. Soon after being awarded the honor, the female professor received a personal call from her male department leader who asked her to prepare a 30-minute online presentation about her award-winning research program for the forthcoming faculty meeting. She was not keen to do so because she had previously experienced a similar situation that turned out badly for a female colleague at another institution. Nevertheless, the professor respected her department leader's decision and came to the virtual session with a prepared slide deck and a planned talk in hand. But what happened next was puzzling. The department leader never invited her to present the speech he had personally requested she prepare. Near the end of the Zoom gathering, however, he did congratulate her on winning the two awards. But what made the situation even more bizarre was that he addressed her not by her professional name (Dr.____), but with the surname of one of the most excessively entitled faculty members in the department, the one to whom he purportedly assigned extra office space due to that person's IDC contributions. This Freudian slip suggested that excessive entitlement had a significant bearing on what happened in the meeting – albeit stoked by what took place behind the scenes. What is more, the department leader offered no apology following the mix-up. Neither did a check-in meeting with the professor take place. The two major awards and the mess created in their aftermath disappeared in thin air – never to be mentioned again.

Restorying the story: One might ask: What possibly could have occurred between the male leader's invitation and the meeting whose agenda he personally planned and enacted? Metaphorically, what took place between the cup and the lip? As with the first story amalgam, sketchy details make it impossible to arrive at any solid conclusion. For example, readers do not know if the male leader happened to share the invitation he issued with someone or others who scuttled the planned celebration because they were excessively entitled and/or had concerns about how other excessively entitled department faculty would react. Or was what happened perhaps something darker? Was the leader himself jealous of the female professor and intentionally set out to embarrass her, making it clear to everyone in the department that those in the disciplines and bringing in mega-dollar grants were respected more than those enhancing the university's reputation with world-class honors? We will never know. But the fact that the female professor was explicitly addressed by an excessively entitled person's name suggested that she did not receive her due as presaged – despite her never demanding or expecting it. Ultimately, the leader's behavior, whether self- or other-driven, temporarily quashed her best-loved self, which to that point in time, had been fully satisfied by the original online awards event.

Then, in an unanticipated turn of events came a surprise "that upset the expected" (Bruner, 2002, p. 8). The double-awarded professor, who initially had put the awards behind her, seemed disappointed in how she was treated in the faculty meeting. After all, being called another person's name – an excessively person's name at that – was unconscionable – by anyone's standards. She began to experience internal waves of excessive entitlement, which is not surprising, given that excessively entitled feelings are an "altogether human tendency..." (Doyran & Hacıfazlıoğlu, 2021, p. 20). Here, we see how those who are excessively entitled have a distinct way of inciting like behaviors in other faculty as well. But this time around, a subtle shift happened. While it is true that the professor's legitimate accomplishment was disparaged in the online faculty meeting, it is also true that she recognized that she still had a powerful force at her disposal: She was in charge of how she responded to the incident as a well-respected female role-model. Cognizant of her personal power, her fleeting bout of excessive entitlement morphed into an empowered kind of entitlement (Ratnam, this volume) where she shifted her attention to the impact of the situation on everyone: all known others around her and her – not just herself exclusively.

INTERPRETIVE TRANSITION

This chapter features two carefully developed story amalgams: one about graduate students and awards; the other, concerning a celebration that was not for a tenured professor who was doubly awarded by an esteemed organization. In both instances, the idea of individuals anticipating due – and then not receiving what they were led to expect or promised – prevailed. In both cases, potential plotlines were pieced together based on the barebones facts available. In between, there was plenty of conjecture and interpretation – with some meanings being deeply nested and convoluted, and others being shadowy and mean and even verging on sinister. At the end of the day, the whole academy's history sets the backdrop for the conferring of awards and what happens to people, their relationships, and their preferred selves in the process of winning honors and in their aftermath.

So far, we have learned that nothing is as simple as it seems in academia. The experiences and mindsets that professors bring to their work *and* the experiences and mindsets that they take away from it complicate even simple matters. Also, as the literature introduced earlier suggests, to get past excessive entitlement is to become more equity sensitive. But how might that be accomplished, given the plethora of complexities evident in the two small story amalgams featured in this chapter?

CONCLUSION

Put otherwise, given the circumstances, how might we move beyond excessive entitlement? How might due be exchanged in more reciprocal ways? Returning to the selection of the graduate student award, the winner could have been chosen by independent ballot, with the task fully centered on the nominated students and their accomplishments. This way, for example, other students' prior winning and who their doctoral advisors were would not cloud the decision-making process. These matters would have no bearing whatsoever on the overall decision. Individual student candidates would be seen and treated as I-Thou's rather than being made into I-It's, judged among many other I-It's in context (Buber, 1970). They would receive respect as unique persons in one-of-a-kind circumstances.

As for the awards celebration scenario, colleges need to establish departmental/institutional processes and systems that outline what will happen when faculty receive noteworthy external awards. Like graduate students, faculty deserve to be treated as I-Thou's and not downgraded to I-It's through others' questionable decision-making interventions. Once again, advance preparation would ensure that neither leaders nor professors would experience discomfort and/or feel compromised in the process. In this way, more informed and just actions would result through empowered entitlement (Ratnam, this book) – with everyone becoming more satisfied with how honor individually and collectively is bestowed. Lastly, weighing these possibilities in advance and leaning into them by carefully following agreed upon decisions would ensure that an attitude of generous scholarship (Craig, 2020b) informed by the best-loved self would prevail, with future interactions being less manipulated and more genuinely celebratory. These ideas make sense, given that all faculty have more important grants and/or scholarship to attend to than to be focused on how those deserving of honor and respect are mistreated – on and off the scene – by the excessively entitled.

REFERENCES

Asadi, L., & Ali, S. (2021). A literature review of the concept of entitlement and the theoretical informants of excessive teacher entitlement. In T. Ratnam & C. J. Craig (Eds.), *Understanding excessive teacher and faculty entitlement* (pp. 17–24). Emerald Publishing Limited.

Bruner, J. S. (2002). *Making stories: Law, literature, life*. Harvard University Press.

Buber, M. (1970). *I and Thou*. Simon and Schuster.

Buchanan, J., & Holland, W. (2021). Learning difficulties: On how knowing everything hinders learning anything new. In T. Ratnam & C. J. Craig (Eds.), *Understanding excessive teacher and faculty entitlement: Digging at the roots* (pp. 117–131). Emerald Publishing Limited.

Campbell-Meiklejohn, D. K., Bach, D. R., Roepstorff, A., Dolan, R. J., & Frith, C. D. (2010). How the opinion of others affects our valuation of objects. *Current Biology, 20*(13), 1165–1170.

Clandinin, D. J., & Connelly, F. M. (1998). Stories to live by: Narrative understandings of school reform. *Curriculum Inquiry, 28*(2), 149–164.

Clandinin, D. J., & Connelly, F. M. (2000). *Narrative inquiry: Experience and story in qualitative research*. John Wiley & Sons.

Colby, G., & Fowler, C. (2020, December 9). Data snapshot looks at full-time women faculty and faculty of color. *Academe Blog*. https://academeblog.org/2020/12/09/data-snapshot-looks-at-full-time-women-faculty-and-faculty-of-color/

Connelly, F. M., & Clandinin, D. J. (1990). Stories of experience and narratives of inquiry. *Educational Researcher, 19*(5), 2–14.

Connelly, F. M., & Clandinin, D. J. (Eds.). (1999). *Shaping a professional identity: Stories of educational practice*. Teachers College Press.

Craig, C. J. (2013). Teacher education and the best-loved self. *Asia Pacific Journal of Education, 33*(3), 261–272.

Craig, C. J. (2017). Sustaining teachers: Attending to the best-loved self in teacher education and beyond. In X. Zhu, A. L. Goodwin, & H. Zhang (Eds.), *Quality of teacher education and learning* (pp. 193–205). Springer.

Craig, C. J. (2020a). *Curriculum making, reciprocal learning, and the best-loved self*. Palgrave Macmillan.

Craig, C. J. (2020b). Generous scholarship: A counternarrative for the region and the academy. In C. J. Craig, L. Turchi, & D. M. McDonald (Eds.), *Cross-disciplinary, cross-institutional collaboration in teacher education* (pp. 351–365). Palgrave Macmillan.

Craig, C. J. (2021). Back in the middle (again): Working in the midst of professors and graduate students. In T. Ratnam & C. J. Craig (Eds.), *Understanding excessive teacher and faculty entitlement: Digging at the roots* (pp. 165–178). Emerald Publishing Limited.

Craig, C. J. (2023). The intersection where excessive entitlement and the best-loved self meet: Stories of experience. In *Studying teaching and teacher education* (pp. 231–242). Emerald Publishing Limited.

Dewey, J. (1934). *Art as experience*. Putnam.

Dewey, J. (1938). *Experience and education*. Basic Books.

Doyran, F., & Hacıfazlıoğlu, Ö. (2021). In between wellness and excessive entitlement: Voices of faculty members. In *Understanding excessive teacher and faculty entitlement* (Vol. 38, pp. 191–204). Emerald Publishing Limited.

Gallop, C., & Chamorro-Premuzic, P. (2022, April 18). Stop criticizing women and start questioning men instead. *Harvard Business Review*. https://hbr.org/2022/04/stop-criticizing-women-and-start-questioning-men-instead&a=D&source=docs&ust=1656769776071742&aug=AOvVaw0A7Boky4DW_8oeHb_l1XoB

Hopkins, N., Reicher, S., Stevenson, C., Pandey, K., Shankar, S., & Tewari, S. (2019). Social relations in crowds: Recognition, validation and solidarity. *European Journal of Social Psychology*, 49(6), 1283–1297.

Lyons, N. (Ed.). (2010). Reflection and reflective inquiry: Critical issues, evolving conceptualizations, contemporary claims and future possibilities. In *Handbook of reflection and reflective inquiry* (pp. 3–22). Springer.

Meho, L. I. (2021). The gender gap in highly prestigious international research awards 2001–2020. *Qualitative Science Studies*, 2(3). https://direct.mit.edu/qss/article/2/3/976/103157/The-gender-gap-in-highly-prestigious-international

Murphy, M. S. (2004). *Understanding children's knowledge: A narrative inquiry into school experiences*. Unpublished doctoral dissertation, University of Alberta, Edmonton, Canada.

Nelson, H. L. (1990). *Injured identities, narrative repair*. Fordham University.

Peters, M. (1999). Neoliberalism. In *The encyclopedia of philosophy of education*. http://www.vusst.hr/ENCYCLOPAEDIA/neoliberalism.htm

Pinnegar, E., & Craig, C. J. (2023). Tribute to Jean Clandinin. In C. J. Craig, J. Menho, & R. G. Kane (Eds.), *Teaching and teacher education in international contexts: ISATT 40th anniversary yearbook* (pp. 7–9). Emerald Publishing Limited.

Ratnam, T., & Craig, C. J. (Eds.). (2021). *Understanding excessive teacher and faculty entitlement*. Emerald Publishing Limited.

Roehling, M. V., Roehling, P. V., & Boswell, W. R. (2010). The potential role of organizational setting in creating "entitled" employees: An investigation of the antecedents of equity sensitivity. *Employee Responsibilities and Rights Journal*, 22, 133–145. https://doi.org/10.1007/s10672-009-9130-6

Schwab, J. J. (1954/1978). Eros and education: A discussion of one aspect of discussion. In I. Westbury & N. Wilkof (Eds.), *Science, curriculum and liberal education: Selected essays*. University of Chicago Press.

Schwab, J. J. (1969). The practical: A language for curriculum. *The School Review*, 78, 1–23.

Spence, D. P. (1982). Narrative truth and theoretical truth. *Psychoanalytic*, 51(1), 43–62. https://doi.org/10.1080/21674086.1982.11926984

CHALLENGING STRUCTURES OF EXCESSIVE ENTITLEMENT IN CURRICULA, TEACHING, AND LEARNING THROUGH DIALOGIC ENGAGEMENT

Richard D. Sawyer[a] and Joe Norris[b]

[a]Washington State University Vancouver, USA
[b]Brock University, Canada

ABSTRACT

In this chapter, we purport that "excessive entitlement" is directly linked to concepts of selflidentity with the belief that how we come to regard self in relation to the Other is implicitly and explicitly taught. We view excessive entitlement as a manifestation of the privilege and infallibility of educators who take for granted the correctness of their actions. Through a critical examination of personal stories, theoretical literature, and common school practices, we create a collage of thoughts that highlight some of the complex factors that intersect with excessive entitlement, albeit considering what may be determined "excessive" and by whom.

We use a dialogic format, in this chapter, but do not engage in an actual duoethnography. We address the following questions: How does one (a) create an ethical habitus, constantly being aware of one's responsibility toward the Other, (b) reflexively and humbly practice self-accountability in a manner that recognizes one's positionality and status that is grounded in historical privileged, personal power dynamics, and systems of oppression, (c) develop dialogic ways of being in a neoliberal ethos of systemic accountability within prescriptive curricula, and (d) as teacher educators, assist students in understanding and practicing such dispositions.

We discuss how developing dialogic ways of being, treating others with respect, practicing humility in the face of other people, and learning to respect and build on difference disrupt excessive entitlement. We also explore complexities around the attempt to create "safe spaces" for students, given risks of self-deception and appropriation of students' meaning-making.

Keywords: Excessive teacher entitlement; collaborative reflexive practices; dialogic; duoethnography; neoliberalism; polyvocal

Unison: This chapter is a form of dialogic research, written in a polyvocal style. We, its authors and cocreators of *duoethnography* (Norris & Sawyer, 2012; Sawyer & Norris, 2013), employ some of its features – although we do not consider it a duoethnography – as we examine past experiences and beliefs using the frame "excessive entitlement." With the belief that a duoethnography is both a research methodology and pedagogical approach (Brown & Barrett, 2017), we suggest that duoethnography can counter excessive entitlement by modeling a disposition of being in the world that invites an "I-Thou" relationship with the Other as opposed to an "I-It" (Buber, 1958) one, with excessive entitlement being one manifestation of I-It.

We write in the first person, using the term "unison" when speaking as one voice and "Joe" and "Rick" to identify each of us separately. Juxtaposing singular and plural voices, we highlight a sense of unity within difference. Still, we recognize that "identity" is an ambiguous construct with multiple definitions as no one is truly separate from the Other. Our definitions are (a) fluid as we believe identity can change in the "face of the Other" (Burggraeve, 1999) and (b) interrelational/communal, as we also believe that, by being dialogic, we recognize the impact we have on each other. We are not singular beings. We not only influence each other's beliefs – a dialogic stance also brings responsibility to the Other:

> A relationship between persons that is characterized in more or less degree by the element of inclusion may be termed a dialogical relation…instinct enters into communion with the fellow-man and into responsibility for him as an allotted and entrusted realm of life. (Buber, 1947, p. 125)

By being polyvocal, we challenge the hegemony of the expository essay's position as being the primary style of academic discourse, which could be considered a form of systemic excessive entitlement, privileging one form of knowledge dissemination over another. It also decenters a solitary voice by creating a "third-space" (Bhabha & Rutherford, 1990) between each author where readers can enter the conversation, juxtaposing their present position with the coauthors. The style implicitly communicates that meanings are not fixed in a text; rather, they are constantly recreated when encountering an Other, in this case, Rick and Joe.

Also, its polyvocal style does not use organizational traditions such as methodology, literature review, themes, and conclusions. It is more organic and holistic in style, with ideas flowing naturally. It is written as a conversation. Some readers have informed us that they have found this format to be more accessible, enjoyable, and invitational, as they naturally entered the conversation internally speaking between the coauthors.

Its informality, however, does not imply the lack of rigor. A literature review is conducted, as evident below, but rather than being a separate section, it is integrated where appropriate. The natural style suggests that the conversation took place over one setting. This is far from the case.

> Like *My Dinner with Andre*, (Malle, 1981) a collection of conversations, amassed over a period of time, are distilled into a cogent summary that has the appearance of one conversation [... ...] Similar to the making of a good scotch, it goes through many rigorous conversations/distillations over a period on time, with aging periods between the conversations. (Norris & Sawyer, 2020, p. 404)

In our early work with duoethnography, we sometimes took notes on road trips to meetings and conferences. We also made notes separately and checked in from time to time, writing in a conversational style and bouncing ideas off each other. The scripts (later defined as a duoethnography) emerged over time. More recently, *Zoom* played a major role. For this manuscript, we met four times over 6 months with online software transcribing the last three sessions for us. We also wrote individually and made notes between sessions as ideas came to us and emailed proposal drafts back and forth. Ultimately, using the final transcription as a guide, we made extensive analyses of our collective life experiences that assisted us in coming to understand excessive entitlement beyond a denotative definition.

But we stop short of calling this chapter a duoethnography. While it shares many characteristics such as its polyvocal style, it lacks the transtemporal nature of *currere* (Pinar, 1975). We do not use the present to reconceptualize the past, nor the past to reconceptualize the future, a tenet that we consider essential to duoethnography. As well, unlike our first duoethnography where we discussed differences in sexual orientation and highlighted how dialogue about those differences reinformed us, we found ourselves more in agreement on the topic. We encourage duoethnographers to have and take different perspectives. Our conversation was/is in the form of collaborative, nonlineal "hermeneutic spirals" (Motahari, 2008, p. 99) of theories and practice as we made revisions during each encounter. The following is our final synthesis.

In our conversations, we returned to the value of difference as a counterbalance to excessive entitlement. We view excessive entitlement as a manifestation of the privilege and infallibility of educators who take for granted the correctness of their actions. This narcissistic, self-serving stance forecloses self-awareness and equitable relations with others (Craig, 2020; Ratnam & Craig, 2021). Excessive entitlement extends beyond the individual to include structural components, including, for example, societal norms, school policies, educational traditions, and sometimes even laws (Ratnam, 2021; Sawyer, 2024).

THE CONVERSATION

Joe: So here we are again, Rick, having another dialogic conversation where we hope that our collective insights and experiences can assist both of us in expanding our understanding of what is meant by *excessive entitlement*.

Rick: So, we've been working together for almost 20 years now, and almost all of our work together has "implicitly" examined the topic of excessive entitlement, without labeling it as such, and the constructed regulatory codes of the symbolic power embedded within traditions and ideologies (Bourdieu, 1983, 1991). Writing this chapter has given us an opportunity to think about how our work with developing dialogic ways of being, about treating others with respect, about practicing humility in the face of other people, and about learning to respect and build on difference disrupts excessive entitlement, a topic we have never explicitly explored before. This now gives us an opportunity to make new connections with this topic and reconceptualize our work with duoethnography (Sawyer & Norris, 2015).

Joe: …and through it, ourselves…

Rick: …and once more intertwine and pull a few new strands together.

Joe: I think for a few reasons, it's timely. I must admit that I'm so discouraged right now. When reading the news, I find there's a lot of what we could call "self-righteousness." The call for parental rights is being co-opted by some to disavow and oppress others who are different from themselves. Right now, in Canada, we are experiencing a lot of transphobic and homophobic marches, and there seems to be a lot of excessive entitlement to the rhetoric. However, I do feel a bit of hope in that some are standing up and saying, "No." There's a strong counternarrative against the homophobia and transphobia. But I still feel discouraged. I thought we, as a society, had grown beyond that. I feel the need for this book, and I also feel the need for this conversation, for this chapter…

Rick: So, let's bounce ideas off each other and see where it goes…

Unison: We will edit later.

Rick: Joe, to build on your "discouragement," there is a tension between this being the best of times and the absolute worst of times. Yes, there are many people talking truthfully and bravely about equity in meaningful ways; but then, there other people either appropriating and subverting this progressive message or actually directly erasing it.

One of the questions that we're going to consider is how dominant discourses frame and propel excessive entitlement forward, normalizing power for a particular group of people.

Joe: And for me, some of that means both of us enter our conversation with a sense of humility, saying, "We don't know."! We are here to learn from this conversation with the hope that our readers will make some connections that will be of use to them. As Barone (1990) suggests, we use "the narrative text as an occasion for conspiracy" (p. 305), an occasion for us to collectively reflect…

Unison: Nor do we want to profess.

Joe: I find it kind of ironic that we're called professors because professing is far from the approach that I take. I prefer "invite" and "question" to "profess." "Profess" has a trace of entitlement to it.

Buber (1947) warns us about "self-righteousness," and I believe that anyone can become entrenched and fixed in one's perspective and, in that, fail to learn and grow. Professors are not immune. Nor is an ideology. Both the far right and far left can have such entrenchment as characterized by Captain Nemo in *Twenty Thousand Leagues Under the* Sea (Verne, 1874) who waged war to end war. So, I ask, "How do we teach humility in the face of self-righteousness?"

I think that the so-called "freedom movement" in North America right now is oppressive and moves us in a dangerous direction. As a personal example from Canada, the freedom convoys that we had as our response to COVID-19 policies, from my perspective, demonstrated excessive entitlement in the name of freedom. I can no longer look at anybody flying the Canadian flag in the same way again as it was used as an icon by self-righteous protestors. While I question nationalism, regionalism, and highschoolism that encourage an I-It relationship with others, I find that the flag has now come to represent the radical right that moves toward hate, and that this group's rhetoric is an example of excessive entitlement. Frankl's (1963) recommendation "that the Statue of Liberty on the East Coast be supplemented by a Statue of Responsibility on the West Coast" (pp. 208–209) is apropos. Responsible action takes the Other into account.

Rick: Right! And I think they're also the voice of a corporate structure that really just wants to empower and engorge itself. And so, they flame hatred among dissatisfied people who feel they are losing a sense of entitlement in a changing world. And then, there is the corporate influence. For example, recently, I've been reading about the fossil fuel industry in Alberta, which has been actually trying to control some of the curriculum of public schools.

Joe: That's partly why I've accepted writing this chapter and the cause beyond it – to provide a counternarrative. I ask, "How do we create narratives that help us question our own positionalities?" That is part of our challenge. But we must be careful not to turn to finger pointing that moves us to self-righteousness – "that we're okay, but everybody else isn't." It's very important for us to question all of our rhetoric and enter into this project with this in mind. As we emulate with duoethnographic work, "Can one dwell between the space of you and me?" as opposed to waving another dangerous flag.

Rick: It's incredibly difficult to do...to talk about other people and examine your relationship to them with a genuine sense of humility and humanity. And I think that's our goal with this chapter – to examine excessive entitlement in order to uncover deeper structures that marginalize teachers as well as those who express complex onto-epistemology ways of being that threaten dominant and often narrow structures.

Joe: Yeah. So, for me, part of this type of research is always entering into it with a certain amount of self-doubt. So, I turn the lens on myself, looking at past experiences with the aim of reconceptualizing them.

Recently, I applied for a deanship position, and part of the institution's mission statement was that they wanted their students to enter the world with "confidence."

And maybe, that's partly why I didn't get the job because while I said yes to "confidence," I also questioned it, by suggesting adding humility, because I think we all have the responsibility to question self. That's a very different way of being in the world but one, if practiced, abates excessive entitlement. My hope is that by being reflexive (Miller, 2011), modeling it, and writing about it through personal narratives for our teacher education students, they would come to regard such a disposition as an essential part of their teacher identity (Watson, 2006). I believe that this can help us move us beyond excessive entitlement.

Over this chapter, we will reflect on four interconnected stories about the teacher/student relationship, that exemplify my personal struggle/challenge to move beyond self, as a teacher, employing Scudder's question, "How can one teach with authority as an expert in a discipline, without violating the integrity of students?" (1968, p. 133). It is a stance that Henderson (1992) may call an "unbounded question" (p. 50), one that we can ask daily but one that we will never fully answer. We can only respond to such questions as they guide our practice. They are "haunting" questions (Norris, 2004, p. 14).

Joe Story 1: A few years ago, I gave drama students an assignment to find different styles of performing similar material because I wanted them to explore how the material changes meaning, based upon the style of representation. One student approached me, and, as expected, she asked, "Can I do it like Disney?"

My analysis of her was that she was caught in that rut. Everything that she did was Disney. Everything she did was like a musical and for readers who have watched one of the contest reality shows; some of the judges made it very clear that they did not like musicals. It is a different genre.

I was hesitant, and I believe that she could tell that I was hesitant. As I looked into her hopeful eyes, I questioned myself, my power and said, "If you think it will work? See how you can make it work?" and she went off and did a very effective but clichéd Disney scene.

Joe: Now is that excessive (and for whom)? Maybe, maybe not. But I do think that it is an example of a habit of recognizing a teacher's power and one that I try to emulate.

Rick: That's an interesting story both about the student *and* about our relationship to students – how do we ask our students to break their broken-record routinized way of seeing the world. We have a responsibility to do that – as we build and maintain a relationship with our students. There are just so many levels of ethics involved in this situation. How do we act? How do we ask our students to be moral? And, perhaps most importantly, how do we treat them in ways that are moral? Part of the behavior is, of course, just trying to "do no harm." But to be ethical, we as teachers need to listen to and build on students' funds of knowledge, voice, and inherent value, inviting them to explore with us.

Joe: Rick, how do you scaffold the learning of your undergraduate and graduate students to expand their funds of knowledge from the traditional means – ends curriculum that they are accustomed to, to situational, interpretive, and critical – theoretical ones that Aoki (2005a) discusses?

Rick: Well, I think to do this, we need to create a lived and embodied curriculum, one that is organic to the lived experiences of the students and – in relation to excessive entitlement – also focused on larger power dynamics. But, of course, it's difficult to structure a class in which the students and teacher together act as scaffolds to begin to unpack and understand the tension between the planned and lived curriculum that Aoki mentions.

For me, as the teacher trying to structure a meaningful dynamic, I try to consider many of the nested and shifting contexts. First are the broader structural issues – those deeply entrenched discourses central to North America which stem back to Europe. These discourses privilege Caucasian male property owners at the expense of all others (Tozer et al., 2009).

There are also public schools and school districts, which are both artifacts and channels of these entrenched traditions, which make these traditions – imbued with ideology – appear normative. Examples here include accountability measures which sort students according to predefined norms defaulting to these traditions: some students readily advance into more academic and enriched programs, while others track into basic skills, industrial education, or, in more extreme cases, prison. It's not surprising, for example, that schools were one of the main instruments of settler colonialism with First Nations and Indigenous boarding schools. It's especially tragic when students begin to internalize these messages. Bill Pinar (Pinar et al., 2008) mentions that a leading purpose of public education is to forge student identity.

And then, we have the personal level. This includes our critical consciousness and lived positionality in relation to these discourses and traditions, again, constantly shifting are crucial to our challenging excessive entitlement. How do teachers and administrators critically examine themselves as agents of these traditions?

And these are just a few of the complex dynamics undergirding excessive entitlement. So how do I try to combat excessive entitlement in my own practice? Well, I have to say that although I relentlessly try to combat this problem, I'm sure I constantly fall short. My own sense of inadequacy here does, however, propel me forward.

Joe: Can you give me an example or a story?

Rick: Let me describe one hopefully helpful assignment that I do in a teacher research class. In this class, I have students do a photovoice study. We do this as a self-study since we examine our own perceptions of culturally sustaining assessment in relation to each other's views. Educators normally think of assessment as being established from an infallible and external location (the teacher authority), which is then used to evaluate the difference between what students know and what we want them to know. We all know this example of deficit pedagogy, but we don't always recognize it as an example of excessive entitlement. Correct answers are often culturally biased.

So in this photovoice assignment, I have students examine their own thinking about culturally sustaining assessment, so that we learn from each other, expand our views, and begin to construct routines that critique and dismantle our thinking, at least, in excessively entitled ways. And part of this assignment calls for a critical examination of the relationship between our thinking and larger systems of power. In this way, we also begin to challenge our thinking about these systems as the first step to begin to reconceptualize our own stance toward them. We work in dialogic pairs in this assignment, thus, ideally, creating a generative and heteroglossic (Bakhtin, 1981) dynamic.

I take part in this assignment as well. Yes, I'm guiding it, but I'm also one of the participants, and I learn about myself as I learn about the students and really the changing nature of the hegemonic forces acting to regulate and colonize different cultures. I think one way to challenge excessive entitlement in schools is to live within generative and collaborative educational situations.

I don't know. This is one thing I do. But it's difficult as a teacher to be truly present (and be accountable to others) and to create generative multiplicity within curriculum (Aoki, 1993). And, of course, it's important to be aware of students' lived experiences as well as co-constructed curricular plans to attempt to dismantle the broader socialcultural structures of oppression are dynamic and ephemeral. And different situations call for different measures.

Ethics are central to the work of Aoki. Joe, how do you see our responsibility as educators to engage with our students ethically?

Joe: A comment by Nell Noddings also relates and haunts me:

> As we build an ethic on caring, and as we examine education under its guidance, we shall see that the greatest obligation of educators inside and outside formal schooling is to nurture the ethical ideas of those with whom they come in contact. (1984, p. 49)

Rick: Yes!

Joe: Yet, at the same time, it's problematic because different cultures have different perspectives. Different people have different perspectives, and currently, the homophobia and transphobia in Canada is under the rhetoric of protecting family values. So, even that ethic of care is problematic because it, like most tools, can be used to liberate and can be used to subjugate.

Rick: People can – and do – care for others in very self-serving ways.

Joe: Yeah, I completely agree. And Rick, both of us, I believe, define ourselves as left of center and will come across that way in this chapter, but at the same time, I ask, "What is the common good; how is it being defined and co-opted; and by whom?" For example, standardized tests have always claimed to be for the common good, i.e., "Do well on the test and succeed in university." We know there's statistical evidence of systemic racism within the standardized test itself, item analysis for example, adjusts to the norm. And we can go on...

Rick: Standardized tests have NEVER been for the common good, rather for the "uncommon" elite.

Joe: We can also use the rhetoric of the common good to help control people because they want what's best for their kids, and that means getting the best score on a very narrow perspective of what the world is. That's definitely not the common good. That's excessive entitlement; that's assimilation.

Rick: So, for me, part of excessive entitlement goes back to the whole concept of the curriculum from an axiological perspective: what are the values that undergird the curriculum? If students see themselves as merely consumers of knowledge and feel compelled to always "please the teacher," we've failed.

Joe: Rick, I find weaning students from seeking teacher adulations a constant struggle as I find when they do, they ironically, most often create better work. Any suggestions?

Rick: I know. This is difficult. This gets back to Aoki's belief in encouraging students to find their own voice. I don't seek an authentic voice – as the one essential voice – but rather a polyvocal work in progress, such as in the photo-voice project I described. I don't know. I try to give them as much space as I can in the classroom. Sometimes, I don't think they're even aware of my presence...

Joe: Can the curriculum itself with its testing regime be considered excessive entitlement, as we have a small group of people deciding what is the common good? That's excessive to me. And it's systemic violence. And it's...

Rick: For me, I go as far as calling it systemic bullying of children.

Joe: Me too.

Rick: Yes. I wrote a paper with Steve Farenga and Dan Ness (Farenga et al., 2015), in which we discussed standardized testing as a form of systemic bullying of kids. And it's not only the kids who are lucky enough to know more than one language or feel open to love in non-normative ways, it's all the kids – it is everyone. We are all harmed by biased and hateful forms of accountability.

Joe: Like a frog being boiled, we are largely unaware what's beyond the frame. "Like Neo, do we dare take the red pill" (Wachowski & Wachowski, 1999)? This connects with Chomsky:

> The smart way to keep people passive and obedient is to strictly limit the spectrum of acceptable opinion, but allow very lively debate within that spectrum – even encourage the more critical and dissident views. That gives people the sense that there's free thinking going on, while all the time the presuppositions of the system are being reinforced by the limits put on the range of the debate. (1998, p. 43)

Rick: Yes. That's another layer of excessive entitlement. When we look at curriculum, we need to think about the values that undergird it. What are those values, and what do they mean? We're revamping yet again our teacher preparation programs at my university in line with benchmarked and precisely (and externally) defined standards, right? And all the standards are presented as neutral. Although a consideration for "culturally sustaining pedagogy" is given as part of the standards, the language is so generic that it can mean anything. Instead, I suggest that we frame what we do with a sense of ethics focused on the value of difference – on an acknowledgment of the conceptual richness of multiplicity and different onto-epistemologies. And of course, as Tom Barone (1995) continues to advocate, for more space for art.

Joe: So, it's not only about accepting our students based on where they are. We have a moral responsibility to change them at the same time, especially if we feel that they're hateful individuals. Education is about growth, but who decides? So, it gets really difficult to do. This comes back to the concept of invitation. It, in the long run, has more to do with an invitation to change than demanding change because you don't get that same form of resistance, of back-and-forth student/teacher power. It reminds me of a story from early in my university teaching.

Joe Story 2: I was teaching a concept about directing in my teacher education class and had the Dean of the Faculty of Fine Arts observing me. The class was asked to take notes when watching the next set of peer performances. One of the students said, "I don't like taking notes; it ruins the experience." I responded, "Well, as a director, you will need to take notes, so this will give you some practice with that."

I reflected on this in my teaching journal, connecting it to Scudders' question about teacher/student power dynamics, adding my own thoughts. I called it the "common dance of resistance/insistence" where, when students resist, teachers insist, and explored how we could break such a cycle. The next class, I read some of my theoretical musings to the students.

After reading it, she (I can still remember her name) said, "You're talking about you and me, right?" How astute!

Later, I spoke to the Dean, explaining both the initial event and my follow-up. He had no problem with my initial act, while I found it excessive.

Again, this is about the power of the teacher and how I question myself and my own power. I try to teach in a way that invites change by creating a collaborative dance. But could this be manipulation? I still have my jury out on that, even after many, many years.

Rick: Well, let me ask you this, since this paper is about your creating an ethical habitat (for education), how do you do that in your life, in your teaching, in your career? How do you face that question and try to have that guide you?

Joe: I would say, by:

- Implicitly questioning myself.
- Explicitly modeling it with my students.
- Giving reflective practice assignments.
- Holding debriefing circles where varied perspectives are accepted and celebrated.

Joe Story 3: I was a participant in a drama exercise where the facilitator asked each of us to toss a big bouncy ball and then analyze how we threw it. When I threw my ball, I put a back spin on it, and it always came back to me. I found that it could be used as a metaphor for the way that I teach. I throw ideas out, but I'm also ready for them to come back and respond to what I receive, making the relationship dialogic. I try to set up situations that are two-way. In keeping with Freire (1986), I send out invitations (consumers) with their responses (producers) directing what we do next. It is an emergent (Osberg & Biesta, 2008) curriculum, not a prescriptive one that is excessively, top-down. So, I would add to the list "the ethic of care that continually listens and responds in a way that treats the other with respect."

EXCEPT when I perceive potential violence directed toward another that seldom, but occasionally happened when I taught junior high students.

Rick: That's good. It's about how we're positioned in relation to a situation. You know what is our positionality, and it's always, it's always changing, and we have to be aware, we have to be open to reflexivity and to change in ourselves in relation to greater systems of privilege. Yes, we need, as Jersild (1952) says, to face ourselves because we are fallible. We now have a culture of specialists and experts, and by their positions, they know more than others, and they don't make mistakes. But once you begin with that premise, you're in trouble. The concept of infallibility protects people as they then engage in harmful projections, shadowing our students with our anxieties, fears, deficits, and even wishes. So, we have to be really careful.

Joe: Do you have an example of when your students witnessed you being fallible in a way that gave them courage to move beyond fear to taking risks, perhaps by using artistic musings?

Rick: Recently, I "came out of the closet" to my teacher preparation students. This was the first time that I did this in a long teaching career. Immediately, in the same class, other students began to describe their intersectional identities. This example isn't about fallibility so much as vulnerability, which is a companion to the acknowledgment of fallibility as a teacher. And yes, as I try to teach in generative and dynamic ways, I bring in the arts. Recently, I had my students listen to Boni Wozolek's recordings made by her students of "what learning sounds like" (Wozolek, 2022, p. 1). The subsequent discussion in class was about the limited ways that we consider learning and really our root metaphors of what we think learning is and the boundaries of our "authority" as facilitators of learning.

One thing I try to explore is how as teachers we want to change our students – and why. I remember reading an article by Alim and Paris (2017), who were discussing culturally responsive pedagogy. And in it was a line that really, at first, I didn't understand. They wrote about valuing our students' intuitive knowledge. I kept thinking, Yeah, we're leading them – we're trying to transform them into our own likeness or social/educational ideal. And we keep enforcing the deficit between what we want them to know and to do, and they're already existing, inner knowledge – grounded in diverse cultures and funds of knowledge. Yet our goal is to transform them into something else – into this neat circle or square. And this is another example of why we need an ethical framework to guide our actions.

Joe: This reminds me of the work of colleagues at Santa Rosa Junior College in California (Harrison et al., In Press) on translanguaging "an approach to language pedagogy that affirms and leverages students' diverse and dynamic language practices in teaching and learning" (Vogel & García, 2017). This is more mutualistic than conforming to a hegemony in whatever form. Rick, I recall you talking about a similar experience when you taught senior high school English.

Rick: When I taught high school English, I always tried to consider language in a fluid and hybrid way. We played with the overlap of different vernaculars of English as well as other languages, such as Spanish (Sawyer & Liggett, 2012).

In terms of curriculum, I think we have to value emotion and imagination over externally imposed rubrics. Tom (1984) reminds us that teaching is a moral craft, and that we need to teach to support the common good, not just benefit a particular group of empowered people. In fact, we should be looking at the groups of people who are the most powerless and voiceless and use how we work *with them* as our measure for success.

Joe: This connects with Chopra's concept of alchemy:

> In the West, Wizard is primarily thought to be a magician who practices alchemy, turning base metal into gold. Alchemy also exists in India (in fact, it was invented there), but the word alchemy is really a code word that stands for turning human beings into gold, turning our base qualities of fair, ignorance, hatred, and shame into the most precious stuff there is: love and fulfillment. So a teacher who can teach you how to turn yourself into a free, loving person is by definition an alchemist – and has always been one. (1995, p. 3)

Rick: Yeah, yeah, it's a good quote. And then I think it's also important to frame our actions with views of social justice and Paolo Freire's (1986) concerns for liberation pedagogy and making sure that we give voice to people to understand larger systems so that they have the power to change things themselves. So, we're not just the, you know, sage on the stage. But we're part of this together as the collective good, and collective engagement, not individualistic effort.

Joe: I've transformed the adage, "Don't be the sage on the stage, be the guide on the side" extending it as I also question the "guide on the side," as even the guide may have a little too much power. I add being the "joker in the middle" who is willing to be as lost as his/her/their students as we all grapple with these important issues.

Years ago, Olenka Bilash and I (Norris & Bilash, 1993) presented a paper called, "Dealing with the pain of mid-wifing uncertainty: Do we want to lessen or lesson the pain?" While many students were thankful for this mutualist (Norris & Bilash, 2016) approach (according to course evaluations), some students rejected that concept. They want us to be the know-it-all teacher, who tells them the right answer and were disappointed when we do not. I think courage is a requirement of being an alchemist because we're trying to be "counter hegemonic," and of course I would define the hegemony as excessive entitlement.

Rick: As the prescribed curriculum is founded on a certainty and infallibility, its writers believe that they know best, there needs to be real courage to challenge it on many levels. Just in terms of, you know, breaking the mold and trying to conceptualize things in a new way. But then, moving that goal into the classroom is really difficult to do because we're talking about teaching in ways that are relational and grounded in the lives of our students – and in our own lives. Right? That's really difficult to do, especially in this climate: we're supposed to be the expert knower, to have certainty about everything. Instead, I try to be guided by Ted Aoki's (2005b) conception of teachers living in that liminal space between the planned-and-the-lived curricula. This is an ethical space, and to be present to our students, we need to let them be present to us, and thus, we need to listen deeply to them. We have to be aware very deeply of the people that we are and try to understand where they're coming from. As teachers, we are both part of this process and outside it.

Joe: It's this dual lens that defines who a good teacher is, and it is hard. I believe that a score of a 100% for teaching should be suspect because we have different students with different learning styles. Not everyone will like everything. So, they're more opinion questionnaires than they're evaluation tools. Maybe a score of a 100% is actually not a good score at all. I could give some great lectures, and students like them, and I could be evaluated in the very traditional way and increase my teaching scores. While I've received teaching awards, I believe that the criteria are flawed. Could we be teaching to the test? Is meritocracy skewed in favor of certain ways of being? The tyranny is that excessive entitlement can be implicit, an illusion of freedom within a certain frame, as Chomsky believes.

Joe: …and we tend to play freedom within that frame, but we seldom challenge the boundaries of that frame, hence the need for this chapter/book. In writing this, I find myself actually proud that I didn't get a university-wide teaching award because I contracted grades with my students. The students wrote wonderful testimonies about how they felt about it. They had voice and power, but the hegemonic powers that defined what good teaching is, found it/me suspect. Maybe that's courage. Maybe that's stupidity. Maybe that's arrogance. I don't know. But at the same time, I think we tried to cocreate a new world other than the ones in which we were brought up, with our own sense of integrity. Tradition can be excessive. Still, we always need to question our definition of integrity as we recognize that meaning could negatively frame someone else's behavior.

Rick: Well, yes, it does. Evaluation is another example of excessive entitlement, including the concept of grade point averages. Where I work, we were in the habit of admitting people into our programs based on their grade point average as a marker of their future performance: the higher the grade point average, the more promising the student, right? But somebody who's gotten all A's with lots of different types of teachers and professors, with a range of styles and ideologies – what does that say about the student's integrity? Now I try to look at the grades and the narrative of the grade point average.

Joe: In doing so, we are basically controlling and encouraging conformity through the grade itself. You know, I often celebrate the outliers. When we're in an in-class conversation, and someone challenges me, I often say, good! Let's run with it, you know, fight me, and I mean that, and not in a negative way. Rick, like your and my use of duoethnographic conversations, we really try to see different perspectives that challenge us to think beyond ourselves. As Lévinas claims (Kearney, 1984), we need the Other, of difference, to better understand ourselves and our places in the world. If we were the only entity in the universe, we could not know ourselves because we would have nothing to compare ourselves with. Lévinas recognizes we need others of difference to help us. Having such a disposition reduces the likelihood of excessive entitlement, and I am compelled to teach it, especially to teachers.

Also, what's exciting for me right now is the music and dance competitions on television. Currently, there is a diversity of people performing right now, and the judges are celebrating that diversity in ways you didn't see 10 years ago, including some of the judges who 10 years ago probably would have rejected it are now celebrating it.

Still, I see excessive entitlement of the curriculum and its evaluation still trying to lead toward conformity rather than celebrating difference.

Rick: Yeah, unfortunately, that's why it's there. The humanities are being dominated by an emphasis on students' preparation for the workplace. Science, technology, engineering, and mathematics (STEM) now emphasize careers. STEM is not science per se, or mathematics per se. It's about getting jobs in a scientific field. (It's hegemonic.) And maybe if the student is lucky, they get to learn about STEAM (A = Arts). And appropriation of the arts for career preparation is another form of excessive entitlement.

Joe: And that is very much a narrow approach that falls into a neoliberal agenda that Mark Spooner (2020) and others talk about (See https://mirror-theatre.ca/drama-in-education/public-engagement-and-the-politics-of-evidence-2/) where the major purpose of university is to get jobs. And I saw that happening over 25 years ago in my career. And it scared me then, and it's now here. From my perspective, it is excessive entitlement of a very narrow perspective of how one lives in the world, how one "dwells," as Aoki (2005c) would say.

So, I think Rick, you and I am trying to live in the world that moves us into an appreciation of difference and an acceptance and a celebration of difference. And I think for me, excessive entitlement can't live in that type of disposition. Right?

Rick: Yeah, I agree. I think it makes it really difficult because its excessive entitlement thrives on power and the control of power, and unfortunately (or fortunately) democracies are messy. With democracy, you have multiplicity and a plurality of viewpoints. And multiplicity is the enemy of excessive entitlement.

Joe: Unfortunately, when things become polarized and entrenched, understanding difference is nearly impossible. Going back to our early duoethnographies and Scudder's question, I continue to ask, "How do we use, abuse, and misuse our power?" It's a haunting question that, if we can instill in our students, by modeling it, by talking about it, by making it explicit, by naming it as opposed to letting it be the hidden curriculum, we expose the hidden curriculum of excessive entitlement.

Rick: We've always included the arts into duoethnography to help generate a critical free-association through, for example, the analysis of artifacts. And duoethnography (and the arts) is embodied, as it is set in a script format, with the intertwining of participants' voices and dialogue – an embodied dialogue. And to really scaffold deep personal (and societal) change, we can't only focus on critical consciousness – privileging thinking in the reconceptualization process. I mean, yes, it is about consciousness, but then that's only part of it.

Joe: Descartes' mind–body split... (Cottingham, 2016).

Rick: Right. And with us, ontology has also been really important and how we live – are – in the world and with each other.

Joe: I've almost finished the next edition *of Playbuilding as Arts-based Research...* (Norris et al., 2024), and in it, I expand the epistemology, ontology, and axiology trio of the discussion of knowledge, now adding two more, the aesthetic and the pedagogy. And through our writings, we try to generate and disseminate knowledge in a way that's more dialogic and open to the Other than didactic.

Rick: Yes, we've always considered duoethnography a pedagogical method (Norris & Sawyer, 2016). With it, we examine ourselves as a curriculum of self and how the self is pedagogical. How do we learn from each other? How do we learn from ourselves? How do we learn in relationships?

Joe: And this ties in with concepts of identity; is identity fixed or fluid? The Prime Minister of Italy claims that Italy's culture is under attack because there are too many immigrants. Basically, she is trying to maintain a fixed identity that doesn't exist. Nor should it exist.

Joe: Rick, in closing, I return to your question, "How do you do that (questioning power) in your life, in your teaching, in your career?" and respond with another story about a teaching experience.

Joe Story 4: One year, when teaching a course about the playbuilding (Norris, 2009/2016) methodology, one student continually monopolized the debriefing sessions, always with her profound insights. Her voice was appreciated, but the result was that many others, as a result, were silenced. One day, I came to class with a ball of yarn, and during our circle debriefing session, I passed it out with the instruction that we would pass it to the person who asked to speak next. The yarn unraveled, mapping our conversation of the day on the floor in front of us. While it did not indicate how long each speaker spoke, it did record how many times. I then asked the class to take note of this day's pattern, noting that on different days, some would speak more and others less.

When reading their daily journal logs, this student, similar to the student in Story 2, discussed how she deduced that the activity was kindly directed to her. She appreciated the approach and changed accordingly. Others spoke more during the debriefing sessions, and in my opinion, we achieved a better balance, albeit I did miss some of her insights.

Rick, I try to provide occasions for students to come to their own conclusions, in this case, excessive monopolization of conversations. This can mitigate the excessive entitlement by both teacher and student, achieving balance.

Unison: In keeping with duoethnography's tenet of creating a "third-space," we are resistant in providing our own set of conclusions as we encourage readers to find their own between our thoughts. We thank our readers in traveling this far with us and wish them well in continuing the conversation, albeit it with us in spirit.

Rick: Thank you, Joe. As always, I've enjoyed talking and have learned more about my own positionality in relation to excessive entitlement.

Joe: Ditto. See you on Zoom.

Closing note: Duoethnographers do not believe that there is a first author as dialogue is mutualistic. Citation styles do not adequately address this. Joe and Rick, Rick and Joe continually flip first author; another structure defines identity by order and status.

REFERENCES

Alim, H. S., & Paris, D. (2017). What is culturally sustaining pedagogy and why does it matter? In H. S. Alim & D. Paris (Eds.), *Culturally sustaining pedagogies: Teaching and learning for justice in a changing world* (pp. 1–24). Teachers College Press.

Aoki, T. (1993). Legitimating lived curriculum: Towards a curricular landscape of multiplicity. *Journal of Curriculum and Supervision, 8*(3), 255–268.

Aoki, T. (2005a). Interests, knowledge and evaluation: Alternative approaches to curriculum evaluation. In W. F. Pinar & R. L. Irwin (Eds.), *Toward curriculum inquiry in a new key: The collect works of Ted T. Aoki* (pp. 137–158). Lawrence Erlbaum Associates.

Aoki, T. (2005b). Spinning enspiriting images midst planned and lived curricula. In T. T. Aoki, W. Pinar, & R. L. Irwin (Eds.), *Curriculum in a new key: The collected works of Ted T. Aoki* (pp. 413–423). Lawrence Erlbaum Associates, Publishers.

Aoki, T. (2005c). Teaching as in-dwelling between two curriculum worlds. In W. Pinar & R. Irwin (Eds.), *Toward curriculum inquiry in a new key: The collect works of Ted T. Aoki* (pp. 158–165). Lawrence Erlbaum Associates Publishers.

Bakhtin, M. M. (1981). *The dialogic imagination*. The University of Texas Press.

Barone, T. E. (1990). Using the narrative text as an occasion for conspiracy. In E. W. Eisner & A. Peshkin (Eds.), *Qualitative inquiry in education* (pp. 305–326). Teachers College Press.

Barone, T. (1995). The purposes of arts-based educational research. *International Journal of Educational Research, 23*(2), 169–180.

Bhabha, H. K., & Rutherford, J. (1990). The third space: Interview with Homi Bhabha. *Identity: community, culture, difference*, 207–221. Lawrence & Wishart.

Bourdieu, P. (1983). The field of cultural production, or the economic world reversed. *Poetics, 12*(5–6), 311–356.

Bourdieu, P. (1991). On symbolic power. In J. B. Thompson (Ed.), *Language and symbolic power* (G. Raymond & M. Adamson, Trans.) (pp. 163–170). Harvard University Press. (Original work published 1979).

Brown, H., & Barrett, J. (2017). Duoethnography as a pedagogical tool that encourages deep reflection. In J. Norris & R. D. Sawyer (Eds.), *Theorizing curriculum studies, teacher education and research through duoethnographic pedagogy* (pp. 85–110). Palgrave Macmillan.

Buber, M. (1947). *Between man and man*. Kegan, Paul, Trench, Trubner and Company Limited.

Buber, M. (1958). *I and Thou* (R. G. Smith, Trans.). Charles Scribner's Sons, MacMillan Publishing Company.

Burggraeve, R. (1999). Violence and the vulnerable face of the other: The vision of Emmanuel Levinas on moral evil and our responsibility. *Journal of Social Philosophy, 30*(1), 29–45.

Chomsky, N. (1998). *The common good, interviews with David Barsamian*. Odonian.

Chopra, D. (1995). *The way of the wizard: Twenty spiritual lessons for creating the life you want*. Harmony Books.

Cottingham, J. (2016). Descartes. In *Consciousness and the great philosophers* (pp. 75–84). Routledge.

Craig, C. (2020). *Curriculum making, reciprocal learning and the best-loved self*. Palgrave Macmillan.

Farenga, S. J., Ness, D., & Sawyer, R. D. (2015). Avoiding equivalence by leveling: Challenging the consensus-driven curriculum that defines students as "average". *Journal of Curriculum Theorizing, 30*(3), 8–27.

Frankl, V. E. (1963). *Man's search for meaning*. Pocket Books.

Freire, P. (1986). *Pedagogy of the oppressed*. The Continuum Publishing Corporation.

Harrison, T., Ledezma, K., Morgan, A., & Morgan, M. (In Press). The language of submission: A four-way duoethnography exploring translanguaging pedagogy. *Language Learning and Teaching*. https://doi.org/10.1080/17501229.2024.2311840

Henderson, J. (1992). *Reflective teaching: Becoming an inquiring educator*. Maxwell Macmillan Canada.

Jersild, A. (1952). *When teachers face themselves*. Teachers College Press.

Kearney, R. (1984). Emmanuel Lévinas: Prefatory notes. In R. Kearney (Ed.), *Dialogues with contemporary continental thinkers* (pp. 47–70). Manchester University Press.

Malle, L. (1981). *My dinner with Andre*. Saga Productions Inc.

Miller, J. (2011). Autobiography on the move: Poststructuralist perspectives on (im)possible narrative representations of collaboration. In *Paper presented at the Narrative, Arts-based and Post Approaches*, Tempe, AZ.

Motahari, M. (2008). The hermeneutical circle or the hermeneutical spiral? *The International Journal of Humanities, 15*(2), 99–112.

Noddings, N. (1984). *Caring: A feminine approach to ethics and moral education*. University of California Press.

Norris, J. (2004). Shadows: Examining the power relationships in the field experience through audience participation theatre. In G. Germain, C. Mills, N. Marchand, & M. Rogers (Eds.), *Proceedings of the Western Canadian association for student teaching* (pp. 13–19). Western Canadian Association for Student Teaching.

Norris, J. (2009/2016). *Playbuilding as qualitative research: A participatory arts-based approach*. Routledge.

Norris, J., & Bilash, O. (1993). Dealing with the pain of mid-wifing uncertainty: Do we want to lessen or lesson the pain? In *Paper presented at the Annual Conference of the Journal of Curriculum Theorizing*, Bergamo Center, Dayton, Ohio. (no senior author).

Norris, J., & Bilash, O. (2016). A journey toward mutualist teaching and learning: A collaborative reflective practice on community building and democratic classrooms. In R. D. Sawyer & J. Norris (Eds.), *Interdisciplinary reflective practice through duoethnography: Examples for educators* (pp. 41–75). Palgrave Macmillan. https://doi.org/10.1057/978-1-137-51739-5_3

Norris, J., Hobbs, K., & Mirror Theatre. (2024). *Playbuilding as arts-based research: Health, wellness, social justice, and higher education*. Routledge.

Norris, J., & Sawyer, R. D. (2012). Toward a dialogic methodology. In J. Norris, R. D. Sawyer, & D. E. Lund (Eds.), *Duoethnography: Dialogic methods for social, health, and educational research* (pp. 9–39). Left Coast Press.

Norris, J., & Sawyer, R. (2016). *Interdisciplinary reflective practice through duoethnography: Examples for educators*. Springer.

Norris, J., & Sawyer, R. (2020). Duoethnography: A polytheoretical approach to (re)storing, (re)storying the meanings that one gives. In P. Leavy (Ed.), *Oxford handbook of qualitative research* (2nd ed., pp. 397–423). Oxford University Press.

Osberg, D., & Biesta, G. (2008). The emergent curriculum: Navigating a complex course between unguided learning and planned enculturation. *Journal of Curriculum Studies, 40*(3), 313–328.

Pinar, W. (1975). Currere: Toward reconceptualization. In W. Pinar (Ed.), *Curriculum theorizing: The reconceptualists* (pp. 396–414). McCutchan Publishing Corporation.

Pinar, W. F., Reynolds, M. W., Slattery, P., & Taubman, M. P. (2008). *Understanding curriculum*. Peter Lang.

Ratnam, T. (2021). The Interaction of culture and context in the construction of teachers' putative entitled attitude in the midst of change. In T. Ratnam & C. J. Craig (Eds.), *Understanding excessive teacher and faculty entitlement* (Vol. 38, pp. 77–101). Emerald Publishing Limited.

Ratnam, T., & Craig, C. J. (Eds.). (2021). *Understanding excessive teacher and faculty entitlement (Advances in Research on Teaching)* (Vol. 38). Emerald Publishing Limited. https://doi.org/10.1108/S1479-368720210000038001

Sawyer, R. D. (2024). In the shadow of traditional education: A currere of school entitlement and student erasure. In C. Craig & T. Rathnam (Eds.), *After excessive teacher and faculty entitlement: Expanding the space for healing and human flourishing through Ideological becoming*. Emerald Publishing.

Sawyer, R. D., & Liggett, T. (2012). Shifting positionalities: A critical discussion of a duoethnographic inquiry of a personal curriculum of post/colonialism. *International Journal of Qualitative Methods, 11*(5), 628–651.

Sawyer, R., & Norris, J. (2013). *Understanding qualitative research: Duoethnography*. Oxford University Press.

Sawyer, R., & Norris, J. (2015). Duoethnography: A retrospective 10 years after. *International Review of Qualitative Research, 8*(1), 1–4.

Scudder, J. J. (1968). Freedom with authority: A Buber model for teaching. *Educational Theory, 18*(Spring), 133–142.

Spooner, M. (2020). Technologies of governance in context: Four global windows into neoliberalism and audit culture in higher education. *Qualitative Inquiry, 26*(7), 743–747.

Tom, A. R. (1984). *Teaching as a moral craft*. Longman.

Tozer, S., Senese, G. B., & Violas, P. C. (2009). *School and society: Historical and contemporary perspectives* (p. 544). McGraw-Hill.

Verne, J. (1874). *Twenty thousand leagues under the sea* (4th ed.). Ballantyne and Company. https://www.google.ca/books/edition/Twenty_Thousand_Leagues_Under_the_Sea/tsXjGPG_fVQC?hl=en&gbpv=1&printsec=frontcover

Vogel, S., & García, O. (2017). *Translanguaging*. City University of New York, Publications and Research.

Wachowski, A., & Wachowski, L. (1999). *The matrix*. Warner Brothers.

Watson, C. (2006). Narratives of practice and the construction of identity in teaching. *Teachers and Teaching: Theory and Practice, 12*(5), 509–526.

Wozolek, B. (2022). "What does learning sound like?": Reverberations, curriculum studies, and teacher preparation. *Northwest Journal of Teacher Education, 17*(3), 27.

GENERATING LIVING-EDUCATIONAL-THEORIES WITH LOVE IN TRANSFORMING EXCESSIVE TEACHER ENTITLEMENT

Jack Whitehead

University of Cumbria, UK

ABSTRACT

This chapter explores the implications of acknowledging one's own excessive entitlement and living contradictions in contributing to Living-Educational-Theory Research. The analysis emphasises the importance of accepting one's educational responsibility for one's own continuing professional development in inquiries of the kind that address this query: 'How do I improve my professional educational practices in education with values of human flourishing?' This responsibility includes making public evidence and values-based explanations of educational influences in learning, in contributing to the global knowledge base of education.

The notion of excessive teacher entitlement was coined by Ratnam to characterise the putative deficit view of teachers that is projected onto them. Craig (2013) developed Schwab's concept, the teachers' 'best-loved self', to embrace teachers' input in promoting the learning and well-being of all in the institutions they serve (Ratnam & Craig, 2021). My experiences of being a living contradiction are grounded in a tension between my best-loved self and my experience of excessive entitlements. Living educational theories research in which individual practitioner-researchers generate their validated, evidence- and values-based explanations of educational influences in their own learning, in the learning of others and in the learning of the social formations that influence their practice with values of human flourishing, have helped me leverage the potential for growth afforded by this tension. The perspective draws insights from the disciplines of education including Habermas's Critical Theory. It also includes insights from other methodologies such as autoethnography, action research, phenomenology, self-study and narrative inquiry.

Keywords: Excessive entitlement; living-educational-theories; professional development; values of human flourishing; practitioner-research; best-loved self

My purpose is to share valid, evidence and values-laden explanations of the implications of accepting my educational responsibility for addressing my own excessive entitlements in relation to my 'best-loved self' (Craig, 2020) in living values of human flourishing as fully as possible and helping others to do so too. These values include a flow of life-affirming energy with one's best-loved self. This responsibility is expressed in my continuing professional development in inquiries of the kind, 'How do I improve my professional educational practices in education with values of human flourishing?' It involves the recognition of myself as a living contradiction and includes making public, evidence- and values-based explanations of educational influences in learning, in contributing to the global knowledge base of education. Experiencing oneself as a living contradiction is not viewed as negative, or in seeing oneself as a problem, as it stimulates the imagination to create possible ways of enhancing the flow of values of human flourishing.

BORN INTO EXCESSIVE ENTITLEMENT

I was born on 29 August 1944, when Normandy was liberated after the D-Day landings on 6 June 1944. During the battle of Normandy, over 425,000 Allied and German troops were killed, wounded or went missing. Concentration camps were murdering millions of people. I shall begin by acknowledging how much I owe to those who gave their lives to uphold the values of human flourishing in the face of these crimes against humanity. In benefitting from these sacrifices, I have been able to live in security, to live within democratic governance, benefitting from health, economic and educational opportunities and choices in decisions about leading a productive life. I continue to draw inspiration from Frankl's (1946, 2019) and Eger's (2017) responses to their experiences of being concentration camp survivors at the end of World War 2. They both focus on the choices we have in responding to conditions that sometimes negate our values of human flourishing. As Frankl concludes, 'Say Yes to Life in spite of everything'.

Because of these sacrifices of others and the opportunities/entitlements provided for me by the individuals who survived the war and rebuilt the United Kingdom on democratic values, I have enjoyed the benefits of excessive entitlements when compared to the opportunities of many millions across the globe, over a career-long commitment to education. My experiences of being a living contradiction are grounded in a tension between my best-loved self and my experience of excessive entitlements in benefitting from these entitlements in the economic, political, health and educational contexts that have influenced my life and learning.

Charles' (2007) ideas of 'guiltless recognition' and 'societal reidentification' have helped me not to feel guilty for these excessive entitlements. Guiltless recognition is 'a process of acknowledging the humanity of the other without feeling guilty for the historical and present injustices that one's group has inflicted on the other's group' (Charles, 2007, p. 237), and societal reidentification is 'a process of redefining one's identity in relation to the other, in a way that transcends the binary oppositions and hierarchies that have been imposed by colonialism and racism' (Charles, 2007, p. 238). Charles' ideas highlight the importance of a recognition of my excessive entitlements in sustaining a flow of life-affirming energy, without experiencing a debilitating feeling of guilt. This recognition serves to highlight the conditions under which many millions are living, whose quality of education and opportunities would be enhanced, through accessing such entitlements. My best-loved self motivates me to contribute to enhancing the quality of life and educational opportunities with those who at present are not as fortunate as myself. I do this by working and researching with those who are seeking to enhance the flow of values of human flourishing with Living Educational Theory Research.

PERSPECTIVE

My perspective is that of Living Educational Theory Research in which individual practitioner-researchers generate their validated, evidence- and values-based explanations of educational influences in their own learning, in the learning of others and in the learning of the social formations that influence their practice with values of human flourishing. The perspective draws insights from the disciplines of education including Critical Theory (Habermas, 1987). It also includes insights from other methodologies such as autoethnography, action research, phenomenology, self-study and narrative inquiry. I do not want this range of interpretative stances to distract from the focus of generating my own living-educational-theory from experiences of myself as a living contradiction between my excessive entitlements and my best-loved self. Yet, the insights from different methodologies are important. Autoethnography emphasises the importance of placing oneself within cultural influences. Action research emphasises the importance of the action-reflection cycles of planning, acting, evaluating and modifying in responding to practical problems. Phenomenology emphasises the importance of beginning from within the experiences of the phenomenon one is seeking to understand. Self-study emphasises the importance of including 'I' within an educational inquiry, and narrative inquiry emphasises the importance of recognising that an explanation of educational influences in learning will be presented within a narrative.

My best-loved self is grounded in a flow of life-affirming energy with values of human flourishing, including love. The perspective is humanistic, rather than religious, while recognising the importance of religious faiths in the lives of many people across the world. As a humanist, my living-educational-theory perspective includes what I experience as a cosmic flow of life-affirming energy that I attach to my productive orientation to life. I use Fromm's (1947) distinction between a productive and a marketing orientation to life in relation to resisting the pressures of the policies of economic rationalism that lead to de-valuation and de-moralisation. Economic rationalism is a term that not only suggests the primacy of economic values. It expresses commitment to those values in order to serve particular sets of interests ahead of others. It disguises that commitment in a discourse of 'economic necessity' defined by its economic models. In facing the living contradictions, in the tensions between one's best-loved self and excessive teacher entitlement, we can move beyond the reductionism which leads all questions to be discussed as if they were economic ones (de-valuation). We can move out of a situation where moral questions are denied completely (de-moralisation) in a cult of economic inevitability (as if greed had nothing to do with it) (McTaggart, 1992, p. 50). I am not underestimating the difficulties of moving beyond this reductionism by retaining one's integrity in living values of human flourishing as fully as possible. One way in which I have continued to avoid this reductionism is to emphasise the importance of using values of human flourishing in explanations of educational influences in learning. In my supervision of living-educational-theory master's and doctoral degrees, I have emphasised the use of these values as explanatory principles and living standards of judgment in evaluating the validity of the knowledge claims.

Fromm (1956) alerted me to the idea that giving form to life itself is a form of art, and that one of the greatest arts is the 'Art of Loving'. I continue to emphasise the importance of living as loving a life as possible, in enhancing the values that carry hope for the flourishing of humanity. I also seek to unite with the world in the spontaneity of love and productive work rather than seek a kind of security within economic rationality that destroys my integrity and freedom (Fromm, 1942). Hence, I identify with Saunder's (2023) point that 'It's OK to be Angry about Capitalism.' Using Critical Theory (Habermas, 1987), as I earlier presaged, has helped to unmask the sociohistorical and sociocultural influences of capitalism in what I do and understand, as I generate my living-educational-theory. I am seeking to live as fully as possible, values of human flourishing with the art of loving and my experience of excessive entitlement within the world as it exists. In the present, this means recognising and responding to wars between Russian and Ukraine and Israel and Hamas among others. In response, I see myself as a global educator who understands the need to campaign for the strengthening of international treaties and laws that can guarantee peace and security within internationally recognised sovereign borders.

Before I explain how I am responding to my excessive entitlement, with guiltless recognition and societal reidentification, I will clarify my meaning and experience of excessive entitlement as they have been evolving over my professional life-time in education starting with the professional and economic opportunities opened up to me from within my particular social contexts through passing various academic examinations, beginning with the 11+ in 1955 up to the present award of an honorary D.Litt. degree from the University of Worcester in 2023 (Whitehead, 2023a).

MY PROFESSIONAL EXCESSIVE ENTITLEMENT

In 1955, my passing of the 11+ examination in England opened up the opportunity to attend Morecambe Grammar School. Passing or not passing the 11+ was understood as a defining moment in many lives, with education viewed as a central influence in enhanced social mobility. Passing 3 advanced-level and 2 scholarship-level science subjects in 1961 enabled me to attend University (Durham), along with some 4% of the school population. I received a full grant from the State. Compare that with today when more than 40% of young people start undergraduate degrees – but it comes at a heavy financial cost. Today's students leave with debts of £40,000 and upwards to pay back over the course of their working lives. My science degree, awarded in 1965, opened up an extensive range of professional and economic opportunities. I chose to study for my Diploma in Education for a further year to begin my lifelong professional engagement in education.

In 1967, at a time of full employment, with no sense of my excessive entitlement, I began as a comprehensive school science teacher at Langdon Park School in London's East End. Between 1968 and 1970, I studied for my Academic Diploma at the Institute of Education at the University of London. This Diploma was based on the disciplines approach to Educational Theory in which this theory was held to be constituted by the philosophy, sociology, psychology and history of education. While studying for a master's degree in the psychology of education between 1970 and 1972, I began to question the validity of the discipline's approach to Educational Theory. My rejection of this approach changed my sense of vocation from being a science educator, to that of being an educational researcher contributing to the generation of a valid form of Educational Theory. The master's degree opened up opportunities to enter Higher Education. In 1973, I accepted an appointment as a Lecturer in Education at the University of Bath where I worked with a tenured appointment until 2009 with my last doctoral supervisions successfully completed in 2012. The award of my doctorate from the university in 1999, my successful supervisions and my publications opened up offers of Visiting Professorships at Liverpool Hope University, the University of Cumbria, Edge Hill University, Ningxia Teachers University in China and North-West University in South Africa. These opportunities are continuing at the time of writing in 2023.

When I began teaching in 1967, as I have said, I had no sense of excessive entitlement in the sense of the privilege I enjoyed. By passing the above examinations, I understood that I was entitled to the opportunities opened up by these accreditations. My awareness of how these entitlements could be understood as excessive entitlements developed with my understanding of being a global citizen and global educator with educational responsibilities for enhancing the influences of values of human flourishing, especially the value of equality. I now look upon the benefits I have enjoyed as entitlements as excessive entitlements when judged from the value of equality from an international or global perspective. My experience of being a living contradiction is grounded in the tensions I experience between my best-loved self and responding to the inequalities I see from the global perspectives analysed by Brown (2021), in terms of global health, climate change and environmental damage, nuclear proliferation, global financial instability, the humanitarian crisis and global poverty, the barriers to education and opportunity and global inequality. I am not responding from any sense of guilt but from the experience of hope and worthwhile activities involved in actions that are intended to enhance the flow of values of human flourishing. Hence, I am stressing that I experience my excessive entitlement, in relation to my best-loved self, as an opportunity to contribute as much as I can to enhancing the flow of these values in overcoming inequalities and injustices.

DEALING WITH MY LIVING CONTRADICTIONS

The responses to my contradictions (in bold below) were grounded in the relations between my excessive teacher entitlement and my best-loved self as I persisted, in the face of hostile pressures, to produce publications with my values of human flourishing (Whitehead, 1977, 1980, 1985, 1989, 1992). My Educational Theory was not considered legitimate at the time as my new scholarship rubbed against the old establishment and their entitlements. My persistence is perhaps best illustrated below in responses to my experience of being a living contradiction within the University as I held together a judgement from the University Secretary and Registrar that my writings were not consistent with my duties as a University Academic with my own judgement that my writings were consistent with my duties as a University Academic. The conclusion of a Senate working paper that was established to inquire into prima facie evidence that related to a breach of my academic freedom was that my academic freedom had not been breached, but this was because of my persistence in the face of pressure that could have dissuaded a less determined individual. I video-taped a re-enactment of a meeting with the Senate Committee to respond to a draft report in which they concluded that my academic freedom had not been breached, but there was no mention of my persistence in the face of the pressure I had been subjected to (Whitehead, 2013, video 4, p. 6). The video referenced here shows how my best-loved self has rechannelled my anger in having my persistence in the face of pressure, ignored. 'This persistence was possible through remaining open to the flows of loving dynamic energy in the passion for improving practice and contributing to educational knowledge' (Whitehead, 2008, pp. 117–118).

Following are the living contradictions and my dialectical response to them through publications. The contradictions are emphasised in bold, with the publications in italics:

1976 Living contradictions – I am a University Academic. I am not;
1977 Improving learning in Schools – an in-service problem;
1980 In-service Education, The Knowledge-Base of Education;

1980 Living contradictions – I am a creative academic. I am not a creative academic. I can question the judgements of examiners. I cannot question;
1985 An analysis of an individual's educational development – the basis for personally orientated action research;
1987 Living contradictions – My writings are consistent with my duties as a University Academic. No, they are not;
1989 Creating living educational theories from questions of the kind, 'How do I improve my practice?' 1990 How do I improve my Professional Practice as an Academic and Educational Manager? A dialectical analysis of an individual's educational development and a basis for socially orientated action research;
1991 The actions of a Senate Working Party on a Matter of Academic Freedom;
1992 Paper – How can my philosophy of action research transform and improve my professional practice and produce a good social order? A response to Ortrun Zuber-Skerritt.

METHODOLOGY AND METHODS

The perspective of this chapter includes a Living Educational Theory Research approach to enhancing professionalism in education. A distinction is made between being a professional, in the sense of fulfilling the criteria for membership of a professional body, and being professional in the sense of accepting a responsibility for one's own professional development in a life-time's commitment to research one's own professional practice. This commitment includes a continuing process of improving practice and contributing the knowledge one generates in the course of researching one's practice to the global educational knowledge base.

Issues of validity and rigour are essential in a Living Educational Theory Research perspective. The validity and rigour of draft explanations of educational influences in learning can be strengthened by subjecting the explanations to the mutual rational controls of critical discussion (Popper, 1975, p. 44) in validation groups of usually between three and eight peers. The critical discussions seek to strengthen the validity of the explanations by answering questions that include modifications of Habermas' (1976, pp. 1–2) four criteria of social validity of comprehensibility, evidence, sociohistorical and sociocultural understandings and authenticity. Rigour can be enhanced by applying Winters' (1989) six criteria of reflexive and dialectical critique, risk, plural structure, multiple resource and theory practice transformation. Kok (1991a) has given a very clear demonstration of how this can be done in enhancing the rigour of her Living Educational Theory Master's dissertation on the Art of an Educational Inquirer (Kok, 1991b).

The methodology of Living Educational Theory research is based on the methodological inventiveness of each practitioner-researcher as they generate their explanations of educational influence in learning in transforming excessive teacher entitlement with one's best-loved self. This inventiveness gains insights from self-study, narrative inquiry, action research and autoethnography. Methods include action reflection cycles and the use of empathetic resonance with digital visual data for clarifying and communicating the meanings of the embodied expression of values of human flourishing.

All living-educational-theories are self-studies in that enquiry of the form, 'How do I improve my professional practice with values of human flourishing?' is grounded in the 'I' of the researcher. However, a living-educational-theory has boundaries that distinguish a living-educational-theory from those of many self-studies. The boundaries are constituted by the necessary condition, of Living Educational Theory Research, of producing and sharing a valid, evidence and values-laden explanation of educational influences in learning with values of human flourishing, a term consistent with the best-loved self that I introduced earlier. As long as self-study fulfils this necessary condition, it is a living-educational-theory.

As mentioned earlier, it is important to recognise that every Living Educational Theory Researcher creates their own methodology through gathering inspiration from a range of other methodologies. For example, I drew insights from Connelly's and Clandinin's (1999) approach to narrative inquiry, in an action research master's course on leadership I tutored at Bishop's University in Canada (Whitehead, 1999). A living-educational-theory, as an explanation by an individual of their educational influences in their own learning and in the learning of others, can be understood as a form of narrative inquiry in that it begins with the experiences as lived and told by the researcher. Within the narrative what distinguishes the story as a living-educational-theory is an explanation of the educational influences of the individual in their own learning and in the learning of others. Not all narratives are living-educational-theories, but all living-educational-theories are narratives. Thus, I have also used narrative autobiography (Ellis, 2004), through the generation of my Living Educational Theory Research (Whitehead, 1967–2023).

Living-educational-theories are also phenomenological in that they begin from the experience of the phenomenon the researcher is seeking to understand. The purpose of a living-educational-theory differs from the basic purpose of phenomenology in that the purpose of phenomenology is to produce a description of a universal essence while the purpose of a living-educational-theory is to produce a unique explanation of the individual's educational influences in learning. I am using phenomenology by starting within my experience of the phenomena I am seeking to understanding in asking, researching and answering my question, 'How do I improve what I am doing in my professional practice with values of human flourishing?'

I want to be clear about an important distinction between Action Research and Living Educational Theory Research, in generating living-educational-theories with love in transforming excessive teacher entitlement. I first explicated my use of action-reflection cycles in Whitehead (1976) in a local curriculum project with six teachers over 18 months that focused on improving learning for 11–14-year-olds in mixed-ability science groups. I continue to use the action-reflection cycles, from action research, of acting, planning, evaluating and modifying, in seeking to resolve the practical problems I encounter in my inquiries, 'How do I improve my professional practice with values of human flourishing?' However, there is no requirement, in these action-reflection cycles, of generating and sharing valid, evidence- and values-laden explanations of one's educational influences in one's own learning, in the learning of others and in the learning of the social formations within which the inquiry is grounded. This requirement is a defining characteristic of Living Educational Theory Research.

As a Living Educational Theory researcher, I identify more with autoethnography while recognising other methodologies such as Narrative Research (Connelly & Clandinin, 1990, 1999), Self-study Research (Tidwell et al., 2009), Phenomenological Research and Action Research (Corey, 1953; Creswell, 2007), which have also influenced me. I particularly like the following about autoethnographic texts:

> In these texts concrete action, dialogue, emotion, embodiment, spirituality, and self-consciousness are featured, appearing as relational and institutional stories affected by history, social structure, and culture, which themselves are dialectically revealed through action, feeling, thought, and language. Ellis and Bochner (2000, p. 739)

In the course of generating my living-educational-theory I have found it necessary to create the method of empathetic resonance (Delong et al., 2013) using digital visual data, for clarifying the meanings of the expressions of embodied values in the course of their emergence through practice. These are the values that I use as explanatory principles in explanations of educational influences in learning. Feyerabend (1975, p. 17) alerted me to the importance of clarifying the meaning of an embodied expression of a value in the course of its emergence in practice. In using the method of empathetic resonance, a cursor is moved backwards and forwards along digital visual data from one's educational practice to the point of greatest resonance that communicates the expression of a value of human flourishing that one uses as an explanatory principle in an explanation of educational influence in learning.

I want to emphasise a limitation of a printed text-based medium of communication for communicating meanings of the embodied expressions of values of human flourishing. Part of the limitation is because of what Vasilyuk (1991) refers to as 'The Energy Paradigm'. Flows of energy are involved in whatever we do. Hence, it is necessary to include flows of energy in the explanatory principles we use for explaining our educational influences in what we are doing. My continuing motivations, for supporting the generation of living-educational-theories, include a flow of life-affirming energy with values of human flourishing. The problem with printed text-based media for communicating meanings is that they are limited in being able to communicate the meanings of the expressions of flows of life-affirming energy with values of human flourishing. This limitation has been analysed in Whitehead and Huxtable (2006a, 2006b). The 2006a paper is a multimedia presentation at the World Congress of Action Learning, Action Research and Process Management (ALARPM). The 2006b paper is a printed text-based presentation produced for the proceeding. This followed the instructions for inclusion in the proceedings and had to be a printed text-based presentation. The differences between the two presentations illustrate what can be communicated with the aid of digital visual data in relation to the expressions of embodied values and what is omitted in these communications in printed text-based communications. This has implications for the communication of the meanings of one's best-loved self in responding to living contradictions with excessive entitlements. It is my contention that these communications will require the use of digital visual data in valid and evidence-based explanations of educational influences in learning. This difference in meaning can perhaps be best illustrated by differences between lexical definitions and ostensive expressions of meaning. My studies of ethics and education between 1968 and 1970 focused on the lexical definitions of values in which the meanings of values were defined in terms of other words using a Kantian form of transcendental deduction in which given proposition x is true; if it can be demonstrated the proposition y is implied in x, then there are good grounds for believing that proposition y is true. The limitation for me in this approach to defining values was that my embodied expressions of my meanings of values could not be clearly defined by this method. Hence, I developed the method of empathetic resonance for clarifying and communicating the meanings of my embodied expressions of my values.

FINDINGS

The findings I share here are related to the planning process for the fourth International Conference on Transformative Education Research and Sustainable Development, to be held in Indonesia in 2024. The previous three conferences were hosted by the University of Kathmandu in Nepal and the Proceedings of the Third Conference can be accessed (TERSD, 2022). I am benefitting from my excessive entitlements in having the economic security to spend whatever productive life-time I have left in doing whatever I chose. My choice in supporting the planning group for Transformative Education Research and Sustainable Development (TERSD) 2024, with this excessive entitlement, is focused on the desire of my best-loved self, to make a contribution to sustainable development with values of human flourishing. My findings in relation to the Indonesian Transformative Education Research Group (TERSD, 2023–2024) are focused on the living posters that each participant has produced, with details of their context, practice and values. I am contributing to the generation of each participant's living-educational-theory by encouraging each participant to generate a values- and evidence-based explanation of their educational influences in learning. For example, Yuli Rahmawati's original living poster includes the claim that 'I endeavour to empower my student teachers, as social agents, to participate in creating a better world?' A video recording of a conversation with the group includes my focus on the importance of gathering data that can be used to justify a claim that Rahmawati is empowering her student teachers to participate in creating a better world. The video includes my encouragement of all the participants to analyse each other's living poster, for such values-laden claims, and to respond with suggestions about the data that need to be gathered and to be used as evidence in justifying the validity of an evidence-based explanation of educational influences in learning.

The findings are also related to the support I am giving to the generation and sharing of Living Educational Theory Research in the Centre for Excellence in Learning and Teaching at Durban University of Technology in the Academic Induction Programme (DUT, 2023). This homepage presents the evidence that each participant in the programme has produced and shared their living poster with the details of their values and research as they begin the generation of their living-educational-theory.

The findings in over 50 living-educational-theory doctorates (LET, 2023) provide the evidence to show how generating living-educational-theories with one's best-loved self can transform excessive teacher entitlement in improving educational practices with other values of human flourishing. I draw your attention to these doctorates as I supervised over 30 of these as an expression of my productive life in education in using the benefits of my excessive entitlements in realising the values of my best-loved self. Hence, I now focus on how living educational theories with my best-loved self have been used to transform excessive teacher entitlement to improve educational practice. My excessive entitlement in my work at the University of Bath between 1973 and 2012 included my tenured appointment. This protected my economic security and academic freedom, a protection not currently given to a majority of university academics throughout the world. This protection meant that I could pursue unpopular activities without fear of losing my employment. For example, I could support practitioner-researchers in doing research which included 'I' within the title. I could champion the inclusion of digital visual data in explanations of educational influences in learning. I could also encourage the clarification of embodied values and their use as explanatory principles in explanations of educational influences in learning.

For example, the first doctorate at the University of Bath with love in the title was Lohr's (2006) 'Love at work: What is my lived experience of love, and how may I become an instrument of love's purpose?' The significance of this thesis is in bringing love, as an academic standard of judgement, into an original contribution to knowledge. It is focused on making explicit the embodied experience of love in a pedagogy of presence that includes action research, phenomenological, hermeneutical, physical, emotional and spiritual knowledge.

Briganti (2021) takes a global perspective in her Living Theory of International Development. This includes her value of gender justice in supporting women in Afghanistan to create a women's taxi service. In August 2021, the Taliban took back control of the country and closed down such enterprises as well as stopping the educational opportunities for girls and young women. This example serves to emphasise the importance of the political context in influencing the generation of living-educational-theories for human flourishing with one's best-loved self. Another example of Living Educational Theory Research that highlights the influence of politics is in South Africa where Nelson Mandela was influential in including the value of Ubuntu in the 1994 South African Constitution. In my 2011 Inaugural Nelson Mandela Day lecture, at the University of Durban (Whitehead, 2011), I outline the importance of including the values of Ubuntu in the creation of living-educational-theories. In this outline, I especially draw on Charles' (2007) living-educational-theory doctorate in which he brings Ubuntu as a living standard of judgement into the Academy. This original contribution to knowledge is a significant finding in moving beyond decolonisation through societal reidentification and guiltless recognition.

I find the idea of guiltless recognition very helpful in making positive responses to my excessive entitlements, especially my entitlement to economic security due to my academic Charles' thesis also included digital visual data to help with clarifying and communicating the meanings of his embodied values. My academic tenure enabled me to contribute to a Senate Working Party that recommended a change in the regulations governing the submission of research degrees, to include the submission of e-media.

Other findings of Living Educational Theory Research, in relation to responding to living contradictions in the tensions between excessive entitlement and best-loved self, can be seen in the living-educational-theory of the Indian researcher Swaroop Rawal (2006, 2011, 2023). Rawal acknowledges the importance of Hindu spirituality in her motivations to support the most vulnerable children in India. This focus is on the use of a life-skills programme she developed, based on drama. Without proselytising, Rawal acknowledges the importance of Hindu values and beliefs in her own motivations while accepting and valuing different spiritualities with values of human flourishing.

REFLECTING ON MY VULNERABILITIES

My thinking about my experience of excessive entitlement was taken forward by the dialogical exchanges with the peer reviewers. I am thinking particularly of my recognition of both the positive and negative aspects of vulnerability, thanks to the dialogue I have had with Tara Ratnam and Jacqueline Ellett. Their questions about my own vulnerabilities and about how my vulnerabilities provide a way of reflecting on excessive entitlement provided a motive to think further and deeper on it. My experience of vulnerability is complex. In a positive sense, I think of my vulnerability in terms of an empathetic awareness of the feelings of others. This includes an openness to the feelings of distress and pain and others. In a negative sense, I think of vulnerability as a response to pain, distress and hostility that can hinder the expression of one's professional educational responsibilities. This kind of pressure can sometimes affect one's mental health to the detriment of fulfilling one's professional responsibilities. For example, the conclusion of a Senate working paper was that my academic freedom had not been breached. My persistence in the face of pressure that my freedom was breached could have dissuaded a less determined individual. In my experience, some individuals that have been subjected to such threats to their employment have experienced the negative vulnerability of their mental health being affected to the extent that they can no long perform their professional responsibilities.

I have found Freud's (1966) analysis of 10 defence mechanisms we can use to strengthen the negative sense of vulnerability very helpful in sustaining my own robust mental health:

So far as we know at present, the ego has these ten different methods at its disposal in its conflicts with instinctual representations and affects. It is the task of the practicing analyst to discover how far these methods prove effective in the processes of ego resistance and symptom formation which he has the opportunity of observing in individuals (p. 44).

CONCLUSION AND SIGNIFICANCE

Each one of us will have a different experience of how excessive teacher entitlements are influencing the generation of our living-educational-theories. Each of us can exercise choice in the way we respond to these external conditions (Eger, 2017).

The significance is focused on facing and responding to the living contradictions grounded in holding together our valuing of our best-loved self with responses to our excessive entitlements that are related to the global contexts defined by Brown (2021) and Saunders (2023). The significance is related to the productive orientation of our best-loved self. In answering the question, 'What is it to produce something as a human being?' I draw on Bernstein (1971, p. 48), from the early writings of Marx, in which he explained that each of us would have been twice affirmed in producing something as a human being.

In producing and sharing my living-educational-theory and in your use of insights from my theory, we are twice affirmed. In my production, I objectified my individuality and its particularity, and in the course of this activity, I enjoy an individual life. In viewing my living-educational-theory, I experience the individual joy of knowing my personality as an objective, sensuously perceptible and indubitable power. In your satisfaction and your use of insights from my living-educational-theory, I have the direct and conscious satisfaction that my work satisfied a human need, that it objectified human nature and that it created an object appropriate to the need of another human being:

> I would have been the mediator between you and the species and you would have experienced me as a redintegration of your own nature and a necessary part of yourself; I would have been affirmed in your thought as well as your love. In my individual life I would have directly created your life, in my individual activity I would have immediately confirmed and realized my true human nature. Bernstein (1971, p. 48)

The life-affirming flow of cosmic energy that I experience, within my best-loved self, motivates my productive life in supporting the generation, sharing and enhancing of living-educational-theories with values of human flourishing. I recognised above that I have benefitted from excessive entitlements in the economic, political, health and educational contexts that have influenced by life and learning. In responding to the living contradictions of my best-loved self, responding to these excessive entitlements, I continue to live a productive life in the generation of my living-educational-theories and in supporting others to do so too. In supporting others to do so too, I draw your attention to an article in the *Malaysian Action Research Journal* (Shaik-Abdullah et al., 2023). These authors acknowledge the insights they have gained from my Living Educational Theory and its contribution to promoting human flourishing. This is illustrative of the freedom I enjoy, as part of my responses to my excessive entitlements, with my best-loved self in continuing to respond to requests for support in different global contexts, in the generation and sharing of Living Educational Theory Research (LET, 2023).

In generating living-educational-theories with love in transforming excessive teacher entitlement, I continue to value the public sharing of such living-educational-theories (Delong & Whitehead, 2023; Whitehead, 2023b; Whitehead & Huxtable, 2016, 2023). This public sharing, for example, in this book, is important, testing the validity of the ideas and offering an invitation to others to use those ideas they find valid and useful in the creation of their own living-educational-theory. I make myself more vulnerable within this chapter in the positive sense above, through deepening and extending my sociocultural and sociohistorical understandings, in my concerns, activities and responsibilities as a global citizen.

In continuing to defend and strengthen my own robust mental health, I acknowledge a resistance to eliciting empathy and understanding of the struggles and tensions I have experienced through self-narratives that focus on overcoming threats to mental health. I have chosen to focus on the expression of a professional, educational responsibility in responding to living contradictions between my best-loved self and my excessive entitlements. I have done this in the hope that this may be useful to readers in the generation and sharing of their own living-educational-theories, with values of human flourishing their best-loved selves.

REFERENCES

Bernstein, R. (1971). *Praxis and action*. Duckworth.
Briganti, A. (2021). *My living-theory of international development*. Graduated University of Lancaster. PhD Thesis. https://www.actionresearch.net/living/ABrigantiphd.pdf
Brown, G. (2021). *Seven ways to change the world: How to fix the most pressing problems we race*. Simon & Schuster.
Charles, E. (2007). *How can I bring Ubuntu as a living standard of judgement into the academy? Moving beyond decolonisation through societal reidentification and guiltless recognition*. University of Bath. PhD Thesis. https://www.actionresearch.net/living/edenphd.shtml
Connelly, F. M., & Clandinin, D. J. (1990). Stories of experience and narrative inquiry. *Educational Researcher*, *19*(5), 2–14.
Connelly, F. M., & Clandinin, D. J. (Eds.). (1999). *Shaping a professional identity: Stories of educational practice*. Althouse Press.
Corey, S. M. (1953). *Action research to improve school practices*. Bureau of Publications, Teachers College.
Craig, C. J. (2013). Teacher education and the best-loved self. *Asia Pacific Journal of Education*, *33*(3), 261–272.
Craig, C. J. (2020). *Curriculum making, reciprocal learning and the best-loved self*. Palgrave Macmillan.
Creswell, J. W. (2007). *Qualitative inquiry & research design: Choosing among five approaches*. Sage.
Delong, J., Campbell, E., Whitehead, J., & Griffin, C. (2013). How are we creating cultures of inquiry with self-studies that transcend constraints of poverty on empathetic learning? In *Presented at the 2013 American educational research association conference in San Francisco with the theme: Education and poverty: Theory, research, policy and praxis*. https://www.actionresearch.net/writings/aera13/lcjdcgaera13jwopt.pdf
Delong, J., & Whitehead, J. (2023). *You and your living educational theory. How to conduct a values-based inquiry for human flourishing*. Routledge.
DUT. (2023). *Durban University of Technology living-poster homepage*. https://www.actionresearch.net/writings/posters/dut23.pdf

Eger, E. (2017). *The choice: Even in hell hope can flower*. Ebury Publishing.
Ellis, C. (2004). *The ethnographic I: A methodological novel about autoethnography*. AltaMira.
Ellis, C., & Bochner, A. P. (2000). Autoethnography, personal narrative, reflexivity: Researcher as subject. In N. Denzin & Y. Lincoln (Eds.), *Handbook of qualitative research* (2nd ed., pp. 733–768). Sage Publications.
Feyerabend, P. (1975). *Against method*. Verso.
Frankl, V. (1946). *Man's search for meaning*. Beacon Press.
Frankl, V. (2019). *Yes to life: In spite of everything*. Penguin.
Freud, A. (1966). *The ego and the mechanisms of defence*. International Universities Press.
Fromm, E. (1942). *The fear of freedom*. Routledge and Kegan Paul.
Fromm, E. (1947). *Man for himself: An inquiry into the psychology of ethics*. Rhinehart.
Fromm, E. (1956). *The art of loving*. Harper & Row.
Habermas, J. (1976). *Communication and the evolution of society*. Heinemann.
Habermas, J. (1987). *The theory of communicative action (volume two): The critique of functionalist reason*. Polity.
Kok, P. (1991a). Rigour in an action research account. In *Presented to the international conference of the classroom action research network, University of Nottingham, 19–21 April 1991*. https://www.actionresearch.net/writings/peggyrigour.pdf
Kok, P. (1991b). *The art of an educational inquirer*. MA Dissertation, University of Bath. https://www.actionresearch.net/living/peggy.shtml
LET. (2023). *Living educational theory doctorate's homepage*. https://www.actionresearch.net/living/living.shtml
Lohr, E. (2006). *Love at work: What is my lived experience of love, and how may I become an instrument of love's purpose?* PhD Thesis, University of Bath. https://www.actionresearch.net/living/lohr.shtml
McTaggart, R. (1992). Reductionism and action research: Technology versus convivial forms of life. In C. S. Bruce & A. L. Russell (Eds.), *Transforming tomorrow today* (pp. 47–61). University of Queensland.
Popper, K. (1975). *The logic of scientific discovery*. Hutchinson & Co.
Ratnam, T., & Craig, C. J. (2021). Introduction: The idea of excessive teacher entitlement: Breaking new ground. In T. Ratnam & C. J. Craig (Eds.), *Understanding excessive teacher and faculty entitlement. Advances in research on teaching* (Vol. 38, pp. 1–13). Emerald Publishing.
Rawal, S. (2006). *The role of drama in enhancing life skills in children with specific learning difficulties in a Mumbai school: My reflective account*. PhD, Coventry University in Collaboration with the University of Worcester. https://www.actionresearch.net/living/rawal.shtml
Rawal, S. (2011). *Learning disabilities in a nutshell*. B. Jain Publishers Pvt. Ltd.
Rawal, S. (2023). *Play, practice, pursue: 10-day bagless school approach to pre-vocational education*. Himalaya Publishing House.
Saunders, B. (2023). *It's ok to be angry about capitalism*. Allen Lane.
Shaik-Abdullah, S., Noor, M. S. A. M., & Whitehead, J. (2023). Delving into living educational theory (LET) research: A conversation with Jack Whitehead. *Malaysian Journal of Action Research*, *1*(1), 11–22. https://www.actionresearch.net/writings/jack/MARNManuscript.pdf
TERSD. (2022). *Proceedings of the 3rd international conference of transformative education research and sustainable development*. https://www.actionresearch.net/writings/tersd/proceedingsTERSD2022.pdf
TERSD. (2023–2024). *Transformative Education Research Group homepage*. https://www.actionresearch.net/writings/posters/indonesiangp23.pdf
Tidwell, D., Heston, M., & Fitzgerald, L. (Eds.). (2009). *Research methods for the self-study of practice*. Springer.
Vasilyuk, F. (1991). *The psychology of experiencing: The resolution of life's critical situations*. Harvester Wheatsheaf.
Whitehead, J. (1976). *Improving learning for 11–14 year olds in mixed ability science groups*. Wiltshire Curriculum Development Centre. https://www.actionresearch.net/writings/ilmagall.pdf
Whitehead, J. (2013). A living logic for educational research. In *A presentation at the 2013 annual conference of the British Educational Research Association, University of Sussex, 5th September*. https://www.actionresearch.net/writings/bera13/jwbera13phil010913.pdf

Whitehead, J. (1967–2023). *Jack Whitehead's writings.* https://www.actionresearch.net/writings/writing.shtml
Whitehead, J. (1977). Improving learning in schools – An in-service problem. *British Journal of In-Service Education, 3*(2), 104–111. https://www.actionresearch.net/writings/jack/jw1977bjie.pdf
Whitehead, J. (1980). In-service education: The knowledge base of educational theory. *British Journal of In-Service Education, 6*(2), 89–92. https://www.tandfonline.com/doi/abs/10.1080/0305763800060205#.UvK9z_ZicUM
Whitehead, J. (1985). An analysis of an individual's educational development – The basis for personally orientated action research. In M. Shipman (Ed.), *Educational research: Principles, policies and practice* (pp. 97–108). Falmer. https://www.actionresearch.net/writings/jack/jw1985analindiv.pdf
Whitehead, J. (1989). Creating a living educational theory from questions of the kind, How do I improve my practice? *Cambridge Journal of Education, 19*(1), 41–52. https://www.actionresearch.net/writings/livtheory.html
Whitehead, J. (1992). How can my philosophy of action research transform and improve my professional practice and produce a good social order? – A response to Ortrun Zuber-Skerritt. In C. S. Bruce & A. L. Russell (Eds.), *Proceedings of the second world congress on action learning, action research and process management.* ALARPM Inc. https://www.actionresearch.net/writings/jack/jw92zuberskerritt.pdf
Whitehead, J. (1999). *Jack Whitehead's curriculum proposal for programme GS 570 on 'A special topic in educational leadership' on 'Action research approaches to educational leadership' at Bishop's University, Lennoxville, 5–16 July 1999.* https://www.actionresearch.net/writings/bishops/bish99.pdf
Whitehead, J. (2008). Using a living theory methodology in improving practice and generating educational knowledge in living theories. *Educational Journal of Living Theories, 1*(1), 103–126. https://ejolts.net/node/80
Whitehead, J. (2011). *Notes for Jack Whitehead's Mandela day lecture on the 18th July 2011 in Durban, South Africa, with a 63 minute video of the presentation.* https://www.actionresearch.net/writings/jack/jwmandeladay2011.pdf
Whitehead, J. (2023a). *Jack Whitehead's graduation with a D.Litt. degree Honoris causa from the University of Worcester on the 12th September 2023.* https://www.actionresearch.net/writings/jack/jacksdlittgraduation120923.pdf
Whitehead, J. (2023b). Developing international scholarship of teaching and learning with living educational theory research. In *Presented at the 2023 conference of the international society for the scholarship of teaching and learning (SoTL) at Utrecht University 8–11th November.* https://www.actionresearch.net/writings/jack/jw2023issotl051123.pdf
Whitehead, J., & Huxtable, M. (2006a). How are we co-creating living standards of judgement in action-researching our professional practices? In *Multi-media text presented at the world congress of ALARPM and PAR 21-24 August 2006 in Groningen.* https://www.actionresearch.net/writings/jack/jwmh06ALARPMmulti.pdf
Whitehead, J., & Huxtable, M. (2006b). How are we co-creating living standards of judgement in action-researching our professional practices? In *Printed text in the conference proceedings of the world congress of ALARPM and PAR 21-24 August 2006 in Groningen.* https://www.actionresearch.net/writings/jack/jwmhalarpmtext06.pdf
Whitehead, J., & Huxtable, M. (2016). Creating a profession of educators with the living-theories of master and doctor educators. *Gifted Education International, 32*(1), 6–25. http://www.actionresearch.net/writings/gei2015/jwmh.pdf
Whitehead, J., & Huxtable, M. (2023, September). Why a focus on 'what is educational?' matters so much in reconstructing education? *Irish Educational Studies.* https://www.actionresearch.net/writings/jack/IESeducational180923.pdf
Winters, R. (1989). *Learning from experience.* Falmer.

SOCIETAL NARRATIVES OF TEACHERS AS NONPERSONS AS AN EXPRESSION OF SOCIETY'S EXCESSIVELY ENTITLED ATTITUDE

Celina Dulude Lay[a], Eliza Pinnegar[b] and Stefinee Pinnegar[a]

[a]*Brigham Young University, USA*
[b]*State Canyon Youth Center, USA*

ABSTRACT

In this chapter, we explore the ways in which media postpandemic responses communicate clearly the excessive entitlement reflected in the public discourse about teachers. During the pandemic, we noted many parent posts on social media lauding teachers. They expressed gratitude for the challenges teachers faced in teaching students on distance platforms and moving learning forward. Yet, we noted that the media reports following the pandemic were noticed a shift in the discourse following the pandemic. Thus, we became interested in exploring how teachers were represented in public discourse following the pandemic. Since the public discourse on teachers has consistently reflected a deficit orientation, given the praise of teachers during the pandemic, we wondered if this acknowledgment of teachers' sacrifice and service might shift the discourse after the pandemic to more positively represent teachers. To pursue this inquiry, we collected and analyzed narratives and examples from postpandemic media representations where teachers and teacher educators were represented as nonpersons. We also collected anecdotes and research and media reports to examine the ways in which teachers were represented. We identified three themes: lack of teachers' voices, the teacher shortage, and loss of learning. Our analysis identifies how teachers and teacher educators are positioned within society and the impact of treating teachers as nonpersons on teachers and the teaching profession. Such depictions fail to represent the vital role of teachers in the progress of society.

Keywords: COVID-19; nonpersonhood; excessive teacher entitlement; excessive public entitlement; teacher shortage; teachers' voices

We began this inquiry with contrasting news stories, occurring at the end of COVID-19 school-based quarantines. In some school districts around the United States, regardless of the threat to the life of teachers and fellow students, parents protested mask-wearing mandates and, in their protests, there is seldom mention of the risk to teachers' health posed by unmasked children who have COVID-19 (Markowicz, 2021). When teachers objected, parents were unsympathetic and indifferent to the threat their child might pose to teachers, staff, and other students. Parents were willing for their children to infect teachers and potentially cause disability and death from the spread of COVID-19 (https://www.cnn.com/2021/08/13/us/teacher-parent-fight-face-masks-trnd/index.html). The media represented the story as parental rights, not focusing on the potential risk on others with whom their child might interact. The story the press reported was about a teacher who had a history of allergies and so she had misidentified her COVID-19 symptoms as her typical struggles with allergies. Post COVID-19, it was especially difficult for schools to get substitutes, and so even though she did not feel great, she went to school masked. She took off the mask to help a struggling reader. This child and eight others as well as fellow teachers got COVID-19. The media represented the teacher as uninformed and incompetent. No analysis indicated the teacher might have gotten COVID-19 from helping students or other school personnel or visitors who were not masked. In this story, the teacher was considered the only possible source for the spread of COVID-19.

With these two contrasting stories, the untold story was the lack of attention to the impact of unmasking on the health and safety of teachers. Teachers, it seemed, were responsible for COVID-19 outbreaks in schools, and children and parents were immune. This led us to explore public discourse about teachers found in the media particularly after the pandemic.

During the pandemic, parents often posted about how much they valued teachers and the difficult task of teaching students, especially as parents took on this task when students were quarantined (Shepherd, 2020). After the pandemic, the discourse reverted to prepandemic representations of teachers as nonpersons interchangeable with each other and uniformly lacking in skill and knowledge and being generally careless and apathetic. This representation echoed previous attitudes showing public entitlement (Darling-Hammond & Bransford, 2007), villainizing teachers and negatively impacting their identity and limiting their ability to educate students. Nonpersonhood is defined as a thing with no social or legal status and where the entity is interchangeable with others in the same category. Waller (1932) argued that the pressures on teachers in schools result in representations of teachers as easily interchangeable (as things rather than humans).

We collected and analyzed narratives and examples from postpandemic media representations where teachers and teacher educators were represented as nonpersons. We also collected anecdotes, and research and media reports to examine the ways in which teachers were represented. We identified three themes: lack of teachers' voices, the teacher shortage, and loss of learning. Our analysis identifies how teachers and teacher educators are positioned within society and the impact of treating teachers as nonpersons on teachers and the teaching profession. Such depictions fail to represent the vital role of teachers in the progress of society.

In developing countries, attention to preparing strong educational systems emerges quickly, but in the United States, this is less true. Educators are treated as interchangeable and often seen as deficit – the importance of education is minimized. The United States faces a drastic reduction in the teaching force, yet the discourse about teachers represents them as deficit, recalcitrant, and less intelligent. Even in the face of the need for better prepared teachers, some developed countries, such as the United States, fail to provide not only underwhelming financial support but more importantly not treating teachers or the profession with the respect and emotional support needed to teach in the challenging environments they face. Currently in the United States, regular classroom teachers must educate all students (including special education, emotionally distraught, and second-language learners) within the regular classroom, and they are held accountable for uniform standards of adequate yearly progress regardless of the motivation, learning ability, or language issues.

OBJECTIVES/PURPOSES

We first became interested in teacher nonpersonhood given our perusal of numerous entries on social media from parents about their gratitude to teachers and attitude of cooperation during COVID-19 when students were being taught at home (Shepherd, 2020). We noticed that those sentiments had burned out by the time students started coming back to school. For example, the tenor shifted as parents, who had initially expressed support for protecting the health of vulnerable populations, now showed frustration about students being required to wear masks at school. We began to be interested in this concept of entitlement in this shift and wondered if we would find similar tensions expressed in the main media.

PERSPECTIVE(S)/THEORETICAL FRAMEWORK

The deficit orientation to teachers coupled with their representation as nonpersons, which makes them victims of other people's excessive entitled attitudes, has had an impact on teaching and teachers. Part of the representation of teachers as deficit and interchangeable was already a problem for the education system before the pandemic. In addition, while there has been a concern about students not making adequate yearly progress, after the pandemic, the concern deepened.

Educational leaders and the media raised the alarm that students were falling even further behind, and there was a sense of despair over their ever catching up. Another ongoing issue that schools faced was teacher attrition, but after the pandemic, there was an actual and pervasive lack of adequate teaching staff, and the teacher attrition problem morphed into a more severe and widespread teacher shortage after the pandemic. In fact, teacher shortages have always existed, albeit not as pervasive as after the pandemic (Craig et al., 2023; Flores & Craig, 2023).

The increasing demand that teachers be tested since the public discourse consistently has for many years presented teachers as less intellectually competent than those in other professions and an insistence that teachers have a woeful lack of higher order thinking skills. Yet, research has demonstrated that the intellectual skills and content knowledge of education graduates match or exceed graduates in other fields (Darling-Hammond & Bransford, 2007).

The public perception is that teachers are less–less qualified, less creative, and under prepared, and the perception persists in spite of evidence to the contrary. Darling-Hammond (2006) argued:

> ...many lay people and a large share of policy makers hold the view that almost anyone can teach reasonably well – that entering teaching requires, at most, knowing something about a subject, and the rest of the fairly simple "tricks of the trade" can be picked up on the job. These notions – which derive both from a lack of understanding of what good teachers actually do behind the scenes and from tacit standards for teaching that are far too low – lead to pressures for backdoor routes into teaching that deny teachers access to much of the knowledge base for teaching... (p. 2)

Based on the view of teachers as deficit and the knowledge needed for teaching being focused on developing tricks of the trade rather than deep knowledge and conceptual understanding, states have spawned increasing numbers of quick-fix less-than-rigorous teacher preparation programs and teacher development. Teachers prepared in this way are those most likely to provide poor-quality teaching and leave teaching even more rapidly, yet teacher education and teachers are often judged by the quality of these teachers who are represented as being typical of all teachers. The faulty assumption that all teacher education is the same is yet another myth that is alive and well in American society (Flores & Craig, 2023).

A deficit representation of teachers contributes to the past and current representation of teachers as nonpersons. In the media and public discourse and the interaction of teachers with parents, students, and administrators, teachers are treated as nonpersons – as things that could be interchangeable. Any person should be allowed to teach even if they have little knowledge and poor-quality preparation (or no preparation whatsoever). Indeed, there is a long-held belief that people only become teachers because they are not capable of doing anything else. When a teacher disciplines a child, comments on pay inequity or the lack of supplies or economic support for the classroom, this is often perceived not as carefully constructed pleas for support but as whining. The pervasive treatment of teachers as nonpersons makes it difficult for teachers to get the educational, emotional, and economic support needed to offer students strong educational experiences. Research has indicated that teachers spend hundreds of dollars from their salaries to buy the tools they need to educate students.

The representation of teachers and schooling in the media communicates the orientation of entitlement, but this influences the public orientation to teaching. The knowledge needed for teaching, the difficulty of the work, and the complexity of teaching are seldom articulated in the public discourse. Arguments teachers make in asking for better support of teachers and education are generally dismissed. These beliefs about the demands of teaching and the capability of teachers presented in the media have made it difficult for teachers to gain the support needed to provide quality education for students. After the pandemic rather than the public insisting on lowering class size, providing more classroom aids, and improving materials, teachers are seen as the main reason for the inability of schools to support students in overcoming learning gap the media and districts insisted had emerged after the quarantine of students and teachers during the pandemic.

Little attention is paid to the fact that most teachers were required to shift from in-person to online teaching within a few days. As teacher educators, we have designed online teaching materials (Richards et al., 2021). Educational companies, online schools, and universities have spent years and millions of dollars designing even a single course, yet teachers were required to do this in a few short days. The discourse about lost learning fails to take this absence of realistic expectations into account. Online programs generally require that students have adequate computer tools and computing support, all of which was woefully inadequate or unavailable during the pandemic. Sometimes, children had to engage in their online education using a single cell phone or computer shared among several children in a household. However, in representing the difficulty of ameliorating pandemic effects on education, teachers alone were considered the culprits – lack of quality online teaching. Other contributors to the learning gap such as lack of commitment and motivation by children and parents, poor-quality access tools, and poor-quality programs or inappropriate educational materials were not considered. During the pandemic, posts about teachers on social media platforms such as Facebook and Instagram (e.g., #teacherappreciation or #teacherlove between 2019 and 2021) were initially tributes, more inclined toward gratitude for what they do. Later, as students returned to school and families and communities began to be more frustrated with pandemic regulations, social media discourse became more oriented to critique of teachers and increased teacher stress (e.g., #schoollife or #teachersoffacebook between 2020 and 2022). In this inquiry, we were interested in how the media represented teachers postpandemic. In this study, we sought to uncover the themes of excessive entitlement toward teachers reflected in the media stories postpandemic.

METHOD, DATA SOURCES, AND ANALYSIS

For this media literature review, we kept the parameters of our search to US online news sources. Given our focus on public responses to teachers within the

United States and even our own state of Utah, we targeted articles written in the public press during the COVID-19 pandemic and just after students returned to school. To do this review, we searched using online news platforms that were conservative and those that were considered more liberal. We made a chart of articles and pulled quotes and summarized stories that seemed most relevant about how teachers were represented.

The sources we perused came both from our own interactions with news coverage of the pandemic in education at the time and a more formal postpandemic search conducted using a range of news platforms. For this search, we met twice weekly for one month and then once a week for 2 months. One of us focused on more conservative news sources, and the other focused more on liberal news coverage. The third author covered social media. We filled in our chart, which included the date published, the news source, a summary of highlights or relevant quotes, and the link.

While our process was systematic, it was not intended to be a comprehensive systematic review. We thoroughly researched four online sites. First, we chose the more liberal sources, Cable News Network (CNN) (www.cnn.com/EDUCATION/archive/) and National Public Radio (NPR) (www.npr.org/sections/education/). Then, we studied news coverage of teachers from a more conservative source (www.foxnews.com/category/us/education). We also found information from Politico (www.politico.com/education). As we started noticing certain trends, we added a search into local news in the state of Utah (www.ksl.com/news/utah/education).

The news articles we analyzed ranged from March 2020 to October 2023. We initially focused our search on the 2021 school year because that was the year most students and teachers returned to school, which comprised our most thorough search. When we noticed a relevant topic or theme, we would follow it, honing search terms and moving a year in both directions.

We met together in person in order to engage in dialogue to share what we found, compare perspectives that were represented, and wonder about recurring themes. In the moment, we would record our observations, sometimes including our own thinking as notes in our chart.

FINDINGS AND DISCUSSION

Our analysis of postpandemic media reports revealed the orientation of excessive entitlement held by the public and represented in the public discourse about teachers. We uncovered three themes that support our assertion that the public discourse held an orientation of excessive entitlement toward teachers. We found that in these media reports, the voices of teachers were mostly absent. We also found an orientation of excessive entitlement in discourses about the teacher shortage. The third theme was the loss of student learning.

Missing Voices of Teachers

As we reviewed the news stories about education regardless of source, we found that seldom were teachers interviewed for the stories or were their opinions sought. In one example, an article claiming to represent the views of "Utah teachers" turned out to be hyperbole, since three teachers from just one school in one school district were quoted (https://www.ksl.com/article/50337352/utah-teachers-speak-out-about-frustration-burnout-that-comes-with-teaching-through-a-pandemic). Often, in news stories where teachers were quoted (instead of just administrators or union representatives), only one teacher was cited, or if more than one was quoted, they were from the same school. In an article on how important substitutes are to supporting quality education, one substitute was represented as a hero (https://www.npr.org/sections/ed/2015/05/22/406524776/an-irreplaceable-replacement-this-sub-gets-the-job-done). She was praised as an unusual case even though in the authors' own experiences with five school districts and personal acquaintances who act as substitutes, in their substitute roles, they act in ways similar to the lone substitute lauded in the news article.

The media seldom sought the voices of groups of teachers who prepared to be teachers through higher education-based teacher education including mentored school placements. Usually, the media quoted administrators or union representatives from the National Education Association (NEA) or American Federation of Teachers (AFT). Weingarten, the president of AFT, was the most often quoted person because of recommendations she made to the Centers for Disease Control and Prevention (CDC) about guidelines for opening schools. Media pundits argued that the guidelines for masking or quarantine proposed were too strenuous and unnecessary (consider again the story of the media assertion about the impact of a single teacher removing a mask for a reading lesson). Instead of teachers, legislators developing laws and policies for schools following the pandemic were also quoted as the voices and representatives of schools and teachers because of legislative work on policies and laws for education (consider such legislators were being pressured by parents, who were their electors, to ignore guidelines).

We are fairly sure that news media personnel could easily have located teachers who could be interviewed. Local schools are spread across a community, and teachers are a highly educated and articulate population. The teaching force makes up 2.5% of the entire working population (Staake, 2023). This suggests that news personnel took a nonpersonhood orientation to teachers and probably did not think of them as individuals but a uniform population who would know little about education and educational issues. Further, they probably believe the ongoing and absolutely wrong myth that teachers are not smart (see Darling-Hammond). Media almost always referenced teachers as deficit and unknowing about what support schools and teachers needed. This is revealed in their reliance on administrators, union representatives, or voices from national organizations.

Since we found very few teachers' voices in articles on education, classrooms, and learning in schools in national news, we looked then at stories in local news. The teachers cited in local stories were almost uniformly teachers who were certified through alternative routes and teachers who taught in charter or private schools. Teachers who were certified through education and preparation rather than alternative routes were seldom cited, and usually only a single teacher was quoted. A typical story reported on a change in a district; the story cited one teacher and used the quotes from her as if she represented the opinion and knowledge of all teachers in that district – again an example of the orientation to teachers as holding nonpersonhood.

Teacher Shortage

While researchers have been studying teacher retention and attrition for at least three decades (see Cochran Smith & Zeichner, 2009). The first meta-analysis was conducted in 2008 (Borman & Dowling). More recently, a second meta-analysis on research studies was conducted from before the pandemic published in 2019 (Nguyen et al.). Such research compiles research findings across multiple studies. For example, Nguyen et al. (2019) reviewed and identified 26,000 studies on teacher attrition conducted since the review by Borman and Dowling (2008). However, in their decisions about which studies they would include, all qualitative studies (since they do not produce results that can be utilized as data in meta-analysis) were excluded. From those 26,000 studies, only 120 studies were actually included in this meta-analysis.

The criterion for selection of studies for inclusion is a way that quantitative studies of teacher characteristics or actions present teachers as objects or nonpersons. The other 25,680 qualitative studies, related to particular teachers, their voices, and individual stories of leaving, were excluded from further analysis or discussion. Yet their inclusion in the larger narrative of why teachers leave teaching would allow for the development of a more nuanced account of teacher attrition. In other words, such studies usually treat teachers as individuals and not as deficit in their decision to leave teaching. In the Nguyen et al. (2019) study, the authors actually only included studies where individual teacher accounts and reasoning disappear. Teachers are not presented as individuals with specific reasons for leaving but as a collective, and individual personhood and personal reasons for leaving the profession disappear. Clandinin et al. (2015) found that the narrative about teacher attrition, which they labeled as teacher leaving, is flawed when the problem is approached from a collective perspective. Each teacher's path to becoming teachers or leaving teaching is captured in the story their lives tell and not in a collective analysis of reasons for leaving.

Further, the narrative about teacher attrition treats this phenomenon as a waste of societal resources; yet, researchers have found that the things teachers take with them from their training as teachers remain, and they continue to use their learning to support good things in society (Pinnegar et al., 2018). Just like the public has an expectation that teachers should buy the tools needed in their teaching, all teachers have a moral obligation to sacrifice all to both become and act in the role of teachers. The stories of teachers leaving the profession communicate a pervasive sense that teachers should continue as teachers regardless. This is an important part of the attitude of excessive entitlement the public holds toward teachers. The individual lives and realities of teachers are not important in the eyes of the public, and they should sacrifice all (see Bullough & Baughman, 1997; Clandinin et al., 2015; Spencer, 1984).

The public narrative about teachers represented in the media is an easy story, where teachers are presented as less than competent. This results in an erosion of respect for teaching or being a teacher since the public discourse carries the notion that anyone can be a teacher, communicating a lack of understanding of the demands (Spencer, 1984). Even before the pandemic, schools were confronted with the problem of teacher attrition and increasing numbers of early retirement. Since the pandemic, the problem of teacher shortage has spread beyond North America and is becoming a worldwide problem. Yet, in the face of the need for more teachers, the media rhetoric presents this as a catastrophe story. There is little or no attention to what really needs to be done. Implicit in the narrative is the sense that if teachers leave, they are stupid, and if they stay, they are stupid. If teachers mention issues of pay, they are whining. Teachers whose compromised health resulted in their leaving, which often occurred because children were not required to mask and they felt their health was compromised, are seen as having a lack of commitment.

Loss of Learning

Student testing has always been a hot topic in the media, and this was true during the pandemic and after students had returned to school. Often though, these media reports were emotional and alarm-raising, "Steep drops in reading and math scores among 9-year-olds show effects of COVID learning loss" (https://www.foxnews.com/media/chart-sharp-declines-math-reading-scores-during-covid). Many discussions about learning loss did not reference testing results since testing was not administered according to the usual schedule while students' schooling was interrupted. Thus, reports of huge learning loss are often lacking in evidence. One article that cited learning loss in 9-year-olds used National Center for Education Statistics (NCES) data from a sample of 7,400 9-year-olds from 410 schools (https://nces.ed.gov/nationsreportcard/ltt/). Yet this report from the National Assessment of Educational Progress (NAES) did not follow its usual administration schedule of every 4 years and did not follow the same students but relied on a random sample. Therefore, it is not an all-inclusive report or accurate for each state or local school's experiences during and after the pandemic.

Other articles used inflammatory language, such as "fears for the future of students who don't catch up" and "the future of American children hangs in the balance" (https://www.foxnews.com/us/online-school-put-us-kids-behind-some-adults-have-regrets). Yet policymakers were not always clear what the best trade off would be for protecting the health of families versus the isolation of at-home learning. This is evident in the various and often conflicting ways each state, school district, and community approached the timing and procedure of returning to school. High on the list of concerns for many teachers is the fear that learning gaps will widen between advantaged and disadvantaged students.

In articles that report teachers' responses to the learning gap, the teachers' focus is on students. In contrast, the media presents this learning gap as a catastrophe narrative. The discourse around the learning gap on teachers focused on testing rather than on the complicated demands of teaching. There is little acknowledgment that in a regular classroom, 25% of the students are at or below the poverty line which means they may come to school hungry, tired, or without proper clothing. As many as 20% of students in regular classrooms struggle with learning disabilities or other disability challenges, 15% speak a home language other than English, and at least 40% are culturally, ethnically, and racially diverse.

All teachers face the challenge of responding to this diverse array of students so that the learning of all students in the classroom moves forward. In reporting on teaching, the media often focused on testing or testing results for students and teachers rather than teacher action in the face of these challenges. Such reports talk about the results of quantitative measures and not on what students learn and teachers teach. The public discourse does not report on how teachers are responding to the challenge of the learning gap. The media seldom, if ever, reports on parents' and students' commitment to learning and how they take up this challenge.

There are two extremes in the discourse around these issues. Conservative viewpoints simply insist that public education is broken and cannot be revived. Liberal views evince concerns about the learning gap and teachers' failure to overcome that gap, but they argue for the need for more inclusion and more kindness and acceptance of diversity, yet just being fair does not teach kids to read. Both camps seem convinced that each year, there is a finite amount of learning that must be achieved rather than recognition of achievement and learning as part of a natural flow which can lag, eddy, and occur with rapid acceleration. Most parents have the view if my child is not outperforming all others with minimal commitment from the parent or the child, then what's wrong with the teachers?

CONCLUSION

In this chapter, we report a study that provided evidence of the ways in which media and public discourse promote an attitude of excessive entitlement toward teachers through an orientation of deficit and a representation of them as nonpersons. We inquired into the ways in which teachers are represented in media-based public discourse following the pandemic. What led to our interest is that during the pandemic on social media, parents and other members of the public posted compliments to teachers in recognition of their efforts as teachers. Because students and teachers were quarantined during the pandemic and much of the responsibility for supervising student learning fell to the parents, parents became aware sometimes potentially for the first time how hard teachers worked to educate their students and the economic, intellectual, and emotional sacrifices teachers made for their students. As parents took up the task of education for their children, in many cases, they realized that in public school, teachers paid attention to the learning of multiple students who might be culturally, intellectually, and linguistically diverse. From the time we began our teaching careers, between 20 and 40 years ago, teachers have usually been represented in the public discourse as silly and less competent in their practices. The praise and gratitude for teachers on social media suggested the tide had turned, and the public seemed aware of the complex and compelling demands of teaching. We were interested in whether the public discourse about teachers would continue to represent teachers in a more positive light and whether there would be recognition of the prowess of teachers.

Thus, we took up this inquiry to investigate how the postpandemic discourse found in the media characterized teachers. Through an analysis of stories in specific conservative and more liberal media outlets, we inquired into the themes in the discourse about teachers. We uncovered three themes: the lack of the representation of teacher voices in explorations of the educational issues, issues of teacher leaving or teacher attrition, and an overwhelming concern with lost learning (with implicit messages about teachers' inability to overcome this challenge). We recognized through this examination that in spite of the gratitude toward teachers articulated during the pandemic, afterward as schools reopened, teachers were again represented as nonpersons and deficit.

One of the implications of this representation of teachers has contributed to the increase in alternative routes to teaching where the knowledge provided for teacher candidates in order to teach today's students lacks rigor (Darling-Hammond, 2006), focuses on speed rather than depth, and continues the orientation of nonpersonhood in characterizations of teaching and teachers (Rice et al., 2014; Waller, 1932). Across the world, countries are increasingly faced with a shortage of teachers; thus, the orientation of legislators is to authorize more and increasingly shortened and shallow teacher preparation schemes. The pandemic has made clear the need for more and stronger teachers; however, the public discourse postpandemic continues to represent teachers as nonpersons and deficit. The recommendations for what is needed to prepare powerful teachers articulated by Darling-Hammond (2006) are still a clear representation for what is needed. The public discourse is produced by media who speak with excessive entitlement and imply that anyone can teach, that once committed and prepared to teach, teachers should be willing to sacrifice economically, emotionally, and mentally to continue as teachers because the public is entitled to that.

REFERENCES

Borman, G. D., & Dowling, N. M. (2008). Teacher attrition and retention: A meta-analytic and narrative review of the research. *Review of Educational Research*, *78*(3), 367–409.

Bullough, Jr, R. V., & Baughman, K. (1997). *"First-year teacher" eight years later: An inquiry into teacher development*. Teachers College Press.

Clandinin, D. J., Long, J., Schaefer, L., Downey, C. A., Steeves, P., Pinnegar, E., Roblee, S. M., & Wnuk, S. (2015). Early career teacher attrition: Intentions of teachers beginning. *Teaching Education*, *26*(1), 1–16. https://doi.org/10.1080/10476210.2014.996746

Cochran-Smith, M., & Zeichner, K. M. (Eds.). (2009). *Studying teacher education: The report of the AERA panel on research and teacher education.* Routledge.

Craig, C. J., Hill-Jackson, V., & Kwok, A. (2023). Teacher shortages: What are we short of? *Journal of Teacher Education, 74*(3), 209–213. https://doi.org/10.1177/00224871231166244

Darling-Hammond, L. (2006). Constructing 21st-century teacher education. *Journal of Teacher Education, 57*(3), 300–314.

Darling-Hammond, L., & Bransford, J. (Eds.). (2007). *Preparing teachers for a changing world: What teachers should learn and be able to do.* John Wiley & Sons.

Flores, M. A., & Craig, C. J. (2023). Reimagining teacher education in light of the teacher shortage and the aftershock of COVID-19: Adjusting to a rapidly shifting world. *European Journal of Teacher Education, 46*(5), 772–778. https://doi.org/10.1080/02619768.2023.2294697

Johnson, L. M., & Mossburg, C. (2021, August 13). *California teacher is hospitalized after he's allegedly attacked by a parent over face masks on the first day of school.* CNN. https://www.cnn.com/2021/08/13/us/teacher-parent-fight-face-masks-trnd/index.html

LaTronic-Herb, A., & Noel, T. K. (2023). Understanding the effects of COVID-19 on P-12 teachers: A review of scholarly research and media coverage. *Frontiers in Education.* https://doi.org/10.3389/feduc.2023.1185547

Markowicz, K. (2021, September 30). Parents fight school mask mandates for kids-just follow the science they plead. *Fox News.* https://www.foxnews.com/opinion/parents-fight-school-mask-mandates-children-karol-markowicz

Nguyen, T. D., Pham, L., Springer, M. G., & Crouch, M. (2019). *The factors of teacher attrition and retention: An updated and expanded meta-analysis of the literature* (pp. 19–149). Annenberg Institute at Brown University. https://edworkingpapers.com/ai19-149

Pinnegar, S., Lay, C. D., Andrews, A. B., & Bailey, L. R. (2018). The enduring characteristics of teacher identity: Narratives from teacher leavers. In D. Garbet & A. Ovens (Eds.), *Changing practices from changing times: Past present and future possibilities for self-study research* (pp. 481–483). University of Auckland.

Rice, M. F., Newberry, M., Cutri, R., Pinnegar, S., & Whiting, E. (2014). Exploring teacher educator identity through experiences of non-personhood. In D. Garbet & A. Ovens (Eds.), *Changing practices for changing times: Past, present and future possibilities for self-study research. Proceedings of the tenth international conference on self-study of teacher education practices* (pp. 183–185). Self-Study of Teacher Education Practices SIG.

Richards, E., Quintana, C., Schell, L., & Wong, A. (2021, March 21). *A year after COVID-19 shut schools, students and teachers share what shook them–and what strengthened them.* USA TODAY. https://www.usatoday.com/in-depth/news/education/2021/03/21/covid-online-school-1-year-teachers-kids-share-powerful-quotes/4652348001/

Shepherd, M. (2020, September 5). An open 'thank you' letter to teachers in a Covid-19 world. *Forbes.* https://www.forbes.com/sites/marshallshepherd/2020/10/05/an-open-thank-you-letter-to-teachers-in-a-covid-19-world/?sh=3cf437ef39da

Spencer, D. (1984). The home and school lives of women teachers. *The Elementary School Journal, 84*(3), 283–298.

Staake, J. (2023, January 11). *How many teachers are in the US?* We are teachers. https://www.weareteachers.com/how-many-teachers-are-in-the-us/#:~:text=How%20many%20teachers%20are%20there,2.5%25%20of%20the%20working%20population

Waller, W. (1932). *The sociology of teaching.* Wiley.

SECTION III
BRINGING TO CONSCIOUSNESS THE *UNTHOUGHT KNOWN*

TROUBLING EXCESSIVE ENTITLEMENT: A TEACHER'S REFLECTIVE JOURNEY

Jackie Ellett

Piedmont University, USA

ABSTRACT

Like most in education, I rarely take the opportunity to question and slow down enough to reflect on ideas and intentionally notice the subtle shifts in my thoughts. Life is hurried, and finding quiet reflective moments is difficult but not impossible. Encouraged to confront experiences of excessive entitlement in relation to the social, cultural, and political world, I learned that as with much in life there is a give and take, a negotiation of sorts, which if allowed leads to understanding. The interconnectedness of practitioners' varying experiences with administrators and educational policies raises the question of who affects whom and causes me to reflect on my research questions: 1. What is my relationship with excessive teacher entitlement? 2. Am I implicit in its production? If so, how and why?

In this chapter, I reflect on my cognitive and emotional relationship with excessive entitlement as an embodied experience through autoethnography methodology and phenomenology. By troubling or worrying the notion of excessive entitlement, I confront my beliefs through conversations with student teachers and veteran teachers, examining the interconnectedness of how people are implicit in its production. As a researcher and participant, the theoretical underpinnings of phenomenology allow me to orient myself to my lived experiences as an art teacher, teacher leader, and faculty member and leader at a private university. Pulling from journal entries, emails, written "ponderings," noted conversations, and memory, data support the notion that excessive entitlement occurs at all levels in education, and awareness is the first step toward understanding.

Keywords: Excessive teacher entitlement; teacher narratives; autoethnography; phenomenology; bridling; awareness

> Once again, I stand at the gate that is ajar. Now that my life has followed the course of the winding arabesque, I find myself once more at the place where I started. (Shammas, 1988, p. 226)

Much like Shammas (1988) in *Arabesques*, I find myself returning to the places where I first began teaching and, through the process, grew from my encounters with excessive entitlement. The reflective revisiting of my past, like the winding, intricate tendrils of the arabesque, can be extended beyond the patterned ends through reflexivity. This critical exploration evolves from autobiographical narratives of lived experiences as a practitioner for over 37 years. I begin with my first year of teaching out of a janitor's closet and end where I am today, a private university within the Piedmont or "foot" of the Appalachian Mountains.

As one who has become so hurried due to overscheduling, large teaching loads, excessive advising commitments, and this thing called life, my reflections throughout this writing begin and quickly are hijacked by the subsequent fire that needs extinguishing or the next crisis that requires my attention. I live in a place that is messy in the sense of contradictions and changes, much like qualitative research, where conversations and reflections often shift from what was thought to be understood to the act of questioning. Since March 2020, life has cranked up the intensity even more. So, I begin at the beginning and welcome you in; as my friend Philip Davis would say, "Come on in, but excuse the mess; we've been busy living here."

REFLECTION

> I began teaching in 1986, about 40 minutes outside Atlanta. I had interviewed for the art position at an elementary school. Once I walked through the entrance doors, I immediately felt it was a place where I belonged. I remember the day I went for my interview; I was rushing to leave the high school art classroom where I was student teaching. I had mapped out my route the evening before and had that feeling in the pit of my very core; it was a mix of fear and excitement, nervousness. I would be their first art teacher if the job were offered to me. It was early May when I interviewed at the elementary school. May can be scorching in Georgia, and this year was no exception. I arrived for my interview 30 minutes early, but much to my chagrin, I found I had arrived at the wrong school. You see, both elementary schools have the same name and are located off the same main road. The schools are 23 minutes from each other, and, according to the principal and secretary, "this happens all the time." This was a time when there was no Google, and my first bag phone was not for another two or three years. I arrived at the correct school, sweaty, shaking, and rushed, and asked by the secretary to wait as the principal finished with the interview he was still having. As I waited, I walked around the entrance area and felt a sense of peace and belonging within that space.

Despite the air conditioning chilling my sweat and causing me to shiver, I felt a deep warmth in this moment of knowing. Merleau-Ponty explains this experience as a "response to situations rather than reactions to stimuli" (as cited in Moran &

Mooney, 2002, p. 424). My hurriedness and anxiety heading to my interview, the unsettling feeling on the realization of arriving initially at the wrong school, and later, the overwhelming warmth and sense of peace and knowing are experiences that you too may have felt. This phenomenon of a bodily memory or "lived body" is often linked to phenomenology and the notion we are always bodily within the world. Van Manen (1990) further explains that when we meet someone in their world [context], we first meet them through their body or what we see. The same holds true for ourselves. When we meet someone physically, we reveal something about ourselves. However, we also conceal something simultaneously, whether consciously or unconsciously, despite our efforts. Although I am using an autoethnographic approach as it affords an "insider's perspective on the practices, meanings, and interpretations of cultural phenomenon/experience" (Adams et al., 2015, p. 31) to trouble my experiences with entitlement, I use phenomenology to highlight the shifts in my understandings (Mertens, 2000; Moran & Mooney, 2002) through a continual reflect journaling technique that K. Dahlberg et al. (2008) termed as "bridling" after the bridle worn by a horse. There are three actions to bridling: First, like "bracketing," bridling is "the restraining of one's pre-understanding in the form of personal beliefs, theories, and other assumptions that otherwise would mislead the understanding of meaning and thus limit the research options" (pp. 129–130). Second, it is also about the "understanding as a whole" not just the "pre-understanding" – this is done so as to not "understand too quickly, too carelessly" (p. 130); it is an "open and alert attitude of activity waiting for the phenomenon to show up and display itself within the relationship" (p. 130). Third, it is forward-looking rather than backward-looking, allowing "the phenomenon to present itself" (p. 130).

Phenomenology questions the essence of the lived experience for an individual or group of people and explores such questions as what does it feel like to find a place where you belong? How do we, as educators, recognize, identify, and interpret the phenomenon of entitlement without making assumptions? How do our experiences impact us both cognitively and emotionally? I attempt to flesh out or give more substance to my encounters with entitlement based on my interpretations of my lived experiences within the culture of education/school. I move reflectively between time: the past, the present, and the future in search of answering the questions: What is my relationship with excessive entitlement, and am I implicit in its production? If so, how and why? Are we, as educators, aware of our involvement in excessive entitlement, or does this occur subconsciously, our unawareness contributing to this cycle that may be adopted and passed on by our students and colleges?

PURPOSE AND RESEARCH QUESTIONS

Practitioners are rarely encouraged to confront experiences of excessive entitlement in relation to the social, cultural, and political world. I hope to contribute to the ongoing scholarly conversation concerning the notion and influences of excessive teacher entitlement, the relationship between these influences, and possible ways to regenerate understanding. Freire warns that as we experience and live under oppression, we may, in turn, become oppressors. This thought makes me wonder if our experiences make us teachers of a pedagogy of the oppressed (Freire et al., 2020). The interconnectedness of practitioners' varying experiences with administrators and educational policies raises the question of who affects whom and causes me to reflect on my research questions that guided this self-study:

- What is my relationship with excessive teacher entitlement?
- Am I implicit in its production? If so, how and why?

LITERATURE REVIEW

Theory of Experience and Reflection

Teachers, over time, develop "a store of practical knowledge" (Elbaz-Luwisch, 2005, p. xi) that is unique and personal to each yet has commonalities with others in the teaching profession. While the commonalities of theory and practice learned in teacher preparation courses and in-service meetings give teachers a common language, individual interpretations of personal experiences provide the rich dialogue often shared. These dialogues result in the storied experiences that give voice to practical knowledge for a better understanding of the teaching world (Bruner, 1994; Clandinin & Connelly, 2000).

The nature of experience is both an active and passive element, with the "active hand... we do something to the thing," and the passive "we do something with it; then we suffer or undergo the consequences" (Dewey, 1938/2004, p. 133). Dewey elaborates that experience involves change, but unless this change connects to a consequence, which can be either positive or negative, it is meaningless; little or nothing is learned (Ellett, 2011b). Using reflection to analyze self-data within an autoethnographic lens opens up the opportunity for change within the culture of the phenomenon of excessive teacher entitlement. Polkinghorne (2004) refers to this interaction as the cultural understanding that provides people with "a pretheoretical understanding that gives them a sense about others, the world, and themselves" (p. 152). It provides an immediate understanding of how to get things done and what is needed to accomplish the task. When we encounter a complex problem, the background does not necessarily help us by itself; we extend it by employing the "reflective mode of understanding" (Polkinghorne, 2004, p. 153). "Interaction, then, is the first important element of experience. The second, ... is continuity" (Rodgers, 2002, p. 846).

Interaction and continuity are inseparable; one informs the other. As educators move from one situation to another, their world grows and moves in different directions, making connections and expanding knowledge. This process is learning from experience.

Essentially, continuity allows us to use what we have learned from past experiences, helping us make sense of and gain understanding from new experiences. However, remember that Dewey does not claim all experiences to be educational or constructive; sometimes, they are "mis-educative," meaning they do not allow one to develop further or grow.

Mis-educative can be an area in which excessive teacher entitlement grows as it has the potential for experiences to lead to "callous, and sensitive, and generally immoral directions" (Rodgers, 2002, p. 847), leading to routine actions where an individual will act without an awareness of their actions or the consequences of their actions on others. Thinking of excessive teacher entitlement, I think of mis-educative action routines where a quick response without an offered explanation is short, quick, and sometimes "callous" and insensitive. Dewey cautions that because experience is not cognitive, it is linked within time – the past, present, and future; thus, an experience is incomplete unless meaning is given to it. To offer meaning, autoethnography uses one's experience with the presence of the other, in this case, the culture of school, to connect to the phenomenon of excessive entitlement. Reflection, then, is used to make meaning and study interactions and continuities of an experience. It is the meaning we bring to our experiences that makes us human. It is what brings value to our lives.

Our reflections vary and can happen at the moment. This think-on-your-feet type of reaction is common among teachers and often developed from years of experience (Schön, 1983). Not reflecting on one's practice has the potential of mechanical or stagnant teaching. Dreyfus and Dryfus (1986) distinguish various experience levels from novice to expert. *Experts* know what to do because of years of teaching practice. Their craft has become so much a part of who they are that teaching becomes natural to what they do. When things are proceeding normally, an expert teacher does not solve problems but does what works typically. While most expert performance is ongoing and nonreflective, when time permits, and outcomes are crucial, an expert will deliberate before acting and thus reflect on their intuition. The rules and theories about teaching and learning are internalized and slowly become automatic and a part of the teacher's intuition (Postholm, 2008).

We live in a series of circumstances inseparable from our experiences. Autoethnography helps capture the interplay between the individual and the social and cultural aspects of the phenomenon of excessive entitlement and how they mutually shape each other. Continuity and interaction work hand-in-hand in allowing one to bring the past into the present to create new reactions, thus developing new experiences. The reciprocity of continuity and interaction is why we each have different experiences and points of view, even if participating in the same event. This chapter offers a way of connecting to the larger experience of excessive entitlement that takes place within the culture of school.

Researching Lived Experiences: Phenomenology

Reflecting on my career experiences and troubling the notion of excessive teacher entitlement, my narratives offer the possibility for understanding how my knowledge of the phenomenon has become shaped by the complex historical, personal, communal, and professional landscape of schools (Clandinin &

Connelly, 2000; Ellett, 2011b). By exploring and presenting my experiences and self-meanings, my intention is that a greater understanding will be afforded to those who are questioning the active reciprocal roles teachers (myself) and those who work with/against them play. Often used to get to the essence of a lived experience or action "performed within everyday life" (Van Manen, 1990, p. 4), phenomenology seeks to support understanding phenomena by describing how one orients themselves to the lived experience. Systematic reflection is essential; Husserl explains phenomenology as "self-evidently given... in perception, experienced as the thing itself-in immediate presence, or, in memory" (as cited in Moran & Mooney, 2002, p. 167). It reduces the everyday human encounters of the lifeworld to their very essence of the everyday experience (Moran & Mooney, 2002). This intentional act of being is core for phenomenology; deep description is essential to understanding the act of being. Dodgson (2023) explains that "all phenomenological research is descriptive (rather than explanatory)," focusing on the lived experience from the onset is essential (p. 39). The researcher uses a first-person perspective (I/my) due to the personal perceptions of living and thinking in the lifeworld, explored primarily by Merleau-Ponty, who expressed the idea "as our being *to* the world...a world of perception" (Dahlberg et al., 2008, p. 37).

Intentionality is a critical concept explained by Dahlberg et al. (2008) as "the relationship between a person and the objects or events of his/her experience, or more simply, one's directed awareness of an object or event" (p. 47). Intentionality is the relationship between a person and the item or thought through "comportment" or a practical relationship with the things we know; Heidegger often referred to moving beyond comportment as "being-in-the-world" (Moran & Mooney, 2002, p. 247). We often overlook and do not notice our relationships with everyday encounters, such as excessive entitlement; thus, we are missing out on meaningful connections that can be made and growth that can occur through the recognition and understanding of excessive entitlement. Intentionality was troubled or continually questioned through the use of bridling to move through the relationship between my autobiographical experiences with excessive entitlement to recognition and understanding. While phenomenology is trying to capture the essence of the experience, my collected autobiographical descriptions of excessive teacher entitlement give me the data to dissect. There is a continual pressing forward and questioning in phenomenology that does not always happen in autoethnography. The personal narrative takes one back to an experience as it was in its context; phenomenology reflects back on the experience as being in that moment but pushes forward so that one gains a deeper emotional understanding, and bridling supports the questioning at all stages. As van Manen (1990) explains, phenomenology "offers us the possibility of plausible insights that bring us in more direct contact with the world" (p. 9), thus helping to illuminate the experience of excessive entitlement.

Autoethnography: A Study of Self

Starting with the study of the self, I am coming to my understandings from a personal, autobiographical perspective reflecting on my narratives of teaching and being in the culture I call school.

Stories have been integral to my life, and using stories as data remains appealing to me. Like narrative inquiry, autoethnography is relatively young in qualitative research, focusing on telling stories of the self within a culture. While the writing of Heider and others was implicit to autoethnography, it was not until the 1980s that the term "autoethnography" began to be applied by researchers personally engaging in their research. In the 1990s, Ellis and Bochner began creating texts "encouraging others to delve into their own lives to explore sociocultural milieus" (Glesne, 2006, p. 199). The autoethnographic approach was a natural method to "unveil, interpret, and/or critique the social structures and underlying power dynamics" through personal experiences (Keles, 2022, p. 2026). Allowing me to create "relevant descriptions of a group to which one belongs based on a structured analysis of one's own experience and the experience of others from one's group" (Karra & Phillips, 2008, p. 547). While I am using an autobiographical approach, it is not in opposition to the broader net of cultural focus that occurs with autoethnography; rather, my narratives allow me to bring the cultural focus to respond to the questions of this study.

Through deep descriptions of my personal experiences and discussions with others, I tried to uncover and express my interactions with excessive teacher entitlement within the culture of school. I found reflecting on my lived experiences from three different points of time within my career: beginning, mid-point, and recent interactions; the blended methodology of autoethnography within the theoretical framework of phenomenology helped create connections between personal experiences in the culture of school with an understanding of my part in the narrative of excessive teacher entitlement and "the shifting connections they forge among past, present, and future" (Riessman, 2008, p. 705).

(August 25, 2023)

My computer was updated earlier today. Programs were removed, and others were added. What should've taken 30 minutes took most of the morning and afternoon. I am frustrated and exhausted. I feel like a child; I want to bury my head under a pillow and scream and cry! Not having a working computer most of a day during the first week of classes is not okay. Technology in 2023 should not be this difficult. I do not understand the constant turnover at this school. We can't keep people in IT- ridiculous. My computer was finally working just as I was leaving my office a little after 5:00 p.m. to attend the museum opening, which I was required to attend, and I did so gladly. The artist is someone I know from when I first began teaching. It was absolutely wonderful seeing her and her husband! My frustrations are not because of attending the exhibit but because I had not had a working computer since 11 a.m. It is now after 10 at night, and I have been home for about 40 minutes. I truly do not understand how we, as educators, are expected to complete everything we need when we are constantly fighting against access to basic technology.

I, like many educators, have a high demand placed on my time and am overworked and stretched thin. My teaching load is what is known as a four/four. This means that I teach four courses in each of my two contracted semesters. This would be fine; however, I also carry overloads. This past spring and summer, my university had many professors resign from the College of Education. Loss of faculty has created a tremendous burden on those of us who have been left behind to pick up the pieces.

Autoethnography and phenomenology have allowed me to deeply explore the notion of excessive teacher entitlement and how the outside demands are implicit in my role in this phenomenon.

Bridling to Understand Excessive Teacher Entitlement

Van Manen (1990) explains, "The problem of phenomenological inquiry is not always that we know too little about the phenomenon we wish to investigate, but that we know too much" (p. 46). Knowing too much remained a concern for me during the research process, and bridling my assumptions and preunderstandings through the act of questioning helped. This process gave me that place I needed to think, to ponder. I have found that often, rather than finding answers, I found more questions. During the bridling process, I came to some understandings but ended with more questions. To better understand bridling, I offer an example (excerpt Bridling Journal Entry, November 2009):

> What does it mean to stay? Is staying just a physical act? Is it holding steadfast to what you believe in, hold dear? Is it done because there is nowhere else to go...or if there is another place, is it no better than where you are? Why do I choose to stay? For convenience, for comfort, security? Why does anyone stay anywhere? How often are people forced to leave- to go against their will? To be displaced- to feel abandoned by a system, a person? It will be interesting to hear why....

When working on my study of teacher narratives, I found it impossible to separate myself from my research (Ellett, 2011a). I decided to embrace the problem by allowing my thoughts and experiences to run parallel with my participants. The use of bridling allowed me to concentrate on my participants while giving me a place for my voice to better hear my participants' individual voices. Dewey (1938/2004) informed us that our lives are intertwined with our experiences, and that our experiences are what education is based upon. Understanding my role in excessive teacher entitlement and whether I am the oppressor, the oppressed, or both can be troubled through the process of bridling.

Dahlberg (2006) introduced bridling as a metaphor based on her experiences with horseback riding. Rather than bracketing one's assumptions and putting them aside, Dahlberg embraced them and recognized that our experiences influence us to some extent. Bridling draws on Merleau-Ponty's philosophical perspective of the *threads of intentionality*, which connect us with the world that could never be cut off but could be tightened and loosened (Ellett, 2011b). Dahlberg felt that the analogy of bridling while horseback riding accomplished much the same thing; the rider can draw (tighten) and slacken the reins on the horse to cause the horse to move directionally (Ellett, 2011b). This metaphor is a straightforward visual for me and anyone who has ever ridden a horse. The process of bridling is questioning that causes the researcher to tighten or loosen up on their inquiry, a place to create lists and thoughts or brain dumping, which I have been doing more of in my personal life.

> (May 9, 2022)
>
> A vote of no confidence. I am the vice-chair of the faculty senate. Today was hard and uncomfortable. I took up and counted the results. I checked and made sure there were no duplicates. Today, the faculty concluded and passed a vote of no confidence for our president and "administration," but the focus was on the president. I like him. He has always been friendly, and I felt supported, though I never asked for anything. But this is not about me – or is it? A beer has helped take off the edge, but I feel sick. I cannot help but to reflect on excessive

entitlement. Am I applying the practice of excessive entitlement? Am I using my power to do harm to someone else? Am I representing the faculty? Am I representing myself? Am I representing others in administration? Is this an example of excessive teacher entitlement? Is this what happens, or is it the result of being micromanaged/oppressed? We turn to oppressing others because of my own dealings with angst and oppression. Am I now, as Freire says, becoming the oppressor? Is this a vindictive act? Is this something I can consciously say is, okay? I cannot help but think that I am part of this problem. Perhaps there could have been something else I could have done. I don't like where I am. I don't like this process. As a leader, I accepted the role of representation, but I do not like it – this is emotionally very hard, and I cannot help but place myself in his shoes. I cannot help but feel hurt for him. I want to fix it – but I can't.

Methodology and More Questions

Using phenomenology as my theoretical framework to investigate the social and cultural factors of my subjective experiences of excessive teacher entitlement allowed me to come closer to understanding the phenomenon. Using autoethnography as my methodology along with bridling, I was able to reflect on my personal experiences with excessive teacher entitlement within the broader cultural context of school.

My theoretical framework was derived from what made sense to me as I reflected on my cognitive and emotional relationship with excessive entitlement. As an embodied experience (Moran & Mooney, 2002) and my past love of the narrative, it became apparent during my discussions with colleagues that writing narratively through an autoethnographic lens made sense. I have confronted my beliefs by reflecting on my conversations and my lived experiences as an educator. However, this is an ongoing process that does not just end but continues. Experience and reflection become synonymous with one another as I bring forth memories of personal experiences of excessive entitlement and question if I, too, am guilty as an educator and leader of "excessive teacher entitlement," even if unintentionally (Ratnam & Craig, 2021, p. 1).

As with all autoethnographic practices, as the researcher, my voice surfaces throughout because reflection and intuitive knowing are constant in the midst of writing. As I researched, I focused on unpacking the experience based on reflective practice (Schön, 1983). We [researchers] often get in the way of our research (Mertens, 2000). So, I intentionally step back, leave, and return to look at my musings from a fresh viewpoint by discussing my thoughts with others. This practice allowed me to distance myself further and delve deeper into my meanings. To further push myself out of the way, I used a bridling journal (Dahlberg et al., 2008) for deeper questioning and noticing those things on the fringe of my memories. As my past professor, Dr St. Pierre, once said, "Qualitative research is like nailing Jell-O to the wall; you see what sticks, and you begin working from that." It is messy; bits and pieces stick, and others give away to smudges of revelations, but in the end, we come a little bit closer to multiple understandings. However, there remain questions, more questions as I struggle with understanding. Life is like this as well; it is messy, and our interactions with others are not always predictable but often intentional, even if they are subconscious.

REFLECTIONS OF EXCESSIVE TEACHER ENTITLEMENT

My reflections in this study are a blend of journal entries, emails, written "ponderings," and noted conversations. I use italicized text to note journal and bridling entries.

Narrative #1

In August of 1986, I began teaching. I do not know the exact date, but I do have a journal entry from the 19th that I will include.

> *It is my first day at Rockbridge Elementary. An art room was not included when the school was first built in 1966, nor is one in the plans for the addition that is expected to be completed by the coming spring. I am the first art teacher to enter this building with a paid position. I feel welcomed, excited, and somewhat nervous as I do not have any supplies, a classroom, or a place to call "home." In just seven short days, I will start being an art teacher. What will I do? I continue to add to my list of things "to do" – order a cart, find a room or an empty closet, introduce myself to the custodian. (Dr Nix told us often in class, "make sure you know your custodian! They are often the first person you go to when you need something!") Maybe I should meet the custodian first.*

As with many in the field of education, starting is always exciting. We aspire to be teachers who will save lives, make a difference, and move our students to accomplish big things. Movies such as Blackboard Jungle (Brooks, 1955), Dead Poets Society (Weir, 1989), Mr. Holland's Opus (Herek, 1995), and Akeelah and the Bee (Atchison, 2006) have all helped to feed these dreams and inspire teachers and those who would be teachers to embrace this rewarding profession. I am a teacher; I absolutely love what I do most days. However, teaching is complex and seems more difficult than when I first began, or is it? In talking with educators and my students, the actual teaching of subject matter does not seem to be the problem. According to these groups, student behaviors, administrative and parental support, and technology that is not current and works unpredictably are the most significant issues educators face.

In January of 2023, the Association for Supervision and Curriculum Development (ASCD) published an article based on the collected data from Brown University and the University of Albany documenting teacher prestige and job satisfaction, noting both are at or below the lowest point in the past 50 years. During the onset of the 2020 pandemic, teachers were hailed as heroes because they quickly adapted to online teaching, adjusting to meet students' needs. Just as quickly, teachers were blamed for education shortcomings. This fame and blame tug-of-war of public opinion may be one factor in a decline in interest in teaching by high school students (Ingram, 2023). Craig et al. (2023), in "Teacher Shortages: What are We Short of?" grapples with this question and concludes that "we are mostly short on the will to enact widespread and sustainable change" (p. 73). What does this mean? First, teacher shortages are not new. In 1986, when I was first hired as a teacher, there were not enough teachers in Georgia, especially in low-income schools. Kozol (1991) speaks of teacher shortages in the 1980s and 1990s, especially in poor urban areas in the North and Midwest. When I first went to human resources (HR) to investigate my retirement in 2016, I was told that 2015–2019 would be a time when many in my school system would be retiring, and that there was a concern about whether there would be enough teachers. The pandemic hit a few years later, creating a more significant problem because many who were near retirement age and could afford to leave left. Craig et al. support my conversations and note that "New York City specifically, has 20% less teacher education candidates than in prior years" (p. 72). According to Sparks, "American teachers teach 200 more contracted hours per year than their global peers" (as cited in Craig et al., 2023, p. 72).

In 2011, I wrote, "Many good art teachers, those who had planned on teaching forever, are leaving the profession as soon as they qualify for retirement. The stressors of the economy, educational mandates, fears of displacement and job loss loom heavily on those in education, especially in the areas that are not looked upon as core curriculum, such as the arts" (Ellett, 2011b, pp. 1–2). Teacher attrition is not new. I have to agree with Craig et al. that we are short on "useful data" (p. 73). From my conversations and personal experiences, I believe that part of the reason for this shortage is that teachers are experiencing excessive entitlement within their jobs. "Teachers need an environment, where they can reclaim what is rightfully due to them, in other words, what they are, justly, entitled to, respect, voice, and autonomy" (Ratnam & Craig, 2021, p. 3).

I am on a 5-day collaborative retreat with educators teaching in the South. In the evenings, we discuss all things education, even items unrelated to the project we have been brought together to complete. This is downtime. Like educators everywhere, we talk school. I brought up the notion of excessive entitlement in teachers and whether we are part of the problem. The conversation was fascinating. As we talked and discussed this topic, some important things stood out to me. First, there is the element of time or lack thereof. The small group I was talking with discussed how we, as faculty of universities, colleges, and teachers in k-12 schools, carry more than our "fair workload." "Schools really don't seem to take retention of teachers critically enough," was a comment, and the discussion stayed there well into the night.

When asked what strategies they felt would keep teachers in schools, the ideas were simple: recognition for accomplishments both in and outside the school and support to visit other teachers. Within this small group, it was felt that the general populace needs to be educated in what education is. Those not in the field of education consume it but don't understand it. "The population does not seem to treat teachers as professionals – they will hire a 'professional' to fix their dishwasher but feel they can tell us how to teach history." Currently, parental control over education is a hot topic in the United States. Many news stories show disgruntled parents addressing school boards on issues such as critical race theory and the teaching of Black History in schools. Some outcomes include book banning, curriculum rewrites, and course deletions. One educator noted, "As a professional educator, I can expose children to a variety of viewpoints; I can expose them to information they wouldn't get if they stayed home." The discussion moved to online teaching and the difficulties of education during COVID-19. The topic of students not showing up to class and teachers being mandated to falsify passing grades was also discussed.

(Bridling Journal 10/23)

I wonder, is this too an example of excessive entitlement? Am I implicit in disseminating these actions and reactions myself? In and to my students? Are we all implicit to excessive entitlement at some level? Do I avoid the reality of excessive entitlement, shying away from it, running? Is this truly something that happens and is out of our control? Through this bridling, I seem to be able to hold these thoughts in front of me, move from the past to the present, and think about the future. How can I keep from imposing my power on my students? Can I? Is it possible? I wonder if this is possible. A realization – we ALL have been part of excessive entitlement, whether consciously or subconsciously. Ah, this, too, is a point to further ponder and trouble.

Narrative #2

(Journal, January 18, 2011) It was announced today that the school system in which I work would have more cuts. Our county has the highest number of foreclosures in the nation for 2010, a 25% decrease in tax revenues, and the school system is 85 million dollars short. Every employee in our system would have to take 13 furlough days in order to break even. The governor of Georgia announced earlier this week that there would be no more furlough days. What did this all mean? There was an anxious buzz that swarmed around the school as we tried to wrap our heads around this new announcement. We had just been told two months earlier that things were getting better, the economy was improving, and our school system was financially sound even though other counties around us were experiencing more teacher cuts, school closings, and the possibility of losing programs. How could this happen? What were we going to do? As I sat in my 15-year-old black pickup I looked out the window across the emptying parking lot. Many of the staff were leaving or had already left; the sky was appropriately gray as if to reflect the heaviness we all felt. I turned the ignition; the truck rattled as it started up; the weatherman was talking of the possibility of more snow. I knew what this all meant....more cuts, more jobs lost, more teachers leaving, but not because of choice.

I remember this day. I remember it well. "The Great Recession of 2008 to 2009 was the worst economic downturn in the US since the Great Depression... What started as a classic tale of greed and deregulation ended in a global crisis that caused six million households to lose their homes" (Duggan, 2023, para. 1–2). As a teacher during this time, it was stressful. Like so many, I was worried about my job, making ends meet, and paying my mortgage. I was fortunate, though, and was able to pick up an adjunct position to supplement some of my pay loss. Not all school systems felt the cuts equally. The gap in inequality in education became greater in rural schools because small school boards could not raise property taxes (Salzar, 2020). Class sizes increased, and many teachers and staff lost their jobs because they were the last hired or were part of a fine arts or Reserve Officers' Training Corp (ROTC) program, which had been eliminated. We "all" had to make sacrifices, yet we "all" did not; this was experienced differently in each school district. One area where there was an increase in revenue was in state universities, where tuition in one school rose 50% between 2008 and 2011. Excessive entitlement continues to happen in education, and while Kozol may have focused on the extremes of wealth and poverty in large urban schools, the effects of the Great Recession are felt today as school systems try to catch up on reviving eliminated programs and resetting salaries.

My assumptions of excessive teacher entitlement began with my thoughts of *entitlement* within the context of social media. We hear of many acts of entitlement in alignment with feelings of deserving of positions, things, and services. The image of "Karen's" immediately came to my mind, as this term has become synonymous with a woman who feels entitled to certain rights based on her self-assumed position in society as the keeper of the laws or unspoken rules. An example would be a woman (or man) getting upset and confronting someone in a parking lot to discipline them for not returning a grocery cart to the receptacle or jumping in front of someone waiting to pull into the coveted store parking space. These entitlements are usually presented in an accusatory confrontation. They may include videotaping of the event, which has become so popular as a brain-numbing pastime on such platforms as Instagram and TikTok. When I hear someone as being entitled, I think of undeserving societal rights, such as being allowed within a certain exclusive establishment by way of proxy because a parent may be someone of power. In each circumstance, the connotation is always negative and "has become part of our collective lexicon" (Fisk, 2010, p. 103).

Within my bridling journal, I brain-dumped a list of words to describe entitlement.

(Bridling Journal February 2022)

Entitlement ... excessive entitlement ... the words that come to mind are "self-centered," "owed," "undeserving," and "privileged," to name a few. These are all negative connotations, but what if entitlement is not negative? As I continue listing words such as "bully", "not earned", "better than others", and phrases began to emerge. This question: "Can entitlement mean confidence in one's professional knowledge?"

I did what any self-respecting 21st-century woman would do; I googled the question, "What is meant by excessive entitlement?" I discovered that my thoughts align with the many articles that popped up, and that entitlement is a personality trait often associated with narcissism (Adams, 2018). Adams pointed out that entitled might not always be negative. "Sometimes we mistake entitlement for a sense of self-confidence projected by competent, assured, often charismatic others," and sometimes a moment of a "fleeting, situational rush of entitlement can be a good thing; it can increase creativity and lead to novel, unusual solutions to problems, the kind of out-of-the-box thinking that organizations and employers encourage" (para. 2).

What about teacher entitlement? Does this help explain and support those moments when teachers override students' opinions? Is this the positivity in entitlement or at least gives an excuse as to why teachers will say, "No, that's not correct" or "This is how/why it is done this way"? Perhaps this is why teachers do not always go along with changes in curriculum and ways of teaching "that seemingly were in their students' and their own best interests" (Craig & Ratnam, 2021, p. 274). This is a frustration that I have felt in trying to help students understand a concept, and they are unwilling to yield to my explanation. Perhaps this is an example of excessive teacher entitlement. I often end a session of bridling with more, not less, questions.

Narrative #3

(October 14, 2023)

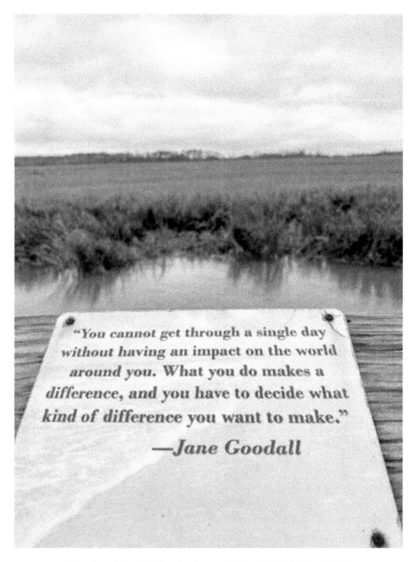

Fig. 1. Sapelo Island. *Source:* Photo by J. Ellett 2023.

You cannot get through a single day without having an impact on the world around you. What you do makes a difference, and you have to decide what kind of difference you want to make.
—Jane Goodall (UGAMI, 1990)

Today, we drove around in Sapelo. We went to Hog Hammock and, on the way, saw an alligator. It was small, probably 4 feet in length, but I'm not 100% sure as we only saw his head; I only imagined the body a little bit longer. We visited the post office and came out on the dock, and that's where I found the quote by Jane Goodall (UGAMI, 1990).

How appropriate! As I am reflecting on excessive teacher entitlement, I cannot help but connect how her words ring true in 2023. I feel a deep sadness as I think about my colleagues. I really wish they would have stayed and waited out the transition, no matter how hard it might be. Part of me felt like I was being abandoned. Actually, I still feel this way, but I know deep down that they left because they had to. Sometimes there is not a choice. Sometimes, we do what is best for our mental and physical health. Living in an environment of fear and uncertainty is hard. Especially if your family is depending on your income for support. One of my good friends left because of the distress of the feeling of uncertainty, of feeling the caustic effects of excessive entitlement that comes out of power. A job opportunity came, and they had to take it. "I did not realize how caustic a place I was in until I left." Life does not have to be a place where you live in fear and uncertainty, not knowing what might happen next. This type of emotional bondage causes not only emotional grief but also physical illness. I am glad that we are moving away from this place, yet I feel a sense of guilt.

Sometimes, we do things we don't want to because we feel we have no choice. Sometimes, the decision is not to do that thing, whatever it may be, so we leave. Polkinghorne (2004) explains that meanings are not concrete because we continuously reconstruct them. I have been constantly interpreting and (re)constructing meaning throughout the entire research process. Each of us is aware only of our own unique realm of meaning, making the study of meaning dependent upon self-reflection.

CONCLUSIONS

I end where I began. I have gone full circle in reliving remembered experiences and have realized that we are all in this constant mode of traveling through and in our experiences to understand our effects upon the world and others. Life is messy, and if we are honest and allow ourselves to walk into that place where we have been living, we may find that place of understanding. I am beginning to understand, but I am only beginning. I have more questions, and only through reflection will I be able to better understand the complexity of excessive teacher entitlement. As Ratnam and Craig (2021) note, "the problem lies not in them [teachers], but in our inadequate understanding of this phenomenon" (p. 3). The real problem, then, is understanding the active reciprocal roles teachers and those who work with/against them play. More research is needed, and perhaps it should start with our students (October 2023), "...we are always taught that teachers are entitled to respect, but we are not taught that students are as well."

ACKNOWLEDGMENT: REFLECTION OF AWARENESS

Writing this chapter has been a journey of personal growth. Through reflection and dialogue, I have come to know and understand the power that excessive teacher entitlement has directly and indirectly on the lives of those in education.

Tara Ratnam and Cheryl Craig encouraged me to continue questioning and expanding my autobiographical narratives to better inform the reader. I also informed myself. As an educator, I have come to realize my position cannot only do harm but also has the potential, through awareness, to do good. Being open to awareness often takes courage. The impact of excessive teacher entitlement is a two-way encounter that can be healing. I did not understand this until Tara and I began conversing via email. Initially, I struggled with developing a deep understanding of the repercussions of excessive entitlement, but the dialogic process we have been engaged in opened the gates to a collaboration of meaning-making and provocation, which led to an epiphany. In that moment of clarity, I discovered I was living Freire's theory! The dialogic process allowed me to become an active agent by living a "pedagogy of question[s]" rather than answers (Brass et al., 1985, p. 9). During this revelation, I became aware that the "book itself is an outcome of the dialogic meaning making process we advocate as a healing touch to excessive entitlement" (personal communication with Tara, December 29, 2023). Honest dialogic exchange has the great potential to heal. Being curious and reflective, asking questions, allowing students to ask questions, and, most importantly, daring to listen deeply are actions that pave the way to awareness and change.

REFERENCES

Adams, J. (2018, January 15). What we mean when we talk about entitlement. *Psychology Today*. https://www.psychologytoday.com/us/blog/between-the-lines/201801/what-we-mean-when-we-talk-about-entitlement

Adams, T., Holman Jones, S., & Ellis, C. (2015). *Autoethnography*. Oxford University Press.

Atchison, D. (2006). *Akeelah and the bee [Film]*. Lionsgate.

Brass, N., Macedo, D. P., & Freire, P. (1985). Toward a pedagogy of the question: Conversations with Paulo Freire. *The Journal of Education*, *167*(2), 7–21. https://www.jstor.org/stable/42742089

Brooks, R. (1955). *Blackboard jungle [Film]*. Metro-Goldwyn-Mayer (MGM).

Bruner, D. D. (1994). *Inquiry and reflection: Framing narrative practice in education*. State University of New York Press.

Clandinin, J. D., & Connelly, F. M. (2000). *Narrative inquiry: Experience and story in qualitative research*. Jossey-Bass.

Craig, J. C., Hill-Jackson, V., & Kwok, A. (2023). Teacher shortages: What are we short of? *Journal of Teacher Education*, *74*(3), 209–213.

Craig, C., & Ratnam, T. (2021). Excessive teacher/faculty entitlement in review: What we unearthed, where to from here. In T. Ratnam & C. J. Craig (Eds.), *Understanding excessive teacher and faculty entitlement: Advances in research on teaching* (Vol. 38, pp. 1–13). Emerald Publishing Limited.

Dahlberg, K. (2006). The essence of essences – The search for meaning structures in phenomenological analysis of lifeworld phenomena. *International Journal of Qualitative Studies on Health and Well-Being*, *1*, 11–19.

Dahlberg, K., Dahlberg, H., & Nystrom, M. (2008). *Reflective lifeworld research*. Studentlitteratur.

Dewey, J. (1938/2004). *Experience and education*. Kappa Delta Phi.

Dodgson. (2023). Phenomenology: Researching the lived experience. *Journal of Human Lactation*, *39*(3), 385–396.

Dreyfus, H., & Dryfus, S. (1986). *Mind over machine: The power of human intuitive expertise in the era of the computer*. Free Press.

Duggan, W. (2023, June 21). A short history of the Great Recession. *Forbes Advisor*. https://www.forbes.com/advisor/investing/great-recession/

Elbaz-Luwisch, F. (2005). *Teachers' voices: Storytelling impossibility*. Information Age Publishing.

Ellett, J. (2011a). Narrative and phenomenology as methodology for understanding persistence in art teachers: A reflective journey. *Marilyn Zurmuehlen Working Papers in Art Education, 2011*(1), 1–14. https://doi.org/10.17077/2326-7070.1407

Ellett, J. (2011b). *Narrative and phenomenology as methodology for understanding persistence in art teachers: A reflective journey*. [Doctoral dissertation, University of Georgia]. UGA Campus Repository. https://doi.org/10.17077/2326-7070.1407

Fisk, G. M. (2010). "I want it all and I want it now!" An examination of the etiology, expression, and escalation of excessive employee entitlement. *Human Resource Management Review, 20*(2), 102–114. https://doi.org/10.1016/j.hrmr.2009.11.001

Freire, P., Ramos, M. B., & Macedo, D. (2020). *Pedagogy of the oppressed*. Bloomsbury Publishing.

Glesne, C. (2006). *Becoming qualitative researchers: An introduction* (3rd ed.). Pearson Education.

Herek, S. (1995). *Mr. Holland's opus [Film]*. Paramount.

Ingram, N. (2023, January 18). *Is the teaching profession in decline?* ASCD. https://www.ascd.org/blogs/is-the-teaching-profession-in-decline

Karra, N., & Phillips, N. (2008). Researching "back home": International management research as autoethnography. *Organizational Research Methods, 11*(3), 541–561. https://doi.org/10.1177/109442810629

Keles. (2022). Autoethnography as a recent methodology in applied linguistics: A methodological review. *Qualitative Report, 27*(2), 448–474.

Kozol, J. (1991). *Savage inequalities: Children in America's schools*. Broadway Paperbacks.

Mertens, D. M. (2000). *Research, evaluation, in education and psychology: Integrating diversity with quantitative, qualitative, and mixed methods*. Sage Publications.

Moran, D., & Mooney, T. (Eds.). (2002). *The phenomenology reader*. Routledge.

Polkinghorne, D. E. (2004). *Practice and human sciences: The case for a judgment-based practice of care*. State University of New York Press.

Postholm, M. B. (2008). Teachers developing practice: Reflection as key activity. *Teaching and Teacher Education, 24*, 1717–1728.

Ratnam, T., & Craig, C. J. (2021). Introduction: The idea of excessive teacher entitlement: Breaking new ground: Digging at the roots. In T. Ratnam & C. J. Craig (Eds.), *Understanding excessive teacher and faculty entitlement: Advances in research on teaching* (Vol. 38, pp. 1–13). Emerald Publishing Limited. https://doi.org/10.1108/S1479-36872021000003800

Riessman, C. K. (2008). *Narrative methods for the human sciences*. Sage Publications.

Rodgers, C. (2002). Defining reflection: Another look at John Dewey and reflective thinking. *Teachers College Record, 104*(4), 842–866.

Salzar, J. (2020, May 7). Georgia revisits lessons of the Great Recession with the new economic downturn. *Atlanta Journal-Constitution, 72*(128). https://www.ajc.com/news/state–regional–govt–politics/georgia-revisits-lessons-great-recession-with-new-economic-downturn/UUuBkNTQUXACdAF7qZ7I6J/

Schön, D. A. (1983). *The reflective practitioner: How professionals think in action*. Basic Books.

Shammas, A. (1988). *Arabesques*. Harper & Row Publishers.

University of Georgia Marine Institute at Sapelo Island [UGAMI]. (1990). *Jane Goodall...* [Wooden plaque]. Long Tabby Complex.

Van Manen, M. (1990). *Researching lived experience: Human science for an action sensitive pedagogy*. State University of New York Press.

Weir, P. (1989). *Dead poets' society* [Film]. Paramount.

IN THE SHADOW OF TRADITIONAL EDUCATION: A *CURRERE* OF SCHOOL ENTITLEMENT AND STUDENT ERASURE

Richard D. Sawyer

Washington State University Vancouver, USA

ABSTRACT

In this study, I use currere *to examine excessive entitlement in my own high school education. By "excessive entitlement," I emphasize teachers' actions and systemic conditions related to an excessive educational mindset justifying (and manifesting) self-infallibility. Teachers displaying excessive entitlement might take for granted, for example, the correctness of their actions, closing self-awareness, and more equitable relations with others (especially students). On a structural level, it includes, for example, societal norms, school policies, educational traditions, and often laws. Specifically, I present findings examining three levels of curriculum – the formal or explicit, the implicit or hidden, and the null or present/absent. I offer my own story as a case study of how schools and teachers may silence and erase student identity and culture as well as how more inclusive and dialogic teaching approaches (and methods of inquiry) can counteract and offer alternatives to such oppressive forces. My framework includes professional ethics, moral ethics, and social justice ethics. Looking back at my history as a gay high school student, I discovered that my school's explicit curriculum provided teachers with a safe haven for bigotry and hostility toward LGBTQ students (as well as female students and students of color), and its hidden curriculum projected messages that privileged such a curriculum (and denigrated epistemologies more on the margin). It was only in the null curriculum that I began to experience a sense of liberation and inclusion and an awareness of the multiplicity of epistemology and ontology.*

Keywords: Excessive teacher entitlement; *currere*; queer gay history; educational ethics; autoethnography; null curriculum

> The act of telling itself changes the tale. The mind cannot help but make meaning out of what it knows, and the meanings we make of our lives changes how and what we remember. (van der Kolk, 1994, p. 193)

In the above quote, van der Kolk (1994) affirms that our process of thinking – engaging in interior or exterior dialogues – alters our relationship between memory and trauma. The trauma from the past often lingers through our lives and continues to change, shadow, and haunt us as we grow older.

I was thinking about this quote as I began this paper on excessive entitlement. For the past 40 years or more, I've been drawn into particular memories of trauma related to my high school experience. As a white but closeted gay high school student in the 1970s in Seattle, I was subjected to unique forms of excessive entitlement. But shortly after graduating from high school and beginning college I experienced a catharsis and refreshing new sense of liberation in my life. Slowly, insidiously, however, working in different educational institutions, I've been pulled back into the trauma of my conceptions of those early memories.

And those memories have been framed by excessive entitlement. By excessive entitlement, I don't refer to teachers' attempts to inhabit an ethical space (possibly at odds with school policies and media representations) for themselves and their students. Rather, and in contrast, I emphasize teachers' actions and systemic conditions related to an excessive – pervasive and dominant – educational mindset justifying (and manifesting) teacher self-infallibility. Displaying excessive entitlement, teachers take for granted the correctness of their actions, closing self-awareness and more equitable relations with others (especially students) (Craig, 2020; Ratnam & Craig, 2021). Structural components of excessive entitlement include, for example, societal norms, school policies, educational traditions, and sometimes even laws. These structures maintain the privilege and power of the dominant group, over marginalized groups.

In this chapter, I examine one specific historical but still pertinent example of excessive teacher (and structural) entitlement. My goal is to explore and excavate deeper meanings associated with my exposure to excessive educational entitlement. In my stories, the official, the hidden, and the null curricula intertwined. Throughout school, I encountered the official curriculum on a daily basis. This was a curriculum of entitlement for some and subjugation for others, enforced by deficit-based tests and quizzes. This official curriculum was shadowed by the hidden curriculum, communicating norms of power and student value (Portelli, 1993). Finally, sitting in class, I constructed and dreamed a null curriculum (Flinders et al., 1986), one which manifested through its glaring absences new meanings about tolerance of difference and hopeful possibilities for the future.

Using the curriculum theory-based methodology of *currere* (Pinar, 1994; Pinar et al. 2008), I revisit my conceptions of my high school education as a gay man. In this paper, I discuss the process of how *currere* facilitated a re-entry into the images and events incubating in my historical memory and provided a means for a meaningful reclamation of my views of my past: without explicit self-study, the growing memories surrounding my exposure to excessive entitlement in high school festered and grew, slowly changing into root memories and metaphors for my life; *currere* has helped me to unpack and replace that process with an affirmative reading of the past. (For a more detailed discussion of this study – its methodology and findings – please see Sawyer, 2022a, 2022b).

To qualify excessive entitlement, I start with ethics. The field of ethics helps educators rise above themselves – their anxieties, biases, distorted memories, and self-interests. It provides a safe, countervailing lens to examine life events. Ethics help educators replace dominant traditions that benefit some students at the expense of others, related to inequity, tracking, and biased school funding. Ethics are of paramount importance in schools overshadowed by industrial-scale oppression – which is often normalized and remains invisible.

In my study, partly based on the examination of artifacts (primarily old photographs), I explore and identify excessive teacher entitlement related to the official curriculum, the hidden curriculum, and the null curriculum. As a framework, I use the literature on educational ethics to analyze my data, with a goal of fostering personal reflexivity and of moving from the trauma surrounding excessive entitlement to a larger sense of the egalitarian possibilities benefiting a rich multicultural country.

EDUCATIONAL ETHICS: DOING THE RIGHT THING

In medicine, there is a term called "iatrogenesis," which means to do no harm (Farenga et al., 2015). Although in education no one actively seeks to harm students, many educators as well as educational structures and policies do great harm.

According to Maxwell and Schwimmer (2016), educational ethics include moral, social justice, and professional ethics. Moral ethics acknowledge that since teachers work as agents of student transformation, there is a moral obligation for them to interact with students in ways that are good or worthwhile. These actions include those supporting care, empathy, and democratic relationships (Tom, 1980). Care ethics are defined as "a relational approach to morality that values emotion, imagination, and context over externally imposed rubrics of normative decision making" (Hamington, 2013, p. 32). Part of this relationship emphasizes teachers' personal and critical reflection about their own positionality in relation to difference – and their acknowledgment that yes, they can do harm and that they are not infallible.

Social justice ethics draw from the foundational work of Paolo Freire (1970). It centers on raising teachers' awareness of social exclusion and the public school as a site for social justice. Included is a sense of teacher preparation focused on teachers acting as agents of social justice and equality. Similar to moral ethics, it calls on teachers to critique their positionality in relation to structures of power and equity.

The third dimension, professional ethics, stem from a lived and grounded consensus from practitioners about how to enact ethics in the classroom as a frame for teacher professionalism (Biesta, 2015). Professional ethics acknowledge that teachers maintain the integrity and professional autonomy of teaching and are responsible to society, communities, their academic discipline, and the profession. Professional ethics also implies that teachers engage in and enact social justice in their classes in and for society. Finally, professional ethics has a lived, organic component, and a goal is for educators to develop and use a language grounded in their own collective practice for social justice and ethics.

CURRERE: EXPLORING IDENTITY AND AGENCY IN CULTURAL WORLDS

Before I discuss how I used *currere* in my inquiry, I first provide a brief overview of *currere*. *Currere* is a curricular form of qualitative inquiry. As curriculum, it allows inquirers to examine self as curriculum and pedagogical text (Pinar et al., 2008). As qualitative (self-study) research, it builds on a search for understanding – how people make sense of their worlds and construct their regulation and agency within it (Baszile, 2017). As a methodology, *currere* moves this focus toward a postmodern framing of being uniquely situated – how specific people make sense and meaning within their environments – and as phenomenological experience – how they create new meaning in the process of engagement (Sawyer & Norris, 2013). It provides a means for inquirers to examine their relationship to a particular phenomenon, ideally in ways that foster a sense of reconceptualized and increased agency over that perception in their life (Pinar et al., 2008).

Methodologically, *currere* has two trans-conceptual steps, analysis and synthesis (deconstructing and reconstructing) and two transtemporal steps, regression and progression (remembering the past and reconceptualizing the future) (Pinar, 1994). Using these steps, inquirers examine how they are socialized into particular beliefs, values, and stances consistent with or in reaction to dominant discourses and how those discourses have moved through and continued to frame their lives. The use of these steps creates a sense of dialogue and movement within the inquiry. Again, ideally, those engaging in *currere* begin to conceptualize and then reconceptualize how they tell stories about life phenomena. As they engage in this process, they are able to surface and identify important events, traditions, and ideologies that have coursed through and stratified their lives.

Finally, as Pinar (2012) mentions, an important dynamic within *currere* is free association. Here, people don't just remember events based on their accumulation of normative framings over time, but reenter those underlying perceptions of experience in a fluid and creatively new way. For example, Kimiecki (2022) mentions that he asks students as a form of self-study to mix free-association with creative interactivity to facilitate new forms of expressive writing in health and medicine.

I also add an arts-based mix to *currere*. Arts-based inquiry destabilizes routine and taken-for-granted meanings. It asks authors and participants (readers, audience members) to view the inquiry as "text[s] seeking a response" (Sameshima & Irwin, 2008, p. 3). These responses are dialogic, awakening new ways of understanding within the inquiry (Leavy, 2009).

In this particular study of excessive entitlement, I examined both formal photos taken by student photographers from my high school appearing in the high school yearbook as proxies for the formal and enacted curriculum at my high school. I also examined my own informal photos (from my high school photography class) that I took with a camera using conventional film which I developed myself. These photos evoke images of the hidden and null curricula (Pinar et al., 2008; Portelli, 1993; Sawyer, 2022b). The photographs – now decades old – are so far removed from their sources, that they've lost their contextualized narrative coherence. To create an alienating effect, I played with the photos, borrowing from the defamiliarization technique of László Moholy-Nagy (Taschen, 2007), examining both positive and negative images. This arts-based approach allowed me to tear specific details from their comforting and normative surroundings. Through photography, I was then able to strip back layers of meanings and associations and examine phenomena in an existential, raw state. The taken-for-granted routines at my school, the way the teacher treated students, how the school formulated its grading policy, how the school tracked students, how the school communicated value and worth or the lack thereof to students, and how the school was embedded in deeper and larger narratives of inequity in society and the country – all these became apparent in the analysis.

THE HIGH SCHOOL

I attended public high school in Seattle, in the northwest corner of the United States. In Seattle, my school was located in the central part of the city, which was considered more diverse than the northern part of the city. With approximately 2,000 students, it was a comprehensive high school, preparing some students for college and others for the workplace. In terms of the faculty, the ratio was 42 male teachers to 29 female. In some subjects, male teachers outnumbered female teachers: in social studies, the ration was nine to one; in math, six to one; and in science, three to zero. However, women outnumbered men in three subjects: in business administration, with a ration of five to one; in language arts, five to two; and in foreign language, three to one. I recall a number of kind teachers, especially a female art teacher (who complimented me on my carvings of geometric shapes), a female student teacher who had us read Simon and Garfunkel songs as poetry ("Hello darkness my old friend..."), and a male social studies teacher, who had us read Marshall McLuhan ("Class, the medium is the message."). The building itself, massive in sandstone blocks, was constructed in the early 20th century. At the time that I attended high school, both the Civil Rights Era and the Vietnam War were winding down.

FINDINGS

The photographs in the high school yearbook were vivid and, it seemed to me, left little to the imagination. With captions pulled from Shakespearean texts, the photos reified power held by heterosexual white males.

The first noteworthy thing about the yearbook is its cover. The theme of the yearbook is Shakespeare's line, "All the world's a stage." Given that statement's nod to performativity, I have to say that on some level I liked the theme. Next to the name of the school (that of a long-dead British monarch), there is a drawing of William Shakespeare, quill pen in hand, sitting on the steps of the school, getting ready to add captions to photos in the yearbook. In case the connection between the monarch, Shakespeare, and the school isn't sufficiently obvious, a plaque on the wall behind Shakespeare presents the name of the school – again, that of a British queen. I need to make clear that I don't intend with my comments to disparage the artist or even the art. The drawings and sketches in the book are, to me, genuinely good.

Given the possibility of intertextual connections within the pages, I'm going to describe a few of my highlights in the order in which they appear. Presenting a few of these photos might help the reader to visualize them:

Here, I describe a few of the photos shown in Fig. 1.

- A male football player, with shoulder pads, helmet, and tight single striped sweatpants, breaks through a large paper banner that says, "We Like our Team." To the side, three female and one male pep squad leader all jump into

Fig. 1.

the air. The caption reads: "Life's but a walking shadow, a poor player/That struts and frets his hour upon the stage/And this [*sic*] is heard no more. –Macbeth"
- A hand holds an open pair of scissors to the face of a young male student with a flattop hair style. An accompanying photo to the left shows what is either a face mask or a carved pumpkin on a pole. The caption reads: "Sans eyes, sans taste, sans/teeth, sans everything. –As You Like It"
- A female student with bangs in a long sleeveless cardigan and carrying a thick notebook has a surprised look on her face. The caption reads: "The naked truth of it is,/I have no shirt. –King Henry VI [*sic*]"
- An accompanying photo shows a male student holding a crutch and his foot is in a cast resting on a footstool. The caption reads: "Wishing his foot were equal to his eye. –Love's Labour's Lost [*sic*]"
- Two referees wearing black-and-white striped polo shirts throw their arms stiffly in the air on the football field. Another referee is blowing a whistle. No caption.
- Another girl in a sweater vest writes on a piece of paper in the library, with an open book in front of her. The caption reads: "The rest is silence. –Hamlet"
- On the first of two facing pages, the Men's Club Officers are pictured. In the lower photo, four student officers all smiling, are dressed in evening attire (black slacks and jackets, white shirts, black bowtie) standing in front of an expensive, LA-style restaurant. In the top photo, the same four students, again smiling widely and looking debonair, are standing around what appears to be a bar; drinks and straws are on the bar in front of them. No caption.
- On the opposite page is the "Girls [*sic*] Club Officers." In the bottom three photos, there is a shot of the faculty advisor and two photos of the female officers engaging in public functions, probably in an auditorium. In the top photo, five of the officers are at a viewpoint near the school, standing in front of a sculpture with a well-known city landmark behind them. They are dressed similarly in long (stewardess-like?) sleeveless argyle sweaters, white knee-high socks, black skirts, and white shirts. No caption.
- On the same page, photos of the Ski Club and of the Swim Team show these to be the only two co-ed sports groups. On the facing page, a photo shows 15 members of the Girls [*sic*] Volleyball team, the team that appears, based on yearbook photos, to be the only team open solely to female students (including golf, tennis, and gymnastics).
- A male student, puckering his lips, is camping it up, holding out a limp (disabled?) hand and opening his trench coat to the waist. No caption.
- A male student with a long, crooked smile and gleaming eyes, is holding a small noose. He is looking with a twisted smile right into the camera. No caption and no additional information: the image hangs on the page.
- Two male students, one of whom appears slightly overweight, sit at a cafeteria table strewn with food wrappers. The caption: "Sweets are uses of adversity. –As You Like It"
- On the same page, another slightly heavy male student is looking into the distance. The caption reads: "Love goes towards love/As school boys from their

books; /But love from love,/Towards school with heavy looks. –Romeo and Juliet"
- A female student is reading a book, possibly in the library. The caption reads: "There is nothing either good or bad/But thinking makes it so. –Hamlet"
- On the facing page, a male student with a bald or shaven head smiles disarmingly at the camera. The caption: "There's no time for a man to recover his hair/that's grows bald by nature. –Comedy of Errors"
- Lower on the same page, four male students, two of whom are standing, circle around a female student who is apparently saying something with (mock?) annoyance. The caption: "The lady doth protest too much, me thinks. –Hamlet"

Here are a few observations about the photos. First, they present a clear ideal student: white, male, athletic, and sometimes blond and shirtless. Only one person of color – standing in the background on some steps – exists in the candid photographs. In the photos, the males are standing or engaged in action. The females are sitting. The males are dressed in power outfits (for examples tuxedos or sportswear). The females are often (not always) wearing matching (and sexist) outfits. The males are often arranged in groups (like little armies). The females are often surrounded by males or are responding to a male gaze in the photos.

The captions – again, Shakespearean quotes taken out of context and given new meanings in their juxtaposition with the photos – mock, belittle, and insult people who look or act differently from the ideal. These captions operate as narration.

Missing are photos of students of color, disabled students, and students engaged in protest or dissent. Aside from the photos of the athletic clubs, there were 69 photos of male athletes in action and none of female athletes.

Interestingly, queer representation does exist in some of the margins of the yearbook – in the drama club and among the male cheerleaders (called yell-leaders). Otherwise there is no LGBTQ+ acknowledgment. I interpreted the limp-wristed male in the earlier photo as a stereotype mocking gay people.

It's clear that the yearbook's images and texts – both present and absent – push an ideology that entitles straight almost entirely white, affluent males within a context of oppression of all others (but within a rigid pecking order). The story of the photos is told both by what is included and what is excluded, by images present and images absent. A total of three black students were shown in the candid photos (although approximately 10% of the students at the school were Black). I didn't do a formal tally of the number of students who were pictured a number of times in the yearbook, but there were approximately 100 students who were shown multiple times. There were also, based on my own photographs of students around the school, large numbers of students who were not acknowledged at all, who were not pictured even once.

I was able to do some quick statistics of the yearbook, using the ratio of students who did and did not have their photos taken for the yearbook, in relation to statistics from the alumni website, from about 35 years later. The website lists students who have been in touch with the alumni association, students who have died since graduation, and students "who are missing," those probably still alive but simply not in touch (my category). What is interesting is a high correlation between the absent students and those with no formal portrait.

Slowly and insidiously over decades, these images and authoritative discourses began to dominate my memories of school. They became the definitive representations for me of my lived school experiences that were complex and non-monolithic. To counter these associations, I turned to my own photography from high school. Digging through a trunk of personal artifacts, I encountered bundles of old black and white negatives of the pictures I took in high school. To view these negatives, I bought a film converter that digitized them (poorly), while still providing a two-by-two inch window onto my past. I had originally developed these negatives in a grade 11 photography class where I had access to the dark room. I must say that the teacher of this class (who was ex-military and sported a flattop haircut) was at times hostile to me and dismissive of my attempts at photography. Once in class, I took sanctuary in the darkroom, a murky space of covered lights, bleach-stained tables, trays, chemicals, and drying lines hanging from the ceiling. Encountering these implements, the contact sheets slowly revealed images in their chemical baths. In my photos, I sought to capture the concrete tonality of life – the natural and spontaneous interactions of students claiming the margins of my school. Most of the photos are rapid, somewhat blurred snapshots, but a few are sharply focused and show their subjects' cryptic awareness of thoughts beyond the reach of the camera. These old photos, dimly lighted and poorly focused, re-engaged me in the moment of their creation. And they shattered the historical strata enveloping their memories: these old photos have now become untethered from the normal appearing and regulatory narratives in which they were embedded at the time.

These photos are important for this study for a number of reasons. They firstly contrast with the formal photos shown in the yearbook, thus helping to delineate official discourses within those photos. Secondly, they evoke a more complete representation of my experience, ideally providing me with the means to begin to destabilize the hegemonic character of the school's formal curriculum and its yearbook representations. Finally, related to the first two reasons, these reconstructed and more complete memories then scaffolded *currere's* goal of reconceptualizing past views and generating future possibilities.

I now take a closer look at the photos. They provide a cascade of associations, sounds, images, and smells from my high school days. I arrived at school every day at 8:20 and left at 3:10. My lunch was in the early afternoon. Throughout the day, small but loud metal bells followed you everywhere, ringing every 55 minutes. Behind closed doors, teachers balanced classroom management with content delivery.

But within that tight schedule, an openness and randomness dominated my time at school. During lunch, I would look through my camera and frame light-and-shadowy landscapes, fresh-appearing flowers, and strikingly beautiful students moving individually or sitting in comfortable groups.

I tried to be a good student and followed the teacher's list of assignments. One day, I took photos of flowers: now, in the present, raindrops still sit on daffodils with light-and-dark creases: a white rose is sharply focused against a hotrod Buick. The freshness of the plants evokes colors and smells. I took many landscapes. Houses perch geometrically on the steep hillside and create underlying shapes – often triangles – to their arrangement. Rooftops slide down steep slopes and chimneys rise alarmingly. These photos promise alienation but engage with secret complicity. Now, an old car seen from a third floor window rounds a corner across from the new gym building for male basketball players. Strangely, the old jalopy sports red circles on its side, as if in a cartoon.

Against this backdrop of animated alienation, other photos such as those in Fig. 2. opened vistas of teenagers in action: playing kickball in the alley, hitting each other with sticks in the street, and jumping in the air. The more intellectual teens sit on stoops and talk quietly, seriously. Is that a paperback copy of Sartre in someone's pocket? Or is it Genet? Or Kerouac? For 3 months, I personally favored the novels of William Burroughs, whose stream of consciousness writing really spoke to me.

After lunch, I attended art class, where I dug into elemental shapes and images: a cube, a cylinder, a screw, a hole. Changing shapes hide past design incarnations; the process becomes the product; the ending holds the beginning.

Reading these sketches I feel happy. I and those I identified with lived on the fringes of the school, alienated by the curriculum and erased by the teachers. But there we debated the best way to protest the war in Vietnam, called politicians fascist flunkies, danced to Sly and the Family Stone, and lived artful lives. One of the portable classroom buildings on the courtyard by the cafeteria had a yellow submarine from the Beatles song painted on its side. No one defaced the mural with graffiti, although everyone had strong and possibly negative reactions to that omniscient tune (*Yellow Submarine*).

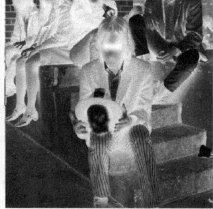

Fig. 2.

In my study, I intertwined my personal photos with the formal photos from the yearbook. My initial thoughts starting this study triggered anxiety in me. I obsessed on the powerful entitlement of the formal curriculum. But re-entering my space has allowed me to reactivate it. I've replaced the void with creativity, depression with dynamic possibilities, and singular alienation with communal passion.

For me, the informal curriculum around the edges of the school became a liminal space. In this space, the missing collectivity and plurality within the classrooms' informal curriculum manifested. Within this subversive null curriculum – grounded in collective voice – our dynamic and emergent cultural worlds generated agency and, at the very least, circumnavigated the discursive regulation surrounding the school. This agency subverted the harmful beat of the relentless call for patriotic duty. Instead, new possibilities of equity, justice, and peace emerged.

EXCESSIVE ENTITLEMENT

A number of dynamics of excessive entitlement played out in my school in a complex way. Some were rendered visible in the formal curriculum and the pictures of the yearbook, and some were rendered invisible. The invisible null curriculum provided strategies to resist excessive entitlement.

The different levels of agency and power for some and regulation and control for others were both product and generator of entitlement. The formal curriculum, a product of historic structures and systems benefiting a particular group of students almost entirely white and predominantly male and heterosexual, reinforced privilege. This privilege can be seen on almost every page of the yearbook: good looking young men, all white, embody power in their every movement, for example in sports and in the club governance structure of the school. This power is also a subtext of the yearbook, as the photographs appear, to me, to reflect an internalized male gaze.

The yearbook itself both reflected and enacted regulation. The photos operate to fetishize white females in the yearbook and socialize them as passive and bookish. And this regulation and control is often situated in settings of future promise, like the library.

The photos also reflect in complicated ways existing laws. Since racism in public schools became illegal in the United States in 1954 following *Brown versus the Board of Education* (a US Supreme Court case), racism entered a gray zone in the school, and in contrast with the treatment of white females in the yearbook, the identities, presence, and contribution of people of color was simply erased. This was the case as well with queer students at the school who were erased both within the curriculum as well as the photos.

When considering entitlement, it is necessary to do so from the vantage point of those who are being marginalized. Again, in this situation, we are talking about people of color, LGBTQ+ individuals, and in more explicit ways, young women. And although in the study I am not looking at assignments or curriculum, almost 100% of the literature in my language arts classes was written by white males with a strongly gendered point of view (e.g., Hemingway). Sports were the exclusive terrain of males. And the tracking of young women and students from poor families away from careers and intellectual pursuits and into, for example, home economics, secretarial work, auto-class, and vocational trades was routine and systematized into the curriculum. On a surface level, this entitlement operated to regulate advancement and civic engagement within society. On a deeper level, it also operated to socialize students into an identity consistent with this entitlement or marginalization (Pinar et al., 2008).

ETHICS

As educators are socialized into the very norms which we are attempting to critique, our use of an educational ethics framework provides us with a revealing and demystifying viewpoint. Each of the three large categories of educational ethics – care ethics, social justice ethics, and professionalism ethics – offers unique analytical opportunities. As we seek to change and transform our students' identities and knowledge, our work carries enormous responsibilities. And part of this responsibility is for us to first examine ourselves – our biases, values, and narratives – before we begin to work in relational ways with students.

It seems clear to me that although ostensibly the educational experience at my high school involved the care and respect of students, it was so only for a particular group of students. The closer a student was to the dominant and empowered culture – the ideal white, male, athletic, and financially privileged – the more *he* (intentional word choice) was essentially cared for. However, I suggest that all students are failed in an environment that projects societal and national insecurities onto students in order to maintain control of and privilege for some at the expense of others: an educational climate that traumatizes some groups of people may not traumatize all groups of people, but does harm all (if only on a psychic level).

And the oppression at my school was nuanced, with the treatment of students varying by race, class, gender, ability, and sexuality. The more a particular group contrasted with and actually represented a level of threat to the dominant group, the more members of that group became visible targets of excessive entitlement at my school. As a young gay student living at a time when homosexual activity was actually illegal and could and did lead to prison time, I represented absolutely no threat to the order of things at my school. Yes, I was traumatized, both by the formal and the hidden curricula, but almost as an afterthought. I would suggest that the group that represented the biggest threat to the ideal at my school, based on the yearbook photos which were again a proxy for the formal curriculum, were white female students who on some level were involved in feminism and changing the order of things. Instead of receiving any care, empathy, or an acknowledgment of intellect and imagination, in the photos, this group of students was sexually harassed, intellectually debased, and encircled and corralled by males and their gaze. The identities of students of color, disabled students, and those resisting the status quo were simply erased.

Social justice ethics did not enter my school. I would say there was no sense of social critique in hopes of dismantling systems of oppression and redistributing power. A sense of critical consciousness simply did not exist. In fact, the opposite existed: discourses of oppression favoring and promoting the ideal were the norm and moved as ideology through the school.

Finally, professional ethics, which are grounded in moral and social justice ethics, were, at least from my vantage point, missing from the school. I do recall teachers who acted with kindness and intelligence, who inspired me and whose words I think of to this day. However, I did not get a sense of a "public moral language" (Coombs, 1998, p. 564) emanating from the teachers. Today, I do get a sense that teachers are developing a collective voice in relation to oppression. But at that time, decades ago, not too far removed from the McCarthy Era (for further reading, see, for example, Foster & Davis, 2004), teachers at least at my school were more agents of oppression than agents of liberation.

Examining the ethics of my school, I am compelled to conclude that the school was, at the very least, approaching moral bankruptcy. Many of the students who did not appear or perform as ideal were excluded or actively marginalized. Going from situated and lived experience to a larger structural framing, this study highlights multiple structural biases grounded in racial, class, ability, sexuality, and gender differences.

And this examination of ethics at my school delineates not only a deficit mentality but also the missing contribution of diverse knowledge, emergent creativity, and generative ways of engaging.

It is also alarming that teachers' professional ethics seemed complicit with these examples of excessive entitlement. In my view, this is unconscionable. Again, it's important to stress that this characterization is not primarily about individual teachers but rather about structural issues threaded deeply through the systemic history of education in North America and appearing in specific examples.

CONCLUSION

So many decades later, before doing this study, at times I felt as if I was still suffering from posttraumatic shock, a morphing, and expanse of trauma, stemming from my high school days. I have since come to know that trauma, even that projected onto the past, is experienced and expressed in the present time. Yes, it may be based on harmful experiences in the past, but how you continue to remember and engage it is based on your lived experience in the present and your hopes for the future.

For me, so many years later, when I examine the candid photos in the yearbook, I feel immensely sad for those who were silenced and abused in them. But I also now realize that those photos were not hegemonic (regardless of their intention) or definitive. This study, focused on story, underscores the power of story to help people re-story and claim their own narratives.

This study has also provided me with a new healing lens to reapproach this trauma and reconceptualize the lived basis of my memories from the past. In many ways, this study has provided an opportunity for me to actually shatter my views of the hegemonic, evolving, and discursive power of excessive entitlement at my school (both then and now).

ACKNOWLEDGMENT

I'd like to thank the editors and reviewers for their feedback – which opened new insights for me as a writer examining my personal stories.

REFERENCES

Baszile, D. T. (2017). On the virtues of currere. *Currere Exchange Journal, 1*(1), vi–ix.
Biesta, G. (2015). Teaching, teacher education and the humanities: Reconsidering education as a Geistewissenschaft. *Educational Theory, 65*(6), 665–679.
Coombs, J. (1998). Educational ethics: Are we on the right track? *Educational Theory, 48*(4), 555–589.
Craig, C. (2020). *Curriculum making, reciprocal learning and the best-loved self*. Palgrave Macmillan.
Farenga, S. J., Ness, D., & Sawyer, R. D. (2015). Avoiding equivalence by leveling: Challenging the consensus-driven curriculum that defines students as "average". *Journal of Curriculum Theorizing, 30*(3), 8–27.
Flinders, D. J., Noddings, N., & Thornton, S. J. (1986). The null curriculum: Its theoretical basis and practical implications. *Curriculum Inquiry, 16*(1), 33–42.
Foster, S. J., & Davis, O. L. Jr (2004). Conservative battles for public education within America's culture wars: Poignant lessons for today from the red scare of the 1950s. *London Review of Education, 2*(2), 123–135.
Freire, P. (1970). *Pedagogy of the oppressed*. Seabury Press.
Hamington. (2013). A performative approach to teaching care ethics: A case study. *Feminist Teacher, 23*(1), 31–49.
Kimiecki, J. (2022). The feel of currere. *Currere Exchange Journal, 6*(1), 63–73.
Leavy, P. (2009). *Method meets art*. Guilford Press.
Maxwell, B., & Schwimmer, M. (2016). Professional ethics education for future teachers: A narrative review of the scholarly writings. *Journal of Moral Education, 45*(3), 354–371.
Pinar, W. (1994). The method of *currere*. In W. Pinar (Ed.), *Autobiography, politics and sexuality: Essays in curriculum theory 1972–1992* (pp. 19–27). Peter Lang.
Pinar, W. F. (2012). *What is curriculum theory*. Routledge.
Pinar, W. F., Reynolds, W. M., Slattery, P., & Taubman, P. M. (2008). *Understanding curriculum: An introduction to the study of historical and contemporary curriculum discourse*. Peter Lang.
Portelli, J. (1993). Exposing the hidden curriculum. *Journal of Curriculum Studies, 25*(4), 343–358. https://doi.org/10.1080/0022027930250404
Ratnam, T., & Craig, C. J. (Eds.). (2021). *Understanding excessive teacher and faculty entitlement. Advances in research on teaching* (Vol. 38). Emerald Publishing Limited. https://doi.org/10.1108/S1479-368720210000038001
Sameshima, P., & Irwin, R. L. (2008). Rendering dimensions of liminal currere. *Transnational Curriculum Inquiry, 5*(2). https://doi.org/10.14288/tci.v5i2.28
Sawyer, R. D. (2022a). Queer narrative theory and currere: Thoughts toward queering *currere* as a method of queer (curricular) self-study. *Journal of Curriculum Theorizing, 37*(1), 23–38. https://journal.jctonline.org/index.php/jct/article/view/981

Sawyer, R. D. (2022b). Confronting normative autobiography conventions at the intersection of queer literary theory and currere: A fluid high school homecoming. *Currere Exchange Journal, 6*(1), 2–14. https://cej.lib.miamioh.edu/index.php/CEJ/article/view/193

Sawyer, R. D., & Norris, J. (2013). *Duoethnography: Understanding qualitative research.* Oxford University Press.

Taschen, B. (2007). *Berlin: Portrait of a city.* Taschen.

Tom, A. R. (1980). *Teaching as a moral craft.* Longman.

van der Kolk, B. A. (1994). The body keeps the score: Memory and the evolving psychobiology of posttraumatic stress. *Harvard Review of Psychiatry, 1*(5), 253–265.

A REFLECTIVE LOOK AT EXCESSIVE FACULTY ENTITLEMENT IN DOCTORAL SUPERVISION

Marie-Christine Deyrich

Université de Bordeaux, France

ABSTRACT

This chapter investigates the experiences of doctoral students and supervisors in the doctoral process, focusing on the potential impact of imbalances in the distribution of power. In this respect, there are troublesome manifestations of excessive faculty entitlement that appear to be a source of inequality and injustice. These phenomena call into question the crucial relationship of support expected of doctoral students, as thesis supervisors have a fundamental role to play in guiding them towards the doctorate and ensuring their successful entry into the research community. Looking at the issue from the angle of the theory of social fields, I examine instances of dysfunction in supervisory experiences. Such problematic practices tend to conform to the relationships and traditions that sustain and (re)produce the practices of the academy, constraining the establishment of what Bakhtin describes as a dialogical relationship, between doctoral students and supervisors. I examine this problem from my own experience, both as a doctoral student and as a supervisor. I approach the question by combining self-study and narrative inquiry to make use of the data from my experience to analyse the issues raised during the supervision of doctoral programmes. I connect accounts drawn from literature, real-life testimonies and a corpus of discussions and notes to explore the manifestations of excessive faculty entitlement in the form of asymmetries and difficulties that can negatively impact the quality of supervision.

Keywords: Doctoral supervision; excessive faculty entitlement; self-study; narrative inquiry; reproduction; dialogism

Aspiring researchers tend to conceive of doctoral research as a privileged period that calmly leads to an academic career. This view rarely corresponds to the reality experienced by students who are not always aware of the many challenges they will have to face in committing to this path (Marcel & Broussal, 2020; McAlpine & Akerlind, 2010). This undertaking sometimes brings them face to face with the harsh reality leading them to life-changing decisions and sacrifices needed to persist on the doctoral path (Bitzer et al., 2018; Haag, 2018; Rockinson-Szapkiw & Spaulding, 2014). With time, however, and following the successful completion of their thesis and their progression in the academic world, university professors tend to forget the difficulties they personally encountered along the way (Halse, 2011). Such is the case with my own doctoral journey, which I tend to revisit with a positive emotion while forgetting the difficulties and pitfalls that punctuated it (Hawley, 2010). Professors are caught up in the pressure of university duties, academic research and administrative tasks, which only allow them to get ahead without ever having the time to consider how the relationship with the doctoral students they are responsible for unfolds (González-Ocampo & Badia, 2019; Grant, 2005). Admittedly, it can be difficult to look back in this context, but the time spent could well prove beneficial in resolving the tensions that sometimes emerge openly or broodingly in doctoral supervision. The question of supervisory liability in these problematic cases deserves to be raised and examined in greater depth. To this end, among the phenomena that have been identified as likely to shed light on the issue, I focus here on the notion of excessive faculty entitlement, which Ratnam documented in her co-edited book with Craig, *Understanding Excessive Entitlement* (2021).

In the challenging and critical context of doctoral support and supervision, resorting to the notion of excessive faculty entitlement is intended to 'identify and better describe situations that are obstacles to the development of inclusive, good quality education for all and a fair, non-discriminatory education concerned with respect for diversity' (Kohout-Diaz & Deyrich, 2021, p. 54). This leads me (Deyrich) to explore ethical issues and manifestations of potentially noxious power asymmetry. Taking a retrospective view, I will provide some contextual explanations. The aim here is to put into perspective the experience of doctoral supervision as experienced by doctoral students and supervisors. From this relational angle, I will examine the difficulties and problems that frequently arise during the doctoral process, leading to many dropouts.

A combination of concepts that complement each other in data presentation and analysis of this study is outlined below under the theoretical methodological frameworks.

THEORETICAL FRAMEWORK
Excessive Entitlement

My conception of excessive faculty entitlement has to do with the professional authority of position given to the faculty in relation to the students. This authority is meant to be used benevolently in guiding and nurturing the students.

However, when this power makes them arrogant, and they become unreasonable by wielding it to dominate and oppress their students, albeit unintentionally, then their unreasonable actions are seen as manifestations of excessive entitlement (Ratnam & Craig, 2021). Excessively entitled supervisors/faculty are generally unaware of the problems that their attitude can cause, both for students they supervise and their colleagues. The experience of supervising doctoral students deserves to be studied from this angle of excessive entitlement because such entitled attitudes of supervisors have the danger of creating a prejudicial asymmetry (Deyrich, 2023) between supervisors in a dominant position on one hand and doctoral students whose fate depends on their supervision and judgement, on the other.

Bourdieu's Social Theory of Reproduction

Despite the harmful effect of excessive faculty entitlement and the associated problems in the academic world, excessive faculty entitlement attitudes tend to be perpetuated in practice, even becoming a form of power-holding tradition (Prata-Linhares et al., 2021). This could be seen in the light as Bourdieu's social field theory (1989) which highlights the network of relations, representations and discursive practices that support and (re)produce traditional practices and representations shaped by habitus. These practices 'are immediately perceived as such only by those agents who possess the code' (Bourdieu, 1989, p. 19). Bourdieu uses the concepts of habitus and field to explain how individuals act and interact in society. Habitus is the set of dispositions, preferences and skills that are acquired through socialisation and that shape one's actions and perceptions. Field is the social arena where different forms of capital are at stake and where different agents compete or cooperate. In the network of relations of power, habitus and field are considered in their social inscription as mutually constitutive and as each other's accomplices. In referring to fields as spaces of social positions and relations, Bourdieu explains that the practices of/in a field 'cannot be accounted for without considering the structure of the power relations among the members' (1998, p. 70) of that field. Adapting to the demands of a field requires a certain 'sense of the game' (Bourdieu, 1990, p. 66). Like a game, social fields are constructed with specific structures and rules. The relative fluidity of the game/field often hinges on the players' blind acceptance of and respect for these rules, even if they may seem arbitrary. In this social game, each field generates its own habitus or system of embodied 'lasting, transposable dispositions'. Such is the case of the academic world in the preservation of a universe that is taken for granted. The game metaphor provides insight into 'the reproduction of social structure and its patterns of domination' (Burawoy, 2012, p. 189). The phenomenon of excessive faculty entitlement, likewise, based on domination, can be reproduced without being openly challenged in the social game of doctoral supervision. Bourdieu helps identify the specific nature of this phenomenon of harmful reproduction (Bourdieu, 1998) and its social inscription (Bourdieu (1997/2000).

METHODOLOGICAL FRAMEWORK

Both self-study and narrative inquiry frame the methodological orientation of the study by providing tools to facilitate my inward journey to understand my excessive entitlement and its negative consequences on the doctoral students I supervise.

Self-Study Research

Self-study research is used by educational researchers as a means of seeking to understand the lived experience of their educational practices and contexts (LaBoskey, 2004; Loughran et al., 2007). It is a 'study of the self and the others in practice' (Pinnegar & Hamilton, 2009, p. 12), with the aim of creating meaning and involving 'a moral commitment to improving practice' (Hauge, 2021).

Narrative Inquiry

Among the numerous research methods used in the self-study genre, narrative inquiry is the research method I have chosen. This approach (Clandinin, 2022) facilitates researchers in addressing the question of excessive faculty entitlement in supervision by shedding light on the issue through the narratives of experiences. This is based on the recognition that all humans use narratives to find meaning (Craig, 2021) in their experience. My exploration deals with stories embedded in experience and more precisely a confrontation of experiences, that of the doctoral student and that of the supervisor on the doctoral path, or in other words the combination of the two lived experiences seen from a narrative point of view. For my purpose, the strength of this methodology lies in the fact that it allows for a holistic view that situates the personal histories of individuals in relation to their social context. As Mertova and Webster (2019) state: 'Narrative inquiry attempts to capture the "whole story" [...]. It studies problems as forms of storytelling, involving characters with both personal and social stories' (p. 2).

Storying and 'Restorying' Framed by Bakhtin's Notion of Dialogism

In this 'storied life' study, my personal commitment as an educational researcher is essential and therefore requires self-reflection, which self-study can help to achieve. The result is a tangle of narratives with different perspectives that can be interwoven and echo each other in search of meaning: 'Storying and restorying help excavate meaning' (Craig et al., 2016, p. 134). Self-study comes into play at several levels here: supervisory experience as a supervisor and past experience as a doctoral student. For Smith (2006): 'Narrative practices provided a way of bridging different worlds and connecting learning experiences' (p. 473). This narrative inquiry is informed by Bakhtin's dialogism, which helps to create a space of dialogical conversation with my past experiences. Bakhtin's dialogism opens our understanding to a multiplicity of perspectives and voices, consisting of open connections since things do not exist in themselves but only in their relationships (Holquist, 2003). In the approach proposed by Bakhtin (1935), life is seen as a dialogue and a shared event. To live, then, is to take part in a dialogue, not just with other people but with the self and everything in the world. Meaning is therefore supposed to emerge from dialogue, at every level. This highlights the importance for the researcher of creating a space for dialogical exchange specific to the research question, by combining data from past and present experiences. For Yumarnamto (2022), this dialogical space makes it possible to go beyond the main narratives and thus 'bring repressed narratives to the surface' (Yumarnamto, 2022, p. 104). Placing narratives in a dialogical manner should thus allow a plurality of consciousnesses to emerge.

Problems of supervision that may fall within the category of excessive faculty entitlement will thus be considered on all narrative experiences. Bakhtin's dialogical perspective will be used to examine the difficulties and problems that frequently arise and are echoed during the doctoral process. This should shed light on some of the most sensitive points on which further research is needed.

Participants, Data Sources and Analysis

For my self-study, I draw on my personal experience both as a former PhD student and as a supervisor using my diary notes. I also use email exchanges with students and notes from my phone conversations with them to capture the experiences of the 12 doctoral students I supervised between 2008 and 2015. These qualitative data were then examined by means of a thematic study (Braun & Clarke, 2012) to identify salient themes, analyse and interpret patterns of meaning. These themes were then compared with elements of the literature on supervision issues to support and validate my analysis.

ISSUES OF POSITIONALITY AND RESEARCH QUESTIONS

The difficulties and problems encountered in doctoral supervision can be highly sensitive and alarming and should thus be a serious cause for concern for the faculty (Doyran & Hacıfazlıoğlu, 2021). Yet, as explained by Cotterall (2013), 'writing and supervision practices are common sites of tension, but the prevailing culture of silence militates against systemic change' (p. 174). Taking a stand against this practice of the wall of silence would seem to be a challenge in the university context. I would nevertheless like to take the untrodden path in order to unearth the manifestations of excessive faculty entitlement in the context of doctoral supervision.

Epistemic Positioning

Successive research projects on the notion of excessive teacher/faculty entitlement brought me into contact with researchers (Ratnam & Craig, 2021; Ratnam et al., 2019; Russell, 2021), most of them English speaking, whose work in the field of education was based on self-study research, autoethnography and/or narrative inquiry. I was previously unfamiliar with these research methodologies, which were not used by French researchers in the educational sciences. In the French context, the epistemic positioning of educational sciences researchers is predominantly based on experience (Deyrich, 2007), but it must involve forms of exteriorisation, as Albero (2019) explains. From this point of view, distancing is required to ensure the articulation of the epistemic, pragmatic and axiological dimensions of experience in research. It is therefore not surprising that self-study and autoethnography are very rarely mentioned in the field of qualitative research in the French-speaking literature. The presence of self-study in languages other than English remains a rarity, as observed by Thomas and Guðjónsdóttir (2020). In literature, there are a few marginal cases in French-speaking Canada, such as Rondeau (2011), who explain this methodology as reflexivity centred on the individual's singular experience. Examples are even rarer in the French context. Bullock and Bullock (2020) present the methodology to the French educational research community as a challenge to be met. My decision to use this procedure represents a real challenge and a risk-taking exercise, since in the research culture where I evolve, talking about yourself, having a self-centred discourse as the basis for a study could hardly be considered as an approach that would be taken seriously as scientific research. I decided to overlook this criticism and take advantage of the possibility offered by this approach to pursue my research on excessive supervisor entitlement from a different angle, focusing on the self to develop insights that may provide the basis for more promising research.

INVESTIGATING EXCESSIVE ENTITLEMENT IN THE FRENCH 'SOCIAL GAME' OF SUPERVISION

My heuristic pathway is based on experience in the French context and is in many respects broadened by connections with English-speaking research. In the background, a dialogical link is established between multiple lived or narrated experiences and in interaction with literature. This collection of elements is used to provide an insight into the problems related to excessive faculty entitlement in relation to the students they supervise. The point is neither to transpose observations on cases of dysfunctional supervision to all contexts nor to assume in a deterministic way that all doctoral supervision goes badly but to begin to reflect on the supervisory process as well as on how to guard against an attitude of excessive entitlement.

The questions I feel are important to address at this stage are as follows: (1) What contribution will this study bring to a better understanding of the phenomena of excessive entitlement observed or experienced in doctoral supervision? and (2) To what extent will self-study research shed new light on the challenges posed by excessive faculty entitlement in my personal experience of supervising doctoral students?

Excessive Faculty Entitlement Affecting Doctoral Students

The difficulties of doctoral students confronted with supervision issues are rarely tackled in a direct way in the French context, although the question should be on the agenda to clearly raise the question of the relationship between these difficulties and manifestations of an excessively entitled attitude that may be seen among university professors.

Path to a doctorate as an obstacle course: Only a minority of PhD students complete their thesis. Denis and Lison (2023) have noted the very high dropout rate in French-speaking countries. In France, the dropout ratio is strikingly high, as indicated by figures from the Ministry of Higher Education. At the beginning of the 2021 academic year, 71,500 students enroled in doctoral studies, and only 13,600 doctoral students obtained their diplomas (EESRI, 2022). The many cases of students dropping out of doctoral studies testify to the extent of the problem. In the path to a doctorate, candidates must negotiate difficulties of several types, which sometimes become obstacles that are hard to overcome in the limited time allowed forcing them to give up.

Need for a Relational Understanding of the Problem of Dropout

Mainstream literature looks at the problem as residing in the individual student. McCray and Joseph-Richard (2020) point out that successful completion of a doctoral thesis requires 'resilience'. They examine the factors influencing the completion of a doctoral programme to propose a model for promoting resilience. Looking at the issue of difficulties in this way from the angle of the individual's mental process of overcoming obstacles in the face of adversity clearly shows the extent of the personal qualities required by individuals on this path strewn with pitfalls to be able to protect themselves. The individual aspect of resilience, however, is not sufficient to explain what leads to success because as these authors explain 'success depends on the establishment of a clear but complex alignment between the personal, family, social and academic relationships they navigated' (p. 683). As for the supervisor's role in this success, it is in a sense downplayed in this analysis: 'for these completers, the best use of the supervisor was that of a facilitator of expert professional guidance and performance outcomes – not as a provider of personal support' (*idem*). This statement leads me to wonder whether it would not be a rather hasty conclusion to deduce that personal support is never needed for this category of students. In addition, focusing on individual resourcefulness in this isolated way may lead to a partial view of the problem. It ignores the sensitive issue of the problems encountered by doctoral students in their relationship with supervisors, namely, the power imbalance arising from issues of excessive supervisor entitlement.

Dysfunctions in supervision, whether minor or major, also raise the question of a lack of respect for individuals, both on the part of the doctoral student and the supervisor. The resulting consequences are sometimes serious and call into question the impact of supervision on well-being of the students and supervisors. Löfström and Pyhältö (2020) emphasise the ethical side of relationships, considering that high levels of burnout and attrition may be indicators of the importance of scrutinising doctoral education practices and supervision from an ethical perspective within the research community.

When the Supervisory Relationship Falls Apart

Problems linked to supervisory issues in the French context are explored in an online article in Le Monde (Raybaud, 2019, https://www.lemonde.fr/campus/article/2019/01/15/quand-la-relation-avec-son-directeur-de-these-vire-au-cauchemar_5409404_4401467.html). This article, which is titled *'Quand la relation avec son directeur de thèse vire au cauchemar/* 'When your relationship with your thesis supervisor turns into a nightmare', is based on a study of 1,700 doctoral students showing the link between relationship difficulties with the thesis supervisor and causes of personal suffering (Haag, 2018). The excerpts below give an idea of the negative impact of inadequate consideration of ethics and human factors (The excerpts below are my English translation from Raybaud's online article in French):

> Lucie, a doctoral student in philosophy in Paris, has only seen her director 6 times in 4 years. Maïa, a psychology researcher, had to wait more than 6 months for her director to sign the papers to get her an office and a computer. [...] On the other hand, others complain that the supervisor is too 'present'. [...] 'You'll see, you'll be in tears, I make all the women I work with have a good cry', is what her thesis supervisor said to Claire at their first meeting.

The article continues:

> Émilie ended up asking to change supervisors after more than a year of toxic relationships and a deep-rooted state of depression. Emilie lost 10 kilos in the battle and was only able to find another supervisor on condition that she started from scratch on a new thesis topic: the world of research is like the King's Court, she sums up, if someone upsets the king, they're not allowed in.

Aside from these very worrying examples, the article fails however to point out that they illustrate several aspects of the systemic nature of the problems that can be encountered in this context. Combes (2022) writes that there is a serious problem undermining the excellence of the French university system: job insecurity, harassment and a culture of silence. This author explains that every year, more than 15,000 doctoral students embark on writing a thesis with passion, but at university, dysfunction breeds abuse. Supervision practices too often tend to conform to the relationships and traditions that support and (re)produce, to varying degrees, the practices of the academy that inflict a 'rite of passage' on doctoral students, i.e. a threshold of obstacles that they are supposed to cross, leading them to accept any sacrifice for the good cause (Bitzer et al., 2018; Rockinson-Szapkiw & Spaulding, 2014). PhD supervisors have a fundamental role to play in guiding candidates through the rite of passage to the PhD and ensuring their successful entry into the research community. This laudable position is not without danger, however, when supervision 'drifts' and risks falling into the abyss of excessive entitlement. I explore this point using a self-study of my personal experience.

BRINGING MY PERSONAL SUPERVISORY EXPERIENCES TO THE SURFACE

When considering the experience of supervision for doctoral students, the issues of supervision criticism, stress and negative emotions need to be addressed (Deyrich, 2023). The self-study approach has encouraged me to examine my supervisory practices and to ask myself to what extent my involvement in supervision might be tainted by excessive entitlement and thus impeded the progress of my doctoral students.

First-Time Oversight of Excessive Entitlement Challenges

I realise now that bringing supervision accounts to the surface, and thus to personal openness, represents a rather disconcerting form of challenge and 'self-discovery'.
Personal narrative # 1:

> Bernard was my first doctoral student. Very respectful of me, he faced a cultural gap that prevented him from communicating and making precise requests. The same discrepancy was present in his writings, notably when quoting in extenso from sources authorized at the political level in his context, with a tendency to systematically conform to institutional texts, and not wanting to stand out from the mainstream. He never asked any questions and never gave any spontaneous news; it was always me who solicited him and waited for his work, which was systematically short and late in arriving. He always agreed with the advice I gave him, but almost never included it in his research. I felt discouraged on several occasions, and the ethical questions I asked myself were not immediately answered: how far did I have to go for him to succeed in his work? For him to agree to conform to the expected scientific standards? It seems to me that my contribution at this stage was to help build a kind of resilience by valuing each of the small advances he made. I was however very anxious, but he eventually managed to defend his thesis on time to obtain 'un précieux sésame' (an essential document), the credential he needed to be promoted to a higher level on his inspector's post in his country.

Thinking back has raised a few questions for me: Did I show excessive faculty entitlement in using my dominant authority of my position to push Bernard disproportionately hard to complete his thesis and submit it for defence despite the residual weaknesses in the final version and the rather mixed defence report that followed? Was I compromising on academic standards by this act of pushing his thesis through despite wanting in quality? This ethical dilemma of whether I did the right thing in letting him get certified on a thesis that did not fully meet the desirable academic standards or whether I should have persisted in supporting him to 'earn' the degree is a point on which I am still undecided.

FURTHER QUESTIONING OF MY EXCESSIVELY ENTITLED APPROACH TO SUPERVISION

When I read the correspondence with the doctoral students, excerpts from which follow, I recognise that the phenomenon of excessive faculty entitlement can be insidious and counterproductive. On several occasions, rereading my documents brought me face to face with my own excessive entitlement in the power I wielded over my students in the belief that it was good for them.

- Caroline

Paradoxically, the most significant case of attitude of excessive faculty entitlement I noticed consisted of a seemingly logical investment to encourage a brilliant doctoral student to go ahead with her research. Teaching full time at primary school, Caroline alerted me on several occasions to the difficulties she was encountering, for example, in connection with the Doctoral School (DS) courses that she was supposed to attend prior to defending her thesis.

Caroline wrote (my translation):

> As a primary school teacher, I cannot attend the training courses given by the DS on Tuesdays and as I must attend 18 hours of teacher training courses as part of national education, I sometimes cannot attend the training courses given by the DS on Wednesdays, especially as from the start of the next school year there will be school on Wednesday mornings.

She added:

> Insofar as I am unable to attend training courses for the reasons given above, it is difficult for me to make an assessment. However, I am going to try next year to attend training courses that will take place on Wednesday afternoons. It's a shame that we can't have distance learning courses.

Caroline was telling me about a problem that was insurmountable for her. Instead of understanding her and giving her space, I tried to involve her in several research projects related to her thesis subject. I felt I had to do my utmost to include her in the world of academic research so that she would not lose touch with her research work. Looking back, I realise that this work had only added to her pressure for time creating a lot of stress. I was totally shocked when I learned that she was quitting for good and there was nothing I could do to dissuade her. I can see now that my insensitivity to the pressure she was under trying to cope with the obligations I subjected her to using my authority of position as a sign of my excessive entitlement.

Personal narrative # 2:

> I now wonder whether I ought not to have considered the question the power I had assumed to myself over Caroline by imposing work that she had no space to handle. What was obvious to me was that my action of exerting my power over her without understanding her from her point became a damaging stumbling block for the doctoral student. A relevant proposal by Kismihók et al. (2022, p. 417) could prove useful in this context. It focuses on the relational aspect by placing greater emphasis on clarity 'on how supervisors should be approached, what is their precise role and how supervisors contribute (e.g., expertise, resources, network) to the aims and objectives of the research project are key (often unclear) challenges for doctoral candidates'. Clarification in the form of a responsible discourse and dialogue could probably have helped to ease the relationship between me and Caroline and the tension she was going through.

This analysis ties in with the issue of excessive supervisor entitlement because it reflects a prejudicial asymmetry between supervisors in a dominant position on the one hand and doctoral students whose fate depends on their monitoring and judgement on the other (Deyrich, 2023). I still regret this unfortunate outcome of my doctoral support, and I still feel guilty and responsible for this. I must admit that my demands were too high, but I did not realise this at the time. I am subjecting myself to this questioning through this self-study provoked by the notion of excessive faculty entitlement.

- Michelle

A few years later, another PhD student, Michelle, sent me a heartbreaking message, which made me realise that what I perceived as a push for her benefit was, for her, an insurmountable obstacle.
Michelle wrote (my translation):

Hello,

Now it's getting difficult because I don't see what kind of short sentence I could add. You asked me for ten lines, I did ten lines :-)!

Besides I'm on my way to my university and tomorrow is a very hectic day. Are you sure that's not enough? or maybe you just use my long abstract to write the sentence that suits you :-)!

Sorry!

To ease her anxiety, I helped her with the rest of her assignment. I also have had to come to terms with the reality that PhD students have their own family life and work that don't leave them the time they would like to carry out all the research they are expected to do. Michelle passed her thesis with flying colours and has since made numerous contributions to our field of research. In hindsight, I think that asking too much of PhD students may represent a lack of empathy, which is inherently a form of insidious excessive entitlement. Thereafter, I tried to be more sensitive to individual cases and to establish more friendly relations, without however inserting myself into the lives and intimacy of the doctoral students.

In these three supervisory experiences, a dialogical relationship is established between two types of discourse, which Bakhtin (1935) describes as discourses of authority ('authoritarian discourse') and personal persuasion ('discourse of internal persuasion'). My findings show that these discourses are in continuous and sometimes marked tension, liable to result in attitudes of excessive entitlement. In the case of Caroline, I thought my advice to her and involving her in academic projects was an internally persuasive discourse for her. However, it turned out as an authoritarian discourse where she felt under pressure to comply with my word because it was coming from a position of authority as her supervisor which she could not brush aside. In the three cases I have cited above, there is a form of internal self-persuasion: the students think the supervisor knows what is best for them, and so they must comply. I have come to realise this is an insidious form of abuse of my authority because students who suffer from it do not acknowledge it as such under the belief that it is in their good. These discourses operate in the relationship between the doctoral student and the supervisor, as well as in the relationships that the supervisor consciously or unconsciously establishes between each of these experiences when being a doctoral student and the experiences as a supervisor who accumulates a corpus of supervisory experiences. For example, Caroline's experience with me was a reproduction of my own experience as a doctoral student in the 1990s. It was sometimes very difficult to conform to the wishes of my thesis supervisor, who was very authoritarian. When I brought her a draft of my thesis, she rejected it very rudely because the list of authors I had referenced was not part of her repertoire. I did not question my supervisor's rejection of my work because it was a normal rule for all thesis students to accept the supervisor's word unquestioningly. Like all my peers I was convinced that no discussion was possible because the supervisor was doing what was best for me, to help me achieve success in my PhD. My doctoral experience was a commonplace one and in tune with the times. The self-persuasion I displayed was therefore logical. Reproduction is thus patent. From the outset of the doctoral experience as a student, the supervisor's subjectivity and identity are forged in a vicarious apprenticeship (Lortie, 2020). This period, which gradually shapes the construction of one's attitudes and identity, is in a way both a reflection of the supervisory practices experienced as a doctoral student and an outline of the supervisory practices for which they are and will be responsible. In other words, this is a process of indirect training or reproduction that develops without our being conscious of this learning.

As opposed to this dominant vertical approach to supervision, in a dialogical approach, meaning is created and transmitted in a different way. When there is dialogue or interaction between two or more perspectives, which includes students' perspectives, several layers of interconnected relationships 'determine the very bases of our ideological interrelations with the world, the very basis of our behavior' (Bakhtin, 1935, p. 682). These considerations lead me to think that, in the absence of a ready-made solution to the problem of excessive supervisor entitlement, I can put forward the idea that all supervisory relationships should enable the actors involved to devote time to the dialogical aspect of the discourse, its mode of address, its ideological anchoring and its potential impact.

SUPERVISION AS AN ONGOING LEARNING PROCESS

The notion of excessive entitlement can be considered to have its basis in several phenomena combining reproduction and inertia, since abusive relationships seem to be both established in the system and often taken for granted in terms of habitus in the social situation (Bourdieu, 1989, 1998). An explanation could lie in the need for faculty to preserve what constitutes the cornerstone of the institution, leading to full compliance within hierarchical practices. Another explanation could be the need to earn access to a status that is rewarding or even prestigious. Such an interpretation of habitus need not necessarily be deterministic. Changing our narratives for a better understanding of sensitivities in asymmetrical interactions should lead to a more self-critical commitment to fairer and more benevolent relations in doctoral supervision. This is where a self-study approach helps us in moving beyond the determinism of Bourdieu's theory of reproduction of 'social structure and its patterns of domination' (Burawoy, 2012, p. 189) to start understanding that things can evolve, and that it is possible to learn to counteract attitudes of excessive entitlement.

Learning From Reflection on Experience

Halse (2011) explains that 'doctoral supervision can be theorised as a perpetual process of subjective and identity formation – of becoming a supervisor' (p. 568). My learning has taken place over time in my continuous becoming:
Personal narrative #3:

> When I was appointed full university professor, a grade which in my context allowed me to supervise doctoral theses, I had already supervised a substantial number of master's projects but had never yet supervised a thesis. I was proud to see that directing a thesis was a new mission in which I was going to invest myself to ensure the success of the doctoral students in my charge. I hadn't had any training in supervision beforehand, and the only experience I could draw on was that of my doctoral studies, which I had carried out in parallel with my full-time teaching job. Here I can mention my initial enthusiasm, my thirst to learn as much as possible about the subject of my thesis, both from the literature and from the colloquia and seminars I willingly attended. I could also mention the hours spent collecting data and the difficulties in organising them, in search of meaning. To this I would have to add that I sometimes had hesitations and even doubts about my ability to carry out this work as such. Thesis supervision as I experienced it as a doctoral student seemed very remote, perhaps my supervisor wanted to give me as much autonomy as possible, but there were also a few rare occasions when my supervisor showed support that I greatly appreciated, for example, by encouraging me to speak at a seminar or to prepare a scientific publication. In this sense, the picture is rather mixed.

My eagerness to invest in my doctoral studies with all my time and energy despite working as a full-time university teacher might be partly responsible for making me believe that my students too were fired by a similar spirit. While I might not have been wrong in my assessment of student interest, I was not aware of other situational demands and pressures that constrained them from investing all their time and effort that my expectations placed on them. I thought I was using my authority for the benefit of my students. I see now how one-sided I was. My neglect to listen to students and understand them from their location had made me excessively entitled to believe that I was right in the way I used my authority as their supervisor. My self-study has made me realise that becoming a thesis supervisor is, above all, a human endeavour where dialogue and empathy play a significant role.

The relationship constructed between supervisor and supervisee is, as Grant (2005) writes, an 'opaque' one, due to the ambiguity that partly 'comes from its contested discursive framing' (p. 12) which result over time in a more psychologising or economic and liberal approach deprived of a consideration of ethical issues. This is also affecting supervisors as observed by Prata-Linhares et al. (2021, p. 189) who explain that supervisors are not only 'perpetrators of entitlement' but also 'common targets' of others' excessive entitlement. Supervisors are often not aware of their excessively entitled attitude that develops tacitly in them in responding to the unreasonable performative demands placed on them and the pressures of work (Ratnam, 2023). As a result, the negative impact of their excessively entitled attitudes on their students remains opaque to them. As victims of the system in which they are entangled, it is difficult for them to take basic human factors into account, thus preventing them from devoting the time they would need to play a more useful, ethical and pedagogical role.

Personal narrative # 4:

> The challenge seems impossible. You must listen to the needs of doctoral students, adopt as ethical an attitude as possible and deal with the many constraints that hamper the potential for positive educational intervention for doctoral students. The different tasks related to teaching, supervision, research and bureaucratic issues, the lack of time to complete all the dimensions of your role can lead to leaving aside the many questions that should be raised from an ethical point of view. I have encountered these challenges myself, having been involved in this system throughout my supervisory missions, and I think that many times I too have had to give up, sometimes to the detriment of the quality of doctoral supervision that I would have liked to maintain.

Like González-Ocampo and Badia (2019), I believe that if the pedagogical dimension of the different areas of activity of professors was incorporated into their evaluation and, consequently, into their career development, it is likely that greater attention would be paid to developing the skills needed to supervise doctoral students. Such developments are possible, but they also require moral commitment on the part of the institutions and the people working in them.

CLOSING COMMENTS

Understanding what is at work in the phenomenon of excessive entitlement in supervision is a vast undertaking. I have done no more than shed light on the subject by putting experiences into perspective, from which I have drawn some insights that are often little known or visible. I hope to have paved the way for further work that may provide additional insights. In this study, it is worth emphasising that my personal involvement, which has resulted in a critical self-reflection, was made possible by a self-study approach, with the constant aim of contributing to the humanist vision that should be prevalent in legitimising the fight against the attitude of excessive entitlement in doctoral supervision.

Personal narrative # 5:

> At the end of this research, which involved my going back to reflect on a whole range of my lived experiences, I realise that when Ratnam (2021) wrote that 'All learning is autobiographical' (p. xxi), she was putting forward the principle of personal reflection. Self-reflection was the driving force that enabled me to develop my perspectives on the concept of excessive entitlement and its relevance to understanding the problems that beset supervisory relationships, such as conflict, stress, dissatisfaction, and supervisee drop out.

Self-Study in the Researcher's Maturation Process

Self-study is more than simply a question of looking back at oneself and one's practices. As Ratnam (2023) points out, becoming conscious of one's excessively entitled attitudes through a self-study should open 'the way for learning and the development of new attitudes towards the self, the other and the world' (p. 221). Self-reflexivity has the advantage of drawing on observational data to bring personal experience into dialogue with other's experiences. Learning from others is an essential part of maturing, since 'the self needs the other (including other perspectives coming from people and abstract theory) to bring them to consciousness' (Ratnam, 2023, p. 227). Progress in achieving maturity should thus involve selectively assimilating the perspectives of others, in a process of self-realisation. It should not simply be a matter of absorbing the other's discourse without taking a step back. I refer here again to Bakhtin (1935) when he describes how a mature subject should learn to reject authoritarian discourse and adopt only those parts of the other's perspectives that are consistent with one's own values and experiences, i.e. one's internally persuasive discourse. This subject would then have an engaged, autonomous and responsible discourse, respecting the autonomy of the alien speech.

I would like to acknowledge that the writing of this chapter has engaged me in a maturation process in the reciprocal learning promoted by my ongoing dialogue with Tara Ratnam and the thought-provoking feedback I received from her, Cheryl Craig and other peer reviewers on my initial drafts.

REFERENCES

Albero, B. (2019). Les sciences de l'éducation au XXIe siècle: Vers une consolidation disciplinaire de la section? *Les dossiers des sciences de l'éducation, 41*, 21–42. https://doi.org/10.4000/dse.3265

Bakhtin, M. (1935). Discourse in the novel. *Literary Theory: An Anthology, 2*, 674–685.

Bitzer, E. M., Trafford, V., & Leshem, S. (2018). The doctoral viva voce as a rite of passage into academia. *A Scholarship of Doctoral Education – On Becoming a Researcher*, 229–248.

Bourdieu, P. (1989). Social space and symbolic power. *Sociological Theory, 7*(1), 14–25. http://www.jstor.org/stable/202060

Bourdieu, P. (1990). *The logic of practice*. Stanford University Press. https://books.google.fr/

Bourdieu, P. (1997/2000). *Pascalian meditations*. Stanford University Press. Pascalian Meditations – Google Books.

Bourdieu, P. (1998). *Practical reason: On the theory of action*. Stanford University Press.

Braun, V., & Clarke, V. (2012). *Thematic analysis*. American Psychological Association.

Bullock, C., & Bullock, S. M. (2020). Exploring challenges to and from self-study methodology: Novice and expert perspectives from a French scholar. In *International handbook of self-study of teaching and teacher education practices* (pp. 483–505). https://link.springer.com/referenceworkentry/10.1007/978-981-13-6880-6_15

Burawoy, M. (2012). The roots of domination: Beyond Bourdieu and Gramsci. *Sociology, 46*(2), 187–206. https://doi.org/10.1177/0038038511422725

Clandinin, D. J. (2022). *Engaging in narrative inquiry*. Routledge.

Combes, A. B. (2022). *Comment l'université broie les jeunes chercheurs. Précarité, harcèlement, loi du silence*. Autrement (Éditions).

Cotterall, S. (2013). More than just a brain: Emotions and the doctoral experience. *Higher Education Research and Development, 32*(2), 174–187. https://doi.org/10.1080/07294360.2012.680017

Craig, C. J. (2021). Back in the middle (Again): Working in the midst of professors and graduate students. In T. Ratnam & C. J. Craig (Eds.), *Understanding excessive teacher and faculty entitlement: Digging at the roots* (pp. 165–178). Emerald Publishing Limited. https://doi.org/10.1108/S1479-368720210000038011

Craig, C. J., Curtis, G., & Kelley, M. (2016). Sustaining self and others in the teaching profession: A group self-study. *Enacting Self-Study as Methodology for Professional Inquiry*, 133–140.

Denis, C., & Lison, C. (2023). L'abandon aux études doctorales : Un problème de direction? *Revue Internationale de Pédagogie de l'Enseignement Supérieur*, *39*(1). https://doi.org/10.4000/ripes.4499

Deyrich, M. C. (2007). Médiations et positionnements: Deux concepts-clés dans la formation des enseignants en anglais. *Document de synthèse présenté en vue de l'Habilitation à Diriger des Recherches. Université Paris*, *3*. https://www.researchgate.net

Deyrich, M. C. (2023). Addressing power asymmetries in doctoral supervision. In C. J. Craig, J. Meno, & R. G. Kane (Eds.), *Studying teaching and teacher education* (Vol. 44, pp. 243–254). Emerald Publishing Limited. https://doi.org/10.1108/S1479-368720230000044024

Doyran, F., & Hacıfazlıoğlu, Ö. (2021). In between wellness and excessive entitlement: Voices of faculty members. In T. Ratnam & C. J. Craig (Eds.), *Understanding excessive teacher and faculty entitlement. Advances in research on teaching* (Vol. 38, pp. 191–204). Emerald Publishing Limited. https://doi.org/10.1108/S1479-368720210000038013

EESRI. (2022). État de l'Enseignement supérieur, de la Recherche et de l'Innovation en France n°16. *Recherche & Innovation*. https://publication.enseignementsup-recherche.gouv.fr/eesr/FR/T744/le_doctorat_et_les_docteurs/

González-Ocampo, G., & Badia, M. C. (2019). Research on doctoral supervision: What we have learnt in the last 10 years. *Traversing the Doctorate: Reflections and Strategies From Students, Supervisors and Administrators*, 117–141. https://doi.org/10.1007/978-3-030-23731-8_7

Grant, B. M. (2005). *The pedagogy of graduate supervision: Figuring the relations between supervisor and student* (Doctoral dissertation, ResearchSpace@ Auckland). http://hdl.handle.net/2292/295

Halse, C. (2011). 'Becoming a supervisor': The impact of doctoral supervision on supervisors' learning. *Studies in Higher Education*, *36*(5), 557–570. https://doi.org/10.1080/03075079.2011.594593

Haag, P. (2018). *L'expérience doctorale: Stress, santé, relation d'encadrement* [thèse de doctorat en psychologie]. Université Paris-Nanterre. https://www.theses.fr/2018PA100020

Hauge, K. (2021). Self-study research: Challenges and opportunities in teacher education. *Teacher Education in the 21st Century-Emerging Skills for a Changing World*, 1–18. https://www.intechopen.com/chapters/75416

Hawley, P. (2010). *Being bright is not enough: The unwritten rules of doctoral study*. Charles C Thomas Publisher. https://books.google.fr/

Holquist, M. (2003). *Dialogism: Bakhtin and his world*. Routledge. https://doi.org/10.4324/9780203425855

Kismihók, G., McCashin, D., Mol, S. T., & Cahill, B. (2022). The well-being and mental health of doctoral candidates. *European Journal of Education*, *57*(3), 410–423. https://doi.org/10.1111/ejed.12519

Kohout-Diaz, M., & Deyrich, M. C. (2021). Entitlement as a promising concept for teacher education research: From displacement to ethical reframing. In *Understanding excessive teacher and faculty entitlement* (Vol. 38, pp. 47–62). Emerald Publishing Limited. https://doi.org/10.1108/S1479-368720210000038004

LaBoskey, V. K. (2004). The methodology of self-study and its theoretical underpinnings. In *International handbook of self-study of teaching and teacher education practices* (pp. 817–869). Springer Netherlands. https://link.springer.com/chapter/10.1007/978-1-4020-6545-3_21

Löfström, E., & Pyhältö, K. (2020). What are ethics in doctoral supervision, and how do they matter? Doctoral students' perspective. *Scandinavian Journal of Educational Research*, *64*(4), 535–550. https://doi.org/10.1080/00313831.2019.1595711

Lortie, D. C. (2020). *Schoolteacher: A sociological study*. University of Chicago Press. https://books.google.fr

Loughran, J. J., Hamilton, M. L., LaBoskey, V. K., & Russell, T. L. (Eds.). (2007). *International handbook of self-study of teaching and teacher education practices* (Vol. 12). Springer. https://books.google.fr/

Marcel, J. F., & Broussal, D. (2020). *Je pars en thèse : Conseils épistolaires aux doctorants*. Éditions Cépaduès.

McAlpine, L., & Akerlind, G. (2010). *Becoming an academic*. Bloomsbury Publishing. https://books.google.fr/

McCray, J., & Joseph-Richard, P. (2020). Towards a model of resilience protection: Factors influencing doctoral completion. *Higher Education, 80*, 679–699. https://doi.org/10.1007/s10734-020-00507-4

Mertova, P., & Webster, L. (2019). *Using narrative inquiry as a research method: An introduction to critical event narrative analysis in research, teaching and professional practice*. Routledge.

Pinnegar, S., & Hamilton, M. L. (2009). *Self-study of practice as a genre of qualitative research*. Springer.

Prata-Linhares, M., da Fontoura, H. A., & de Almeida Pimenta, M. A. (2021). Faculty entitlement: Perspectives of novice Brazilian university professors. In T. Ratnam & C. J. Craig (Eds.), *Understanding excessive teacher and faculty entitlement* (pp. 179–190). Emerald Publishing Limited. https://doi.org/10.1108/S1479-368720210000038012

Ratnam, T. (2021). Foreword. In T. Ratnam & C. J. Craig (Eds.), *Understanding excessive teacher and faculty entitlement. Advances in research on teaching* (Vol. 38, pp. xxi–xxii). Emerald Publishing Limited. https://doi.org/10.1108/S1479-368720210000038001

Ratnam, T. (2023). Excessive teacher entitlement? Going inward and backward to go forward. In C. J. Craig, J. Meno, & R. G. Kane (Eds.), *Studying teaching and teacher education: ISATT 40th anniversary yearbook* (pp. 221–230). Emerald Publishing Limited. https://doi.org/10.1108/S1479-368720230000044022

Ratnam, T., & Craig, C. J. (2021). *Understanding excessive teacher and faculty entitlement. Advances in research on teaching* (Vol. 38). Emerald Publishing Limited. https://doi.org/10.1108/S1479-368720210000038001

Ratnam, T., Craig, C., Marcut, I. G., Marie-Christine, D., Mena, J., Doyran, F., ... Peinado-Muñoz, C. (2019). Entitlement attitude: Digging out blind spots. In D. Mihăescu & D. Andron (Eds.), *Proceedings, the 19th Biennial conference of international study association on teachers and teaching (ISATT), education beyond the crisis: New skills, children's rights and teaching contexts* (pp. 210–219). Sibiu, Romania: Lucian Blaga University Publishing House.

Raybaud, A. (2019). Quand la relation avec son directeur de thèse vire au cauchemar.

Rockinson-Szapkiw, A. J., & Spaulding, L. S. (2014). *Navigating the doctoral journey: A handbook of strategies for success*. Rowman & Littlefield.

Rondeau, K. (2011). L'autoethnographie: Une quête de sens réflexive et conscientisée au cœur de la construction identitaire. *Recherches Qualitatives, 30*(2), 48–70. https://doi.org/10.7202/1084830ar

Russell, T. (2021). Exploring teacher entitlement: Perspectives from personal experience. In T. Ratnam & C. J. Craig (Eds.), *Understanding excessive teacher and faculty entitlement: Digging at the roots. Advances in research on teaching* (Vol. 38, pp. 35–46). Emerald Publishing Limited.

Smith, T. (2006). Self-study through narrative inquiry: Fostering identity in mathematics teacher education. In *Mathematics education research group of Australasia (MERGA) conference 2006* (pp. 471–478). MERGA Inc. https://merga.net.au/Public/Publications/Annual_Conference_Proceedings/2006_MERGA_CP.aspx

Thomas, L., & Guðjónsdóttir, H. (2020). Self-study across languages and cultures. In J. Kitchen, A. Berry, S. M. Bullock, A. R. Crowe, M. Taylor, H. Guðjónsdóttir, & L. Thomas (Eds.), *International handbook of self-study of teaching and teacher education practices* (pp. 1325–1337). Springer. https://link.springer.com/referenceworkentry/10.1007/978-981-13-6880-6_44

Yumarnamto, M. (2022). Dewey, Habermas, and Bakhtin: The epistemology for autoethnography and narrative inquiry. In *Proceedings of the international symposium on transformative ideas in a changing world-the global solidarity crisis* (Vol. 1, pp. 93–106). The Faculty of Philosophy Widya Mandala Surabaya Catholic University. http://repository.ukwms.ac.id/id/eprint/36263

EXCESSIVE (EN)TITLE(MENT) FIGHT? EXPLORING THE DYNAMICS THAT PERPETUATE ENTITLEMENT IN EDUCATION AND BEYOND

John Buchanan

University of Technology Sydney, Australia

ABSTRACT

Education tends to colonize. Established authorities (teachers, curricula, and examinations) instruct newcomers, extending conditional membership. This presents a dilemma for teachers seeking to instill in their students habits of critical, creative, and lateral thinking. In Australia as elsewhere, blueprint educational documents embody lofty aspirational statements of inclusion and investment in people and their potential. Yoked to this is a regime routinely imposing high-stakes basic-skills testing on school students, with increasingly constrictive ways of doing, while privileging competition over collaboration. This chapter explores more informal, organic learning. This self-study narrative inquiry explores my career in terms of a struggle to be my most evolved, enlightened self, as opposed to a small-minded, small-hearted mini-me. To balance this, I examine responsible autonomy (including my own), rather than freedom. This chapter also explores investment in humans, with the reasonable expectation of a return on that investment. It draws and reflects upon events in or impacting my hometown, Sydney, Australia, focusing largely on WorldPride, the Women's World Cup, and a referendum on an Indigenous voice to parliament, all of which took place as I compiled this chapter. Accordingly, the narrative focuses primarily on sexuality, gender, and race. I explore the capacity of my surroundings to teach me and my capacity to learn from my surroundings. The findings and discussion comprise diary-type entries of significant events and their implications for (my) excessive entitlement. The final section of this chapter reviews what and how I have learned.

Keywords: Excessive entitlement; autoethnography; narrative inquiry; learning on Country; self-study; inclusion

BEFORE THE STORY

Acknowledgment of Country: I live, I believe, on the borderlands of the Cadigal and Wangal[1] peoples in today's 'Sydney, Australia.' The border's exact location may now be erased from history. Such is colonization. Some accounts place the border along a ridgeline that my street now follows. The street name, Bulwara, means high place or place of high winds. It was once called Crown Street, not for the Monarch but for the ridgeline crown it traces. That explains an erstwhile Crown Hotel opposite, nowadays a café, with a crown etched above the former name. Somehow, they missed the ridgeline memo. The road led to quarries, where sandstone was extracted for constructing many of Sydney's early buildings, which I dig into in this work below. Local histories and geographies have greatly informed this chapter.

As I write this opening section, Sydney is hosting WorldPride. This festival of LGBTQIA+ culture and achievements is presumably awarded only to 'enlightened,' 'inclusive' cities. Yet, Sydney is founded on gender- and race-based hate and persecution, the cruelty of convict labor, the brutal displacement of the original Indigenous[2] inhabitants, and so forth. These are just some of the dark secrets that Sydney harbors (Lepage et al., 2023). I write in the context of this city of pride and shame, which informs what I see, say, write, and what I might do.

A vignette: The privileges I enjoy

> Dateline: Sydney, on and about Saturday February 25, WorldPride 2023
> *Darlinghurst Gaol: Straightened times*
>
> The term 'gaol' persists in Australia, perhaps as part of a faintly oedipal desire to out-British the British. (King's Birthday is a public holiday here but not in Britain.) Or perhaps because of our convict beginnings upon contact/ invasion. 'Gaol' is etched onto the walls of some older prisons.
>
> Darlinghurst Gaol was built (1822–1824) on a prominent hilltop on the southeastern edge of then Sydney Town, on Gadigal Country, as a reminder

---

[1] The suffix gal in local languages means 'men (of)'. The peoples of Cadi, and of Wan, or Wann, respectively.

[2] I am using the terms (Australian) Indigenous here in reference to Australian Aboriginal and Torres Strait Islander peoples. Most designations in this field are somewhat contentious.

(Continued)

to all that Sydney is/was a prison town. It was built in part by convicts – the serfs building the Master's keep on the hill. With primitive tools, they hewed and laid the sandstone blocks – the jailhouse rock – for the prison walls. Convict markings remain visible on the external walls today. Each convict was assigned his – I believe they were all men, or boys – some transportees were possibly 10 or younger – his own stone markings, as a means of monitoring productivity, and discouraging sluggardliness. (A long sentence, that was.) The Prison, nicknamed 'Starvinghurst,' housed one of Sydney's gallows, for public and private hangings.

The Prison and adjoining Courthouse front Oxford Street, in Sydney's Gay/Queer precinct. In 1978, gay and lesbian protesters demonstrated nearby, to protest against laws that were broken. They were arrested *en masse* and taken to Darlinghurst Police Station, where many were bashed. Their names and addresses were published in the *Sydney Morning Herald* (for which it has since, belatedly (2016) apologized). Oxford Street is the ground/s for today's (tonight's, to be precise) Gay and Lesbian Mardi Gras parade.

Before the decriminalization of homosexuality, the eastern wall of Darlinghurst prison, 'The Wall,' was a gay beat, for men and boys, to hang (surreptitiously (whisper that bit)).

During those protests of 1978, I was a final-year undergraduate at Sydney University, three or four kilometers across town, and a very different order, or class, of sandstone institution. There were no university tuition fees at that time. And I was awarded a scholarship; I was not a stellar scholar – there was a shortage of teachers then (as now).

Not a badge of pride on my part, but I recall nothing of the protest events at the time.

There's more. Around the same time, gay or transgender men jumped, or were pushed, or were death-marched, over Sydney's on-any-other-day-beautiful coastal sandstone cliffs. The beauty and terror (Mackellar, 1908) of Sydney's sandstone is all-around. Police dismissed the deaths as suicides. Some of the perpetrators still live and walk among us. One was recently charged with manslaughter (Noyes & Whitbourn, 2023). Seems a light touch, but I was not there that night and do not know the details. The New South Wales (NSW) Police apologized lately, following accusations of obstructing a Special Commission of Inquiry into Unsolved Suspected Hate Crimes (Beatty, 2022; NSW Government, 2023), and promised to behave better; better, that is, than obstructing an inquiry into Hate Crimes, in the year 2022. Their motto is *culpam poena premit comes* – punishment swiftly follows crime.

Darlinghurst Prison is now an art school, hosting very different hangings. And Darlinghurst Police Station is now an LGBTQI+ museum. Bondi's Marks Clifftop Park, site of numerous gay-hate deaths, now hosts Sydney's annual Sculptures by the Sea exhibition and a monument to the victims. Police now march in the Mardi Gras Parade, along with, tonight, our Prime

(Continued)

> *(Continued)*
>
> Minister. During WorldPride 2023, rainbows proliferate across Sydney, as if from an unseen prism.
>
> That all sounds quite rose-hued. But as you pass the old Prison's cliff-walls on a quiet night, what histories might they whisper?
>
> And his ghost may be heard (Paterson, 1903).
>
> Main source: The Dictionary of Sydney: Darlinghurst Gaol (n.d.)

PURPOSES

The above 'history-in-a-can' serves at least two purposes. It offers a cautionary backdrop for this chapter. More personally, it spotlights some privileges I have enjoyed, and reminds me of what, but for some random fate-twists, my life might have been. I hope the remainder of this chapter might be read, and indeed written, in that light. For what, and to whom, might I need to apologize one day? What might I need to paper-over? Smugness doesn't become me. (Or does it?) Such matters form the basis of my arguments with myself. (I always win.[3]) Specifically, I will examine the dynamics of excessive entitlement, regarding exclusion and inclusion. This chapter will interrogate who and what has entitlement to authority, why and when.

Education, when worthy of the name, bears authority. It stalks and exposes (my) every blind spot, prejudice, hunch, and superstition. I am liable to/for producing antibodies in response. I will strive to counter-colonize others and to 'resist the altogether human tendency of excessive entitlement' (Doyran & Hacıfazlıoğlu, 2021, p. 202), in short, to examine myself otherwise. Events during the time of writing will serve as evidence for the cross-examination.

I will endeavor, simultaneously, to understand, and to willfully misunderstand, myself, as part of my cross-border mind-reading (Mattingly, 2008). Spoiler alert: it's messy in there. In particular, I seek the 'surprises that upset the expected' (Bruner, 2002, p. 8). I like and fear the double meaning of 'upset' here. Komisar (1971, in Russell, 2021, p. 40) speaks of 'root phoniness in teaching.' I anticipate uprootings of my thinking. Like my street and suburb, my mind also houses remnants, that might be rendered visible to the keen eye and the sometimes-less-than-keen mind. The metaphor of isobars emerges for me here. Invisible, except when drawn on a weather map, these lines of equal air pressure exert immense influence on the weather. In some ways, though, I wish to venture beyond the comfortable stasis (Flavian, 2021) of isobars, to places of unequal pressure, with their attendant tensions and torsions. I am unaware of an antonym for isobars. 'Heterobars' sounds somewhat GLBTQI+-unfriendly.

---

[3]We even argue over who is subordinate. Long car trips can become highly tedious. There are times when I end up beside myself.

THEORETICAL FRAMEWORK: SCENE-SETTING

This chapter adopts the self-study genre in the narrative inquiry vein 'drawing on' my multistoried existence and surroundings (Connelly & Clandinin, 2006). It incorporates the 'three commonplaces of narrative inquiry, temporality, sociality, and place' (p. 479). I also appeal to[4] Indigenous pedagogies of learning on, and from, Country (Coff, 2021). I intend to meld this with Vygotskian (Vygotsky & Cole, 1978) sociocultural theory after letting experience in the front door. I am positioning Country as one holding superior knowledge, at whose feet I might learn; my environment as organic curriculum. I hope the process is somewhat radical, root-getting. This self-study is a 'testimony to chart aspects of my experiences' (Carter, 2023, p. 392) and make what I learn available to the profession. I trust and invest that the process is 'improvement-oriented and transformative' (Pithouse-Morgan, 2022) for me. Richards (2008) refers to 'writing the othered self,' describing her inward investigation into 'a different country, with different languages and customs, different laws, different international relations' (p. 1718).

A working definition for 'excessive entitlement' herein is: taking liberties with, sometimes from, others, including the land and its bounty. Accordingly, I recognize 'how cleverly entitlement is hidden from view' (Russell, 2021) and seek 'resistance to any notion of authorial omniscience and objectivity' (Richards, 2008, p. 1720).

My previous Acknowledgment of Country is more extended than I would normally include in a publication. It would typically comprise only the first sentence, positioning me, followed by a statement of respect for the Elders. The extended version is pertinent to my study, however. My street is a metaphorical pentimento or palimpsest. Crown Street overrode, in all probability, an Indigenous walking trail along the ridgetop, as part of eroding, erasing Indigenous presence. I hope to explore boundaries and borderlands. It constantly takes me aback that local Indigenous habitation predates the harbor, which only dates from the last ice age. Local Indigenous people would, similarly, have been taken aback by the rising sea levels. Sometimes we move borders; sometimes they move us. Some Indigenous stories appear to recount these events (Phillips, 2015). Such stories were dismissed as folklore before the science of ice ages was known. The harbor continues to rise, almost imperceptibly, for now. And to the Elders, naturally, respect.

Education is a service rather than a gift, as Russell asserts (2021). But can it be both? If so, I am not the gift but the gift bearer – a Trojan horse? Linking giving to service, my head wants the gift to be useful to the recipient/s, and my heart wants it to be aesthetically pleasing. I accept that the gift analogy falls short, though. The educational gift might not be to one's liking: I don't envisage presenting someone with a voucher for a colonoscopy or for a course in anger management, even if I think the recipient needs such. And anyway, I might get it wrong. My colonoscopy beneficiary might die from rage-related blood pressure or in a fight.

---

[4]At least I hope so.

I am now semi-retired. Retirement offers 'time in the corner,' to think about one's behavior. Accordingly, this chapter primarily explores my entitlement/s as a learner, rather than as a teacher. Labaree (2000, cited in Russell, 2021) claims we should teach ourselves into redundancy, a further call to humility on my part.

On Truth: I occasionally help my sister with gardening. (Don't tell her I enjoy it.) Whatever task I undertake is met with 'that looks great' or similar praise. I appreciate the approbation. It's certainly preferable to unconditional opprobrium, wherein nothing I do suffices. And yet, I am sometimes left wondering how good a job I have really done. Political correctness, otherwise known as courtesy, has its place. It could also be labeled 'being proper' with all the airs of superiority inherent. Unconditional praise might characterize how we speak to ninety-plus-year-olds or to two-year-olds; 'what a lovely jumper you knitted me/ poo you did.'[5] We might be unable to have an other-than-condescending conversation with either of them. Might this parallel a wolf of superiority cloaked in sheepskin's gentility? Or perhaps the Emperor's new clothes, everyone being too polite or fearful to comment, or stare?

Ultimately, this chapter examines power, privilege, and entitlement. Foucault (1976, pp. 92–93) described power as:

> the multiplicity of force relations immanent in the sphere in which they operate and which constitute their own organization: as the process which, through ceaseless struggle and confrontations, transforms, strengthens, or even reverses them; as the support which these force relations find in one another, thus forming a chain or a system, or on the contrary, the disjunctions and contradictions which isolate them from one another.

METHOD AND CONTEXT

This chapter examines both my cognitive and affective responses to what is around and before me (that is, in front of and behind me). It comprises some hearty-thinking, if you will. Given that teachers are change agents (Ratnam & Craig, 2021, p. 6), how might I accept that I need changing? (Disregard footnote 5 in this regard). I will border-cross through time and between my 'interior and exterior worlds' (Royster & Kirsch, 2012, p. 657).

This chapter draws on some dated (yet current) diary-type entries and my reflections thereon. The data are organized – to the extent that they can claim to be organized – chronologically rather than thematically. Data selection was partial in two senses – neither complete nor unbiased. Data were collected primarily from February to October 2023. Three events with local and broader significance predominate during this time: WorldPride 2023, The FIFA Women's World Cup, and a referendum on an Indigenous voice to parliament. Accordingly, three emergent themes are sexuality, gender, and race.

As I endeavored to untangle the links between privileges afforded to me and excessive entitlement, the guiding research questions were: What is the capacity of the land and the events thereon to teach me, particularly regarding my excessive entitlement? Correspondingly, what is my capacity to learn therefrom, and (how)

---

[5]Talking poo is more for children than for elders. Respect.

can I know my limits? More simply, what might the land unearth in me? The iterative nature of the peer review process further enriched my questioning.

Two contextual snapshots:

(1) The Apology: In 2008, then Australian Prime Minister Kevin Rudd offered a national apology to the Stolen Generations, those children of mixed Indigenous and non-Indigenous descent who were removed from their families, in order to erase their Aboriginality (Parliament of Australia, n.d.). The current Leader of the Opposition, Peter Dutton, walked out of Parliament and boycotted the apology, something for which he has recently apologized. I boycotted his apology.
(2) The Voice (not to be confused with the eponymous television franchise): Australians are soon to vote in a referendum to enshrine in our Constitution a Voice to Parliament, which would advise national parliament on matters affecting Indigenous Australians. This proceeds from the 'Uluru Statement from the Heart' (Australian Government, n.d.), compiled by a First Nations National Constitutional Convention, and whose three petitions are occasionally encapsulated as: Voice, Treaty, and Truth. While not having declared his hand, the Leader of the Opposition appears to be resisting the Voice. This chapter also tracks the Voice's (and my) progress or regress.

A further complication, ere the narrative commences: Sydney is sometimes labeled Smug City. Occasionally, Sydney glimpses its reflection[6] in the harbor and falls, all over again, in giddy, adolescent self-love.

FINDINGS AND ANALYSIS

Flashback: November 28, 2022. The National Party, in coalition with the conservative opposition, declares its opposition to the Voice (The Nationals, 2022), before campaigning or explanation (or this chapter) began. Opposition to the Voice appears stronger in 'the bush' (regional Australia – the Nationals' main constituency) than in the cities.

On and about Wednesday, March 8, 2023, International Women's Day.

What do gender equity and equality look like? I want to improve at doing equity. I consulted some lists of 'best countries in which to be a woman.' In those lists, western, and particularly northern, Europe predominates. The ring-ins on some lists are Canada and New Zealand (colonized, like Australia). To determine what determines equality, I listed some features common to many such countries: wealth (possibly the main determinant), cold climate (work to survive), significant Protestant Christian (the 'Protestant work ethic'), White populations; constitutional monarchies, former colonial powers, emigration destinations (people from less woman-enlightened countries appear content to migrate there), men seem to be prospering there also (see wealth, above, and migration), relatively generous

---

[6]An ignoble pursuit of reflective practice.

safety nets (see wealth). Australia ticks most of the previously listed boxes (Papua New Guinea was an Australian colony until 1975); we are wealthier than some of the more woman-friendly countries. It strikes me we can have it all and keep our warmer weather – and beat New Zealand – with just a little more political and social will. I will even attempt it independent of Britain's monarchy. Might equality mean I can anticipate living as long as the average woman? Perhaps longer; I'm highly average. We, men, might aspire to match women's levels of incarceration and crime; gaol might become almost a quaint relic.[7] The crime downswing would mean longer lives for both men and women. More men than women are murder victims in Australia, but almost all perpetrators are men. Domestic violence against women remains a scourge here.

23 March–3 April (1–12 Ramadan 1444 AH): I visit Saudi Arabia

Visiting Saudi Arabia tempts one to be smug about women's status in Australia. But the Saudis might dismiss the West's treatment of women as quite shabby, too, with some evidence. In a moment of idleness, I notice that my Lonely Planet (Walker et al., 2019 – purchased prepandemic) guide undertakes to 'inform, educate and amuse' me (p. 512). Its presumption to educate me fails to amuse. Excessive entitlement on my part, perhaps.

27 March (6 p.m. Saudi time): A woman takes up arms in Nashville and kills six, including three children. Not the kind of equal opportunity I envisaged.

1 April Fools' Day

5 April: the Leader of the Opposition, Peter Dutton, declares the Liberal Opposition's opposition to the Voice.

April 30: A poll indicates a majority yes vote for the Voice in every state and territory (Galloway, 2023) and, *ipso facto*, nationally.

Interrogating why I propose to vote yes to the Voice:

Referenda in Australia: A Brief Overview

A referendum is the only legal means to alter Australia's Constitution. To succeed, a referendum must gain a majority of voters nationally and from a majority of the states. This requires a two-thirds majority of states, four of the six, to succeed. Australia's two territories count toward the national total but not toward the states' total. (I don't understand either.)

This is a high bar. Of 44 referenda since Federation (1901), only eight have succeeded and none without the opposition party's support. The main reason for introducing the Voice constitutionally, rather than through legislation, is that the only way future governments could repeal it would be through another successful referendum. Voting is compulsory.

I propose to vote yes.

---

[7] Linked to the word 'fossil' so I discovered.

I have reservations (a loaded colonial term) about the Voice to Parliament. Potentially, it will achieve little or nothing. Parliament will be unfettered by the Voice's recommendations, which can be politely, or impolitely, disregarded. Indigenous people do not uniformly support the Voice (Tong, 2023). Conceivably, once established, the Voice might crumble into cacophonous conflict. I'm relieved those three words don't begin with Ks. The referendum does ask more of us than did a recent plebiscite on marriage equality. In that instance, the rights of the many were to be extended to the remaining minority. The logic was almost irresistible, irrefutable.

I hope my misgivings prove unfounded. One defensive/offensive tactic by no voters is that 'it's not racist to vote No' (Sydney Morning Herald, 2023). I've not really heard a cogent explanation of this, but in any case, a no vote does side with, and give succor to, the racists. Reports have emerged recently in Australia, as elsewhere, of the rise of neo-Nazi groups. I presume (I have not asked them) that they will vote no. While this is far from my main reason for voting yes, I do not wish to be some neo-Nazi's stooge, goon, or useful idiot. Pride, perhaps. I also see more potential for good than for harm in the Voice, particularly if, as I hope, my misgivings disintegrate.[8]

Fundamentally, it seems reasonable to extend this (dare I call it?) privilege to a group dispossessed, dismissed, discarded, and discredited. Perhaps my main motive for voting yes is that I expect the Voice to be educative. It will get me thinking and learning about the issues raised. I look forward to being disabused.

16 May: US President Joe Biden cancels his Sydney visit, leading to a cancellation of a meeting of the Quad security group (USA, Japan, India, and Australia). Indian Prime Minister Narendra Modi proceeds with his visit and frontlines a rally[9] at a stadium in Parramatta, in Sydney's west (The Guardian, 2023a), near Sydney's 'little India.' At a press conference with Australian Prime Minister Albanese, Mr. Modi denounces graffiti on Hindu temples in Australia. Some of the graffiti was anti-Modi (Times Now, 2023). Mr. Albanese's response invoked freedom of religion in Australia (SBS News, 2023). I might have ventured further, rallying all worthy democracies to do likewise. Recent figures appear elusive, but *The Times of India* (2013) cited 107 deaths of Muslims and Hindus in India. Figures for other faiths (Sikhs, Christians...) appear unavailable. This is not to trivialize defacing a place of worship or to claim that graffitiing a temple is the most egregious commission of persecution against, or by, people of faith in Australia. Nor is it to dismiss the complexity that is religion in India, borne partly of colonization.

11 June: A poll indicates that the yes vote now prevails only in NSW, Victoria and Tasmania (The Guardian, 2023b). NSW and Victoria are the most populous states. Accordingly, there could be a majority yes vote nationally, but the referendum would fail to garner a fourth state in favor; the minority of voters would

---

[8]My fears may have little integrity anyway.
[9]Whose choreography would shame many Bollywood movies.

prevail. At least we could say that the majority voted yes, when facing international opprobrium.

24 June: A poll suggests that the Voice Referendum will fail in every state and territory (The Guardian, 2023b). The cause appears lost.

6 July: The Australian Financial Review publishes a cartoon for the No campaign.
(https://www.news.com.au/national/politics/disgusting-racist-crap-afr-anti-voice-supporters-slammed-for-controversial-cartoon/news-story/de58afcd86624312139c6d47914d19e0)

The cartoon depicts a 'yes' campaign director and Wesfarmers Chair, Michael Chaney, with his (adult) daughter, Kate, a member of parliament, drawn as a diminutive girl, sitting on his lap. He is handing a wad of money, two million dollars, to another yes campaign director, Thomas Mayo, a man of Kauareg (Aboriginal) and Kalkalgal and Erubamble (Torres Strait Islander) descent. Mayo is depicted as a dancing 'minstrel-boy.' Chaney senior is saying 'It's only shareholders money.' The positioning of the daughter on the father's knee arguably smacks of child abuse or incest. An apostrophe is missing.

I found the depiction of Mayo deeply unsettling. I then recalled a search I did some time ago to learn if Jim Crow was a real person, which unearthed the following image, seen in Fig. 1.

20 July–20 August: The FIFA Women's World Cup comes to Sydney – and to some other, inconsequential towns. I jest[10]. While much remains to be done – in terms of pay equity and conditions – toilets and changerooms would be nice – the rapid rise in profile of women's sport in Australia and elsewhere is cause for cautious celebration. FIFA is honoring Indigenous place-names, with the two Sydney venues being labeled Sydney Cadigal and Sydney Wangal accordingly (FIFA, 2023), as per my opening 'position statement.' At the same time, there has been discussion about the ongoing ramifications of concussion in sport, particularly during childhood. It strikes me (so to speak) that our children's brains, education-cured, are the best, perhaps the only, thing we have going for us. More on our children's brains follows.

The Voice: Getting Deeper

There is one further misgiving about the Referendum that I have not dared voice so far. I remain unsure as to what matters apply differentially to Indigenous Australians and other Australians. One mantra in Australia concerns 'Closing the Gap' – the difference in life expectancy between Indigenous Australians and other Australians (Closing the Gap, n.d.). It seems logical to me that if you wish to die like middle-class people (i.e. at about the same age), you need to live like middle-class people. It sounds cringeworthily colonial. Here goes:

Education and health: my advice to the Voice to Parliament[11] might include the following basics: attend school; attend school every day you are well enough

---

[10]Nonetheless, Sydney is proving amply consequential for me.

[11]Hypothetically. I accept that my advice will not be canvassed.

Fig. 1. Jim Crow. *Source:* https://npg.si.edu/object/npg_NPG.2022.102. Provided courtesy of The Smithsonian via Creative Commons.

to do so; apply yourself at school; listen, study, think, be curious, question, test your ideas; proceed with your education as far as your intellect and finances will bear; get a job – one that: serves others meaningfully; is satisfying, rewarding, and fulfilling (see 'serves others', preceding); and one that garners sufficient income to afford some security. Eat healthy, floss and brush regularly (trust me there), exercise moderately, have routine medical check-ups, nonprescribed drugs are better avoided.

As I confessed, it is all quite mundane and middle class, apart, perhaps, from the drug abstinence bit. All quite banal. And not necessarily pleasing to the hearer. Colonoscopy, anyone? But my education compels me to share this advice. I consider myself to have some expertise in education. I believe my advice there is sound. For the health advice, consult medical experts. If their advice differs from mine, follow theirs. The alternative is to leave (Indigenous) people ill-informed, gravely so, thereby condemning them to intergenerational low quality of life, dependence on others, and, ultimately, gap-wise, shortness of breath. I recognize that for some Indigenous people, in remote communities, this will be complex, requiring compromise. And trust; I dislike injections and dental check-ups. I raise this because it is immaterial. It might also require compromises from the rest of us. At the moment, some of the most, in my view, rewarding professions (e.g. teaching and nursing) are remunerated, shall we say, poorly.

I allude to the medical issues mentioned above as one who has entered his seventh decade in relatively good health. I do not wish to be smug about this, lest my health be rude. As outlined above, my health is relative (inherited) and largely an outcome, an outpouring, of good luck and opportunity, to which I am unentitled. I also realize that something lies in wait for me – several things jockeying for first place, probably. As with the land, with myself, what's happening beneath the surface isn't immediately appreciable. Nevertheless, my education compels me to test those ideas. Could my proposals even constitute a case of a sheep in wolf's clothing? It would take some effort to convince me that the above advice constitutes the evil of banality. Such things apply, surely, to those in the third millennium (or century, in Australia), as to those in their 66th.[12] To internal and other voices of dissent, I might respond, why would you despise good health and education, and why would you begrudge another's good health and education?

I still propose to vote yes.

4–7 August *Garma*: Australia's largest Indigenous festival takes place in Arnhem land, in the Northern Territory (Yothu Yindi Foundation, 2022[13]). Garma is a Yolngu (sometimes rendered Yolŋu) word referring to the meeting of salt and fresh waters, a perpetually moving boundary, with the ebb and flow of the tides. The festival was used by the Prime Minister as a platform to promote the yes case for the referendum.

16 August: With Australia now out of contention for the World Cup, I presume our King and Head of State will now root for the English team. A possible exam question: 'If I were a Monarch, I would be prone to excessive entitlement. Discuss.'

18 August: On the 50th anniversary of Australia's withdrawal from the Vietnam War, the NSW Returned and Services League (RSL) of Australia apologizes to returned Vietnam War veterans for its poor treatment of them upon returning home (Burnside & Cole, 2023).[14] Of the 60,000 Australians deployed to the war, 523 died, with nearly 2,400 wounded (Australian War Memorial, 2023). Some of the returnees were refused membership of the RSL, the organization established to support them. Fifty years ago today, I was one-point-something years (and several galaxies) shy of

---

[12]Current evidence suggests that Indigenous people have lived in Australia for about 65,000 years or more (National Museum of Australia, n.d.).

[14]When Indigenous Australians returned from fighting in World War Two, they suffered substantial discrimination, and were excluded from benefits afforded to the non-Indigenous (Department of Veterans' Affairs, n.d.). Australia mythically prides itself on equality.

having my birth date potentially selected in a ballot,[15] to be trained then possibly sent to kill or be killed by Viet Cong or to face prison upon refusal. A further reminder of my fortune. Women were excluded, doubling my chances.

16 August: The Federal Government launches an action plan to tackle domestic violence in Indigenous communities (NITV, 2023).

21 August and thereafter: Now for the hard part. The Women's World Cup is over. Whither gender equity in sport from here? My head reminds me that sport is, largely, inconsequential, and reliant upon confected scarcity – getting the ball, getting the points,[16] etc. But my heart has played happy hostage this past month. I can find no better way of capturing the mood than this: following a particularly intense 20-goal penalty shootout, in which Australia eventually prevailed over France, Australian wheelchair tennis champion Dylan Alcott cried, 'that was the closest I've ever been to standing up.' You had to be there. The tournament wasn't without blemish, here or overseas. Spain's football President, Luis Rubiales, covered himself in vainglory (Valdés, 2023). He remains un(re)moved at the time of writing. Still, both economically and attitudinally, the Cup has moved boundaries. Domestic violence remains a scourge in Australia.

30 August Referendum date announced: 14 October. The Prime Minister's missive is met with applause and cheering, but little surprise, from those present. By the process of elimination (sidestepping football (rugby and Australian football) finals and the wet season in northern Australia), many had pinpointed this date. The no case appears to lead now by about nine points nationally, according to the Australian Broadcasting Corporation (ABC) (YouTube, 2023). If true, the states' tally becomes irrelevant but is also lost. It seems that the yes vote is most predominant among recent migrants, especially those of culturally and linguistically 'different' backgrounds and the young. If so, it is mainly old whites, like so many tissues in the washing machine, causing the blockage.

31 August–9 September: UNESCO's International Council on Monuments and Sites (ICOMOS, 2023) General Assembly convenes in Sydney. The theme is 'Resilience, Responsibility, Rights, Relationships,' resonating richly with the Referendum. Coinciding with this is a campaign to add Indigenous culture to the Greater Blue Mountains' World Heritage listing. An arc of land mainly on the northwestern edge of Sydney, and slightly beyond, is home to a concentration of Indigenous rock art and carvings unmatched anywhere nearby, to my knowledge. Curious and humbling. To my mind, Australian Indigenous culture/s should be added to the United Nations Educational, Scientific, and Cultural Organization's (UNESCO's) intangible cultural heritage list.

10 September Spanish time: Luis Rubiales resigns from his post as the president of the Royal Spanish Football Federation. A new line has been drawn. Might a genuine apology have saved him?

15–22 October: South by Southwest (SXSW)

---

[15]Sounds so democratic!
[16]Clearly, I don't get the point.

I am unsure how Sydney managed to score the first SXSW beyond Texas's borders. The Opera House's 50th anniversary (20 October) may have played a role. Given that SXSW is a festival of, inter alia, the arts, I will invoke the arts to speak about country.

> I have seen tempests, when the scolding winds
> Have rived the knotty oaks, and I have seen
> The ambitious ocean swell and rage and foam,
> To be exalted with the threatening clouds:
> *But never till to-night, never till now,*
> *Did I go through a tempest dropping fire.*
> Either there is a civil strife in heaven,
> Or else the world, too saucy with the gods,
> *Incenses* them to send destruction.
>
> William Shakespeare, 'Julius Caesar', (emphases added)

Visions of Northern Hemisphere firestorms (Hawai'i, Canada, Greece, Algeria...) sparked memories of Australia's 'Black Summer' of 2019–2020, fires that proved to be antediluvian (ABC News, n.d.). Considering my carbon footprint, what might I need to apologize for one day? My willingness to accept responsibility for my environmental impact has been heavy-footed. Nevertheless, there remain glimmers of hope. In recent years, whales have returned in ever-greater numbers to our waters. We can infer greater numbers of koalas in Sydney's southwest than previously thought (through, sadly, increased road-kills disproportionate to growth in traffic). Platypuses have recently been rediscovered in Sydney's outer northwest reaches. This is absolutely humbling, unmerited environmental forgiveness. What, then, when the environment ceases to forgive, unable to tolerate? The following entry is out of order.[17]

14 October: The referendum – a no-win situation

Some tales end unhappily. I would love to have written earlier that 'Australia's women's football team are now world champions. Just saying.' Similarly, I was hoping against hope to announce yes to the Voice. The referendum failed in all six states, and one territory, succeeding only in the Australian Capital Territory. Acceptance of the Voice required, I believe, some pride- (entitlement-)swallowing from both sides. We were unequal – what a sorry word to use in this dis/respect – to the task on this occasion; what a shame. The no vote has unsettling implications for our future nationally. In their defense, Indigenous Australians voted yes in greater proportions for the Voice, as did the educated,[18] vindicating *education* (if not basic skills tests).

I believe our Constitution would benefit from root-and-branch amendments; its authors envisioned a white Australia, through barring all nonwhite

---

[17]Chronologically.
[18]Yes!

immigration (e.g. Wright, 2023). They sought to 'enlighten' (a chilling term in this [dis]regard), Indigenous people by breeding them, through successive generations, with whites. I concede that my ancestors of the day were probably also racist and homophobic and half sexist.[19] Domestic violence remains a scourge in Australia. Maybe you knew.

I *have* a voice, as evidenced by my authoring[20] this chapter. I was naïve to believe that most others would sing along harmoniously, that we could smooth over the disc(h)ord of our racial rifts of historic proportions. Surely, though, listening is a good first step toward renouncing entitlement.

To Indigenous leaders who advocated no, I accept that, individually, you have a prerogative to request not to be consulted. In that spirit, I disregarded you and voted yes. You do not, I believe, have license to erase the opportunity for others/ Others to be heard. And for people whose platform was 'I don't want to be consulted or listened to', you talked a lot.

My hope for our grandchildren's grandchildren is that they will be bewildered and disgusted by our behavior. And I hope they don't play us for noble savages, excusing our ignorant and primitive ways way back when. We knew. We knew.

CONCLUSIONS: BACK TO MY ROOTS

Craig (2021) draws on the Stealers Wheel song *Stuck in the Middle with You* (Rafferty & Egan, 1973) and invokes a British slang term, 'cockwomble' (p. 174), a (male) chauvinist term, to illustrate the behavior of some men in authority whom she has encountered. Perhaps torturing the reference unreasonably, I note that one of the song's composers, Gerry Rafferty, prior to being in Stealers Wheel, was in a band with a less gendered, less presumptuous – let's say less cocksure – name, the Humblebums (Larkin, 2007, p. 1901). This prompts me to ask, how has this chapter furthered my own education? How has it taught me, moved me? Has it helped eradicate, root out my entitlement? Earlier, I observed, flippantly, that I always win my internal disputes. I recognize that improvement is hard to gauge, given that I have been judge, jury and executioner, or acquitter.[21] Nevertheless, I trust this process has honed my skills in questioning, which implies both greater inquisitiveness, even inquisition, and concedes greater ignorance on my part. It is cozy to believe that there remains nothing further to learn (Buchanan & Holland, 2021). Has my alleged enlightenment lightened the burden for some others, leveraging their agency (Ratnam, 2021)? I hope so, but is that condescending? Still, this autoethnographic approach has been liberating. And questioning the constraints irrationally applied to others is surely an emancipatory (Richards, 2008) investment in human capital, mine, and others.

---

[19] Historians might advise us not to judge our ancestors by today's standards. Forbearance for our forebears, rather than unentitled arrogance. What might my descendants find apology-worthy in me?
[20] I trust I have not regressed to authorizing or my teacher voice.
[21] Much as I dislike being called acquitter.

Having observed and reflected on my place through the lenses of sexuality, gender, and race, I find myself 'in a new place.'

The ideas expressed in this work are my own. I have endeavored to record my responses to events around me, sans sanctimony, or cynicism, but, I concede, with some self-censorship; I have drawn boundaries – passageways whose dusty darkness I dared not disturb or divulge their deep-down discoveries. I see this as a failing. I have perhaps chosen my words too carefully. You can't really comment, as you know not what lies unspoken in my chamber of secrets or of any offense averted. Those latter thoughts remain my own. Was the censorship to protect you? Or me? I can hazard[22] a guess.[23] As with the land, with me, some secrets remain interred. Still, education is redemptive. I trust that it has been so for me here, as I set out to interrogate my (en)title(ment) deeds.

Sydney has provided a rich, wonderful backdrop for questioning my entitlement. I have attempted to peel back the layers of my country and of myself. The process has helped me learn my place. It has loosed the learner and the teacher/researcher, that is, the catalyst/analyst, in me; 'pedagogue, teach thyself' (Buchanan, 2006, p. 134). Diarizing and discussing the events of my city – 'Pepyshow' (Pepys, 1825) would be presumptuous – has helped put me in my place. The chapter's contribution might be weighed on the extent to which it can help others with similar encounters, as they 'work from home.'

This is the learning that my self-study in the narrative vein offers my profession. In a context of Indigenous education, Country et al. (2015) speak of decentering human authority. I am unlikely to match the Country awareness of Indigenous Australians, particularly in my time remaining; Indigenous Australians are almost certainly more rooted in this country than I am ever likely to be. Notwithstanding, I believe that I have sharpened my ability to learn from Country. I am of this Country. I live on the western side of Bulwara Road, placing me within Wangal lands, albeit at the margins. I was born on Wangal Country, a few kilometers westward. No one told me then it was Wangal Country; such is colonization. Having lived elsewhere in the interim, I sometimes feel that I have returned home. I find borders moving.

ACKNOWLEDGMENT

I am thankful to Dr Don Carter, Associate Professor, for an insightful response to an earlier draft, and to Dr Helen Russell, for a thoughtful discussion on (my) entitlement and voice. I am also grateful to my friend Julie Robinson, for a thought-provoking discussion on International Women's Day. And to my sister, for letting me loose in her garden.

---

[22]From a Persian word meaning (roll of) the dice, as I discovered.

[23]The only hint I am prepared to divulge is that in restoring the mirror, I restore myself, or at least my image.

REFERENCES

ABC News. (n.d.). *Floods*. https://www.abc.net.au/news/topic/floods

Australian Government. (n.d.). *Uluru statement from the heart*. https://voice.gov.au/about-voice/uluru-statement

Australian War Memorial. (2023). *Vietnam War 1962–1975*. https://www.awm.gov.au/articles/event/vietnam

Beatty, L. (2022). *Police apologise to NSW gay-hate Inquiry over 'offensive' submissions*. News.com.au. https://www.news.com.au/national/nsw-act/courts-law/police-apologise-to-nsw-gayhate-inquiry-over-offensive-submissions/news-story/79cee3f06b42ad55eb8e6c0b874ff46b

Bruner, J. (2002). Narratives of human plight: A conversation with Jerome Bruner. In R. Charon & M. Montello (Eds.), *Stories matter – The role of narrative in medical ethics* (pp. 3–9). Routledge.

Buchanan, J. (2006). Splashing in puddles? What my teaching and research teach me about my teaching and research. In P. Aubusson & S. Schuck (Eds.), *Teacher learning and development: The mirror maze* (pp. 131–144). Springer.

Buchanan, J., & Holland, W. (2021). Learning difficulties: On how knowing everything hinders from learning anything new. In T. Ratnam & C. Craig (Eds.), *Understanding excessive teacher and faculty entitlement. Advances in research on teaching* (Vol. 38, pp. 117–131). Emerald Publishing Limited. https://doi.org/10.1108/S1479-368720210000038008

Burnside, N., & Cole, H. (2023, August 18). *Australians gather to mark 50 years since the withdrawal of troops from Vietnam War*. ABC News. https://www.abc.net.au/news/2023-08-18/50-years-since-australia-left-vietnam-war/102745850

Carter, D. (2023). Intrepid ghosts and writing identities. *Journal of Autoethnography*, 4(3), 392–410.

Closing the Gap. (n.d.). *National agreement on closing the gap*. https://www.closingthegap.gov.au/national-agreement

Coff, K. (2021). Learning on and from country. In M. Shay & R. Oliver (Eds.), *Indigenous education in Australia: Teaching and learning for deadly futures* (pp. 190–201). Routledge.

Connelly, F., & Clandinin, D. (2006). Narrative inquiry. In J. Green, G. Camilli, & P. Elmore (Eds.), *Handbook of contemporary methods in in educational research. American education research association* (pp. 447–489). Routledge.

Country, B., Wright, S., Suchet-Pearson, S., Lloyd, K., Burarrwanga, L., Ganambarr, R., ... & Maymuru, D. (2015). Working with and learning from country: Decentring human authority. *Cultural Geographies*, 22(2), 269–283.

Craig, C. (2021). Back in the middle (again): Working in the midst of professors and graduate students. In T. Ratnam & C. Craig (Eds.), *Understanding excessive teacher and faculty entitlement* (pp. 165–178). Emerald Publishing Limited.

Department of Veterans' Affairs. (n.d.). *Indigenous Australians in service during World War II*. https://anzacportal.dva.gov.au/wars-and-missions/world-war-ii-1939-1945/resources/indigenous-australians-service-during-world-war-ii#6

Doyran, F., & Hacıfazlıoğlu, Ö. (2021). In between wellness and excessive entitlement: Voices of faculty members. In T. Ratnam & C. Craig (Eds.), *Understanding excessive teacher and faculty entitlement* (pp. 191–204). Emerald Publishing Limited.

FIFA. (2023). *FIFA women's World Cup Australia & New Zealand 2023TM match schedule*. https://www.fifa.com/fifaplus/en/articles/fifa-womens-world-cup-australia-and-new-zealand-2023-match-schedule-football-soccer

Flavian, H. (2021). Teachers' role and expectations: Processes versus outcomes. In T. Ratnam & C. Craig (Eds.), *Understanding excessive teacher and faculty entitlement* (pp. 63–74). Emerald Publishing Limited.

Foucault, M. (1976). *The history of sexuality* (R. Hurley, Trans.). Éditions Gallimard.

Galloway, A. (2023). *Yes vote for the voice is leading in every state and territory: Poll*. https://www.smh.com.au/politics/federal/yes-vote-for-the-voice-is-leading-in-every-state-and-territory-poll-20230429-p5d482.html

ICOMOS. (2023). *ICOMOS General Assembly and scientific symposium*. https://icomosga2023.org/

Komisar, B. (1971). Is teaching phoney? In R. Hyman (Ed.), *Contemporary thought on teaching* (pp. 57–60). Prentice-Hall.

Larkin, C. (2007). *The encyclopedia of popular music* (5th ed.). Omnibus Press.

Lepage, T., Triggs, V., & Buchanan, J. (2023). Coming out to Australia: Cosmopolitan vlogging. *International Journal of Education & the Arts, 24*(2). http://doi.org/10.26209/ijea24n2

Mackellar, D. (1908). *My country*. London Spectator.

Mattingly, C. (2008). Reading minds and telling tales in a cultural borderland. *Ethos, 36*(1), 136–154. http://www.jstor.org/stable/20486565

National Museum of Australia. (n.d.). *Evidence of first peoples*. https://www.nma.gov.au/defining-moments/resources/evidence-of-first-peoples

NITV. (2023). *Government releases first dedicated Aboriginal and Torres Strait action plan to end domestic violence*. https://www.sbs.com.au/nitv/article/govt-releases-first-dedicated-aboriginal-and-torres-strait-islander-plan-to-end-domestic-violence/povhr4d8s

Noyes, J., & Whitbourn, M. (2023, February 23). *'This could have been solved within weeks': Brother's fury at 34-year fight for justice*. Sydney Morning Herald. https://www.smh.com.au/national/nsw/scott-white-s-guilty-plea-to-manslaughter-in-scott-johnson-case-20230223-p5cmxp.html

NSW Government. (2023). *The special commission of inquiry into LGBTIQ hate crimes*. https://www.specialcommission.nsw.gov.au/

Parliament of Australia. (n.d.). *Apology to Australia's indigenous peoples*. https://www.aph.gov.au/Visit_Parliament/Art/Exhibitions/Custom_Media/Apology_to_Australias_Indigenous_Peoples

Paterson, A. (1903). *Waltzing Matilda*. Angus & Robertson.

Pepys, S. (1825). *Memoirs of Samuel Pepys*. Henry Colburn.

Phillips, N. (2015, February 14). Aboriginal stories of sea level rise preserved for thousands of years. *Sydney Morning Herald*. https://www.smh.com.au/technology/aboriginal-stories-of-sea-level-rise-preserved-for-thousands-of-years-20150212-13d3rz.html

Pithouse-Morgan, K. (2022). Self-study in teaching and teacher education: Characteristics and contributions. *Teaching and Teacher Education, 119*. https://doi.org/10.1016/j.tate.2022.103880

Rafferty, G., & Egan, J. (1973). *Stuck in the middle with you. (Stealers Wheel)*. Apple Studios.

Ratnam, T. (2021). The interaction of culture and context in the construction of teachers' putative entitled attitude in the midst of change. In T. Ratnam & C. Craig (Eds.), *Understanding excessive teacher and faculty entitlement* (pp. 77–101). Emerald Publishing Limited.

Ratnam, T., & Craig, C. (2021). Introduction: The idea of excessive teacher entitlement: Breaking new ground. In T. Ratnam & C. Craig (Eds.), *Understanding excessive teacher and faculty entitlement* (pp. 1–13). Emerald Publishing Limited.

Richards, R. (2008). Writing the othered self: Autoethnography and the problem of objectification in writing about illness and disability. *Qualitative Health Research, 18*(12), 1717–1728.

Royster, J., & Kirsch, G. (2012). *Feminist rhetorical practices*. Southern Illinois University Press.

Russell, T. (2021). Exploring teacher entitlement: Perspectives from personal experience. In T. Ratnam & C. Craig (Eds.), *Understanding excessive teacher and faculty entitlement* (pp. 35–46). Emerald Publishing Limited.

SBS News. (2023). *Disturbs our mind: Narendra Modi condemns Hindu temple attacks in Australia during Anthony Albanese meeting*. https://www.sbs.com.au/news/article/disturbs-our-mind-narendra-modi-condemns-hindu-temple-attacks-in-australia-during-anthony-albanese-meeting/61bekatct

Sydney Morning Herald. (2016, February 4). *The Sydney Morning Herald apologises to the 1978ers*. https://www.smh.com.au/national/nsw/the-sydney-morning-herald-apologises-to-mardi-gras-founders-the-78ers-20160224-gn26jm.html

Sydney Morning Herald. (2023, June 30). *Not 'ignorant or racist': No voters want their 'legitimate concerns' taken seriously*. https://www.smh.com.au/national/nsw/not-ignorant-or-racist-no-voters-want-their-legitimate-concerns-taken-seriously-20230628-p5dk66.html

The Dictionary of Sydney. (n.d.). *Darlinghurst gaol*. https://dictionaryofsydney.org/entry/darlinghurst_gaol#:~:text=Darlinghurst%20Gaol%20is%20the%20oldest,the%20stonemason's%20art%20in%20Australia

The Guardian. (2023a). *Narendra Modi receives rock star welcome in Sydney as Anthony Albanese hails rich friendship*. https://www.theguardian.com/australia-news/2023/may/23/narendra-modi-receives-rock-star-reception-in-sydney-as-anthony-albanese-hails-rich-friendship

The Guardian. (2023b). *The Voice to Parliament polling tracker: How many people support or oppose the referendum*. https://www.theguardian.com/news/datablog/ng-interactive/2023/jul/26/indigenous-voice-to-parliament-referendum-tracker-news-newspoll-essential-yougov-by-state-australia-latest-results

The Nationals. (2022). *The Nationals oppose a Voice to Parliament*. https://nationals.org.au/the-nationals-oppose-a-voice-to-parliament/

Times Now. (2023). *Shri Shiva Vishnu Temple in Australia smeared with anti-India graffiti, second attack in 4 days*. https://www.timesnownews.com/videos/times-now/india/shri-shiva-vishnu-temple-in-australia-smeared-with-anti-india-graffiti-second-attack-in-4-days-times-now-video-97062109

Times of India. (2013). *Government releases data of riot victims identifying religion*. https://timesofindia.indiatimes.com/india/Government-releases-data-of-riot-victims-identifying-religion/articleshow/22998550.cms

Tong, K. (2023). What are Aboriginal people saying about the Voice to Parliament? *Australian Broadcasting Corporation*. https://www.abc.net.au/news/2023-02-01/what-are-aboriginal-people-saying-about-the-voice-to-parliament/101912918

Valdés, I. (2023, August 21). *Why a non-consensual kiss has marred Spain's first Women's World Cup title*. El País. https://english.elpais.com/sports/2023-08-21/why-a-non-consensual-kiss-has-marred-spains-first-womens-world-cup-title.html

Vygotsky, L., & Cole, M. (1978). *Mind in society: Development of higher psychological processes*. Harvard University Press.

Walker, J., Lee, J., Bremmer, J., Hussain, T., & Quintero, J. (2019). *Oman, UAE & Arabian Peninsula*. Lonely Planet Global Limited.

Wright, T. (2023, September 1). Alfred Deakin architect of modern Australia and white supremacist. *Sydney Morning Herald*. https://www.smh.com.au/national/alfred-deakin-architect-of-modern-australia-and-white-supremacist-20230831-p5e118.html

Yothu Yindi Foundation. (2022). *Garma festival*. http://yyf.com.au/garma-festival

YouTube. (2023). *Casey Briggs looks at the latest polling for the voice referendum*. ABC News. https://www.youtube.com/watch?v=LMjI3QROcjs

SECTION IV
SYNTHESIZING THE CORE IDEAS

LOOKING BACK TO LOOK FORWARD

Cheryl J. Craig

Texas A & M University, USA

ABSTRACT

This "looking back to look forward" chapter addresses narrative threads that began in the Foreword of this book. The Holocaust and other inhumane acts again serve as starting points for discussion. Woven in are passages from an open letter a Holocaust survivor wrote to teachers in the aftermath of World War II. The naming of dehumanizing acts, along with their educated aggressors, segues into a discussion of excessive entitlement, the topic of this volume. This chapter acknowledges that faculty and graduate students wrestle with intractable educational dilemmas ignited by those who are excessively entitled. As they struggle to make sense of off-putting experiences that trace to their peers' excessiveness, they inevitably conclude that dilemmas, by their very nature, can never be resolved definitively. But they can be circumstantially managed. Teachers and principals are highly influential in weighing and managing dilemmas. They are primary role models to others in society because of their sustained relationships with youth over time. Only when teachers and professors consider humanity in its entirety do their in situ understandings of excessive entitlement recalibrate to become empowered entitlement where both self and others are taken into consideration where informed actions are concerned. This chapter ends by reinforcing the importance of the best-loved self, which repeatedly shows itself to be the yin to excessive entitlement's yang. This point is emphatically made in each preceding chapter as well – with all this volume's chapters suggesting how academia could move beyond excessive entitlement with the betterment of humankind in full view.

Keywords: Narrative threads; excessive teacher/faculty entitlement; dehumanizing acts; empowered entitlement; best-loved self; managing dilemmas

THE HOLOCAUST AND OTHER INHUMANE ACTS

This book began with the Holocaust and a discussion of inhumane acts that humans inflict on one another. The opening comment reminded me of a letter I read that a concentration camp survivor had written to teachers following the atrocity. In the open letter, the anonymous Holocaust survivor said he witnessed:

> Gas chambers built by learned engineers. Children poisoned by educated physicians
> Infants killed by trained nurses.
> Women and babies shot and burned by high school and college graduates. (n.d., p. 1)

He went on to say that teaching subject matter is dangerously incomplete if students only learn content. His advice to teachers was this:

> Help ... students become human. Your effort must never produce learned monsters, skilled psychopaths, educated illiterates. Reading, writing, arithmetic are important only if they serve to make ... children more human. (n.d., p. 1)

The point the survivor drove home was that the psychological and the sociological are vital to learning. Subordinating or neglecting one or the other creates fertile conditions for "evil results [to] follow" (Dewey, 1897, p. 77). And, while evil never totally wins, we cannot free ourselves from it because evil never dies (John Steinbeck in a conversation with a friend).

EXCESSIVE ENTITLEMENT AS DEHUMANIZATION

The authors of the chapters of this book have shown readers how an overly aggrandized view of one's contributions, accomplishments, and position results in teachers and, by close association, professors, who act in excessively entitled ways. Their puffed-up sense of entitlement negatively impacts others' pursuits of their preferred visions of self. Because those who are excessively entitled greedily demand attention beyond what others should have to give them, no wiggle room is left for others to thrive. They feel dehumanized and robbed of their humanity. Consequently, their social relations inside and outside of classrooms become "dead spaces" (Dewey, 1938). The robust environment that is requisite for productive learning to happen becomes choked out. The best-loved self of others is quashed, while the best-loved self of those excessively entitled becomes increasingly self-turned.

THE PRIMACY OF TEACHERS AND PROFESSORS

The Holocaust survivor's poignant letter underscored the fact that teachers and professors are paradoxically part of the cause and the solution to the world's most vexing problems. Certainly, they share the same challenges as they too are part of humanity. However, as educators, they are uniquely positioned with respect to youth. This unavoidably puts them in a powerful – yet vulnerable – place. While they are hired to represent the state, they can choose to be much more than that. They can be "agents of education" (Schwab, 1954/1978) in its entirety in classrooms, schools, universities, and society at large. They would not just possess the title of teacher or professor, but they would be educators in the deepest sense of the word. They would profoundly affect "how life [comes] to children" (Dewey, 1897, p. 83).

THE IMPORTANCE OF MANAGING DILEMMAS

It goes without saying that big and small problems defy single solutions. There are no one-size-fits-all answers to the difficulties humans face. All we can do is "manage dilemmas" (Cuban, 1992) as this volume's chapter authors amply showed. The challenges of humans in general (and of the professions specifically) are moral and utterly intractable. However, we can better manage them if we give them our undivided attention despite our flawed natures and errant ways. We recall from Tara Ratnam's Preface that we are able to flag "things" in our experiences, as Dewey (1920) averred. Once a phenomenon like excessive entitlement has a name and is brought to full consciousness, we have a much better chance of addressing it in our own and others' experiences, situations, and contexts. Once we are aware of how problematic and far-reaching its effects are, we are less likely to knowingly play a role in its perpetuation. We learn – through hard-lived experience – to identify it for ourselves and others. At that point, our and others' human tendencies to be excessively entitled may morph into a kind of empowered entitlement (Ratnam, this volume) that queries whether decisions are humane based on close consideration of everyone (self *and* others). A positive aside is that the term begins to "stick" and becomes commonly known and spread in the profession and throughout the world.

EDUCATORS AND THEIR HUMANITY

In managing dilemmas, educators increasingly discover that we are part of a human whole according to the Upanishad as earlier asserted – and that none of us can enact our best-loved self (Craig, 2013, 2020; Schwab, 1954/1978) if the best-loved selves of others are compromised. We are simultaneously being and becoming, as Maxine Greene (1995) pointed out. We are never complete in a fixed and finished sense. As long as we live, we have ongoing opportunities to change.

Hence, we return once more to teachers and professors and recognize that they are among the most widely influential members of society due to their prolonged engagement with youth. They, in Barone's words (2001), "touch eternity." The chapter contributors brought forward for analysis introspective wonderings, ponderings, and difficulties weighing heavily on them. They queried who they were in certain situations; they reflected on roles they and others played; they considered how different results would be achieved if the chronicled scenarios played out otherwise. They also skillfully illustrated how different research methods can be powerfully used to unpack lived, told, and retold experiences. Such experiences are brought together for the first time in this edited volume.

The concentration camp survivor, with whom I began, maintained that everything depends on the teacher/professor, their humanity, and the kinds of examples they set. They must teach youth about the self without losing sight of the self's relationship to others in community. Making everything about themselves is not in the best interests of humanity. Hence, the best-loved self can never be self-concerned and solipsistic in its orientation. Out of necessity, it must be generative and generous – with one's actions and modeling spilling over to others' actions and modeling, all spreading outwardly and simultaneously being received inwardly in both anticipated and unanticipated ways.

TOWARD THE FUTURE

Looking forward, we understand with greater clarity that the flourishing of one inescapably affects the flourishing of another. Through experience, we learn that everything is morally and physically "hitched to everything else" (Muir, 1911, p. 110). Distilled to the essence, we recognize none of us is an island (Donne, 1623). It could not be otherwise. These are the lessons we take with us as we press forward, with confidence, to an unknown future.

> I have learned again, again and again ... that generous scholars focus on being ... not on having ... the spoils of the academy. Having anything – awards, accolades, money, titles, competitive grants, research centers – is a tinny prize if the diminishment of one's best-loved self or the best-loved self of another is the price-of-purchase. Craig (2019)

REFERENCES

Anonymous Holocaust Survivor. (n.d.). *Nazi concentration camp letter to teachers* (after World War II). Posted by Josh Marlo Avinante on Shiv Tandon's Space. Quora.
Barone, T. (2001). *Touching eternity: The enduring outcomes of teaching*. Teachers College Press.
Craig, C. J. (2013). Teacher education and the best-loved self. *Asia Pacific Journal of Education*, *33*(3), 261–272.
Craig, C. J. (2019). *Best-loved self, choice, and action*. Keynote address. International Study Association on Teachers and Teaching. University of Sibiu.
Craig, C. J. (2020). *Curriculum making, reciprocal learning, and the best-loved self*. Palgrave Macmillan.
Cuban, L. (1992). Managing dilemmas while building professional communities. *Educational Researcher*, *21*(1), 4–11.
Dewey, J. (1897). *My pedagogical creed*. Southern Illinois University Press.
Dewey, J. (1920). *Reconstruction in philosophy and essays, 1920*. Southern Illinois University Press.
Dewey, J. (1938). *Experience and education*. Basic Books.
Donne, J. (1623). *No man is an island*. Sermon delivered at St. Paul's Cathedral.
Greene, M. (1995). *Releasing the imagination: Essays on education, the arts, and social change*. Jossey-Bass.
Muir, J. (1911). *My first summer in the Sierra*. Houghton Mifflin Company.
Schwab, J. J. (1954/1978). Eros and education: A discussion of one aspect of discussion. In I. Westbury & N. Wilkof (Eds.), *Science, curriculum and liberal education: Selected essays* (pp. 105–132). University of Chicago Press.

AFTERWORD

Tom Russell

Queen's University, Canada

This second collection of perspectives on excessive teacher/faculty entitlement draws together authors from nine countries to extend the insights developed in the first book assembled by Ratnam and Craig (2021). Overall, this volume represents a powerful guide to all who dare to study the extent to which their teaching displays excessive entitlement. Consider the following broad conclusions about our educational systems from two of the authors: "Excessive entitlement occurs at all levels in education and awareness is the first step towards understanding" (J. Ellett, this volume). "Schools are rule bound institutions where asymmetrical power ensures a firm divide between teacher and taught; the idea that a teacher acts autonomously in this hierarchical system needs to be critically engaged with" (J. Hardman, this volume).

Also consider the following two personal statements, one in the context of doctoral supervision and a second in the context of the impact of personal school experiences:

> I connect accounts drawn from literature, real-life testimonies and a corpus of discussions and notes to explore the manifestations of excessive faculty entitlement in the form of asymmetries and difficulties that can negatively impact the quality of supervision. (M-C. Deyrich, this volume)

> This study has also provided me with a new healing lens to re-approach this trauma and reconceptualize the lived basis of my memories from the past. In many ways this study has provided an opportunity for me to actually shatter my views of the hegemonic, evolving, and discursive power of excessive entitlement at my school (both then and now). (R. Sawyer, this volume)

In her Introduction to this collection, Tara Ratnam offered the following questions about the concept of *excessive entitlement* as it appears in some teachers' behaviors:

> Why are teachers not open to learning and change despite being overly concerned about the success in school and life of the multiculturally diverse students they teach? What prevents them from being flexible, adaptable, and responsive to the needs of their students in the rapidly

changing educational, social, environmental and technological contexts? Why do they blame their students, parents, or administrators for their own failures or shortcomings?

Thus, we must ask, *what is it about the work of teachers and the culture of schools that makes it so easy to develop and hold an excessive sense of entitlement without being particularly aware of it and the significant impact that excessive entitlement can have on the work of teaching?* While the perspective of excessive entitlement is new, powerful tensions in the culture of schools have been with us for decades. Let's briefly review just how much has been accomplished in each section of this new volume on excessive entitlement.

In Section I, several authors demonstrated various ways in which the Cultural-Historical Activity Theory (CHAT) perspective can be used to develop further insights into the origins and potential consequences of teachers' sense of excessive entitlement. Authors from India, China, Brazil, and South Africa introduced a range of relevant concepts, including school culture, the nature of teacher authority, aspects of teaching that contribute to excessive entitlement, and constraints on teacher behavior. They also focused on teachers' defensive and coercive postures, teacher agency, and ways of moving closer to teachers' professional values.

Section II linked excessive entitlement to the concept of the "best-loved self," introduced by Schwab (1954/1978) and addressed more recently by Craig (2013/2020). Authors from the United States, Canada, and the United Kingdom have introduced ideas such as practicing self-accountability, modeling reflexivity in teacher education, engaging in dialogue, researching one's own practice, the general lack of teachers' voices and treating teachers as nonpersons.

Section III provided four examples of teachers studying their own actions from the perspective of excessive entitlement, with research conducted by authors from the United States, Canada, France, and Australia spotlighted. Here, details become even more personal, with examples of confronting personal beliefs as a teacher and faculty member, sharing one's personal history as a gay high school student, analyzing experiences as both doctoral student and supervisor, and exploring what and how a teacher learns from one's own surroundings.

At this point, the discussion draws on personal experiences to indicate how the perspective of excessive entitlement has promoted my own thinking about teaching, teacher education, learning to teach, and the complex nature of teachers' authority. Fifty years ago, as a doctoral student, I found value in R. S. Peters' perspective that a teacher is an authority in the classroom in not one but two senses: A teacher is *an* authority *in* authority (1966, p. 240). In other words, a teacher has two types of authority – the authority of reason (based on scholarship) and the authority of position (based on appointment as a teacher in charge of a group of students). Analysis of several transcripts of the teaching of science teachers revealed that when there is difficulty convincing students using reason (as *an* authority about content), it is possible to move on in a lesson by asserting that a statement is correct (by virtue of the teacher's position *in* authority). Years later, analysis of the dynamics of my teacher education classroom extended Peters' types of authority to conclude that a teacher educator is an authority in authority who also holds the authority of experience. In the following excerpt, the term knowledge-in-action is used to refer to knowledge gained from personal experience.

> The explanatory potential of the authority of experience is evident in the predicament of experienced teachers appointed to faculties and colleges of education. Their knowledge-in-action gives them the authority of experience. But the circumstances of telling their students about teaching unavoidably commits them to the authority of being in charge, and their students are automatically placed under authority. The authority of experience gets transformed into the authority that says, *I know because I have been there and so you should listen.* The authority of experience simply does not transfer because it resides in having the experience. (Munby & Russell, 1994, pp. 92–93)

Although I have not identified extensive research on the timing of courses and practicum experiences, I expect that many postdegree teacher education programs in universities begin with on-campus classes intended to prepare individuals for the tasks of teaching, from planning lessons to enacting lessons to analyzing what has been learned from personal experiences of teaching. In the two academic years 1997–1998 and 1998–1999, the Faculty of Education at Queen's University at Kingston enacted a radically different structure of what was then a two term, 8-month teacher education program for individuals who had already completed a first degree. The first term began with an orientation week and then placed people in schools on the first day of the school year. These teacher candidates made many discoveries, including the fact that on the first day of school, all who are not students must be teachers, not visitors passing through briefly. These teacher candidates stayed for 4 months, interrupted only by a 2-week return to the university after six or eight weeks of teaching. Being present on the first day of school seems to be the dream of every teacher candidate. Course work followed in the second term, which also included two much shorter practicum placements.

In 1999, the program reverted to a 4-week period of introductory classes (Russell, 1999), but the radical change revealed that teacher candidates with such extensive experience respond very, very differently to teacher education classes. Perhaps they were rejecting professors' sense of excessive entitlement; perhaps they had acquired an early sense of entitlement themselves. Inevitably, participants in the program had a range of reactions to early teaching experience; one individual shared his reactions in an extensive and strongly worded statement about the powerful differences that early experience made in his learning to teach:

> How can someone claim to know so much about teaching that her or his input could be so invaluable that it warrants exposure [to future teachers] before an individual has had an opportunity to teach? For someone to tell me that my experiences are less important and will offer me less than what they can 'show' me is, by definition, arrogant and hypocritical! ... They will spray perfumy phrases like "telling is not teaching" or "how you teach is the message." These phrases mean a great deal when I apply them to my own experiences. But when someone tells me that they know more than I can learn on my own, then the principle [underlying] the phrases is lost. In fact, they are modelling what they teach, but their model is based on a double standard. They tell me that "telling is not teaching." How can they tell me that? Let me find out for myself.

> Even sadder is the fact that these faculty members have a tremendous amount to offer, yet it is easily dismissed with inexperience. After six weeks of teaching, I knew what I was weak at. Thus, when I was listening to faculty I could absorb the things I needed most and filter [out] that which was unnecessary. I also listened more acutely. Without those initial teaching experiences, ... I couldn't decipher what was pertinent and what wasn't and therefore I absorbed far less in the initial [orientation] week than [when] each student, with 6 weeks under the belt, had a vast amount to offer to both the faculty and the other students. (D. Day, personal communication, 8 December 1998)

When the relationship begins in a university classroom without prior teaching experience, deep changes in that relationship are unlikely to occur when classes resume after practicum experience. Day suggests that acquiring experience before being told how to teach quickly alerted him to faculty members' display of excessive entitlement. Presumably, a teacher's authority of position contributes significantly to the development of excessive entitlement. A very different teacher–student relationship develops when courses only begin after significant teaching experience. Early teaching experience importantly provides personal experience of acting with authority of position as well as authority of reason.

At the same time, early experience introduces teacher candidates to the many challenges of learning from personal experience. As that learning continues, those learning to teach develop knowledge-in-action that provides the authority that comes with personal experience. When education classes in the university only begin after significant teaching experience, that authority of experience can inspire challenges to the teacher educator's authorities of reason and position. Such challenges can make teacher educator's work more complex, in part by threatening their sense of entitlement that comes with their authority of position.

From the chapters in this collection and its predecessor, I have learned a great deal and have concluded that it is time to extend these analyses into extensive research activity that examines teacher education programs from the perspective of excessive teacher entitlement and its potential for reframing the work of preparing new teachers. Teacher educators need to begin by examining personal practice. Teacher education programs are not easily changed and a friend recently mentioned the reluctance of senior faculty to support changes. Our teaching seeks to prepare people for a productive teaching career guided by learning from experience that generates new insights and practices. We need to do this by actively discouraging a sense of excessive teacher entitlement. How this can be done constructively is a question in search of many answers.

REFERENCES

Craig, C. J. (2013). Teacher education and the best-loved self. *Asia Pacific Journal of Education, 33*(3), 261–272.

Craig, C. J. (2020). *Curriculum making, reciprocal learning, and the best-loved self.* Palgrave Macmillan.

Munby, H., & Russell, T. (1994). The authority of experience in learning to teach: Messages from a physics methods class. *Journal of Teacher Education, 45,* 86–95.

Peters, R. S. (1966). *Ethics and education.* George Allen & Unwin.

Ratnam, T., & Craig, C. J. (Eds.). (2021). *Understanding excessive teacher and faculty entitlement: Digging at the roots.* Emerald Publishing Limited.

Russell, T. (1999). The challenge of change in teaching and teacher education. In J. R. Baird (Ed.), *Reflecting, teaching, learning: Perspectives on educational improvement* (pp. 219–238). Hawker Brownlow Education.

Schwab, J. J. (1954/1978). Eros and education: A discussion of one aspect of discussion. In I. Westbury & N. Wilkof (Eds.), *Science, curriculum and liberal education: Selected essays*. University of Chicago Press.

INDEX

Academia, 139–140
Academic entitlement, 44
Action Learning, Action Research and Process Management (ALARPM), 175–176
Action research, 169, 174–175
Activity
  drawing networked relational model of, 53–55
  system, 49, 54–55, 72
Activity systems model (ASM), 46
Alchemy (Chopra's concept), 160
Amalgams of experience, 142–145
  faculty member example, 143–145
  graduate student example, 142–143
American Association of Teaching and Curriculum (AATC), 141
American Federation of Teachers (AFT), 189
Apology, The, 255
Arts-based inquiry, 218–219
Assemblages, 49
Australia, referenda in, 256
Authoritarian, 69–70
  discourse, 241–242
  style, 71
  teacher's style, 71–72
Authoritative discourse, 20–21, 68, 74
  authority vs. authoritarian, 69–70
  dialogue, authority and teachers' styles, 71–72
  dialogue vs. monologue, 70–71
  teacher and student power relations, 72–73
'Authoritative teachers' style, 72
Authority, 69–72
Autoethnographic practices, 205
Autoethnography, 169, 201–203
Awareness, reflection of, 211–212

#BackonTrack programme, 100
Bakhtin's notion of dialogism, storying and 'restorying' framed by, 234–235
Banking Education, 64–65, 71
Basic Law of the Non-Higher Education System, 127–128
Best–loved self, 138–139, 168–170, 272, 276
  concept, 2–3, 6
  Yin–Yang of excessive teacher/faculty entitlement and, 11–12
Bodily memory, 198–199
Bourdieu's social theory of reproduction, 233
Bracketing, 198–199
Bridling, 198–199
  excessive teacher entitlement, 204–205
Broadening, 141
Burrowing, 141

Cable News Network (CNN), 188
Cami Maths (Software), 82
Care ethics, 217, 226
Catholic education, 128
Change Laboratories, 106
  protocols, 108
  session, 108–109
Chinese basic education system, 124
Classroom discourse, uncovering teacher authority in, 21
Community of practice, 77
Competition, 5–6
Computer software, 94
Computer-based mathematics lessons, 91–93
Concept activity, 74–76

Conceptual complexification, 76
Conceptual inquiry, 77
Conceptual investigation approach, 76–77
Confucianism, 126
Consciousness, 12–13
Conservative viewpoints, 192
Continual reflect journaling technique, 198–199
Continuity, 200–201
Contradictions, 33, 83–84
Convoluted circumstances, 143
Core ideas, synthesizing, 13
COVID-19, 184
Critical theory, 169–170
Cultural inquiry approach, 77
Cultural mediation, 75
Cultural-Historical Activity Theory (CHAT), 8, 11, 22–23, 37–38, 44–45, 54, 65, 78–79, 83–84, 102–104, 108, 121, 276
    activity system, 50–51, 53
    CHAT-informed educational research, 104
    contextualization within, 45–48
    perspective, 118–119
    principles, 112
Cultural–historical theory, 33
Culturally sustaining pedagogy, 157
Currere, 216–219
Curriculum theory-based methodology, 216–217

Darlinghurst Gaol, 250
Darlinghurst Prison, 250
Decision-making processes, 66–67
Defensive pedagogy, 95–96
    analytical framework, 87–88
    computer-based mathematics lessons, 91–93
    context, 86–87
    equivalent fractions, 89–90
    face-to-face lessons, 89
    findings, 89, 96, 109, 113
    instructional rules, 90–91
    method, data sources and analysis, 108–109
    methodology, 86–88
    object in computer-based lesson, 93–96
    purposes, 102–103
    research participants, 86
    theoretical framework, 82, 86, 103, 108
Deficit teacher, 35–36
Deficit view of students, 29–30
Dehumanization, excessive entitlement as, 272
Dialectical process, 70
Dialogic engagement, conversation, 151–164
Dialogic interaction, 69
Dialogic research, 150
Dialogical approach, 242
Dialogical relationship, 241–242
Dialogical science education (*see also* Traditional education), 68–74
    authority *vs.* authoritarian, 69–70
    dialogue, authority and teachers' styles, 71–72
    dialogue vs. monologue, 70–71
    teacher and student power relations, 72–73
Dialogical–authoritative educational framework, 74
Dialogic–authoritative process, 77
Dialogism, storying and 'restorying' framed by Bakhtin's notion of, 234–235
Dialogue, 70–72
Dichotomies, 68
Digital technologies, 100–101
Dilemmas, importance of managing, 273
Dilemmatic spaces, 120–121
    excessive teacher entitlement, 119–120
    Lee's narrative account, 124–126
    narrative inquiry as research method, 122–124

Ping's narrative account, 126–127
(re-) telling and (r-) living in stories of teachers, 124–129
theoretical underpinnings, 119–122
transformative agency, 121–122
Wang's narrative account, 127–129
Direct teaching, 91
Discourse, 241–242
District Institute of Education and Training (DIET), 24–25
Doctoral School (DS), 240
Doctoral students, excessive faculty entitlement affecting, 236–237
Doctoral supervision
  Bourdieu's social theory of reproduction, 233
  bringing my personal supervisory experiences to surface, 239
  epistemic positioning, 235–236
  excessive entitlement, 232–233
  first-time oversight of excessive entitlement challenges, 239
  further questioning of my excessively entitled approach to supervision, 239–242
  investigating excessive entitlement in French 'social game' of supervision, 236–238
  issues of positionality and research questions, 235–236
  learning from reflection on experience, 243–244
  methodological framework, 234–235
  narrative inquiry, 234
  participants, data sources and analysis, 235
  self-study in researcher's maturation process, 244–245
  self-study research, 234
  storying and 'restorying' framed by Bakhtin's notion of dialogism, 234–235
  supervision as ongoing learning process, 242–244
  theoretical framework, 232–233
Double stimulation
  experiments, 106
  as method of intervention, 26–27
  as unit of analysis, 27
Drawing-based network model, 52
Dropout, need for relational understanding of problem of, 237–238
Due, 140
Duoethnography, 150–151, 162
Dysfunctions in supervision, 237–238

Earned entitlement, 47–48
Economic rationalism, 169–170
Education, 100, 157–158, 252–253
Educational ethics, 217–218, 226
Educational leaders, 185–186
Educational process, 20–21
Educational theory (*see also* Living–educational–theories (LET)), 171
Educational transformation, 102
Educators, 226
  and humanity, 273–274
Elimination process, 261
Emancipatory dialogic activity, 70–71
Empowered entitlement, 4, 273
  development, 6–7
  from excessive entitlement to, 33–34
'Energy Paradigm', The, 175–176
English as a Foreign Language (EFL), 102
English as Second Language (ESL), 2, 18–19
Entitlement concept, 43–44, 119, 140
Epideictic discourse, 73–74
Epideictic oratory, 73–74
Epideictic-Esperantist discourse, The, 74
Epistemic positioning, 235–236
Equivalent fractions, 89–90
Esperantist-Epideictic discourse, 74
Ethics, 156, 226–227
Evaluation, 161

Excessive entitlement, 2, 18, 44–45, 48, 101–102, 138, 168–169, 171, 216, 219, 225–226, 232–233, 242–243, 253, 273
- amalgams of experience, 142–145
- back to my roots, 263–264
- background literature, 138–140
- best-loved self, 139
- cultural-historical view of, 4–5
- as dehumanization, 272
- due, 140
- excessive faculty entitlement affecting doctoral students, 236–237
- experience, 139
- findings and analysis, 255–263
- first-time oversight of, 239
- in French 'social game' of supervision, 236–238
- higher education contexts, 139–140
- interpretive transition, 145
- mainstream view of, 4
- method and context, 254–255
- narrative inquiry research method, 140–141
- need for relational understanding of problem of dropout, 237–238
- positionality, 141–142
- purposes, 252
- supervisory relationship, 238
- the voice, 258–263
- theoretical framework, 253–254

Excessive faculty entitlement affecting doctoral students, 236–237

Excessive teacher entitlement, 2, 64, 78–79, 84, 86, 130, 209, 217
- analytical framework, 87–88
- background and questions for study, 23–25
- bridling to understand, 204–205
- computer-based mathematics lessons, 91–93
- concept, 18–19
- conquering excessive entitlement to develop beneficial aspect of teacher authority, 21–22
- context, 86–87
- continuing learning through emergent problem situation, 32–33
- developing professional and transformative activist stance, 32
- double stimulation as method of intervention, 26–27
- double stimulation as unit of analysis, 27
- enriching notion of, 2–4
- equivalent fractions, 89–90
- face-to-face lessons, 89
- findings, 27, 33, 89, 96
- government school in India, 23–24
- implications for teacher education, 35–36
- inconsistency between teacher espousal and practice, 19–22
- instructional rules, 90–91
- methodology, 86–88
- notion of excessive entitlement, 36–37
- object in computer-based lesson, 93–96
- participants, sources of data and analysis, 25–27
- perspective framing study, 22–23
- primary contradiction, 28–29
- problem situation, 24–25
- reflecting on process, 33–34
- reflections of, 206–211
- research participants, 86
- resistance to excessive entitlement, 34–35
- secondary contradiction, 29–31
- signposting contributions of study, 38
- space of becoming, 38
- teacher as researcher, 23
- teacher authority and links to, 20–21

Index

tertiary contradictions, 31–32
theoretical framework, 82–86
uncovering teacher authority in classroom discourse, 21
Excessive teacher/faculty entitlement, 8, 275
excessive entitlement as teacher resistance to change, 5–6
healing touch to, 5–7
humanizing pedagogy with resistance for change, 6–7
Yin–Yang of, 11–12
Expansive learning, 26–27
Experience
amalgams of, 142–145
learning from reflection on, 243–244
theory of, 200–201

Facebook, 187
Faculty member example, 143–145
Fictionalization, 141
Field, 233
FIFA Women's World Cup, 254
Formative initiative, emergence of, 24–25
Fourth Industrial Revolution (4IR), 100
Freedom movement, 153
French 'social game' of supervision, investigating excessive entitlement in, 236–238

Google Classroom, 110
Government school in India, 23–24
Graduate student example, 142–143
Guiltless recognition, 169–171

Habitus, 233
High school, 219
Higher education contexts, 139–140
Historical analysis, 33
Holocaust and inhumane acts, 271–272
Human ideological becoming process, 38

Humanity, educators and, 273–274
Humanizing pedagogy with resistance for change, 6–7

"Iatrogenesis", 217
Imaginative artifact, 52
Inclusion, 252
India, Government school in, 23–24
Indirect costs (IDC), 139–140
Indulgent teachers, 72
Inflammatory language, 191
Informal curriculum, 225
Information and communication technologies (ICTs), 82
Inhumane acts, holocaust and, 271–272
Instagram, 187
Institutional Framework of Teaching Staff in Non-Higher Education Private Schools, 127–128
Instructional rules, 88, 90–91
Instrumental dialogue, 70
Intentionality, 202
Interaction, 200
Internally persuasive discourse, 20–21
International Conference on Transformative Education Research and Sustainable Development, 176
International Council on Monuments and Sites (ICOMOS), 261
International Study Association on Teachers and Teaching (ISATT), 141
Interpretive transition, 145
Intervention, double stimulation as method of, 26–27
Invisible college, emergence of, 2–4
Inward-looking process, 22

Learning
through emergent problem situation, 32–33
by expanding concept, 77
loss of, 191–192

from reflection on experience, 243–244
Lee's narrative account, 124–126
Liberal views, 192
Lived body, 198–199
Living contradictions, dealing with, 172–173
Living Educational Theory Research approach, 169, 173–175, 177–178
Living Educational Theory Researcher, 174–175
Living–educational–theories (LET), 174, 180
  born into excessive entitlement, 168–169
  dealing with my living contradictions, 172–173
  findings, 176–178
  methodology and methods, 173–176
  perspective, 169–170
  professional excessive entitlement, 171–172
  reflecting on vulnerabilities, 178–179

Master Maths (Software), 82
Mathematics, 82, 85–86
Media literature review, 187–188
Mediation, 76, 82–83
Mediational artefacts, 106
Mis-educative, 201
Mobile dictionaries, 105–106
Monological-authoritarian teacher–student interaction, 73–74
Monologue, 70–71
Moral ethics, 217

Narrative analysis, 129
Narrative inquiry, 234, 253
  as research method, 122, 124, 140–141
Narrative Research, 175
National Assessment of Educational Progress (NAES), 191

National Education Association (NEA), 189
National Party, The, 255
National Public Radio (NPR), 188
Networked relational model, 50, 52–53, 57
  applying, 55–59
  drawing networked relational model of activity, 53–55
  excessive entitlement, 45–48
  excessive entitlement as performative networked relational model, 48–50
  of learning, 51
  method, 53–55
New South Wales Police (NSW Police), 250
Nonpersonhood, 184
Null curriculum, 216–217

Online programs, 187
Ontological dialogue, 70

Pandemic, 184
Participatory formative interventions, 106
Pedagogy dehumanization, 5–6
Peer review as self-reflexive tool, 7–8
Performative networked relational model, excessive entitlement as, 48–50
Permissive style, 71
Permissive teachers, 72
Personal persuasion, 241–242
Personal supervisory experiences to surface, 239
Phenomenological Research, 175
Phenomenology, 169, 201–202, 205
Photo voice assignment, 155–156
Ping's narrative account, 126–127
Political correctness, 254
Politicians, 224
Polyvocal style, 150–151
Positionality, 141–142
  issues of, 235–236
Postpandemic media reports, 188

Power, 254
Practitioner-researcher, 173–174
Practitioners, 199–200
Primacy of teachers and professors, 272–273
Primary contradiction, 28–29
Principal investigator (PI), 139–140
Professional activist stance, 32
Professional development, 168
Professional ethics, 218, 227
Professional excessive entitlement, 171–172
Professional living, 118–119
Professionalism ethics, 226
Professors, primacy of teachers and, 272–273
Progress in International Reading Literacy Study (PIRLS), 100

Quality education system, 100–101

(R-) living in stories of teachers, 124–129
(Re-) telling in stories of teachers, 124–129
Reconceptualization process, 162
Referenda in Australia, 256
Referendum, 256
Reflections
  of excessive teacher entitlement, 206–211
  theory of, 200–201
Reinforcement pedagogy, 91
Reproduction, Bourdieu's social theory of, 233
Research, 73
  issues of research questions, 235–236
  methodologies, 235–236
  narrative inquiry as research method, 122–124
Researcher's maturation process, self-study in, 244–245
Resistance, 6
  to excessive entitlement, 34–35

Resource persons (RPs), 25
Restorying framed by Bakhtin's notion of dialogism, 234–235
Returned and Services League (RSL), 260–261
ROTC program, 208

Saturday group, The, 25–26
School encapsulation, 74, 76–77
Science, technology and society approach (STS approach), 66
Science education, 68
  teachers' commitment to absolute truth in, 65–68
Science teachers' power, teachers' style and epistemological dimension of, 73–74
Science-Technology-Engineering-Mathematics (STEM), 139–140, 162
Scientific Esperantism, 73
Scientific inquiry, 77
Scientific instrumentalism, 66
Scientific–cultural inquiry (*see also* Narrative inquiry), 74–77
  concept activity, 74–76
  mediation and conceptual complexification, 76
  towards overcoming school encapsulation, 76–77
Secondary contradiction, 29–31
Self-realisation, 245
Self-reflexivity, 245
Self-righteousness, 153
Self-study
  genre, 253
  research, 175, 234
  in researcher's maturation process, 244–245
Situated learning, 26–27
Siyazama Primary School, 87
Social activity, 72
Social justice ethics, 217, 226–227
Social media platforms, 187

Societal narratives of teachers
  findings, 188–192
  loss of learning, 191–192
  method, data sources, and analysis, 187–188
  missing voices of teachers, 188–190
  objectives/purposes, 185
  perspectives/theoretical framework, 185–187
  teacher shortage, 190–191
Societal reidentification, 169–171
Sociomaterial approach, 48, 50–51
South Africa, 82
Spatial sociology, 120–121
Standardised materials, 105–106
Stories, 203
Storying framed by Bakhtin's notion of dialogism, 234–235
Student testing, 191
Supervision
  investigating excessive entitlement in French 'social game' of, 236–238
  as ongoing learning process, 242–244
Supervisory relationship, 238
Systemic excessive entitlement, 150
Systems view, 59

Teacher education
  implications for, 35–36
  insights for, 36–37
  programs, 278
Teachers, 32, 186
  agency, 102
  authority and links to excessive teacher entitlement, 20–21
  commitment to absolute truth in science education, 65–68
  conquering excessive entitlement to develop beneficial aspect of teacher authority, 21–22
  entitlement, 209
  ideological becoming, 32
  inconsistency between teacher espousal and practice, 19–22
  missing teachers voices, 188–190
  narratives, 204
  nonpersonhood, 185
  primacy of professors and, 272–273
  as researcher, 23
  resistance, 19
  (re-) telling and (r-) living in stories of, 124–129
  shortage, 190–191
  and student power relations, 72–73
  style and epistemological dimension of science teachers' power, 73–74
  styles, 71–72
  uncovering teacher authority in classroom discourse, 21
Teaching, 18
Teaching–learning process, 74–75
Tertiary contradictions, 31–32
Theoretical endeavour, 65
Traditional education
  Currere, 218–219
  educational ethics, 217–218
  ethics, 226–227
  excessive entitlement, 225–226
  findings, 220–225
  high school, 219
Transformative activist stance, 22, 32
Transformative agency, 4, 119, 121–122
Transformative agentive side up, 23
Transformative potentials, 102–103
'Transformative process of teachers' ideological becoming, 34
Translanguaging, 159
Trends in International Mathematics and Science Study (TIMSS), 82, 100
Trinomial, 75
Troubling excessive entitlement autoethnography, 202–203

Index 289

bridling to understand excessive teacher entitlement, 204–205
literature review, 200–205
methodology and more questions, 205
narrative, 206, 208–211
purpose and research questions, 199–200
reflection, 198–199
reflection of awareness, 211–212
reflections of excessive teacher entitlement, 206–211
researching lived experiences, 201–202
theory of experience and reflection, 200–201

United Nations Educational, Scientific, and Cultural Organization (UNESCO), 261
United States, 185
Universal education, embodiment of, 23–24
Universities, 139–140

University Academic, 172

Value-seeking phenomena, 55
Values of human flourishing, 168–172
Visual representations, 57
Visually accessible networked relational model, 57–58
Voice, The, 255, 258, 263
  recommendations, 257
Vygotsky's triangular model, 9

Wang's narrative account, 127–129
Western Cape Education Department (WCED), 100

Yin–Yang of excessive teacher/faculty entitlement and Best Loved Self, 11–12
Yrjö Engeström's activity systems model, 44–45

Zone of proximal development (ZPD), 82–83
Zoom, 151

Printed in the USA
CPSIA information can be obtained
at www.ICGtesting.com
JSHW011759031224
74704JS00004B/103